INTRODUCING CATHOLIC THEOLOGY
Series editor: Michael Richards

Further titles in preparation

INTRODUCING CATHOLIC THEOLOGY

BEING HUMAN
A Biblical Perspective

Edmund Hill

GEOFFREY CHAPMAN
LONDON

A Geoffrey Chapman book published by
Cassell Ltd
1 Vincent Square, London SW1P 2PN

© Edmund Hill, OP 1984

First published 1984

ISBN 0 225 66358 9

Nihil obstat: Anton Cowan, *Censor*
Imprimatur: Monsignor Ralph Brown, *V.G.*
Westminster, 14 July 1983

The *Nihil obstat* and *Imprimatur* are a declaration that a book or pamphlet is considered to be free
from doctrinal or moral error. It is not implied that those who have granted the *Nihil obstat* and
Imprimatur agree with the contents, opinions or statements expressed.

British Library Cataloguing in Publication Data

Hill, Edmund
  Being human: a Biblical perspective. —
  (Introducing Catholic theology; 3)
  1. Man
  I. Title   II. Series
  128   BD450

Phototypesetting by Georgia Origination, Liverpool
Printed in Great Britain at the University Press, Cambridge

Contents

Foreword

Introducing Catholic Theology has been conceived and planned in the belief that the Second Vatican Council provided the Church with a fundamental revision of its way of life in the light of a thorough investigation of Scripture and of our history, and with fresh guidelines for studying and reflecting upon the Christian message itself. In common with every other form of human enquiry and practical activity, the Christian faith can be set out and explained in ways appropriate to human intelligence: it calls for scientific textbooks as well as for other forms of writing aimed at expressing and conveying its doctrines.

It is hoped that these volumes will be found useful by teachers and students in that they will supply both the information and the stimulus to reflection that should be taken for granted and counted upon by all concerned in any one course of study.

Conceived as expressions of the Catholic tradition, the books draw upon the contribution to the knowledge of God and the world made by other religions, and the standpoint of other patterns of Christian loyalty. They recognize the need for finding ways of reconciliation where differences of understanding lead to human divisions and even hostility. They also give an account of the insights of various philosophical and methodological approaches.

The series began with an examination of the Christian understanding of the process of revelation itself, the special communication between God and humanity made available in the history of Israel and culminating in the person of Christ; its second volume was about the Catholic understanding of Christ, the Word of God and the source of the New Testament faith. This present volume offers an account of the nature and purpose of human life in the light of that faith. It is hoped that the series will eventually cover the full range of theological themes.

Michael Richards

Preface

Christian theology, after the apostolic age of the New Testament, began and developed for the most part as a homiletic reflection on the scriptures. Much of the best theology of the Fathers is contained in their sermons. And even when they were composing apologies or treatises rather than preaching sermons their whole style was rhetorical, because their culture was rhetorical and literary through and through.

However, they envisaged a wider audience for their sermons and their writings than just the communities of their fellow Christians. They also addressed themselves, as bearers of the gospel of salvation, to unbelievers. And to make contact spiritually and mentally with unbelievers they spontaneously found themselves arguing and explaining things in terms of the philosophies with which educated pagans were acquainted, Platonism, Stoicism, Aristotelianism. So began the long symbiosis of theology and philosophy.

In the Middle Ages this produced a totally new style of theology, which is called scholastic. Theology is now more the business of the *schools* (i.e. the universities) than of the pulpit or the forum. It is therefore studied *systematically*, divided into treatises, and in technical language which is to a very great extent the language of philosophy, above all of Aristotelian philosophy. This style of theology continues to this day. For most modern theologians the philosophy they employ has changed, and I doubt if you will find many openly Aristotelian ones. Instead they are very properly elaborating their theology in dialogue with Heidegger or Husserl, with Hume and Kant and Hegel and Marx and Wittgenstein. The schools have of course changed, but I think the theology, or much of it, written by Rahner or Schillebeeckx or Lonergan, by Bultmann or Ian Ramsey, can still properly be called scholastic.

One great weakness of mediaeval scholastic theology was that its practitioners had very little sense of history. Their theology failed to do justice to the inescapable historical element in Christian faith; and it also became more and more separated from its biblical roots, until we reached the highly unsatisfactory situation in which biblical exegesis and systematic or dogmatic theology were regarded as quite separate disciplines. Indeed they are still so regarded for practical purposes in most theological institutions (at any rate in Catholic ones), and it is unfortunately possible to breed from these institutions biblically illiterate dogmatic theologians, and dogmatically illiterate biblical exegetes.

At the present day studies in all disciplines, including theology, are marked by a strong sense of history. In the theological field this is as yet more truly the case with biblical studies than with those in systematic theology (the two are still a long way from being fused once more into their proper unity). But it is now also respectable and proper to give theology a historical rather than a philosophical structure and style.

That is almost, but not quite, what I am trying to do in this book. The brief I was given was a theology of man. I distrust the word 'man' as a general term, the subject of even such innocuous generalizations as 'man is a rational animal' – one has, after all, come across specimens in whom even this statement can only with difficulty be verified. So I did not think I could profitably attempt a scholastic theology of man geared to any particular philosophical anthropology. On the other hand my dislike of the generalization 'man' is mild compared with my aversion to the excessively common generalization 'modern man', or variations of it such as 'Western man'. And these are generalizations that are thrown around with the greatest freedom nowadays by people who are explicitly and deliberately taking the historical dimension into account. It is true, they are usually doing it very badly, in ways that should make any self-respecting professional historian squirm. But still, 'modern man' is a historical generalization, implicitly contrasted with 'ancient man', or (God preserve us!) 'primitive man', or 'mediaeval man'.

In any case, while the Christian revelation contained in scripture is certainly historical, to talk about salvation history and to treat the biblical narratives as simply historical without qualification is to run the risk of creating in the student expectations that simply cannot be satisfied; expectations based on what modern professional historians do and write. But nowhere in the Bible is there history as history is written and practised by modern professional historians.

So I have preferred to approach the theology of man as the study of the *drama* of the relationship between God and the human race, and all its members from the beginning to the end of time. Drama is a literary category. Though few if any of the biblical writings fall strictly into this category (the Song of Songs, perhaps, or Job?), still they are all of them much more evidently literary than philosophical or systematic writings. And to see them all as constituting one gigantic dramatic script seems to me an illuminating way of viewing the Bible and the divine revelation it records. It obliges us to bring to exegesis, and to theology, techniques of literary analysis and criticism. In this way theology is coming back once more to a style that has a greater affinity to that of the Fathers.

So I begin the book, after a few introductory chapters, with theological reflections on human origins, based on the texts of Genesis, and conclude it with reflections on the ultimate destiny of mankind or eschatology, based mainly on New Testament texts, and above all on the book of Revelation. But of course there is absolutely no question of rejecting the contribution made by scholastic theology of all kinds to the theological tradition. By and large I draw on it, mainly in a historical manner, in the central part of the book, between the two little interludes entitled *Selah*, that mysterious word which is interjected from time to time into the text of several of the psalms.

When I was asked to contribute this volume to the series I had already written a course of lectures on Christian doctrine for an ecumenical correspondence college in Johannesburg, the Theological Education by Extension (TEE) College. One section of that course was on the subject of man. I am therefore very much obliged to the TEE College, Johannesburg for allowing me to make use, not wholesale but to a considerable extent, of my lectures for this book.

Bl. Jordan House, Maseru, Lesotho   *Edmund Hill, OP*
on the feast of Bl. Jordan of Saxony,
14 February 1983

Abbreviations

ACW   *Ancient Christian Writers*: a series of patristic translations
AV   Authorized Version of the Bible
CTS   Catholic Truth Society
CUP   Cambridge University Press
D   Deuteronomist
DLT   Darton, Longman and Todd
Dz   Denzinger-Schönmetzer, *Enchiridion Symbolorum*
E   Elohist
ET   English translation
J   Yahwist
JB   Jerusalem Bible
LXX   Septuagint Greek version of the Old Testament
NEB   New English Bible
OP   *Ordinis Praedicatorum*: of the Order of Preachers
OUP   Oxford University Press
P   Priestly Code
par(r).   and parallel(s) in other gospel(s)
PG   *Patrologia Graeca* ⎱ 19th-century collection of Greek and Latin
PL   *Patrologia Latina* ⎰ Fathers, edited by J. P. Migne
RSV   Revised Standard Version of the Bible
SCM   Student Christian Movement Press
SPCK   Society for the Propagation of Christian Knowledge
STh   *Summa Theologiae* of St Thomas Aquinas

1

Placing a Theology of Man

A. THE STUDY OF MAN'S RELATIONSHIPS WITH GOD

'We need a theology of work'; 'The definitive statement of a theology of leisure is yet to be made'; 'When are we going to get a theology of sport?'; 'Much research needs to be done before we can construct a viable theology of communications'; 'Professor X has gone some way to providing a much needed prolegomenon to a theology of infancy'; '... a theology of industry...'; '... a theology of seafaring...'; '... a theology of science...'; '... a theology of dress...'; '... a theology of space...'; '... a theology of feet...'; '... a theology of ...': '... a theology of ...'.

These are not, I confess, real quotations from contemporary theological journals – but they well might be. It is all, indeed, part of the laudable modern urge to make Christian faith and doctrine relevant to the real world of our contemporaries. And in such a stylistic climate it may seem unnecessary to place, or justify, so obvious a theology as a theology of man. All the same, that is how I think we should begin, if only to save the word 'theology' from being diluted into a kind of meaningless mush that tastes of nothing in particular.

Theology, strictly speaking, is about God. That is what the word means, in its derivation. Even more particularly, by a precision given to the concept in Christian tradition, it is about God's revelation of himself to us. So strictly speaking it is only God, and God as revealing himself (not God as otherwise discoverable) that you can have a theology of.[1]

Theology (that is, Christian theology, which is the only kind that concerns us in this book) is the study of God's revelation of himself, because it is essentially an exercise of Christian faith, and faith is the response to and acceptance of God's revelation or self-manifestation. Theology, in St Anselm's famous phrase, is 'faith seeking understanding', faith in God seeking understanding of God.[2]

So we can make our first elementary but basic point: in no way is it permissible to leave God out of theology. If you do, you are just left with '-logy', which means you are just left with words, verbiage signifying nothing.

How then can you have a theology of man, or of anything else, from feet to work, via industry and infancy? You can only do so insofar as these subjects are somehow related to God and his revelation, insofar as God 'has said something about them'.

But has God said anything about them? Has there been any need for him to do so? Confining ourselves to our own subject of man, or being human (and nearly all the things of which people require or offer theologies today are really aspects of being human, so that nearly all such theologies are reducible to the theology of man), is there really any need for God to say anything to us about us? Here, after all, we are – extremely accessible to ourselves, and very curious about ourselves; and all we have to do is to study ourselves and each other as we are, which we do with great resource, enterprise and originality. We have developed endless variations of 'anthropology', which is the proper name for the study of man (*anthrōpos*), as 'theology' is for the study of God (*Theos*). That is what those university faculties generally known as *humanities* or *arts* are really all about: men and their achievements, their cultures, languages, histories, laws, politics, economies; archaeology, psychology, human biology, social anthropology, sexology, criminology, philosophy; these, and a host of other academic disciplines besides, are all valid ways of studying a part of what it means to be human. And they don't require God to start them off or to complete them, by telling us something about ourselves that we couldn't otherwise find out for ourselves.

However, one important thing about ourselves which we are not in a position to study through any of these various 'anthropologies' is our relationship with God. This is because God is not accessible to us, not 'there' for our observation and study or our discovery, like other things – for the very good reason that God is not 'another thing'. He is not a thing among things at all. He does, however, disclose himself to us in and through other things, and in disclosing himself he discloses the relationships in which things, and we ourselves, stand towards him. And that is what a theology of man must be about: *our relationships with God*. There has to be such a subject, and it is important to study it (we say this as believers), because being fully human both presupposes such a relationship and requires or works towards such a relationship as its goal or fulfilment.

We say this as believers, I say. But even as unbelievers, or rather perhaps as not-yet-believers, people have felt the questions, where we come from and where we are going, to be unanswerable simply on the evidence of life as we experience it – and have felt these unanswerable questions to be painful gaps in our necessary knowledge about ourselves. The most poignant statement of this sense of need, or loss, is to be found in this famous passage from St Bede's *Ecclesiastical History of the English People* (one of King Edwin's counsellors is addressing him, when they are discussing whether they should receive baptism from Bishop Paulinus):

When we compare the present life of man with that time of which we have no knowledge, it seems to me like the swift flight of a lone sparrow through the banqueting-hall where you sit in the winter months to dine with your thanes and counsellors. Inside there is a comforting fire to warm the room; outside the wintry storms of snow and rain are raging. This sparrow flies swiftly in through one door of the hall and out through another. While he is inside, he is safe from the winter storms; but after a few moments of comfort, he vanishes from sight into the darkness whence he came. Similarly, man appears on earth for a little while, but we know nothing of what went before this life and what follows. Therefore if this new teaching can reveal any more certain knowledge, it seems only right that we should follow it (II, 13; tr. Leo Sherley-Price, Penguin Classics, Harmondsworth, Middx, 1964).

B.   METHOD TO BE FOLLOWED

We are to study our relationships with God, then, insofar as God has revealed these to us. So our method should be governed by the manner in which God has made his revelation.

Now the record of God's saving revelation to mankind, according to Christian faith, is given us in the holy scriptures of the Old and New Testaments. And if there is one thing that is clear about these writings, it is that they are in no sense whatever textbooks. It is really rather odd how Christians of practically all periods in the history of Christianity have been tempted to treat them as if they were, and to try and 'look up the answers' in them to the questions that have arisen and continue to arise about the faith and its application. And so throughout the Church's history Christians have found themselves being disconcerted by the Bible, put off by it because it has not in fact been what they assumed it ought to be. That we should be disconcerted by the word of God is very proper. We need disconcerting, shaking out of our prejudices and false assumptions; but that we should be unnecessarily disconcerted because we insist on opening the Bible with a silly false assumption is a pity, and leads to a great waste of valuable energy.

If the Bible is not a textbook, what is it? On the face of it, it is a *library*, a collection of books, not a single work. And in fact the English word 'Bible' transliterates the Greek plural *biblia*, meaning precisely 'books'. We can best describe this small library of books as the select literature of a particular people, the Israelites/Jews, with a cultural history of something more than 1,000 years from about 1200 B.C. to about 100 B.C. (that is, the Old Testament); topped off with the select literature of a particular sect of the Jews, called Christians, written over a period of considerably less than a century, from about 50 A.D. to perhaps 100, perhaps 120 A.D.

It is through such literature, containing a fairly wide variety of literary forms, that God has chosen to make his revelation known to us.

The literature being that of a people, it both reflects and in part relates the history of that people. So God is making himself known to us through the history of Israel and the Jews, and of Jesus Christ and the first few generations of his disciples. And so we call God's revelation a historical revelation. From this we conclude that our study of man's relationships with God must be basically historical in method, more or less following the record of God's revelation in the Bible from its beginning to its end.

But the word 'historical' is not entirely satisfactory, since it has such a great capacity to mislead. 'History' in modern English means a fairly precise field of study and a certain professional standard and technique of study, geared to a strict, not to say narrow, concept of factual truth. So if we call God's revelation historical, and call the Bible the record of that revelation, we are again very possibly encouraging false expectations and false assumptions in the student of the Bible. He will of course very soon observe that much of the Bible is obviously not historical in form: the Psalms, or Proverbs, or the Song of Songs, for example. But what is not so immediately obvious is that those books which do appear to be historical in form are none of them remotely 'history' in the strict modern sense of the term. In a word, the term 'history' can encourage that textbook expectation again. And once again, it is going to meet with disillusionment.[3]

So while not altogether rejecting the term 'historical' as a description of the manner of God's revelation, since it is all along related to actual events in the past that are in principle open to professional historical investigation, I prefer the term 'dramatic'. From the beginning to the end of his creation God has been engaged in a stupendous drama with that creation, or at least with the human segment of it; a drama of salvation which is also a drama of revelation, of saving by making himself known. And the scriptures are the script, not of the whole drama which engages the whole human race, but of the crucial section which is the key to the interpretation of the whole.

We can then see our theological task as comparable to that of the dramatic critic. Not that we are passing judgement on the drama or its author, but that we are trying to interpret and appreciate it. In this book, of course, we are concerned with only one aspect of it. But even so we must link our appreciation to the course of the drama as it unfolds from the first act to the last. We shall be concerned with the drama of the human race (with its history, in a sense) from its origins to its final destiny in its relationships with God. As we shall see in the next chapter, this historical/dramatic approach accords with the nature of man. For being human is a dramatic, historical mode of being, a becoming, a process.

In the past few centuries there has been a continuous tendency, that has become more and more pronounced, to divide what is called dogmatic or systematic theology from what is called biblical exegesis, and to put them into separate and practically water-tight compartments. With the enormous advance of biblical studies in the last hundred years, biblical scholars have often had reason to complain that too many dogmatic theologians appear to be biblically illiterate. But I fear the boot is also on the other foot, and that too many contemporary biblical scholars are, if not illiterate, then at best not much advanced beyond catechism level in their dogmatic theology. It is time this artificial chasm was bridged. It is my hope, by adopting this dramatic/historical method, tied to the dramatic/historical text of scripture, to contribute something to this necessary 'pontifical' activity.

For though tied in a sense to the text of scripture, we shall certainly not be limited to it. Since our subject is man's relationships with God, we cannot ignore the work of those other anthropologies we have already mentioned. In section D below we shall be discussing briefly the relationship of theology with these anthropologies. But here I simply wish to point out that our method will permit us to stray freely from the strict dramatic/historical path and consider all sorts of questions about the nature of man and society that are bound to arise, and do not call for a dramatic/historical answer, provided all such meanderings are subordinated to the dramatic/historical form of the whole. We shall pause for further reflections on method later on in the book in the unnumbered interludes headed *Selah*.

C. ADAM AND CHRIST

Since, then, we are committed to studying man in his relationships with God from the beginning to the end of the 'divine comedy' of salvation, we can conveniently name the two termini or poles of our course 'Adam' (the beginning) and 'Christ' (the end). In Adam we can study our primary or initial relationship with God, while we scrutinize our ultimate and final relationship with him in Christ.

Adam is presented in Genesis not only as the first man, but also as the archetypal or representative man. The name 'Adam' is indeed just the Hebrew for 'man' – not 'man' as opposed to 'woman' (*ish* and *ishshah* respectively in Hebrew), but 'man' as meaning 'human being', of either sex and any age, like the Greek *anthrōpos*, Latin *homo*, German *Mensch*.[4] And Adam is shown to us in Gen 1 and 2 in the first place as a *creature*. This is our fundamental relationship with God. The basic datum of a theology of man is man's *creatureliness*. 'It is he who made us and not we ourselves', as it says in what is admittedly not the most approved reading of Ps 100:3.[5] This states an extremely important limit, a *terminus a quo*, for all reflection on man. The darkness from which the sparrow comes is the creative hand of God. This rules out any humanist totalitarianism, any limitless claims by man and on behalf of man. Man is not God; man is made by God. And let us remember what this generalization means; it means every single human being is made by God, and no human being whatever (with the one exception that proves the rule, of Jesus Christ himself) is God. When this elementary truth is forgotten or ignored or denied (as it was in Gen 3:4–6), then very unpleasant results inevitably follow.

However, that is only the beginning of the story of man, the basis of the human structure. Like all good stories, it has to have an end, and like all good structures, its basis is laid in order to achieve and sustain a culmination. Man is a creature of God, like everything else in the universe; but according to the creation story of Gen 1 the human race is, even at its creation, the crown of creation, created to be lords of creation; and created for a goal or destiny. That this is so is hinted at in the creation narratives: in the statement of the goodness of all things made by God (1:31); in the statement of man, male and female, being created in the image and likeness of God (1:27); in the statement of God's resting on the seventh day (2:2–3); and it is hinted at in the very different story of the so-called second creation narrative, where the man is given a task (2:15), a command (2:17) and a companion (2:21–24), which taken together all imply an orientation to some end. In a word, the human race is launched into history, set on a course.

But what the destiny is, what the end of the course and the goal of the history, is not finally disclosed until we come to the person of Christ, to the whole story of Jesus Christ and his life, death and resurrection, in the New Testament. Christ, the Son of man, is the last Adam. Christ, above all in his glory, as the heavenly man of the resurrection, represents the *terminus ad quem* of any theology on man, the darkness into which Bede's sparrow flies out again, out of the lighted hall. In him we see that the ultimate and final relationship of man with God is intended to be one of sonship, and of participation in the divine nature (2 Pet 1:4). I said above that Jesus Christ is the exception which proves the rule that no man is God. This man is God; but he proves the rule because he did not make himself God. God became this man; Jesus as man is the *creature* (as much a creature of God as the rest of us) assumed in his very creation to be one person with the divine Word, with God the Son. And while his being God in this way is unique and incommunicable, it is the means of communicating to mankind a share in his *divine* sonship, a share in the divine nature.

This is a dignity of being human that infinitely surpasses any possible aims or claims or ideals of the most absolute humanist totalitarianism. When this too is forgotten, ignored or denied, very unpleasant results again follow, of mutual enslavement and exploitation.

Adam and Christ, then, are the two poles of a theology of man. And I hope that in this book we will be able to explore the whole course between the two poles. Our guiding text will be Paul's words: 'Thus it is written, "The first man Adam became a living being" [Gen 2:7]; the last Adam became a life-giving spirit . . . . The first man was from earth, a man of dust; the second man is from heaven. As was the man of dust so are those who are of the dust; and as is the man of heaven, so are those who are of heaven. Just as we have borne the image of the man of dust, we shall also bear the image of the man of heaven' (1 Cor 15:45, 47–49).

D. THE RELATIONSHIP OF THE THEOLOGY OF MAN TO OTHER 'ANTHROPOLOGIES'

In the universities of mediaeval Europe, theology reigned as 'queen of the sciences', and philosophy was seen as 'the handmaid of theology'. Since those days, clearly, the other sciences, thanks in the first place to the clear-headed reflections of scholastic theologians, have achieved a total independence of theological control – so much so that they mostly ignore theology altogether, and the *quondam* queen of the sciences has become their Cinderella. Few people, few theologians even, any longer regard theology as a *science* at all, in what we take to be the ordinary and proper sense of that word. And everyone, theologians included, would agree that it is simply absurd to intrude God, or any religious considerations, into studies in physics or mathematics, chemistry, engineering, botany or astronomy. It is equally disreputable, intellectually speaking, to draw theological conclusions (or more usually anti-theological or a-theological conclusions) from purely scientific theories, procedures or data, and then to regard such conclusions as scientifically established, to state as a scientist, for example, that science has disproved the existence of God; though not all scientists notice the disreputable absurdity of this so readily.

But when it comes to the 'human sciences' which I have been calling anthropologies, the relationship of theology to them, in particular of the theology of man, is rather more complex. For while nearly all of them are in theory, like physics, astronomy, chemistry or mathematics, simply *descriptive*, i.e. attempting to find out and analyse how things are with man, under all the different aspects of humanity from the anatomical to the psychological, the social and the religious; they also tend in virtue of their subject-matter to be at least implicitly *prescriptive*, i.e. to decide or at the very least to assume how things ought to be. Since they are concerned with man, they can scarcely avoid being concerned with the human apprehension of *meaning* in the world and the human articulation of *values*, and indeed there is no reason why they should try to avoid this.

But whenever you talk about meanings and values, you talk about matters that are the direct concern of the 'sacred teaching', of Christian doctrine, hence of theology. So the Christian theologian of man is obliged to take a great interest in these various anthropologies, from medicine to political economy (especially political economy). He must, of course, try and learn from them, and take account of their genuine discoveries and advancements of human knowledge. But above all he must study them with a truly critical appraisal. To put it bluntly, the Christian theologian must be ready to claim the right to sit in judgement on the values and meanings propounded by these various anthropologists, by doctors and financiers, by sociologists, psychologists, economists and politicians, and to say how far they do or do not accord with the values and meanings disclosed to us men in our relationship with God. Even more, he must insist on the right to judge the prescriptions and the actions of persons who affect our lives so widely as economists and politicians. So it is futile to suppose that religion can be kept out of politics (the most crucial arena of anthropological activity) in the same sort of way as it can be kept out of algebra.

But this responsibility of Christian theological judgement on politics, political theories, philosophies and ideologies is a matter of real delicacy. No Christian, no theologian is of course purely and simply a theologian and nothing else; they would be monsters, two-dimensional abstractions, if they were. But this means that their critical judgement on some ideology or political philosophy, some economic system or practical policy, will not usually be purely and simply a judgement in terms of Christian doctrine. They will not always be capable of the highest degree of detachment or abstraction (a most necessary and desirable technique in its proper place) from their own concrete interests, prejudices, traditions, upbringing and so on, in order to make it so. If they are critical of communism, for instance, as anti-Christian and anti-human, there is the possibility at least that they also fear it as a threat to their economic and class interests. If they are critical of traditional customs in Africa or Asia as superstitious or inhuman, it is probable that they are also repelled by them as unscientific or unhygienic – or un-British.

Likewise if they condemn capitalism or apartheid as contrary to the values of the gospel, it will possibly also be the case that these systems injure their Christian critics in their race or their class, and that they resent them for these personal reasons as well as for offending against the justice of God.

Now there is nothing necessarily wrong with these other, secular, non-doctrinal standards of judgement. But it is a sin against truth to confuse them with essentially Christian standards; not to be aware of the multiplicity of motives underlying one's criticisms and condemnations (or one's plaudits and approvals). It also weakens the force of criticism, it sells the pass. For it is clearly the regular defence of the ideologies or systems being criticized that the 'so-called Christian' attack on them is just a cover for less reputable motives. Thus in South Africa[6] the World Council of Churches and the

South African Council of Churches are called front organizations for communism because of their opposition to the policy of apartheid or separate development and their programmes to combat racism, while in Soviet Russia the Churches are no doubt dismissed, in their criticisms of communist inhumanities and their championing of human rights, as the lackeys of capitalism.

So the waters are muddied – and always by the cloven hoofs of the father of lies working through *his* front organizations, to which most of us only too easily belong at some time or other or in some instances. The remedy is to be found, *not* in the Church keeping out of politics, as the governments of Poland and Paraguay, Soviet Russia and South Africa demand with equal stridency that it should, but in the Christian always trying to be clear-headed and *devoted to the truth* (honest) in his judgements, and *self*-critical in his criticisms of those whom he regards as opponents, in their various -isms, of the creative and saving revelation of God.

E. MEDITATION ON PSALM 8

Psalm 8 makes a very suitable introduction to what God's revelation has to say about man, since it both refers back explicitly to the creation of man, to Adam, and is also interpreted by the New Testament as referring forward to the new man, Jesus Christ. Let us begin by looking at it in its own Old Testament terms.

'O Lord, our Lord, how majestic is thy name in all the earth!' (vv. 1, 9). The psalm is first and last a hymn of praise. The true revealed doctrine of man begins and ends not with man but with God. God, not man, is the first and the last.

The little ones know this: 'Thou whose glory above the heavens is chanted by the mouth of babes and infants' (v. 2). Jesus says that God has revealed his mysteries to little ones, not to the learned and the wise (Mt 11:25). So the first lesson, the first value stressed by the revealed doctrine of man is *humility*, a value that is not often stressed (I don't say never) by secular anthropologies. The first thing that we are advised to consider about ourselves is that we are *little* before God, and in comparison with him.

And not only in comparison with *him*. 'When I look at thy heavens, the work of thy fingers, the moon and the stars which thou hast established; what is man that thou art mindful of him, and the son of man that thou dost care for him?' (vv. 3–4). This is a sentiment often echoed by astronomers today when they contemplate the unimaginable vastnesses of space and time. But with them it seems sometimes to have about it a touch of despair, a sense of human life reduced to total insignificance by the immensity of the stage we stand in.

Not so the psalmist. For besides the basic humility with which he starts, he has on the strength of his faith in God a 'proper pride' in his humanity. 'Yet thou hast made him little less than God, and dost crown him with glory and honour' (v. 5). This could also be rendered: 'Though thou hast made him somewhat less than the gods/angels, still thou hast crowned him . . .'.

Man and gods – for the word RSV renders by 'God' should here, with greater probability, be rendered 'the gods'. The Hebrew has 'the *elohim*', which is a plural form, even when it means 'God'. The old Greek LXX[7] translates it 'angels', and the psalmist clearly meant such superhuman beings, elsewhere sometimes called 'sons of God' (e.g. Job 1:6, Gen 6:1). As for man, the Hebrew in v. 4 has two words for him, *enosh* and *adam*. Both occur as proper names in the genealogy of origins, Gen 5:1–11, Enosh as the grandson of Adam. Both carry connotations of lowliness, *adam* being connected, at least in the minds of biblical writers if not etymologically, with *adamah*, 'soil'; and *enosh* likewise with a word meaning 'weak'. So man in his weakness and earthiness or dustiness is less than these heavenly beings, as indeed he seems less than the moon and the stars. And yet 'thou dost crown him with glory and honour' by making him the lord of creation, 'putting *all* things under his feet' (v. 6); not only the other animals and the fishes of the sea (vv. 7–8), but *all* things, including moon and stars and the immensities of space (which man dominates by his intellect) – and 'the gods'? The New Testament at least will take that 'all things' very seriously.

So according to Ps 8 God reveals us to ourselves as mysteriously paradoxical beings, imaging or echoing the paradoxical mystery of God himself: little yet great, lowly and sublime – and all in praise of the wonderful name of God.

The psalm is often quoted or alluded to in the New Testament: Heb 2:6–9, 1 Cor 15:27–28, Eph 1:22, to name the most significant instances. The writers of these passages, Paul and others, do not alter or distort the fairly obvious interpretation of the psalm just outlined; they merely apply it in person to Jesus Christ, assuming it to be a 'messianic' psalm. The reason, presumably, is the expression 'son of man' in v. 4. This is Jesus' favourite designation of himself in the gospels. We shall consider it in much greater detail in a later chapter. Here it is enough to say that it carries both the littleness and the greatness, the lowliness and the sublimity of which we have been speaking.

What the New Testament writers do by applying this psalm to Jesus is to turn a religious *description* of humanity at large into a prophecy of the Messiah in person, and thus into a *prescription*. The psalm no longer tells us what man in general *is*; it tells what The Man in particular, our model, *does*. So man in general, you and I and everybody else are now given a programme, a road to follow along which Jesus went, and a place to go to where he went to. First along the road of his emptying himself (Phil 2:7) in the littleness of his common humanity, taking the form of a slave down to the depths of lowliness and humiliation in his death on the cross; then on to his goal in his 'glory and honour' through his resurrection and ascension up to the heights of heaven, where seated at God's right hand he is waiting until at the end of the world *all* things (certainly including those 'gods' or angels) will be subjected under his feet.

It might be said that Heb 2 and 1 Cor 15 are only turning a general description of humanity into a particular description of Jesus Christ. But since he is the last Adam, the new and perfect representative and model of the human race, such a description of him (especially when combined with the general reference of the psalm in its first and obvious meaning), is bound to be a prescription or programme for us, for all other human beings. These are our human dimensions, the dimensions of our human destiny.

NOTES

1 Thomas Aquinas, *STh* Ia, 1, i and vii (ET, vol. 1). St Thomas does not use the word 'theology', but the expression 'sacred teaching'.

2 Anselm, *Proslogion, prooemium* (*PL* 158, 225). It is almost the sub-title of this work.

3 For what we do find in the Bible, see below, Chapter 2, A and B.

4 While I support most of the aims of 'Women's Lib', and their insistence on the absolute equality of the sexes, I do not accept some of their methods; for example, their attempt to limit the English language's use of the word 'man'. Sure, the English language is defective here, unlike many, perhaps most, others. But still 'man' does have these two senses, does mean 'human being' like German *Mensch* as well as 'male adult' like German *Mann*.

5 'It is he who made us, and we are his' is almost certainly the correct reading; a difference of one letter in the Hebrew.

6 I am writing this just across the border of South Africa, in the neighbouring country of Lesotho.

7 The Septuagint ('seventy'; abbreviated to LXX), so called because of a legend that it was miraculously produced by seventy scholars all translating independently in separate cells, and yet making an identical translation. The point of the legend is to assert the divine inspiration of the LXX, which was the Bible of the influential Greek-speaking Jews of Alexandria.

QUESTIONS FOR FURTHER DISCUSSION

1 How should biblical learning and dogmatic theology be related? Why is it important that all theology should be biblical theology?

2 How can a properly Christian theology of man help to develop a Christian stance towards the problems facing humanity today?

3 What light does the Adam/Christ polarity throw on God's intentions for humankind?

2

The Process of Being Human

'What is man?', the psalmist asked. An answer, if not the answer, is that man is a process. The question, that is to say, is not best answered, or at least does not have to be answered, by giving a definition of man. Anyhow, that is not the kind of answer the psalmist was looking for. In answer to his own question he simply stated some important things that God had done for man, that had happened to man – a bit of process that man had undergone.

A. PROCESS THEOLOGY

In the early 1970s there was an influential school of theology in America called 'Process Theology'. Its exponents were (are) disciples of the English mathematician/philosopher A. N. Whitehead. Very briefly, Whitehead maintained that the concept of *process* (of becoming, of change, of action) rather than the concept of *substance* (being, essence) is the key to a proper understanding of the world, and indeed of God.[1]

Theological fashions change so fast, especially in America, that perhaps Process Theology is already out of date. All the same, we cannot afford simply to ignore it. Professor Whitehead was a man of great distinction. And while a metaphysics of process is not, in my view, at all an adequate instrument for talking about the mystery of God, nor capable of doing justice to the whole teaching of scripture and tradition about God, still it has some cogent criticisms to offer to a debased and oversimplified metaphysics of being or substance, which we traditionalists are perhaps inclined to relax into. What is more to the point in this book, it does provide a suitable structure of concepts with which to study the physical world, especially living organisms – and especially man and his existence.

We say, for example, 'Life must go on'. And that is precisely what life does do. It goes on. Life *is* a going on, an ongoing process. It is framed in time, and time means change, means becoming, developing, decaying, doing and being done to. And human being, presumably, means human living, it means the human process. We cannot know what it is to be human except by knowing this human process, the process of life from the cradle (and before) to the grave (and after).

It is true, the life process has a unity, a pattern or form. And more than that: this unity or form is not just like the unity or form of a piece of music, for example, or a dance, a pattern of movement which is all there is that gives unity to the object. A life may indeed lack much pattern, like a bad piece of music or a mere noise; but it always has the unity of the living subject, of the self, the 'I' who is born, grows, lives and dies. So, no doubt against the tenets of the purest Process Philosophy and Theology, I think we have to accept that becoming presupposes being, process somehow or other presupposes substance.

And yet, while I would certainly maintain that I am not reducible to the process of my life (or to generalize, man is not reducible to process), I would also maintain that I am only knowable in and through that process. People are only to be known, and *distinguished from each other*, through their life processes, their stories, their histories. It is true that for all our differences we are all human beings. Yes, but what does being human mean? We each have to discover the answer to that question by the process of living, and we each discover it slightly differently. We discover what we are by becoming what we are. And we always run the risk of failing to discover what we are by becoming what we are not.

B.   KNOWING THE HUMAN STORY AND HUMAN STORIES

Our object in this book is not, of course, to know everything about everybody. We prudently leave that to God, who alone is capable of it because, being himself beyond and before and after all process, he is most intimately present to all and each and every process. Our object is to study and learn something about our relations with God.

But these relationships are an element in our lives, and so can only really be studied through our stories. And again, while it is impossible for us to study everybody's story, or even to study and know fully anybody's story, including our own, still there is a common humanity about human stories, and a certain selection of patterns which human stories can fall into, and hence a certain finite set of patterns into which human relations with God can fall.

Furthermore, individual human stories interlock. We are not just individuals, but political and social animals, as Aristotle observed. We don't only live, we live together. We are not only related to God individually, we are related to him together, socially, in communities. So as well as studying human relationships with God in individual stories (in a selection, that is, of *typical* individual stories), we also have to study them in collective or communal or group stories, the stories of societies and nations, in stories that take the form of what we call hi-*stories*. And these too we can only study in a selection of typical histories.

Perhaps a better word than 'typical', which is likely to mislead, would be 'typological', which anyhow has a more satisfying technical ring to it. Now that, by and large, is what we may be said to have in the Bible: a typology of human relations with God, both individual and communal or collective, conveyed in the stories of the persons and communities of which scripture tells us. Analogous typologies are to be found in other literatures besides the biblical, and in other religious literatures, oral as well as written, besides the Judaeo-Christian, and they are well worth studying and comparing with our biblical typology. But for Christians the Bible of the Old and New Testaments, as the record of God's saving revelation and the privileged commentary on it, must hold a unique place. Israel's is the typological history *par excellence* of a people's relationships with God.

As such, however, what the Bible has to say about Israel's history is of primary interest to the student of ecclesiology, the theology of the Church, and that is not our subject in this book. Since our subject is the theology of Man, it is both a narrower topic than ecclesiology because it is about people as individual persons, and a wider one because it is concerned with the whole human race. So of particular interest to us is not what the Bible says about Israel or the patriarchs, but how it inserts their typological histories into the stories of mankind. It does this in Genesis 1 – 11. So it is to these chapters that we shall be referring again and again in the course of the book, and of these that we must say something by way of introduction now.

C.   GENESIS 1 – 11

How did the final editor of Genesis, and indeed the earlier writers whose work he was arranging and editing, conceive of the book? The answer admits of very little doubt: it is an introduction to the account of God's covenant with Israel, the basic charter of the nation's very existence, an introduction that tells us how the nation was chosen in its ancestors, Abraham, Isaac and Jacob. The ancestors were chosen for a purpose, to receive a blessing (a land and descendants), and this not just for their own sake or for the sake of the nation of Israel that would spring from them and with whom the covenant would be made, but that through them 'all the families of the earth might bless themselves' (Gen 12:3, 22:18, 28:14).[2] Israel, through its ancestors, has a responsibility towards the other nations to receive on their behalf a divine blessing and make it available to them. The final editor (or editors) of Genesis, or rather the Pentateuch, the Law or Torah to which it is an introduction, did not know how this would happen, but that it was divinely intended to happen he has placed on record. We know it has happened through the 'offspring of Abraham' 'which is Christ' (Gal 3:16).[3]

Meanwhile, who were these nations, how was Israel related to them, why were they all, including Israel, in need of a special blessing? These are the questions that the editor and his original authors answer in Gen 1 – 11. These chapters are a prologue, therefore, to an introduction to the story of God's covenant with Israel.

Now the story of God's covenant with Israel is a hi-*story*. It is rooted in definite past events, the exodus from Egypt, the giving of the Law on Sinai to Moses on behalf of the people. This is so, however much the narrative of these events may be embroidered by legendary material employed for doctrinal, apologetic and catechetical purposes. So the introductory stories about the patriarchs must also be historical in the same manner. They are envisaged by the writers as the historical roots of Israel's historical covenant with God.

Our immediate question, therefore, is: do we have to say the same about Gen 1 – 11, the prologue to the 'historical' introduction to the history of the covenant? The answer will have to be qualified and complex. Basically, it is 'Yes'. The writers and editor deliberately gave historical form to their narratives in these chapters. They include in them genealogies, which are the ancient form of historical chronology. Having embarked on a history of Israel's relations with God, the history of the covenant, and having gone behind that history to its antecedents in the ancestors, they decided to push the 'pre-history' right back to the beginning of time. 'In the beginning God . . . ' (Gen 1:1).

'Prehistory' is perhaps the right word here to show us how we have to qualify our answer as it stands so far. A modern prehistorian differs from a historian in that he cannot offer a narrative of events. He has no evidence for particular events, no records, no names of particular persons. On the evidence of archaeological remains, flints and bones and potsherds and so on, he can merely describe, and in the broadest outlines, a succession of types of culture. Now in the ancient world there were no such disciplines as archaeology or prehistory. Instead there were, yet again, stories: myths, sagas, tales, legends from the remote past. And this is the kind of material we find in Gen 1 – 11. The authors say, in effect, 'The human race existed before Abraham; it had a history, had a beginning, and this history from the beginning is extremely important, because it produced the situation we have today, or at least the situation we had in Abraham's time. Unfortunately we know absolutely nothing about it. But we do know by looking at ourselves and at our actual relations with God something of what that unknown prehistory must have been like. So here are some carefully selected stories to illustrate what human prehistory was like.' These stories then are in the strictest sense typological, type stories; and in no sense whatsoever are they descriptive of actual events. And yet they are historical in the sense that they claim to instruct us about how things must have developed from the beginning.

Gen 1 – 11 is often called a sin history, given as a prelude to the salvation history which begins with Abraham. This is not a complete description of these chapters as we shall see in Chapter 3, but it is true as far as it goes, and it enables us to see how to interpret these stories as typological. In Gen 12:1–3 we are told how God called Abraham and promised him a blessing that would benefit all the families of the earth. Fine; but why did and do they need such a special blessing? Obviously, because they are in a mess, in a state of singular unblessedness. The writers (or one of them) of Gen 1 – 11 analyse this state of unblessedness. Its most obvious and universal mark is conflict and division between different groups and nations; and not just that, but the collective pride which animates such conflicts. How did it all start? 'I haven't the slightest idea', says the author, 'but there must have been a first instance of such a state of affairs, and here is a story about it'; and he tells the typological story of the tower of Babel.

But such collective sin and unblessedness presupposes personal conflict and wrongdoing between individuals; war presupposes murder. And make no mistake – all murder is really fratricide, since all men are kin. How did murder begin? 'I haven't the slightest idea', he says, 'but it must have begun with a first murder, and here is a good story to illustrate it' – and he tells us the typological story of Cain and Abel.

Murder may be the most striking and terrible illustration of the unblessedness of human society; but people don't murder each other unless there is something more profoundly and mysteriously wrong with them, unless, that is to say, they are out of tune with the goodness of God. How do they get that way, and what is the basic and primal sin? He tells us the typological story of Adam and Eve and the serpent and the apple. And all these stories are put in a historical sequence (in the highest degree artificial, of course), because 'there must have been a first time', there must have been a beginning.

So to put our qualified answer in a nutshell, I think we can say that the narratives of Gen 1 – 11 are certainly history; they are not however (and do not purport to be) descriptive history, but typological or symbolic history.

D.   J AND P

I have mentioned the editor(s) and authors of Genesis. It is the common opinion of scholars that the Pentateuch, what the Jews call the Torah or Law of Moses, i.e. the first five books of the Bible, received its present form not long after the return of the Jews from exile in Babylon. A story of the canonization of the Law as sacred scripture is to be found in Neh 8:1-8, and is

associated with the name of Ezra. So we could, speaking purely typologic-
ally, call Ezra the editor, and date the final form of Genesis, as part of the
Torah, to 500–400 B.C.

It is equally the common opinion of the scholars, however, that the
Pentateuch, Genesis included, is a composite work of enormous complexity,
attributable to many hands or authors, whose work covered a span of
centuries. Since J. Wellhausen published his *Prolegomena to the History of
Israel*,[4] four basic strands of sources or traditions have been discerned
(Wellhausen called them documents), to which in order of their antiquity the
names have been given of *Yahwist* (where God is called Yahweh), *Elohist*
(where he is called Elohim), *Deuteronomist* and *Priestly Codex*; always known
by their initials as J (because the Germans spell Yahweh *Jahweh*), E, D and P.
These are commonly dated as follows: J to 950–900 B.C., E to 850–800 B.C.,
D to 650–550 B.C., and P to 550–500 B.C.[5] We are only concerned for the
time being with J and P because it is only these two that contribute to Gen 1
– 11. Of course, we must be aware of treating the common opinions of the
scholars as if they had the same divine authority as the tablets of the Law.
There are some rogue voices, for example, currently raised to date J from the
time of exile, i.e. as almost a contemporary of P. But I think no reputable
scholar any longer rejects the whole hypothesis of the four main traditions.

In the following chapters, while my presentation of the biblical and
Christian doctrine of man will in many ways depend upon the validity of the
distinction between J and P, because I will be contrasting and sometimes
comparing their points of view, it will not be greatly affected by the question
of their dating. So I shall follow the reigning 'orthodoxy' in the matter.

The material of Gen 1 – 11 is divided up between P and J as follows:

P	J
Gen 1:1 – 2:4a: Creation	
	2:4b – 4:26: Paradise, Fall, Cain and Abel, Cain's descendants
5:1–32: Genealogy of antediluvian patriarchs (with one nugget of J, v. 29)	
	6:1–4: Origin of giants
6:5 – 8:14: Flood (a mixture of J and P)	
	8:15–22: Blessing of Noah
9:1–17: Covenant with Noah	
	9:18–29: Sin of Canaan/Ham
10:1–32: Origin of nations	
	11:1–9: Tower of Babel
11:10–32: Final pre-Abraham genealogy	

E. THEOLOGICAL INTERPRETATION OF J AND P AND OTHER SUCH TRADITIONS

I talked in Chapter 1, B about the desirability of bridging the artificial chasm between dogmatic or systematic theology and biblical exegesis. One way of doing this is to give proper theological weight to the different points of view, the different ideas about our relationships with God, for example, that we find expressed by J and P and D, and the many other sources or traditions we find in scripture. It was Wellhausen's historical insight, his sense that the texts that we now call P and D represent two comparatively late and sophisticated interpretations of Israel's history, in conflict with more archaic narratives, which led him to formulate his classic four-document theory of the Pentateuch. It is no accident that this pioneer labour of critical analysis of the text was called by its author *Prolegomena to the History of Israel* (above, D, and below, note 4).

But biblical scholars, with their predominantly historical and analytic or critical interests, have not always fully appreciated the theological potential of their analyses. This means to say they have not been given to studying their texts in the light of revelation as a whole, or to considering what possible bearing they might have, even in a historical perspective, on Christian doctrine.[6]

Theologians, on the other hand, at least Catholic theologians, have either continued unreflectively to treat the Bible as a kind of fall-back or long-stop textbook (these are the ones I have called biblically illiterate), or else, aware of the complex developments in biblical studies and of their own unfamiliarity with them, have simply permitted the chasm between their own field and that of exegesis to continue unbridged. I think even Karl Rahner, SJ, the doyen of contemporary theologians, has tended to take this line. One man who has attempted very painstakingly to bridge the chasm, but only in the field of christology and New Testament studies, is Edward Schillebeeckx, OP, in his two massive volumes *Jesus* and *Christ*.

So in this book I want to make the most of the theological potential of J and P predominantly, but also of other contrasting schools of thought to be found in the scriptures. Doing this, and allowing it to be done without theological anxiety, involves appreciating that divine revelation, at least as received by men and communicated by human authors, is a highly dialectical process. We have already seen that it is a dramatic/historical process, and this in fact requires it to be dialectical. Just imagine a play without any dialogue, indeed without any argumentative dialogue, without any conflict not only between the heroes and the villains but even among the ranks of the heroes! So it is part of the divine condescension that God's revelation should proceed to unfold through the interplay of conflicting points of view, of opposed attitudes, through the high tension between contrasting values strongly cherished – as for example the tension between Peter and Paul (Gal 2:11–21), or on a smaller scale between Paul and Barnabas (Acts 15:36–41).

This dialogue of revelation, furthermore, has a continuity of pattern. The same kind of conflicts and tensions keep on recurring in different guises, and also keep on being resolved, or half resolved, at one level only to re-emerge at a higher (or deeper) one, and so be given a further more comprehensive resolution. It is thus no accident that Paul in his controversy with both Pharisees and Judaizing Christians constantly turns for support to the J sections of Genesis about Abraham, never to P. Of course, he knew nothing about J and P; for him it was all the divine Law, the Torah (the Pentateuch). But in his dialectical confrontation with his opponents he spontaneously picked up the echoes of that older one, in a way that I find of great theological interest.

Good textbooks don't contain inner contradictions. *A fortiori* a divine textbook cannot do so. So if you are misguided enough to assume that the Bible is a divine textbook, everything that has been said here will be a rock of offence to you and a stone of stumbling. You will also fail to appropriate most of the treasures the Bible has to offer you.

For it is not a textbook, but the text of a drama, a comedy, a tragedy, a pantomime, a pageant, presenting you as a matter of course with conflicts and opposing points of view. In this stupendous pageant J and P – and many other traditions or sources – can emerge, if you let them, as real characters, each with something *of their own* to say to us. We must decide *a priori* not to take offence or be scandalized – but as best we can, simply to listen.

NOTES

1 A. N. Whitehead, *Process and Reality* (1929) and *Religion in the Making* (1926); Rem B. Edwards, *Reason and Religion* (1972); Norman Pittenger, *God in Process* (1967); Charles Hartshorne and William Reese, *Philosophers Speak of God* (1969).

2 I prefer the traditional translation, given in the RSV footnote: 'shall be blessed'. I think it is theologically sounder. Perhaps 12:3 and 28:14 talk of 'families' instead of 'nations' because in the perspective of the stories, mankind was as yet divided only into families or clans, not nations.

3 What Paul actually wrote was 'the seed of Abraham', arguing from the word 'seed' used in Gen 22:18 and other texts. The RSV translates it as 'descendants' in those texts, here as 'offspring', and so the apostle's argument is obscured. This is the kind of thing I mean by theologically less satisfactory translations. Paul's argument may be odd, unconvincing to modern minds, and so forth. But there it is, and it seems to me that it is the translator's duty to make it accessible to the English reader.

4 In 1878, in German. It is, perhaps surprisingly, a most readable book.

5 See any commentary, e.g. *Jerome Biblical Commentary*, pp. 1–6: 'Introduction to the Pentateuch'; or the Jerusalem Bible, pp. 7–9: 'Introduction to the Pentateuch'.

6 There have, to be sure, been any number of biblical theologies, of which G. von Rad's

Old Testament Theology (2 vols) is perhaps the most distinguished. One much slighter book, but of particular relevance in our context, is Peter F. Ellis, CSSR, *The Yahwist*. But these are all *biblical* theologies and have all too easily, it seems to me, made yet another little watertight compartment for themselves, so that now we have biblical theology alongside dogmatic theology, moral theology, patristic theology etc., but as yet no co-ordination. A man who is obviously very concerned about this problem is Bernard Lonergan, SJ, who deals with it in *Method in Theology*: a most stimulating book that combines clarity and obscurity, simplicity and complexity in about equal proportions. But I am not sure if the final effect of Lonergan's system is not simply to rationalize the present situation of mutually unaware and indifferent compartments – he calls them 'specialties'.

QUESTIONS FOR FURTHER DISCUSSION

1   How is a theology of man to be related to the other psychological, sociological and philo-sophical studies of man available today?

2   What are the advantages and disadvantages of a historical/dramatic method in this subject?

3   What is the value of 'Process Theology'?

4   What is the theological value of the analysis of the Pentateuch into the sources, J, E, D and P?

5   What can the concept of typology bring to our understanding of being human?

RECOMMENDED FURTHER READING

Thomas Aquinas, *Summa Theologiae*, ET, vol. 1. With its introduction and appendices, it is a very useful introduction to theology and traditional theological method.

Bernard Lonergan, *Method in Theology*: see above, note 6.

Norman Pittenger, *God in Process*, is a convenient introduction to the mysteries of Process Theology.

Julius Wellhausen, *Prolegomena to the History of Ancient Israel* (its present title in ET), is the classic of Pentateuchal criticism. Though in many ways it is now out of date, reading it is a valuable experience, just to see how these mysterious characters J, E, D and P came into being.

Edward Schillebeeckx, *Jesus*, though very difficult and heavy reading, is worth the effort simply as a work of theology that does deliberately set out to dissolve and ignore the artificial divide between the biblical exegete and the systematic theologian. I doubt if it would fit into Lonergan's method.

3

Different Perspectives on Man and his History

(i) Man's history ought to have been totally different

My statement in the last chapter that Gen 1 – 11 constitutes a sin history is true as far as it goes. To be precise, it is true for J's contribution to these chapters, and not for P's. A sin history is J's prelude to the salvation history which it is his chief purpose to tell and which begins with Abraham; a prose epic of God's saving work for his people would be, perhaps, a better way of describing his whole enterprise.[1]

But this means that what J is in effect telling us is that the historical process which constitutes human existence is in itself *radically distorted*, so that it constitutes an inhuman or anti-human existence. This goes on getting steadily worse and worse until God intervenes, with the call of Abraham, to set the remedial salvation process going – though this has in fact been anticipated from the beginning by little indications of the divine forbearance. Remember, for example, how God clothed Adam and Eve with skins when he expelled them from Eden (Gen 3:21), how he put a mark on Cain to stop people killing him (4:15), how he saved Noah from the flood and promised him he would not send a flood again (8:21). J's pessimism about mankind as sinful is not total.

The point is, however, that J is telling us we cannot look at human history to discover what we really are, certainly not what we really ought to be, as human beings. We have this disastrous *penchant* for becoming what we are not, instead of becoming what we are.

And yet this distorted human history, the history of human wickedness, 'the register of the crimes, the follies and misfortunes of mankind',[2] must have started well, J says, from the creative act of 'the Lord, the Lord, a God merciful and gracious, slow to anger and abounding in steadfast love and faithfulness' (Exod 34:6, also a J passage; 'the Lord' is *Yahweh* in the Hebrew).

Thus on the one hand human history begins in paradise (Gen 2); on the other, it has been definitely cut off from paradise, from which the erring couple were expelled to get the historical ball rolling elsewhere, and to which any re-entry was barred by the cherubim and a flaming sword (3:23–24).

Can we say then that the paradise story should give us at least a hint of what human history, in J's view, ought to have been, or rather of what mankind in the persons of the first couple was beginning to be constituted as by its history before it took the wrong turning?

(ii) Man as he should have been

I think we can. But a superficially plausible suggestion to the contrary must at least be considered. This is, that history being what Gibbon said it is, an innocent and happy humanity would have had no history at all, and that it is thus a blissful *state* (not a *process*) that we glimpse in Gen 2. Such a view has at least this to be said for it, that the picture of Eden given in this chapter represents not only the original condition of man, but also a model for his final condition, when process will be complete and at an end. If this was not in the mind of J, it occurred at least to the minds of later biblical writers as the tradition developed. See for example Isa 11:6–9, Ezek 47:1–12 in the Old Testament, and in the New, Lk 23:43, the words of Jesus on the cross to the men being crucified with him, and Rev 22:1–5.

All the same, this anti-process line of thought won't really do. The paradise story is just that, a story: the story of a beginning, a becoming, happenings that are surely meant to lead to other happenings. Whoever heard of a story in which nothing happens? Certainly not ancient storytellers, whatever some modern writers may be able to produce in that genre. The man is fashioned, put in the garden, given a command (this is the dynamic focus of the story, as the sequel shows), shown the animals, provided with a suitable companion, the woman. If there had been no sin, J is therefore implying, history would certainly have been very different, totally different; but some kind of history there would still have been. It would all have taken place inside the 'enchanted garden' (which God would no doubt expand as need arose, to include the rest of the world). According to our actual sin-laden standards it would almost certainly have been excessively dull history, with no battles, tragedies, victories, heroes, villains – 'no wrecks and nobody drownded, Fact, nothing to laugh at at all', as Stanley Holloway put it in his recitation about *The Lion and Albert*.

But something would have happened. The man and his wife would have spurned the temptation, and would have been suitably rewarded.

Irenaeus, among the early Church Fathers, thinks of life in paradise as a childhood condition, and Adam and Eve as children, 'not knowing good and evil'.[3] This phrase is indeed a Hebrew idiom for designating childhood (see

Isa 7:16). The writer, though, fairly obviously pictures them as adults, but with the innocence of childhood, adults who had no need to 'turn and become like children' (Mt 18:3), because they were like that already as they came forth from the hands of the creator. What J emphasizes is the human value of littleness or humility, which we saw was the first value stated by Ps 8. The man is made of the dust of the earth (2:7); he is put in the garden to till and keep it (2:15), a very humble, unassuming, if pleasant occupation. He does indeed name the animals, thereby being permitted to demonstrate his superiority to them (2:19–20), but he exercises no other power over them. Finally, he and his wife are naked and unashamed (2:25). The writer could equally have written 'poor, with no dignity to stand on, and unashamed', for in his culture nakedness was not so much an indication of sexual immodesty as of indignity, something you inflicted on defeated enemies and slaves, something to mock and deride (see, e.g. 2 Sam 10:4, Isa 20:2–4). Yet this is the manner in which the first man and woman, who were also in a sense the ideal man and woman, existed – naked but without dishonour because without pride.

(iii)   A radical criticism of civilized values

From J's picture of the first couple in paradise, and also from his sin stories that follow, it is clear that he was highly critical of the values of civilization. He would have made short work of any nonsense about 'Western Christian civilization', such as Mr Ian Smith and his associates used to talk in the erstwhile Rhodesia of UDI, and such as many white people in South Africa are still talking in all seriousness today. (It is when nonsense is talked seriously, of course, that it is most dangerous and sinister.) Paradise, surely, was the last word (well, in fact it was the first word) in uncivilization, an idyll about innocent children of nature, in modern romantic terms.

Civilization began, in rudimentary form, with the expulsion of the man and woman from paradise *clothed in skins* (Gen 3:21),[4] and progressed rapidly with *Cain*, who was first of all a farmer (a 'higher' form of culture than Abel's pastoral existence) who did not succeed in pleasing God; and then after murdering Abel *founded a city* (4:3, 5, 17). Civilization[5] is built on blood. Compare the story of Romulus and Remus at the origins of Rome, the mother of Western civilization – and just note 1 Kgs 16:34. Furthermore, it is from Cain in J's history that the inventors of the arts are descended: 4:20–22. These men of genius are not merely the descendants of Cain, they are the sons of his most bloodthirsty descendant, Lamech (4:23–24).

After the flood we have a similar rapid progression. Noah, a tiller of the soil like Cain, discovers that other foundational fluid of civilization, alcohol (9:20–21). The *contretemps* that follows his drunkenness and nakedness (now shameful and the object of mockery by Ham/Canaan) brings a curse on Canaan – not on Ham, all racists and white supremacists please note (9:24–27). Now Canaan necessarily represents the Canaanites, whose urban civilization was overthrown by the pastoral nomadic Israelites under Joshua in the name of Yahweh their God.

Finally, there is the episode of Babel (11:1–4), in which the community of civilized man tries to climb up to heaven and rival God – precisely what civilized man, emancipated from the Eden of Christianity,[6] has been doing for all he is worth these last two hundred years or so.

Civilization (so J, as I read him) means pride, strife, greed, cruelty: inhuman and anti-human 'values'. True humanity is to be realized in simplicity of life, close to and almost subordinate to nature, and certainly respectful of it. Although sin has made this total simplicity impossible, it remains an ideal and a standard of judgement.

(iv)   Conditional immunity of innocent man from death

The one notable privilege enjoyed by man at his creation, as J presents him, was a conditional immunity from death. Some interpreters deny that this is implied in J's narrative, but I myself cannot see how any other inference can be drawn from the man's being told that if he eats of the forbidden fruit he will die (2:17). Therefore, if he doesn't, he won't. And you cannot say that the meaning of the divine warning is that eating the forbidden fruit will carry the death penalty, that if he eats it he will be executed, put to death, because when he did eat it he wasn't, and there is not the slightest suggestion, when we come to chapter 3 and the sentences God passes on the sinners, that Adam was in any sense granted a reprieve from execution.

Certainly it is the view of later biblical writers that there would have been no death if there had been no sin. That is how the tradition developed. 'God did not make death' (Wis 1:13); 'God created man for incorruption, and made him in the image of his own eternity, but through the devil's envy death entered the world' (ibid. 2:23–24). If the man, then, had obediently accepted the 'blissful ignorance' and lowliness of his created condition, he would not have died; and since he was the representative of the human race, neither would his consort or his offspring.

The history of a race of non-dying human beings would have been totally different from the history and prehistory we know. It is hard to imagine what it would have been like, but presumably it would have been very much briefer before being brought to its divinely appointed end or eschaton.[7] But it is a just and to my mind inescapable inference from J's style and substance that in his view there would have been, on that hypothesis of a sinless and hence undying human race, such a history and eschaton.

B. MANKIND AND ITS HISTORY ACCORDING TO P

(i) Man's history, though distorted, has followed the same lines as it would have done had there been no sin

P's view of man is in some ways much more 'realistic', less romantic, than J's, and as I see it, his narratives contain some deliberate criticisms and corrections of J. This at least would be likely if, as is the common view, P is to be dated some four hundred years after J.

For P, history as we know it began with creation, whereas for J it began with the expulsion from Eden. Thus after creating man God blessed them, saying (in the P narrative) 'Be fruitful and multiply, and fill the earth and subdue it; and have dominion over the fish of the sea and over the birds of the air and over every living thing that moves upon the earth' (Gen 1:28). Man, that is to say, is created with the positive mandate to exploit and develop the world; and what is this but developing civilization, which could be a very summary description of the whole historical process? P's ideal and goal was not the garden but the city.

Now an implication of this is surely that mankind (in P's view) was created *mortal*. For the historical process as we know it, the development of civilization and the complexification of cultures, is inconceivable without death relieving the current generation of the burdensome presence of too many of their ancestors. P's narrative, we must remember, passes straight from Gen 2:4a, the end of his creation story, to Gen 5, the list of antediluvian patriarchs, who all die, though to be sure they live magnificently long lives.[8] But they all die, and in P there has been no story of the fall. Death for him is natural, not a consequence of sin.

P's correction of J, indeed, starts at the very beginning. Over against J's emphasis on the lowliness of man, P asserts that he is made in the image and likeness of God (1:26–28). A tremendous, divine dignity is man's. Man has by God's creation in P what he aimed at achieving by disobeying the divine prohibition in J: being godlike. And therefore he is the lord of creation, and therefore he has to set out on the historical process to realize his God-given historical destiny.

(ii) Sin and the flood

But man does indeed distort this proper historical process by sin. The one and only sin P mentions in his share of Gen 1 – 11 is *violence* (6:11; cf. 9:5–6). Men should have exploited and developed the earth, and built their civilizations peacefully and harmoniously. Instead, they corrupted the earth by violence ('Well, what else can you expect from civilization?' murmurs the ghost of J – in this, more realistic than P). So God punishes them with the flood.

The flood is for P what the expulsion from Eden is for J. It marks the big break in human history. P presents the flood, as far as he can, as an act of *un-creation*, with the waters of the deep (Gen 1:2) and the waters above the firmament overwhelming the earth God had made by separating these forces of primeval chaos on the second and third days of creation (1:6–10). So with Noah after the flood God makes a new beginning, a new creation, and starts the historical process all over again. But this time he is prepared to put up with evil, and promises in spite of it never to destroy the earth again. This time he also makes a law to check and cope with evil (9:8–17, 4–6; I suspect this is P's endorsement of what J disapproved of as the blood feud in 4:23–24). For the rest, God's first blessing on man and woman is repeated with significant modifications for Noah (9:1–3, 7). Human existence and history have sadly deteriorated since creation, but not radically altered in character. And human beings are still in God's image (9:6), endowed with this tremendous godlike dignity, and therefore, we must infer, with some kind of godlike destiny.

So – where J's 'ideal' of human existence is rather that of the ecologist and conservationist, P's 'realistic' assessment of it is that of the developer and exploiter. For one, the modest man close to nature, adapting his life to nature; for the other, the confident man dominating nature and adapting it to his own ends.

NOTES

1 I say 'his' by a figure of speech, personifying the J tradition or source. I will do the same with P, purely as a matter of literary convenience. I like to think that with J, though hardly with the other traditions, there was a single creative author, or at least a very close group or school of men, behind the tradition. But that is not our concern here.

2 Gibbon, *The Decline and Fall of the Roman Empire*, vol. 1, ch. 3.

3 *Proof of the Apostolic Preaching*, 12; *Against Heresies*, III, 22, 4; cf. III, 23, 5; IV, 38, 1–4. Irenaeus was Bishop of Lyons from 177 to *c*. 200 A.D.

4 Notice that the garments of skin are said to have been made for them by God. So I am not saying that J rejected civilization as evil in itself. No, but it is in his view a consequence of the evil of sin, something therefore to be accepted and endured as willed by God, like death and sickness. And its so-called values are to be regarded with a very sceptical eye because they are so frequently false and bogus.

5 'Civilization' means the culture of a *civitas* or city.

6 But of course man has never really lived there; as G. K. Chesterton drily remarked, the emancipated statement that Christianity has been tried and found wanting is not true, because Christianity has been found difficult and left untried.

7 *Eschaton* is the Greek for 'last'. It has become a theological word for the end of the world, the end of time, and that part of theology that deals with such matters is called *eschatology*.

8 I need hardly repeat that the ages of these patriarchs are not to be taken as literally descriptive. They are symbolic or typological, though of what precisely we can no longer tell. That they are so, however, is indicated by Enoch's age, 365 years (5:23), a year of

years; perhaps he was a symbolic solar man. In purely general terms we may perhaps say that this antediluvian longevity signifies the splendid vigour of mankind as created by God before the degeneration of sin set in. For P, though he has no fall story, and is not, like J, writing a sin prehistory, does not ignore the existence of sin. See subsection B, ii.

QUESTION FOR FURTHER DISCUSSION

1   How do the J and P narratives in Gen 1 – 11 differ in their presentation of the early history of mankind?

4

Questions about the Origins of Man

A. HOW TO RECONCILE THE VIEWS OF J AND P

(i)   What they have in common

We saw in the last chapter that J and P have very different views about the origins, the character and the history of the human race, and we are going to come across similar differences between them several times more in subsequent chapters. But we must not overlook what they have in common.

First of all, they are both within the same Israelite religious tradition, both witnesses to God's revelation through the history of his chosen people.

Both, therefore, are monotheists. J says that Yahweh, the God of Israel, is also the God who created the whole human race, and by implication therefore is the God of all men, by whatever other names he may be known. P says that it is one God who created heaven and earth and the human race, and this one God will in due course reveal his name of Yahweh to his chosen people Israel.

Both insist on the goodness of God's creation, hence on the goodness of man as created.

Both are, by implication, 'Process theologians' as far as a doctrine of man is concerned; that is to say, both imply by their writing of stories and typological histories that mankind can only be known through its histories, its stories.

(ii)   Contrasting emphases, not mutually exclusive doctrines

It is because they have these common foundations that both traditions were included by the final editors of the Pentateuch in what the tradition soon came to regard as the sacred text. Therefore, as believing heirs to that tradition, we cannot suppose that we are compelled to choose between them in the sense of deciding that the teaching of one is true and of the other false. But we can accept them as representing contrasting attitudes and emphases in considerable tension with each other; contrasting attitudes which are bound to generate critical arguments and debates; emphases and points of view between which at any given time we do have to choose.

For the point about two variant emphases is that you cannot emphasize them both at the same time, but you can emphasize each at different times. A play may be acted this way or that way, in modern dress or in period costume, with the producer emphasizing this or that aspect. A producer may at various times produce it in all these various ways without being open to the charge of self-contradiction. But at any given time he has to choose. A pianist won't always play a piece of music the same way with the same emphases and tempo and feeling. How he does it will vary according to his mood, his audience, the place, the historic occasion. And you cannot say that one way of playing is true, all the others false; one way right, all the others wrong. But at any given time you have to choose, and people will argue and disagree about the choice to be made.

So with the emphases of J and P. I remarked at the end of the last chapter that J seems to represent the stance of the ecologist and conservationist, P that of the developer and exploiter of resources. Each stance is taken today by different people with different interests, with varying degrees of passion, and they frequently clash head on in demonstrations as well as in parliamentary debates and in law suits. But it is a gross abuse of reason, the abuse of over-simplification and of stunted logic to treat one as true and the other as false, one as always right and the other as always wrong. Sometimes the developer will have right on his side in a particular instance (in my opinion, but not perhaps in yours), sometimes the conservationist. Sometimes it will be important to stress J's insight into human lowliness and creaturely simplicity, sometimes to stress P's value of man's tremendous dignity as made in the image of God. And often it will not be possible, or at least relevant, to stress them both together. But Ps 8 has already shown us that each is a profound insight into the truth of man's relationships with God, and to deny either in favour of the other would simply be to commit theological bigotry.

(iii)   Each fulfilled in Jesus Christ

So much are the essential teachings of J and P not mutually contradictory that both sets are fulfilled in Jesus Christ. He, if anybody, is the Man for All Seasons, the universal man, in whom the differences between human beings are transcended without being abolished, and thus are fulfilled. So he is 'gentle and lowly in heart' (Mt 11:29), and the servant of God, thus fulfilling J's conception of man; and by his obedience (which was required of J's man) he opens again the gates of paradise which had been closed by J's first man failing to be what he ought to have been.

At the same time Jesus Christ is 'the image of the invisible God, the first-born of all creation' (Col 1:15; cf. 2 Cor 4:4), thus perfectly fulfilling P's ideal of man in his God-given excellence.

The destiny of man, too, as implied by each tradition, is fulfilled in the New Testament *eschaton*, in which the garden (J) and the city (P) are finally united (Rev 21, 22:1–5).

B.   GENESIS 1 AND 2 AND MODERN SCIENCE: EVOLUTION

(i)   No conflict between Bible and science

I think this is a point we need not linger on here. We have already seen that the writers and editors of Genesis were not writing descriptive history, but rather telling typological stories as their way of making sense of prehistory. They were asserting that the human story from its totally unknown beginning has a meaning, to be traced in man's relations with God; and in their own way they were stating their sense of that meaning. Much less, then, were they purporting to write descriptive science. They therefore cannot possibly contradict or be contradicted by modern scientific palaeontology and theories of the emergence and development of living forms – unless scientists stray from their proper field and start making theological (which include anti- and a-theological) assertions.

Evolutionary theories, then, about the origins of the human race, the species *homo sapiens*, are quite compatible with Christian doctrine and commitment to the special authority of scripture. More than this, Christians have no right at all to criticize theories of evolution as such on theological grounds. And again, until theories of evolution are overthrown on scientific grounds, I would say that Christian theologians are bound to acknowledge that the great weight of evidence at the moment tilts the scales massively in favour of such theories.

(ii)   Assumptions underlying theories of evolution

But we must notice some points that are often overlooked. Although evolutionary theories (there are, I understand, more than one propounded by scientists) are strictly theories about the origin of biological species, there are certain non-biological, implicitly metaphysical assumptions presupposed to them; particularly assumptions about value, revealed in such expressions as 'higher and lower forms of life'. Now there is nothing wrong with having such assumptions, provided the biological scientists are aware of them, and aware that these assumptions and presuppositions are in no sense proved by the evidence adduced to prove the theories.

Furthermore (and here is where dangerous and sometimes sinister mistakes can be made) we must be quite clear that the values presupposed in the expression 'higher and lower forms of life' are ontological, *not moral* values. And above all we must be even more clear that evolutionary theories are elaborated and more or less completely verified with respect to the evolution of biological species, and not with respect to the historical succession of human cultures.

This is where sinister side-effects of theories of evolution are most plainly to be observed. Such a Darwinian catchphrase as 'survival of the fittest' is transferred without critical reflection from the biological to the human social field and becomes, for example, a spurious 'scientific' justification of the maxim 'Might is right'. The succession of human cultures from simple to complex, from primitive (which properly speaking only means 'first' or 'original') to developed is viewed in illegitimate biological terms as an evolution from lower to higher, from cultures of less value and moral worth to cultures of higher value and moral worth. The historical, social category of progress (perfectly valid in limited contexts) is given a spurious and invalid universality by being assimilated to the biological category of evolution.

And so we get that sinister development known as social Darwinism, the spurious, pseudo-scientific justification of such nastinesses as racism and anti-semitism and Nazism. Such bogus and anti-human 'scientific' theories, I am happy to say, are in no sense whatever endorsed by Christian doctrine or by scripture, not even by P's underwriting of the values of civilization. He was not mixing up biological and historical or social categories.[1]

C. THE ORIGIN OF THE HUMAN SOUL

(i) *Catholic teaching on the point*

As regards strictly scientific theories on the origins of the species *homo sapiens*, Catholic theology does have two important reservations, both explicitly made in Pius XII's encyclical letter *Humani Generis* of 1950. One is about monogenism, or the human race being descended from one original pair; we will discuss that in the next section. The other, which we shall consider here, concerns the origin of the human soul.

It is said, in effect, that the theory of the evolution of man from lower forms of life can be accepted as regards the human body (man as an organism, we should say), but not as regards the human soul (man as an intelligent being or person, with an eternal destiny). The human soul, according to Catholic teaching, is immediately and directly created by God out of nothing. We are talking of the souls of all human beings, not just the first human beings to have evolved, as regards their bodies, from sub-human ape-like forms. So this point of Catholic teaching is more than just a reservation about the theory of evolution; it is also a reservation about what I imagine are ordinary biological views on the generation of individuals by sexual reproduction. We don't owe our souls, says this teaching, to our parents but immediately to God; only our bodies are derived from our parents; or in the case of the first human beings, from lower forms of life by a process of evolution.

In *Humani Generis* Pius XII says that Catholic faith obliges us to hold that souls are created by God (Dz 3896/2327²). This would appear to mean that the doctrine, according to Pius XII, is *de fide*, an article of Catholic faith. Notice, the Pope was not in this document claiming to define the doctrine as being *de fide*; he merely remarks in an aside that Catholic faith obliges us to hold it. And he omits to give his reasons for saying so – natural enough, perhaps, in an aside. But the fact is that there does not seem to have been any formal and official definition of the doctrine in the history of the Church's tradition. So it is possible to hold that Pius XII was a little too definite about it there in *Humani Generis*.

An article in the *Dictionnaire de Théologie Catholique* on 'Traducianism' (the opinion that souls are not created by God but transmitted by parents; so named from the Latin *traducere*, to transmit) concludes by saying, 'Certainly, no explicit definition has sanctioned as a dogma of faith the creation of each individual soul at the very moment of its infusion into the body it is to animate . . . . But it is a clear consequence of the interventions of the *magisterium*, directly or indirectly referring to traducianism, that this teaching must be regarded henceforth not merely as improbable or lacking doctrinal support, but as positively erroneous. A more severe theological censure cannot, it would seem, be attracted to it' (vol. 15, 1364). It is pointed out in the article that the question of defining the doctrine was raised at Vatican I, but that it was eventually decided to leave the matter alone (*ibid.*, 1360).

Pius XII, however, was probably basing his opinion about the *de fide* character of the doctrine of the immediate creation of the soul on what Thomas Aquinas says about it: 'to suppose that the intelligent soul is caused by the begetter [St Thomas' Aristotelian biology allowed almost no causative efficacy to the female conceiver] is quite simply to suppose that it is not subsistent, and consequently that it perishes with the body. *And therefore it is heretical* to say that the intelligent soul is passed on from begetter to begotten with the seed' (*STh* Ia, 118, ii; ET, vol. 14). In any case it cannot be doubted that the doctrine of the human soul's immediate creation by God has been official, unanimous Catholic teaching for centuries. So it is undoubtedly 'certain' even if not 'of faith'.

(ii)   Difficulties of the doctrine

The problem, to my mind, is that as formulated – 'the human soul is immediately created by God, while the human body is produced by the natural reproductive process, or at the beginning by a natural evolutionary process' – the doctrine is really very unsatisfactory. It is unsatisfactory from the human end because it seems to favour a philosophical view of man that has been devastatingly satirized by Professor Gilbert Ryle in his book *The Concept of Mind* as 'the ghost in the machine' theory, which is in point of fact Descartes' theory of man, which in its turn is an oversimplified or degenerate version of Plato's theory of man and the soul. This kind of philosophical anthropology is neither consonant with the consistent biblical awareness of man, nor agreeable to the dominant contemporary experience and awareness of man, at least in Europe and America.

The word 'soul' is itself so problematic nowadays in English (and I suspect the same is true for its equivalents in other European languages) that a formulation of a *de fide* doctrine of the Church which contains it is rendered *ipso facto* unsatisfactory, since the presence of the word is going to make it difficult to convey to ordinary people what the doctrine is really saying. But we will be seeing much more of this question in our chapters devoted to the subject of 'body and soul'. Here it is enough to remark, by way of balancing what I have just said, that Aquinas accepted and propounded this doctrine, as we have just seen, and he did not in fact subscribe to the Platonic philosophy of man, and cannot justly be satirized as believing in a 'ghost in the machine'.

Again, the doctrine as formulated is unsatisfactory from the divine end. For it appears to subordinate God's action to the actions of his creatures; to tie God to creating and 'infusing' a human soul every time a human couple causes a human body (on this formulation) to be conceived by the male sperm fertilizing the female ovum.

This difficulty is easier to surmount, in my opinion, than the other. Tackling it enables us once more to drive home some very necessary teaching about God. That is that we cannot talk about God's being or his actions in the same way as we talk about the being and actions of creatures, as though they were being and actions in exactly the same sense in each case. They are not. God is not a being among beings, a thing among things, a person among persons, an agent among agents, a cause among causes. To confine ourselves to the correction of the last phrase, he is the cause of causes, the cause in all causes. According to the scholastic tag, *Deus operatur in omni operante*; God is active in every activity (*STh* Ia, 105, v; ET, vol. 14). This in no way subordinates his activity to that of creatures, but on the contrary it is declaring that all creaturely activity, all natural causality, is rooted in and depends on and is enabled by the continuous (and in itself timeless and eternal) providential activity of God. So when a human child is conceived God is operative in the natural causes and actions producing that effect, just as he is when a piglet or a calf or a chick is conceived; but with this additional difference that in the case of human conception God's action consists in making something out of nothing, namely a human soul. We are back with our first difficulty, but have, I suggest, eliminated the second.

But the mere fact of a doctrine, or rather its formulation, being seriously unsatisfactory does not warrant our rejecting it. That would only be so if, in this case, the doctrine were formulated in order to carry through or substantiate or impose an unsatisfactory philosophy of man or of God. But that is not so. The basic concern of the doctrine is quite other. To discover what it is and then perhaps to attempt a more satisfactory formulation of it we must begin by tracing its history.

(iii) History of the doctrine

In the Graeco-Roman world into which Christianity was born the language of 'soul' and 'body' governed all reflection on the nature of man, and especially on man's relationship with the divine sphere. I should say, rather, the language of 'soul' and 'spirit', because there was a fairly universal tendency among all schools of thought to disdain body and matter – a tendency that thoroughly and unhappily infected Christianity. The dominant philosophies, Stoicism and various forms of Platonism, were all highly moral and religious philosophies, and hence concerned to stress man's affinity with the divine rather than with the animal world. Christian thinkers like Origen (d. 253), thoroughly Platonic in their outlook, saw no difference in kind between human souls and angels. Others, more influenced by Stoicism, were inclined to conceive of the soul as an emanation from the divine substance. So it was against such views that the orthodox reaction of the Church came to emphasize that the soul is created by God (and thus is not derived from the divine substance), and moreover is created by God as the soul of this or that human person (and thus is not of the angelic nature). So we have this statement in a credal formula sent by Pope Leo IX in 1053 to the Patriarch Peter of Antioch: 'I believe and preach that the soul is not a part of God, but is created from nothing, and without baptism is subject to original sin' (Dz 685/348).

This mention of original sin brings us to the other context of this doctrine of the creation of the soul immediately by God. The question of the origin of the human soul began to be a matter of keen interest during the controversy conducted by Augustine and his supporters with the Pelagians on grace and original sin. We shall be looking at the whole question of original sin in a subsequent chapter; here we need only state that according to Catholic doctrine it is a condition of alienation from God that all human beings derive, by simply being born into membership of the human race, from the first ancestors of the race. The question is, how is it derived? One answer, which

Augustine found rather attractive, though he never committed himself to it, and remained agnostic about the origin of the human soul to the end of his life, was that it is inherited through our parents because we derive our souls from our parents; our souls as well as our bodies, our whole selves in fact, are procreated. This is the view called 'traducianism'. The point is that original sin, though often talked about on the analogy of disease as an infection, being a moral condition attaches to the soul rather than the body; and if it is to be derived from our first parents, how can this be unless our souls derive from them? We will try and answer the questions in a later chapter (7, A, i).

Thus it appears that the doctrine of the immediate creation of the soul by God has been developed in the Church almost in opposition to the doctrine of original sin, and in no sense as a consequence of it. This, and St Augustine's hesitations on the matter, help to explain how the doctrine never came to be formally defined, or traducianism formally condemned.

But what traducianism logically contradicts, though most, if not all, of its proponents in Augustine's time did not see this, is the spiritual nature of man. It is in fact a materialist doctrine, as Thomas Aquinas saw in the passage quoted above. It is the essential, divinely revealed truth that man is more than just an animal (though a little less than the gods; Ps 8) that is being safe-guarded by this doctrine of the soul's immediate creation by God, this theo-logical reserve about evolutionary explanations of the origins of the human race.

(iv)   Towards a more satisfactory formulation

The unsatisfactoriness of the formula we are discussing is entirely a modern problem, and is due to what you might call the semantic disintegration of the word 'soul'. It has come to such a pass that some people will say they don't believe in the soul, and others say that they do. The soul something to be believed in or not! You might as well talk about believing or not believing in the self or in the life of living organisms. No wonder Professor Ryle ridiculed this notion as the ghost in the machine. But that is what has happened to the word (under the corrosive influence, I regret to say, of half-baked and over-simplified Christian doctrine on all modern European languages). So to say that God creates the soul, and parents (and evolution at the beginning) reproduce the body is inevitably going to mean to almost everybody, believer and non-believer alike, that God creates the ghost, parents and evolution produce the machine. Non-believers (rightly) will scoff, believers stoically endure the mystification.

But the point must be made that the authentic (though not, I rather think, the prevalent) Catholic notion of 'soul' is not that of a ghost in the machine. It is not authentic Catholic teaching that body and soul are two parts of the human being, like peanut butter and bread being the two parts of a peanut butter sandwich. The authentic Catholic teaching, formally declared at the little-known Council of Vienne in 1311, is that the 'rational or intelligent soul is the form of the human body' (Dz 902/481). The soul precisely 'animates' the body, and the soul cannot but be the soul (life principle) of the living body. For the mediaeval scholastics, above all St Thomas, the soul was anything but a ghost in the machine.

Still, the word, I fear, is nowadays irredeemable. So we must try and find a formulation of the doctrine that does not use it. I cannot here suggest a neat formulation. But what we want to assert as believers, surely, is that man (i.e. all human beings without exception, in virtue of their being human) has a direct relationship with God and orientation to God that cannot be predicated of the rest of the material, or animal, world of which man is indeed a part. And this relationship and orientation cannot be derived from the material world, or from man's materiality. It is a quality of his life as precisely being more than animal or biological life, as transcending these levels of life. So man's life, as having this quality, can only derive immediately, creatively, from God. How then, to conclude, did I come to exist? We mustn't say (and the common doctrine of the Church does not in fact say) that part of me was created by God, and the other part was begotten by my father and conceived by my mother. What we do have to say is that in one and the same event I, this human being, was created by God and I, this human being, was begotten by my father and conceived by my mother.

D. MONOGENISM

Pius XII had one other reservation about evolutionary theories in his encyclical letter *Humani Generis*. I suppose that most scientists forming their hypotheses on the subject assume that man evolved from lower forms of life as a species of several members, as a small population. Perhaps some incline to the view that this happened in more than one part of the world. In any case, they do not trace the human race back to a single pair or couple at the beginning.

Now the Pope says in this document that this view of human origins (called polygenism, the origination of humanity from many) is not agreeable to Catholic teaching 'since it is not at all clear how this kind of opinion can be reconciled with what the sources of revealed truth and the acts of the Church's *magisterium* have to say about original sin, which proceeds from the sin really committed by the one Adam, and which being transmitted to all by generation belongs properly to every human being' (Dz 3897/2328).

So according to Pius XII Catholics are committed to monogenism, the view that the whole human race springs from one original couple (which we may certainly suppose came into being by the evolutionary process). But should theologians manage to show that some or any polygenist theory can be reconciled with the doctrine of original sin, then presumably the objection to such polygenism would fall away.

Karl Rahner thinks that this has been achieved by theologians, and briefly gives his explanation in the article 'Monogenism' in *Sacramentum Mundi*. I confess I cannot follow his argument. Meanwhile, we must observe that there is no biological *proof* available of either polygenism or monogenism, nor is there likely to be. There is certainly no reason to dismiss monogenism as biologically impossible, or even improbable, and in some ways, I would have thought, it is scientifically the more economical theory. But that is for scientists to decide.

There is, however, another profound theological argument in favour of monogenism, proposed by St Augustine (*City of God*, XII, 21; *PL* 41, 372). St Augustine, of course, knew nothing about evolution, but he took it for granted that when God created the animals, he created several of each species at the beginning.

But man he created in one single specimen, not indeed to leave him destitute of human society, but to commend to him more insistently by this means the unity of this society and the bond of concord. For in this way men would be connected with each other not only by likeness of nature but also by the sentiment of kinship. Even the woman who was to be joined to the man God preferred not to create in the same way as him, but to make her from him, so that the whole human race might issue from one man.

Unity and concord founded on kinship; we are not just one species, we are one family, one blood. It is serious, urgent and powerful doctrine, a standing criticism against all racial, social, aristocratic exclusivism. And we must remember that perhaps the basic function of the Church of God in the world is to promote and realize this unity, to prompt the human race to become what it is – one, a universal brotherhood. ' . . . The Church is in Christ a kind of sacrament, or sign and instrument of intimate union with God and of the unity of the whole human race' (Vatican II's Constitution on the Church, *Lumen Gentium*, I, 1; cf. II, 9).

Is it sufficient for this close unity, this kinship, to be symbolized in the typological story of the creation of Adam, without its having to be founded in actual genetic fact? I myself would say not, and in indirect support of my view would simply draw attention to the readiness with which all those people who reject and decry the concept of human unity, because it undermines their cherished notions of superiority, have recourse to polygenist theories of human origins. I am not saying that being a polygenist makes you a racist. But I am saying that being a racist makes you a polygenist, and that makes me very chary of polygenism.

NOTES

1 One could not possibly accuse Teilhard de Chardin of social Darwinism. But I do think he makes the mistake in *The Phenomenon of Man* and elsewhere of reducing the historical category of progress to the genetic category of evolution. He says somewhere that history (or progress) is the form taken by evolution once the transition has been made from the 'biosphere' (the field of evolving forms of life) to the 'noösphere' (the field of human history) by the evolution of man from lower forms. According to his line of argument I think you are compelled to say that the life of civilized twentieth-century man is a higher form of human life than that of, say, Aurignacian man 20,000 years ago (and thus, by implication, than that of aboriginal Australian man today), just as human life is a higher form of biological life than that of the amphibians from which it has remotely evolved several million years ago. This does not *necessarily* lead to social Darwinism, because the Chardinists could say that it is the *culture* of modern civilized man that is higher (better) than the *culture* of aboriginal Australian man in their view; not the white European man a higher specimen of the human species than the black Australian man.

But the danger is there, and certainly the mistake of categories is there, with the consequent tendency to take a deterministic view of human history. Teilhard de Chardin was very much a man of the nineteenth century, even though all his work was done in the first half of the twentieth.

2 In Dz references, the first number refers to the section in the 33rd edition (1965), the second to the section in the 31st (1957).

QUESTIONS FOR FURTHER DISCUSSION

1 Are the very different approaches of J and P to man and his condition and history of any contemporary interest?

2 How can we deal with conflict between Christian doctrines on the origins of man and scientific theories of evolution?

3 Is the Catholic teaching about the direct creation by God of every human soul tied to an unsatisfactory philosophy of man? If so, can it be liberated from such a philosophy?

4 How are we to understand the term 'soul' today?

5 Has monogenism any value for a contemporary anthropology?

RECOMMENDED FURTHER READING

Gilbert Ryle, *The Concept of Mind*, for those readers of a philosophical turn of mind, presents a trenchant critique of the Cartesian assumptions that have infected so much 'Christian' language.

Peter F. Ellis, *The Yahwist*, is a useful little book to supplement Wellhausen, and help the reader to put some flesh and blood into these abstractions (even if the flesh and blood are highly tentative).

Pierre Teilhard de Chardin, *Science and Christ* and *The Vision of the Past*, as well as his more central and well-known *The Phenomenon of Man*, give a great Christian's powerful and influential attempt to baptize the discoveries and theories of science since Darwin, and digest them theologically. Teilhard's world-view has met with severe criticism from both scientists and theologians. I have made my own reservations about it clear in note 1 above.

Karl Rahner, *Theological Investigations*, 1, chapter 9: 'Concerning the Relationship between Nature and Grace'.

Etienne Gilson, *The Spirit of Mediaeval Philosophy*, chapter 9: 'Christian Anthropology'.

5

The State of Innocence: Original Justice

A. J'S INSIGHT TO BE PREFERRED TO P'S

In the last chapter I was arguing that the differences between J and P were more matters of perspective and emphasis than of direct disagreement or confrontation. But that is not a complete assessment of the matter. There are points in which one is to be preferred to the other. On this question of the state of innocence the main Christian tradition has certainly endorsed the insights of J rather than of P.

To be sure, until the development of the higher criticism in the nineteenth century, the tradition was itself innocently unaware of the differences between J and P and their divergences. It followed J instead of P on this matter because in fact J has more to say about it. But the divergence between them here is theologically, instructive and merits closer examination.

On the hypothesis we are accepting, J is the older source by some four hundred years or so. And he gives us the picture of man and woman in paradise in Gen 2. Now although, for reasons we saw in Chapter 2, C, we cannot without qualification label this picture and the whole story of Adam and Eve as a myth, it certainly has a great many mythical features,[1] and a kind of myth-like tone to it. The picture is of course drawn in order to emphasize the goodness of man's original condition as established by the creator. But it does more than this; it implies, with its picture of the enchanted garden, of perfect simplicity, and its suggestion of immunity from death and hence from suffering, that such a condition requires a special divine protection from evil; that it is not, to use a word that J knew nothing of, natural. It was precisely an ideal condition, an ideal world, from which nature as we know it and as J knew it represents a catastrophic fall or lapse. These are the later theological terms that are very aptly employed to designate the climax of J's story, though he does not use them himself.

Now P, I suggest, writing during the exile or shortly after, is not at all happy with this mythical element in J. The more I read Gen 1 the more I am struck by what I can only call the rationalism of P. He would have been entirely at home in the eighteenth-century Enlightenment (well, almost; he was no deist, but it was possible to be rational and classicist at that time without being a deist). 'Of course', he says, 'God's creation is very good – and it does not require magical means and defences to make it so. It is very good *as it is*. Man was created as he is now, and that was and is good. Human nature is good as it is, even with its liability to suffering and death, natural concomitants of a material and temporal mode of existence. Of course, men have spoilt things by sin. But they don't need to if they don't want to, and in any case that does not eliminate the basic God-given goodness of human nature, and indeed of all nature.' So before sin (this I think is the implication of P) neither human nature nor the human condition were basically different from what they are now, and from the first moments of its existence the human race set out on its divinely appointed task of development, of mastering the world, of constructing cultures and civilization.

I would say that the only significant differences between P and contemporary rationalists and humanists in their overall view of human history are: first that he was a convinced believer in God, and secondly that he had no evolutionary assumptions colouring his value judgements of 'primitive man'. He never constructed a 'cave-man mythology' of his own: man with club and prognathous features dragging home shrieking female (also with prognathous features but no club) by the hair.

P was the great demythologizer of those times. For him man is in fact Aristotle's 'rational animal', a part of the natural order of the cosmos; the crowning part indeed, but still a part of nature, subject to the laws and processes of nature – and no more.[2]

P's view of man and his origins, then, is one that readily appeals, once it has been perceived for what it is under its very different cultural expressions, to the modern mind, so strongly influenced, *au fond*, by scientific rationalism. But from the standpoint of Christian doctrine it is a view that is very defective. Certainly, it represents a sophisticated critique of J's mythical picture. But in this respect its sophistication is the measure of its superficiality – as with much contemporary sophistication.

J says, in effect, that you cannot simply reduce man to nature, and Christian doctrine very explicitly says the same. We got a glimpse of this affirmation in the last chapter, with the doctrine of the immediate creation by God of the human soul. There is that to being human which is more than just a natural process, more even than the crown and summit and glory of all natural processes. Sin therefore cannot be thought of as a merely natural aberration for which purely natural remedies are available. It is the negation, the cancellation of this 'more' to being human. So man in his innocence, at his origins, must have been in a condition qualitatively different from that in which he finds himself today. He wasn't simply what he is today with the warts removed.

J with his myth-coloured picture of paradise perceives this; P with his acute but more superficial rational critique does not. But even so, the classical Catholic tradition, as represented here by Thomas Aquinas, manages to save what is just and valuable in P's rationalism, and to combine it in a harmonious synthesis with J's supernaturalism – to use a concept that we shall have to look at more closely in a moment.

B.   MAN CREATED IN GRACE

(i)   *The need for elevating grace*

The traditional theological word for this plus quality that characterizes human existence is 'grace'. No, that is not quite accurate. The plus quality of human existence is simply the capacity and need for grace. And by capacity here I mean something entirely passive, like the capacity of a jug or tank to contain so much, a sheer and mere openness. I do not mean a capacity to do things in an active sense. This purely passive capacity for grace is sometimes called in a technical scholastic expression 'obediential potency'.

For this is the paradox of being human at its very base or root; God in his goodness has made us too big for our boots (where boots stand for nature), or perhaps made our boots too big for us (where boots stand both for our original condition and our destiny). Anyway, he has given us, as intelligent beings, a destiny which we are absolutely unable to achieve by our own powers and natural resources; a capacity we are absolutely unable to fill by ourselves. The capacity is for God himself, the destiny is to share his life, to be divinized. We thus have a destiny and a capacity that go beyond our nature. It is our *nature* as intelligent creatures (the same must be true of whatever other intelligent beings may have been created, like angels and cherubim) to have a destiny and a capacity that go beyond our nature. To attain this destiny and fill this capacity we need God's grace, which is just a word for his free giving of himself, and his freely helping us to rise above the limitations of our created nature to achievements beyond our natural powers. In the traditional technical language he 'elevates' us by his grace above our natural limitations, and so this grace is named elevating grace, and the state or condition to which we are elevated is termed 'supernatural'.[3]

But it is not really my task here to talk about us as we are now; rather to discuss 'us' as we were in the first human beings, the first human couple, according to the view preferred in the last chapter, before sin came on the scene. For simplicity's sake let us call them Adam and Eve and be done with it.

Now it is as theologically certain as anything can be that they were created by God in grace, or 'established in holiness and justice' as a more ancient formula had it.[4] The proof text from which Aquinas argues to this conclusion (a conclusion long held in the tradition without this argument to support it) is not from Gen 2, curiously enough, but Qo 7:29: 'God made man upright' ('straightforward/simple': NEB, JB). Now this uprightness consisted in his reason being duly submissive to God, and as a consequence his lower powers being submissive to his reason and his body to his soul (*STh* Ia, 95, i; ET, vol. 13).

But, says St Thomas, this submission of body to soul and lower powers (drives, emotions, instincts) to reason was not 'by nature'. For if it had been, it would have persisted even after Adam and Eve withdrew the submission of their reason to God by their first disobedience, since the specific nature and natural attributes of a thing are not altered by its aberrations, by sin. So as this harmonious submission of lower powers to mind is not verified by experience of human existence after sin, it can only have existed before sin as an effect of supernatural grace elevating man above his natural condition. And hence, to complete his argument, the submission of man's reason to God, of which these two other submissions were the consequence, must also have been a gift of supernatural grace.

It is here, I feel, that St Thomas and the main Catholic tradition with him do some justice to the instincts of P. Sin does not alter nature as such. Man, like other creatures of God, continues to be the same sort of thing with the same sort of essential qualities and structures after the sin factor was introduced as he was before. The differences between St Thomas and P is that P really has no inkling of grace, or of any other dimension of existence for creatures than simply that of creatures – i.e. what we now call the natural. In consequence he has a rather superficial idea of sin and its effects, as we shall see in Chapter 6.

(ii) Human nature in itself

St Thomas' argument, however, implies a very different and much more problematic idea of human nature than any which P may have had. P, as I read between his lines, accepted death as natural and therefore presumably at least a modicum of suffering. But in addition to death and suffering, St Thomas regards as also natural to man a radical disharmony between the component elements of his nature; he regards as natural 'the law in my members being at war with the law of my mind', as Paul puts it (Rom 7:23). So it is not just that man has been made too big for his boots, as we expressed it in the last section, with a supernatural destiny beyond his natural powers to attain. This is true of any intelligent being, and the apparent paradoxicality of this is not in itself absurd or inharmonious; it is simply a consequence of the infinite gap between creator and creature. The oddness of human nature as St

Thomas sees it, is that in addition to this orientation to a destiny beyond itself it is inherently cross-grained, man's intelligence being at odds in many respects and much of the time with his animality. So it would seem that in creating man as he is God created an essentially unstable being, a most aesthetically unsatisfying mixture of incompatibles. How then can such a creation be called good?

Before attempting to answer that question we might as well extend the problem to the whole animal kingdom, indeed the whole biosphere, to use Teilhard de Chardin's word. If death and suffering are natural there, and a constant warfare between the species (nature red in tooth and claw), how can the biological creation be called good either? Surely P's optimism in Gen 1, especially in Gen 1:31, is altogether too facile.

St Thomas' answer here, or one answer, is that Nature (personified for the moment) is not concerned with individuals but with the species; and while the destruction of individuals, whether individual bees or lambs or elephants, is bad for the individuals, it is not bad, and very often is positively advantageous, for the species. He was presumably unaware of the phenomenon of the extinction of species (cf. *STh* Ia, 50, iv ad 3; ET, vol. 9). But I think his argument can be updated without too much difficulty. We can say that what Nature is concerned with is the grand evolutionary process of diversifying evolutionary forms, and that the things that fill us with anthropomorphic horror, for example the disgusting habits of certain predatory spiders, make their proper contribution to the evolutionary symphony.

I think this is a satisfactory answer within its limits, though as we shall notice shortly it is not the full theological or religious answer. But it certainly won't do for man.

For even if it is true that 'Nature' is concerned with the species and not with the individual (and I do not think 'Human Nature' is; that is part of the paradox of man), it is certainly not true of God where human beings are concerned. It is not just the human race but each individual human person that has a God-given destiny, 'boots too big for us'. And here is each human person, unlike each angelic person, equipped with a cross-grained, contrary, discordant, self-destructive 'human nature as such'. Whatever was God thinking of? How can God's work of creation be justified in producing such a monstrosity?

The short and sufficient answer is that God did not produce such a monstrosity. 'Human nature in itself', 'human nature as such', 'the state of pure nature' – these and similar expressions signify an *abstraction*. Abstractions are the creations not of God but of the human mind, and they only exist in the human mind, as ideas and concepts. There, they play a very necessary role in our understanding of the real concrete world; let us have none of the foolishness of pouring scorn on abstractions and abstract thought. In a very important sense abstract thought is the only genuine kind of thought there is. Despise it and you despise thought itself. So I am in no sense rejecting or despising the idea of human nature in itself when I call it an abstraction. I am merely advising the reader that it must not be treated as a concrete reality, or even as a real concrete possibility. In any case, because it is an abstraction and not a concrete reality, God cannot be credited or debited with its creation.

Concretely, human beings have existed in three states or conditions. First, in the state of original justice, in which the elevating grace bestowed on the human race in its first representatives ironed out, checked or harmonized the potential discords inherent in 'human nature as such'; secondly in the state of *fallen* nature, in which grace having been forfeited by sin, these inherent discords assert themselves; thirdly in the state of restored grace, in which human beings are once again converted to God and restored to his favour and friendship (a supernatural mode of being), and yet have to continue to bear the consequences of sin in the burden of that cross-grained nature in which 'the flesh lusts against the spirit' (Gal 5:17), and 'the law in my members is at war with the law of my mind' (Rom 7:23). For indeed in these passages St Paul was not talking about human nature in the abstract but about our actual concrete condition.

Before I leave this topic of human nature as such, or in itself, I just want to deal with the question of what God thought he was about in creating such an ambiguous, paradoxical, potentially discordant creature as man, half animal half angel/devil, matter-bound intelligence, an organism strained to breaking point by super- or transorganic intelligence – however you like to describe it. In doing this we may be able to give a more theologically satisfying and more Christian dimension to that axiom about Nature being concerned with species and not with individuals, which we invoked earlier on to solve the problem of biological suffering and death.

The classical answer is to envisage man as the central microcosm of the universe, the knot tying together the spiritual and the material grades of creation. And I think this is basically the correct answer. It represents an un-ashamedly anthropocentric view of the cosmos, of which I have no intention of being ashamed myself. But its propriety is often obscured by misplacing the emphasis, by assuming that it involves simply seeing the material cosmos as made for man. Now I suggest that it is more just and more Christian and biblical also to see man as made for the cosmos.

God's purpose in creation is to communicate his goodness, according to the Neoplatonic maxim 'goodness spreads itself abroad' (*bonum diffusivum sui*), which was wholeheartedly endorsed by the scholastics and is indeed in harmony with the drift of Gen 1. The most perfect level of such communi-cation (below the uncreated level of the eternal processions of the divine persons) is by God's sharing his nature with creatures (2 Pet 1:4) through being known by them (Jn 17:3, 1 Cor 13:12). But this mode of communication of the divine goodness is only available to intelligent creatures, primarily to those pure intelligences, immaterial but created beings, which we call angels (or demons). It is not available to material creatures as such. The lower, more general participation in divine goodness which we call life is available to material creatures as such, and so we get the evolutionary process of the various grades of life, the material cosmos reaching up towards God, so to speak, and God reaching down towards it. But to know God – that, material being is not capable of, not unless it is also intelligent (or spiritual) material being. And that is what man is. Man enables material being to know God, to communicate at least by proxy in the divine goodness at the highest level.

Man is the mediator, the priest between God and the cosmos, and in that sense a microcosm. It is partly as such that he is depicted in P's creation narrative, in Gen 1:26–28.[5] He is both the divine image, or idol, in the cosmic temple constructed by God himself, and the priest officiating in it and offering God the praises of all creatures, and communicating to his fellow material creatures the saving word and blessing of the creator. The *Benedicite*, the canticle of the three young men in the fiery furnace (Dan 3), is the most outstanding expression in the Old Testament of man's priestly mediation on behalf of all creation.

All this is because God's love of the natural world goes far beyond the concern of Nature for species. Nature may not be concerned with individuals, but God is. 'Not a sparrow will fall to the ground without your Father's will' (Mt 10:29),[6] or as Luke puts it, 'Not one of them is forgotten before God' (Lk 12:6). To be sure, this is only an aside in the discourse of Jesus. 'You are of more value than many sparrows', he continues with a reassuring irony (Mt 10:31, Lk 12:7). But it is for all that a statement of God's universal and concretely particular concern, his *hesed*, his lovingkindness towards every particular thing he has made. And man is called upon to be the instrument of that concern by sharing in the materiality, and hence in the suffering, of all material being. Which of course he does supremely in his supreme and perfect manifestation and representative, Jesus Christ.

And so when mankind is fully redeemed and liberated and glorified in Jesus Christ, then too will the whole of creation share in this liberation and glory, this unimaginable communication of divine goodness to God's creatures. 'For the creation waits with eager longing for the revealing of the sons of God; for the creation was subjected to futility, not of its own will but by the will of him who subjected it in hope;[7] because the creation itself will be set free from its bondage to decay and obtain the glorious liberty of the children of God' (Rom 8:19–21).

(iii)   The Catholic tradition and Protestantism

St Thomas' axiom that sin does not damage nature (above, B, i; *STh* Ia, 95, i; ET, vol. 13) was vehemently rejected by Luther and the other Protestant reformers. Now I am very hesitant about even attempting to summarize Protestant theology on the point, being neither a Protestant nor in the least learned in Protestant theology. So what I will do is present a few texts, first from Paul Althaus, *The Theology of Martin Luther*, and then from Karl Barth, *Church Dogmatics*. Althaus, regrettably, does not give references to Luther's works by name and chapter, but just to various American editions of the *Complete Works*. So my references are simply to Althaus' book, with his quotations from Luther put in inverted commas.

II,12,1: One of the decisive concerns of Luther's theology is to avoid minimising the greatness and seriousness of sin, as though it did not matter. At no other point has he fought against his opponents the scholastic theologians with such passionate seriousness (p.142).

ibid. 3: No one is godly 'purely for God's sake or because it is the right way to be. Nature both needs and likes to have some reason for being godly; it is neither willing nor able to be godly simply for the sake of godliness' (p. 147).

ibid. 'A righteous man sins in all his good works' (p. 149).

ibid. 5: 'Our weakness lies, not in our works but in our nature; our person, nature and entire being are corrupted through Adam's fall.' Man's acts reveal that his entire nature is impure, that is, there is simply nothing in me except sin . . . . Luther and Paul describe this condition by calling man 'flesh' (p. 153).

Just a few observations:

(1)   The scholastic theologians Luther fought with such passionate seriousness for minimizing the greatness and seriousness of sin were probably not the most authentic representatives of Catholic doctrine. It would not, I think, be unfair to describe Luther's teaching as a somewhat extreme reaction to a debased Catholic theology, as well as to much corrupt Catholic practice.

Aquinas can certainly not be accused of minimizing the seriousness of sin, nor can the main Catholic spiritual and ascetical tradition. He treats it as essentially a turning away from God, *aversio a Deo*, the effect of which is to rupture the grace relationship of man with God; a far more serious effect than any mere corruption of nature. According to the ordinary catechetical Catholic teaching, sin destroys the supernatural life of man – a more serious thing than corrupting his natural life.

(2)   Luther and scholastic theologians, whether debased or authentic, were simply speaking different languages. His was the language of proclamation, of the pulpit, oratory directed at the heart and the feelings; theirs the precise technical language of academic analysis. So his contemptuous rejection of many of their concepts and distinctions, including no doubt all the distinctions we have made here, was an impatience with style rather than a rejection of substance. They were at cross purposes.

(3)   When he says that a righteous man sins in all his good works, a Catholic (and also I suspect most ordinary non-theological Protestants) is inclined to bridle at such exaggerated language. But in fact is Luther saying anything different from what the prophet says: 'We have all become like one who is unclean, and all our righteous deeds are like a polluted garment' (Isa 64:6)? And that would be translated into Catholic terminology as saying that without the grace of God, without that conversion to God which only grace can achieve, no human actions have any supernatural value in God's sight. I leave the question of substantial equivalence between this and what Luther says open, because Althaus does not make clear to me the context of Luther's famous utterance.

Karl Barth, *Church Dogmatics* III, *Doctrine of Creation* 2:

> X, 43, 2: The truth of man's being as revealed in the Word of God . . . presents him as the corrupter of his own nature.
>
> *ibid*.: What is sinful and strives against God and himself is not just something in him, qualities or achievements or defects, but his very being (p. 26).

Barth quotes (*ibid.*) the Lutheran hymn writer Cyriakus Spangenberg:

> By Adam's fall
> Corruption's pall
> Has spread o'er human essence (p. 27).

So his view of the corruption of human nature is quite as radical as Luther's. But he goes on to make some extremely significant qualifications:

> *ibid*.: But if we know man only in the corruption and distortion of his being, how can we even begin to answer the question of his creaturely nature? (p. 27)
>
> Sinful man in himself, without regard to the fact that he is also the partner in the covenant which God has made with him, and as such still the creature of God, is an abstract concept which must be excluded no less than the abstraction which would create for us a picture of pure creatureliness which takes no account of sin. Sinful man as such is not the real man . . . . The real man is the sinner who participates in the grace of God (p. 32).
>
> Christ's human nature as such is not different from our own . . . . Human nature in him is maintained in its original essence (p. 51).

Here much more strongly than with Luther I have a sense that Barth's differences with Catholic doctrine are differences of language much more than of substance; of language and method. As a matter of method I would not agree with Barth that we have to exclude abstractions – unless he means by that that we have to avoid regarding them as concrete realities.

When he says the real man is the sinner who also participates in the grace of God, I take it he would also be prepared to add that the real man was also the man before he sinned, who participated in the grace of God, that grace which we call the grace of original justice.

C. THE CONDITION AND EFFECTS OF ORIGINAL JUSTICE

(i) Human nature harmonized

The first mark or effect of the grace of original justice was one we have already referred to several times, what St Thomas calls 'uprightness' or rectitude, by which is meant not the moral virtue of the upright person, but the *rectification* of the whole person, the whole nature of man. In this condition there is no lust of the flesh against the spirit, no law in my members waging war against the law of my mind. Instead there is the harmonious subordination of lower to higher powers, lower to higher appetites, because there is the proper and willing subjection of man's mind or reason to God. In the condition of original justice all men would have enjoyed, in virtue of their engraced nature, that perfect self-possession, self-mastery, self-control, which few if any individuals now attain as a result of life-long training, ascesis, discipline and moral effort.

We should note that this rectitude of the whole person was a gift of grace bestowed by God on human *nature*, or on mankind as such in its first representatives; on the species. Had our first parents not sinned, their offspring would have inherited this condition, have been born in original justice with all its happy effects. The grace of original justice was common to all human beings, just as human nature is. This is perhaps the most important difference between original justice and the redemptive grace of justification in Christ as it is received now by sinful men. This is received personally, not 'commonly'.

(ii) Further effects of original justice

The effect of original justice which is implied in Gen 2, besides this rectitude of nature, is conditional immunity from death and hence from suffering or any deadly perils. If the man and the woman had not sinned, they would never have died. This is firmly entrenched in the Christian tradition. The clearest biblical statement of it is found in Wisdom: 'God did not make death, and he does not delight in the death of the living' (1:13); 'for God created man for incorruption, and made him in the image of his own eternity, but through the devil's envy death entered the world' (2:23–24). It may seem a mythical concept to rationalists like P, but it seems to me a doctrine without which it is hard to make sense of the salvation Christ has brought us and of his victory over death. It is as indispensable to Christian doctrine as that other highly 'mythical' notion, the resurrection of the dead.

More debatable effects are those on man's intellectual condition. One view, represented by Irenaeus in the second century, sees men's intellectual capacity in paradise as that of children. The innocence of Adam and Eve, signified by their unashamed nakedness, was the innocence of children, and so it is assumed that their mentality was that of children. I know of no later representatives of this point of view, though it has an obvious appeal to modern Christian writers, who in harmony with current ideas about evolution and progress talk of modern man having 'come of age', and refer to 'the infancy of the human race', to 'the cradle of civilization', and so forth. All these figurative ways of talking predispose us today to think of the first human beings as endowed with an intellectual capacity little higher than that of cretins. A graphic illustration of this almost universal prejudice against our remote ancestors is to be found in the film, released with great acclaim in 1982, *Quest for Fire*.

In this we are the victims of our own modern myths and the images they employ. More difficult for us to swallow, but a more intellectually rigorous view of original man, one in which the mythical images are at least subjected to some kind of rational criticism, is that held by Aquinas, and regarded as normative by the Catholic tradition. It is that Adam was, on the contrary, an intellectual giant. To put it crudely, he knew everything with an infused knowledge, with a mind enlightened by God's grace, and furnished by divine inspiration with all the necessary insights into the nature of things.[8] This was shown, according to St Thomas, by his naming the animals when God brought them to him (Gen 2:19–20; *STh* Ia, 94, iii; ET, vol. 13), a very shrewd piece of exegesis; by which I mean that here St Thomas is correctly interpreting the mind of J.

Thomas distinguishes between Adam and any offspring he may have had in the state of innocence, had he not sinned. They would have learned things just as we do – only presumably with much greater ease and pleasure and brightness. But the thing about Adam is that he was created as an adult, he personally did not grow from infancy. The same is true (we are talking about the story, of course) of Eve; but I rather doubt if St Thomas credits her with the intellectual perfection of Adam. She did not name the animals; St Thomas would have assumed that she learned their names from Adam, though in so doing she would have seen the rightness of these names in a flash.

To digest all this let us first see the principle on which St Thomas bases it, and then try and translate it into terms that we in the twentieth century can possibly accept. The principle which St Thomas states is that 'in the natural order [I think he means in any natural series] the perfect precedes the imperfect, just as the actual precedes the potential; because things which are potential are not brought to actuality except by some being that is actual' (*STh* Ia, 94, iii; ET, vol. 13.). This is, on the face of it, directly contrary to the evolutionary principle that the perfect evolves from the imperfect, the actual from the potential. Now St Thomas allows that evolutionary principle for *individuals*; it is clear that living organisms *grow*. But, he points out, a living organism growing from seed to maturity presupposes a mature parent organism (or two mature parent organisms). And I think he has a very sound point there, which at least shows up the possible fallacy of simply transposing the concept of growth and development from single organisms to whole species, and to historical groups and so forth, without any qualification. In any case, he infers from his principle that the first man had to be a complete adult (perfect) not only physically so that he could beget others, but also mentally so that he could instruct others. And whereas he couldn't, be he never so adult a male, beget Eve all by himself, he could at least instruct her once God had produced her for him.

That's all very well, we say; but we now know that this story of Gen 2 is not to be taken as literally describing what actually happened. We have to take the evolutionary hypothesis of human origins seriously, according to which the first human beings evolved from some lower form of life, from some kind of anthropoid ape. And in this view of things the less perfect *species* precedes the more perfect *species*. The being that is actual, which makes the whole process possible, is God (or a personified Nature), and that is enough to satisfy St Thomas' ontological principle.

Here we must remember what we have already seen, namely the Catholic proviso to evolutionary theory, that this theory cannot be applied to the human soul (for 'soul' in our present context read 'mind' or 'intelligence'), which in the case of the first human beings as of all others is immediately created by God. This being the case, how do we have to say the first human beings evolved from their non-human animal parents? Did they have to be human from the first moment of their conception, as human beings are now, so that we would have to say that God created their human souls (minds) for them from that moment? Or, in the case of the first human beings, is it not perfectly possible that God should have given to two *adult* individuals that extra quality of intelligent life which we call the human mind; transformed their ape-souls into human souls? I suggest that it is.

But this leaves us still with the enormous imaginative obstacle faced by us moderns. The first human beings cannot have been the intellectual giants St Thomas says they must have been, because all the evidence shows that they were so *primitive*, with the most primitive tools and primitive kinds of culture. Why, the human race had existed for heaven knows how many millennia before even agriculture and writing were invented. These intellectual giants at the origins of the race must have been, mentally, uncommonly lethargic.

Here I must ask the reader to be mentally very alert in the rational criticism of mental *images*. First of all, please, criticize all the images and assumptions contained in that word 'primitive'. We assume that it implies dumb, stupid, ox-like, uncouth, slow in the uptake – but with what justification? There are still 'primitive' peoples in the world who know nothing of agriculture or writing, or who if they do have only learned it within the last century from Europeans. Are their intelligences less acute than those of Europeans? It is only the racist in us, I suggest, (a singularly stupid form of immaturity) that finds it easy and natural to reply in the affirmative.

Secondly, let me remind you of the proverb 'Necessity is the mother of invention', and of the important distinction between active and contemplative life. Lack of the multifarious arts and skills of civilization does not mean lack of intelligence; it simply implies lack of necessity. Now in the state of innocence there was no necessity of that kind; no need for the arts and skills of civilization (this is J's insight). So Adam and Eve did not need to waste their time and mental energy on being clever and inventing things. Instead they could devote all that intellectual power of which St Thomas speaks to the much more valuable and important activity of contemplation, to appreciating the wonders and beauties of the world and of its creator, and to the leisure arts of celebrating these wonders and glories in song and dance and general joy. If, as Christians, we take the superiority of contemplation over activity seriously, then I do not see that such a picture can be dismissed as romantic myth.

Finally – we must not forget that the state of innocence did not last long! Scarcely created (and/or evolved), man sinned and fell. And with his fall he lost that intellectual pre-eminence; necessity, inner and outer, crowded in on him, and launched him on the long, hard, bitter road to civilization. And of course it is only of fallen man that we have any evidence, archaeological or otherwise. The state of innocence or of original justice, with its unique conditions and consequences, is not a sociological hypothesis based on evidence. It is a theological postulate required by the whole Christian view of man, his destiny and his origins, and indicated by divine revelation.

NOTES

1 The most obvious mythologem (i.e. stock mythical symbol) is the tree of life. Then there is its opposite number, the tree of knowledge of good and evil (possibly an original invention of J himself). Other such mythologems are the rivers of paradise, the idea of the garden itself, which I feel justified for this reason in calling an enchanted garden, and the serpent.

2 Well, not much more. P's view of man as created in God's image and likeness does look further than a purely rationalist or humanist conception of man. See also below, note 5.

3 We must be clear how this word is being used. It is not here being employed in the popular sense of 'eerie', of having to do with ghosts, and spirit mediums and so forth. In the sense we are using it here the word applies to the whole Christian life as such, since it signifies a relationship to God that is more than natural. Christians are constantly, I trust, performing supernatural acts that have nothing spooky or eerie about them – acts of faith, hope and charity, for example.

4 The Council of Trent in its decree on original sin (Dz 1511/788). The Council derives the

expression from the regional Council of Quiercy held by the bishops of Gaul in 853 against the monk Gottschalk and the 'Predestinationists'. That Council's expression is 'the holiness of justice'.

5 I fear I have been giving P a rather bad press. But such has not really been my intention. Certainly his outlook was limited in many ways; but these were the limitations of invaluable qualities of a sane and reasonable view of God and the world, which has been a sheet-anchor to Judaeo-Christianity in times of psychological storm and stress, and temptation to religious hysteria.

6 The Greek simply says 'without your Father'; 'your Father's will' is RSV's construction on this. I prefer JB's 'without your Father knowing', because this implies caring, which is the point at issue here.

7 This clause is left prudently unpunctuated by RSV. It certainly suggests a contrast between 'of its own will' and 'by the will of him who subjected it'. There is however no such obvious contrast in the Greek, which runs (literally) 'not willingly but because of him who subjected it in hope'. I suggest the real contrast Paul is making is between 'not willingly' and 'in hope'. So punctuate the clause thus in the RSV translation: 'not of its own free will, but (by the will of him who subjected it) in hope'. Creation was subjected to futility (death and decay) unwillingly, to be sure – the fault was Adam's; but still in hope, because it was after all the good God who so subjected it. The RSV translators seem to be rather voluntarist in their basic philosophy.

8 In scholastic terminology infused knowledge is contrasted with acquired knowledge. All our ordinary knowledge is 'acquired' through the senses, and through our elaborate digestion of what our senses tell us in the apparatus of the brain, what St Thomas called the inner senses of imagination and memory and so on; all of which is then assimilated, judged, expressed, 'known', by the intellect. But God can, and in Thomas' view does, also grant knowledge of certain things, that is intellectual knowledge, without our having thus 'acquired' it. He infuses it, or 'pours it in'. The metaphor is crude, perhaps. But this is no reason for spurning the insight which it is trying to express.

QUESTIONS FOR FURTHER DISCUSSION

1 Is there such a reality as 'pure nature'?

2 Are the concepts of a state of innocence and original justice pure mythology, or are we bound to say as a consequence of our faith in the goodness of God that once upon a time everything in the garden was lovely (mythological language for some genuine reality)?

3 How does a more recent theology of original sin modify previous understanding?

RECOMMENDED FURTHER READING

A. Hulsbosch, *God's Creation*.

Piet Schoonenberg, *Man and Sin: a Theological View*.

6
Sin

Having looked at man in his creational state of original justice we should go on next to original sin. And so we shall. But we cannot talk about original sin unless we first investigate sin. Our friends J and P, in any case, say nothing directly or deliberately about original sin but a great deal about sin. So we must listen carefully to them. But before we do that let us attempt to clarify our understanding of the terms we use in this field.

A. SIN AND EVIL: THE MEANING OF THE TERMS

'Evil' as a noun is a much wider term than 'sin'. All sorts of things are evils that are certainly not sins: death, suffering, famines, droughts, floods, earthquakes, disasters of all sorts. 'Evil', in fact, is the most readily available noun to correspond to the adjective 'bad', though it has much stronger and more vivid overtones. But everything which is bad, from bad weather to bad breath and bad grammar and bad government can be called, if you forget those overtones (don't forget them in the case of bad government, though), 'an evil'; a very little evil, perhaps, but still an evil.

(i)   The evil we suffer and the evil we do

Now we are only concerned with evils as they affect human beings; and in this context they are traditionally classified under two headings: (a) the evils people suffer, and (b) the evils people do; one form of doing in this moral context is also failing to do, so you can do evil simply by failing to do good. It is the second kind of evil we refer to as 'sin'.

The technical scholastic expression for the first sort is *malum poenae*, literally, 'the evil of pain/penalty'; and for the second is *malum culpae*, literally, 'the evil of fault/blame'. They are respectively the evil you are punished with and the evil you are to blame for. Current modern expressions are 'natural evil' for the first and 'moral evil' for the second. The scholastic distinction is more frankly anthropocentric, evil only being considered as it affects man (and other intelligent beings); the modern one perhaps runs the danger of being unconsciously and uncritically anthropomorphic. But use whichever you prefer.

(ii) The evil we suffer, malum poenae, is not absolutely evil

The important point to be clear about is that it is only moral evil, the evil you are to blame for, that is evil in the absolute and strict and unqualified sense; i.e. it is only sin that is evil, full stop. Natural evil, or the evil that you suffer, the evil of pain and punishment, is only evil in a qualified and relative sense. Being damaged or hurt or destroyed is an evil for the particular living organism concerned (can you talk about evil where inanimate objects are damaged or destroyed, except insofar as the damage affects human beings?), but may be a good for one or more other living organisms. 'Change and decay in all around I see.' Indeed; but while it is natural for this to strike a melancholy chord in the human heart – or in some human hearts some of the time – it would be a most peculiar world in which I saw no change and decay anywhere around. Gardeners would hate it, and anyway seeing itself, living itself (material living and seeing) would be impossible.

So natural evil is to be recognized as part of the natural order, contributing as such to the good of the whole. It is also sometimes part of the moral order, when it is just punishment, or correction, for example, also contributing as such to the good of the whole.

Sin, on the other hand, or moral evil or the evil we do or the evil we are to blame for, all this is evil pure and simple. It cannot be reduced to being either part of the natural order or of the moral order. On the contrary, it is moral disorder, and hence a disorder of the human intelligent nature, to which it belongs by nature to perceive and respect the moral order.

There is no consistent correlation between natural evil and moral evil. Even though it is true that most of the evil done in the world, sin, consists of causing others to suffer evil – murder, assault, robbery, rapine, exploitation, oppression, cruelty and callousness – still to cause natural evil is not always a sin; and on the other hand there are forms of sin or moral evil that do not consist in causing suffering or natural evil. We may well come to find that all sin or moral evil entails some natural evil or evil of punishment as a consequence, at least for the evildoer; but that is not to say that the evil done consists in causing evil to be suffered – sins of self-indulgence, for example.

As for causing natural evil, we do it all the time, and even regard it quite correctly as virtuous. A few hours ago I was pulling up weeds on the lawn, and more recently still swatting flies in the kitchen. I was deliberately destroying living organisms, for which actions, had I bothered to draw attention to them, I would (or should) have been applauded by my confrères.

I was doing a good thing from our human point of view, but the weeds pulled and the flies swatted were experiencing evil. However, if the evil they experienced were evil pure and simple, unqualified evil, then my causing that evil could not possibly in any circumstances be regarded as morally good.

Who cares about weeds and flies, you may ask? Well, weeds and flies do – and God. But let us progress up the scale (please observe the anthropo-centrism of my language) to other human beings. We have to say that it is not always sinful and sometimes is morally good, to cause people, both ourselves and others, to suffer or even die. Quite apart from soldiers and judicial executioners, the moral goodness of whose lethal activities is much debated, there are doctors, not to mention parents and schoolteachers and simple friends deliberately causing pain to their patients, children, pupils and loved ones – and being required to do so by their obligations to those they hurt; and there are heroes deliberately going to their deaths for the sake of their friends. We may take it then as established that the evil we suffer, or natural evil, is not absolutely evil, not evil pure and simple. If it were, it could never be good to cause it.

(iii)   Sin, the evil we do, and its divisions

I will leave the proof of the assertion that sin, the evil we do, is evil in the strict and absolute sense to emerge, I trust, in section C. Here I just want to say a little bit more about the word, and then about the division of sin into venial and mortal.

The English verb 'to sin' translates Greek and Hebrew words (*hamartanein, hata'*) whose primary meaning is 'to miss', as when shooting or throwing stones. An instructive text is Jgs 20:16, which describes the accuracy of the left-handed slingers of Benjamin by saying that they could sling a stone at a hair 'and not sin'. RSV translates quite correctly 'and not miss', but both Hebrew and Greek use the word normally translated by 'sin'.

The word's application to the moral sphere is thus originally metaphorical. The basic meaning of the English word 'sin' seems to be 'guilt', 'liability', and so the verb means basically 'to incur guilt'. You might say therefore that it is a less metaphorical word than the Greek or Hebrew. But even so its use in the most common sense is certainly analogical, because guilt strictly speaking is by no means identical with sin.

In any case, the metaphor of missing the mark is one we have in English too – think of all those words beginning with 'mis-', like misconduct and misbehaviour and mischief, and also the way we talk about people going astray, or going off the rails. It is worth remarking in passing that almost all our language about morals is metaphorical, or at least analogical. Right and wrong are originally 'straight' and 'twisted', though with this pair the basic metaphor has long since been forgotten. But even so that particular metaphor is still used very freely, in such phrases as 'fair and square', 'going straight', 'devious behaviour', 'a crook', 'a bent cop', and so on.

We cannot talk about God except in analogical and largely metaphorical language, and we cannot talk about morals except in analogical and largely metaphorical language. What does this indicate? With God, it indicates that he is always *beyond* our here and now experience, and yet to be reached out to from this experience, because he is also *within* this experience. In other words, it indicates the mystery of God, that he is the Beyond within and the Within beyond. If you want the big words for it, it indicates the transcendence and immanence of God. But don't make the mistake of thinking that the big words are any less analogical/metaphorical, or even any more precise, than the little homely ones.

With morals, it indicates something similar, though of course in a lesser degree. The world of morals is clearly not beyond the world of our here and now experience, but an essential part of it. And yet it does involve a going *beyond* from *within*. So the analogical nature of moral language should remind us that our dealings with other persons (which are what morals are nearly all about) are on a different level from our dealings with things. *Doing* (the 'in' word is 'praxis') transcends, goes beyond *making* (poiesis), even though to be good and complete praxis it should proceed from within poiesis, and never be separated from it. The virtuous man must exercise all sorts of *skills* (poiēsis, making) to make his virtues (concerned with *praxis*, doing, doing the right thing) effective.

So, to return from that digression to sin: first let us just not forget that sin, bad moral action, belongs to this transcendent level of existence as much as good moral action. Animals don't sin, any more than they perform virtuous actions, in the strict sense (that is to say in the human, anthropocentric sense). So sin is action at this moral level of existence which misses the mark. But being a bad man who does bad things is different from being a bad shot who shoots badly at Bisley. The bad shot misses the mark, but not deliberately. The bad man misses the mark – because he aims at the wrong one. If the bad shot missed the bulls-eye because in fact he intended to hit the range warden, and did so, he would in fact be a good shot, but a bad man.

What then is the mark which the sinner misses deliberately by aiming at something else instead? While it can be all sorts of things, depending on what kind of sin is being committed, in the last resort and at the heart of the matter it is *God*; God who is our ultimate end, at whom the genuine human life has to be aimed. So to sin, essentially, is to miss God, but to miss him on purpose, and thus *to turn away from God*. Again, I hope the substantiation of this statement will emerge in section C, though if you accept it for the time being, it shows why sin, moral evil, is absolute evil or evil pure and simple, since God is the absolute good, good pure and simple.

Here the statement that sin is essentially turning away from God is enough to enable us also to state the difference between venial and mortal sin. Briefly, it is only mortal sin that is sin in the strict theological sense, because it is only mortal sin that involves a turning away from God, *aversio a Deo*. That indeed is what makes a sin mortal, because God is our true life. A venial sin is that sort of action, bad action indeed, which although bad does not involve turning away from God. In the scholastic expression it is an action which though blameworthy is not *contra finem*, against our true end, but *praeter finem*, beside the point, irrelevant to the end. It is a turning *aside* from the right road rather than a turning *away* from it. Thus, as the moralists say, a thousand venial sins (or a million) do not add up to one mortal sin. The difference between them is not a difference merely of quantity, or degree of gravity; it is a difference in kind. This means, as I see it, that venial sin is not sin in the strict sense, and therefore it is not purely and simply evil. It must belong, in a curious way, to the evil we suffer, *malum poenae*, as well as, or rather than, to the evil we do, *malum culpae*.[1]

B.   P'S DOCTRINE OF SIN

The crucial history of sin, its presentation as the leading adversary of God in Gen 1 – 11, the prelude to the great drama of salvation which begins with the story of Abraham in Gen 12, is the work of J. But we take P first, even though he made his contribution after the exile, some four hundred years and more later than J, simply because his contribution to the doctrine of sin is secondary and less important.

I think it is fair to say that the essence of P's view of sin is that something can be done about it, either by the sinner or by the society, and that only in the last resort does something have to be done about it by God himself as the supreme judge of the society. Not only must something be done about sin, but something *can* be done about it, and by man. P, as we remarked in the last chapter (B, ii), was an optimist. Not only is creation good, and especially man, the lord of creation; but its possibilities and potentialities are good and so are all realizations of them by way of man's subduing the earth and developing cultures and civilizations. Sin damages all this, to be sure. It damages above all the proper order in society between people, and also between people and God. But the damage can be put right. There is, of course, an obligation to put it right, and *the obligation can be met*. To prescribe how it can be met is the chief function of *law*, in particular of that basic law which we call *covenant*. P did not, like J, give us a salvation history, or salvation drama, prefaced by a sin history or drama; he gave us a progressive history structured by a series of *covenants* between God and his creatures. First there is an implicit covenant with the whole of creation (the term is explicitly used in Jer 33:20); next a covenant with Noah and the whole human race (Gen 9:1–6); then the covenant with Abraham and his descendants (Gen 17), and finally the covenant with Israel under Moses (Exod 19–20).

(i) The evidence of Gen 1 – 11

To some extent, therefore, P's contribution to what is now the primordial history of Gen 1 – 11 seems to be devoted to offering a corrective of J's more pessimistic, more radical theology of sin, his more sceptical view of human achievement.

After Gen 1 – 2:4a the next section of P we come to is Gen 5, the genealogy or list of the so-called ante-diluvian patriarchs. Not one of the more thrilling passages of scripture, and what people usually stumble over when they do run through it is the inordinate length of life allotted to these ancients. The shortest is Enoch's 365 years, the longest Methuselah's 969 (father and son, incidentally). But let us forget this chronology for the moment. We can never hope to understand what precisely these figures symbolize, even if P himself did, which is unlikely. Though that they do symbolize something is suggested by Enoch's life span of 365 years – a year of years.

Much more interesting than the ages of these patriarchs are their names, which reveal that this genealogy of Gen 5 is a variant, and possibly a deliberately corrective variant, of the shorter one of the descendants of Cain given by J in 4:17–24. That genealogy is intended to represent a 'brood of vipers'. It represents at once the growth of civilization (vv. 17, 20–22) and the intensification of violent, murderous sin (vv. 23–24), the one inextricably entangled with the other.

P recasts it. He refuses to accept that the progress of sin and of civilization are inextricably mixed up with each other, and so he disentangles them. First he gives us the development of mankind without the faintest whiff of sin. That is what we have, very baldly, in Gen 5, which you must read immediately after Gen 2:4a, forgetting entirely about the intervening J section. P is indeed criticizing this, but not presupposing it in his own narrative. The development is not specifically described, but it is implied simply by the genealogy being a sin-excluding variant of J's in Gen 4.

Then, bang! In the beginning of his version of the flood story, P introduces sin, total sin. It does not in the least disqualify the cultural achievements of mankind, but it simply earns the death sentence for the whole human race. 'Now the earth was corrupt in God's sight, and the earth was filled with violence . . . . And God said to Noah, "I have determined to make an end of all flesh; for the earth is filled with violence through them; behold I will destroy them with the earth" ' (Gen 6:11, 13).

The cardinal sin, the only sin mentioned, is violence, murder and mayhem, and its proper punishment is death. I think P is suggesting, however, that from the creation to the flood there had been no law (cf. Rom 5:13–14), and so violence had gone unpunished by men. Therefore God himself had to step in eventually and pronounce the universal sentence of death, Noah alone excepted (and his family, which was part of him), because like Enoch before him 'he walked with God' (Gen 6:9; 5:24).

And so when the flood is over and God promises never to repeat the treatment, he puts his promise in the form of a covenant, which is a legal contract and creates law: specifically a law to deal with the sin of violence. 'Whoever sheds the blood of man, by man shall his blood be shed; for God made man in his own image' (Gen 9:6). This law will make it possible for man himself to curb violence, or rather to rectify it and put right the damage to the moral order once it has been committed, to nullify sin in fact, and God will not have to intervene again.

(ii)   The evidence of Leviticus

The P document *par excellence* is the whole book of Leviticus, which is one of those books of the Bible that most of us conscientiously abstain from reading. It is worth noting in passing, therefore, that it is from Lev 19:18 that Jesus quotes the second great commandment of charity, 'You shall love your neighbour as yourself' (Mk 12:31 parr.).

But now our concern is with what it has to tell us about P's conception of sin. Lev 4 is all about what you have to do if, in the RSV translation, you 'sin unwittingly', or 'inadvertently' according to JB and NEB. I myself am inclined to question these translations and I suspect that what the Israelites meant by such sins was something much wider than mere faults of carelessness or ignorance. The Hebrew word is *shegagah*, which means 'error', 'going astray', 'wandering'. What I suggest is meant by this on the moral level is any fault or sin, against neighbour as well as against God and his proper worship, that falls short in gravity of those sins which are punishable by death; sins of inadvertence, yes, but also sins of weakness, passion, hasty judgement and so forth.

And the point is that you not only must but you can do something, and something entirely adequate and sufficient, about these sins. You can make up for them, make amends, both to God and to your neighbour. Lev 4 is all about the sacrifices you must offer in order to make amends to God for your *shegagah* sins. In Lev 16 the ritual of the great Day of Atonement is described, in which the nation as a whole, represented by the High Priest, makes up for its sins by the appropriate sacrifices to God, which include a day-long fast.

There were some sins however which could only be atoned for by the death of the sinner. We have already seen that bloodshed is such a sin. The sinner himself didn't atone for these sins, but society did, by putting him to death. Lev 20 gives a list of such sins other than that of violence or bloodshed. The various sins here mentioned may perhaps be considered as all coming under the heading of infidelity to the God of Israel. We are not here concerned, in any case, about why these sins were regarded as capital crimes, but only to illustrate how, in the mind of P, sin has been tamed and contained by being legislated for. Sin is a social and religious disorder of varying gravity. But, however grave, it can be adequately remedied by executing the prescriptions of social and religious law, which sometimes involve executing the sinner. P does not seem to envisage any sinful situation of the people which could not be catered for by the rituals of the Day of Atonement, and by enforcing the sanctions of the Law. In this he differs from a number of the prophets, and from J – and most clearly manifests his theological limitations.

C. J'S TYPOLOGICAL HISTORY OF SIN

(i) The context

Back in Chapter 2, C we ran briefly through J's sin history and so we need not repeat it here. But a few more particular remarks on its context will be useful, before we come to a detailed examination of his story of the fall.

His sin history is a prelude to his salvation history which begins with Abraham. Since he is composing a salvation history, he needs to tell us what we are being saved from. It is sin and its consequences. Here is the fundamental difference between J and P. J does not think of sin as something to be remedied, put right, but as something to be saved from. And how does God set about saving us from our sins? He begins by *choosing* certain people like Abraham, Isaac and Jacob for the sake of all nations (Gen 12:1–3; 22:18; 28:14), *justifying* them (Gen 15:1–6; see Paul's commentary in Rom 4), and making them *promises* to which they respond in one way or another by *faith*. Election, justification and promise are precisely uncovenanted acts of God, acts of divine grace. So Paul sums up God's saving work in two words: *grace* on God's part, *faith* on man's, accepting this grace.

Sin therefore is that from which we can only be saved by God's grace – and by faith as our response to grace. It is not, basically, that for which law is a sufficient remedy. This can only be because sin is perceived as an evil much more radical than a mere bad act. It is a bad act proceeding from a bad will. A bad will, with the distorted intelligence that goes with it, means some kind of corruption of the person at the core of their being; a corruption therefore which the person affected, being corrupted by it, cannot remedy.

The flood story is the only part of Gen 1 – 11 which J shares with P, and

two texts at the beginning and end of his account of the flood illustrate well
how very different his view of sin is. In 6:5–7 he writes, 'The Lord saw that
the wickedness of man was great in the earth, and that every imagination of
the thoughts of his heart was only evil continually. And the Lord was sorry
that he had made man on the earth, and it grieved him to his heart. So the
Lord said, "I will blot out man whom I have created from the face of the
ground".' Then in 8:21 we are told 'The Lord said in his heart, "I will never
again curse the ground because of man, for the imagination of man's heart is
evil from his youth".' The same reason is given, what the rabbis call 'the evil
inclination' of man's heart, both for blotting out the human race, and for
promising never again to blot out the human race. Now this makes no sense
at all if the discussion the Lord has with himself is thought of in legal, or even
in moral terms. So it is clear that J, unlike P, does not see the problem of sin in
moral terms. In such terms it is simply insoluble. He sees God as faced with
the problem of an enterprise that has gone wrong. He has two options: he
can either scrap it altogether, or he can decide to salvage it. First he goes
through the motions of scrapping it. But not thoroughly, because he makes
an exception of Noah and his family; then he states his intention, in fact a
promise, of never scrapping it again, and therefore implicitly of salvaging it.
But the point is made; the problem of sin is nothing less than the problem of
evil in its starkest form, and as such it is a problem beyond the categories of
morals and of law.

(ii)   The first sin, Gen 3

As we saw in Chapter 2, C, J's sin stories, from the sin of Cain to the collective sin at Babel, provide us with the primal archetypes of various manifestations of sin, while his story of the sin in paradise is the primal archetype of
sin as such. It illustrates the basic sin, the root sin of all. Now the first thing
to notice about it is its apparent triviality. It consists of disobeying a specific,
but to all appearances somewhat arbitrary or whimsical, command, given in
Gen 2:17. Is J wishing to tell us that disobedience to a commandment or law
is of the essence of sin? That certainly seems to be the basic principle of D's
covenant theology as expounded in Deuteronomy, a theology that makes
even more of the covenant idea than P does. This theology so came to
dominate the religious thought of Judaism, especially Pharisaic Judaism, that
it has tended to be read automatically into J's story. For D's view of sin as a
breach of the covenant has influenced Christian moral theology quite as much
as Judaism, St Paul's (and Jesus') opposition to it notwithstanding.

But to read it into J's story is, in my view, to get a distorted notion of J's
theology from the start. So I suggest that the prohibition in 2:17 is a purely
formal element in J's story, part of its mechanics or structure but not really a

part of its meaning. If you had asked J, 'Was eating this apple [in Lesotho, I am delighted to discover, they call it a peach, peaches being as common here as apples in England] wrong because it was prohibited, or prohibited because it was wrong?', I am sure he would have answered, 'God forbade it because it was wrong' – a point we shall return to in a minute.

It is the temptation scene which gives us the true nature of the sin, which we must not forget is being presented as *the* sin. There is first of all, on the woman's part, the minimizing of sin, seeing it only in terms of its unpleasant consequence: 'God said, "You shall not eat of the fruit of the tree which is in the midst of the garden . . . , *lest you die*" ' (Gen 3:3); as he might say, 'You shall not touch this trinitrotoluol, or drink this prussic acid, lest you die'. She sees the object of the prohibition purely as dangerous, not as wrong.

Secondly there is the tempter's falsehood, which she accepts; his assurance, 'It is not dangerous at all. God was deceiving you to stop you attaining the benefits of it, which will make you equal to him, make you both gods in knowledge of good and evil, in *wisdom*' (cf. *ibid.* 4). The heart of this falsehood is, 'God is not really your friend, your loving creator. He is a *jealous* God [a P and D phrase! See Exod 20:5; Dt 5:9], in the sense of being a selfish deceiver who does not want to share with you what is really yours for the taking.' The diabolical ingenuity of this falsehood is that it is in some ways true, being a caricature, a distortion of the truth. So there is on the woman's part a readiness to believe the tempter and so start disbelieving and distrusting God. She has already turned away from God. This is the essence of all real sin.

Finally, she eats it and gives it to her husband and he eats it too. Why? What is the motive? 'To be wise, to be like God, knowing good and evil' (Gen 3:6, 5). Pride, *hubris*, the desire, nay the demand as of right to be wholly one's own master, independent, captain of one's soul. That is the specific nature of this sin; and because this is the first and archetypal sin, that is the source and root of all sin.

(iii)   Some further points about the story

Let us go back to the intrinsic wrongness of eating that prohibited apple or peach. In the story, of course, it is not an apple tree or a peach tree, but the tree of the knowledge of good and evil (Gen 2:9, 17); in other words it is not a real tree but a symbolic (or mythical) one, and its name tells us what it stands for. Knowledge of good and evil is just a Hebrew idiom for knowledge of everything. So the tree stands for omniscience, for what the Bible calls the wisdom of God. To eat of this is intrinsically wrong because men cannot achieve, and therefore must not aspire to achieve, divine wisdom or omniscience by their own resources. They can only receive it as a gift from God, as grace. To grab a gift before it is given is wrong in itself – we call it greed. Pride is a form of greed, of wanting for oneself an eminence or greatness which is not proper to one. 'She saw that the tree was good for food and a delight to the eyes [greed], and desirable to make one wise [pride]' (Gen 3:6).

That it was the woman who was first tempted and fell and not the man is another purely formal element in the story, part of its artistic structure. To derive lessons from it, justifying male domination for example, is to misread the story. If people are going to argue like that and say women are more to blame than men, perennial temptresses, then one could answer that on the contrary the man was the more to blame because the prohibition had been given to him directly and in person before the woman even existed. He was the boss, and must accept primary responsibility. Indeed, I suggest that J made the woman the main character in the temptation story, because if it had been the man, that would have left the woman practically guiltless. He wants them to be equally guilty, since this is a story of all *human* sin, committed by men and women alike.

(iv)   The consequent punishments

Finally, about the punishments that followed I think we must say much the same as about the original prohibition. The judicial form of a sentence by God is as purely formal as that prohibition. The point about a judicial punishment, as St Thomas remarks in the article referred to in note 1 below on the distinction between mortal and venial sin, is that it is extrinsic to the sin, having only an incidental, not a necessary connection with it. It is possible, if you are lucky, to avoid it, and the only reason you cannot avoid God's punishments, conceived of as judicial sentences, is because of the total efficiency of God's law-enforcement agencies.

Now that is a P and D view of divine retribution, but not, I suggest, J's. He is using a folklore form of story, a kind of *Just So Story* told to children to explain why snakes don't have feet and why women suffer the pains of childbirth and why men have to sweat it out in the fields, and why finally we all have to die ('aetiology' is the big word for *Just So* stories; I prefer Kipling's phrase): he is using this form of story to teach that the evils we suffer from, above all the supreme evil of death to which all others are subordinate and to which they all lead, are an intrinsic and necessary consequence of sin, not mere 'punishments to fit the crime' imposed from outside. Even if God had not passed this sentence there would have been no escaping these evils, just as it would still have been wrong to eat of the fruit of the tree of knowledge even if he had not forbidden it. For they are disharmonies in our lives, inevitably and intrinsically caused by unharmonious action. Sin destroys the proper harmony between man and God, and therefore there is no harmony any more between man and other creatures, between man and man, man and woman, man and himself, man and his life. That is the radical nature of sin. That is how and why sin is evil pure and simple. That is how sin is basically turning away from God.

NOTE

1 St Thomas deals with the distinction in *STh* Ia IIae, 72, v; ET, vol. 25). I am sure that what I have said here is consonant with what he says there, though at first sight it would seem not to be. For the question he is there asking is whether this distinction of sins in terms of their liability to punishment constitutes a specific difference between sorts of sins, and he answers that it does not. Clearly, we don't classify sins in terms of the punishment they incur, but in terms of their objects, of what they are about; and so picking a pocket will be the same kind of sin as robbing a bank. But on the other hand he says in passing that venial and mortal sin differ infinitely in the kind of inordinateness they involve, in the way I have stated. And from this I go on to draw my conclusion, which I do not think contradicts what he is saying in that article.

It does however contradict what another very venerable theologian once said: Cardinal Newman's remark that the Church holds that it would be better for the whole world to be destroyed, than for one venial sin to be committed (*Lectures on Anglican Difficulties*, VIII).

QUESTIONS FOR FURTHER DISCUSSION

1 How do J and P differ in their approach to sin?

2 Is 'turning away from God' a sufficient definition of sin, and one universally applicable in all ages and cultures?

3 Is there any necessary connection between sin and suffering?

7

Original Sin
I: Definitions and Background

A. THE MEANING OF THE TERM

It is unfortunate that a doctrine so central to Christian faith should be labelled by an expression so fraught with misunderstanding. It is central to Christian faith because it represents the shadow or negative side of the positive affirmation, surely as central to Christianity as you can get, that Christ is the saviour of the *whole* human race, that he died for *all*. All human beings, therefore, without exception need to be saved. That universal need is expressed by the doctrine of original sin.

But in this context neither of these two words means quite what it usually means. In the case of the word 'sin' this cannot altogether be helped; but we have to be very clear about the range of meanings we make the word carry.

(i) The word 'original'

In the case of the word 'original', it might really be possible to find a more accurate term. In current English the adjective 'original', applied usually to a human action or achievement, means not being copied from something else, coming first. Applied sometimes to persons, as in 'X is a very original artist', it means that what X does or makes is never a mere copy or derivative of anything anybody else does or makes.

So when people hear the term 'original sin' they very often, indeed usually, assume that it refers to the *first* sin ever committed, the sin of Adam and Eve in paradise, and in a most peculiar way puts the blame on all the rest of us for that sin as well. But that is *not* in fact what the word 'original' means in this phrase. For it is not what the original Latin *originale* means, and the English is transliterated straight from that. That word, and so 'original' in this expression 'original sin', means 'to do with origins'. 'Original sin' therefore means, not the first sin, nor any particular actual sin which is in no sense a copy of other sins – a brand new kind of sin invented by a very original sinner, like kidnapping fourteen ambassadors at once, let us say, or killing off the great chefs of Europe;[1] no, it means sin which we derive from our origins.

It is in us, our sin, not the sin of the first man or first sinner. A better term therefore would be, perhaps, 'originated sin'. A traditional alternative expression is 'hereditary' or 'inherited sin'. One could, just possibly, call it 'genetic sin'.

For what is in fact meant by the term is a sin we acquire in and through our origins, *a sin of our nature as such*, and not a personal or a particular sin, personally committed. Original sin is specifically distinguished from personal or actual sin, and is indeed defined by St Augustine and all who come after him as 'sin of nature' or 'feebleness of nature'.[2] So I think 'genetic sin' might be quite an appropriate term after all. But it must not be understood in the strict biological sense.

We can now see how original sin is transmitted from one generation to the next, without having to have recourse to the theory of traducianism (above, 4, C, iii); it is simply transmitted with the human nature of which it is the vice or flaw. As one becomes human simply by being conceived and born, so one becomes 'originally-sinfully-human' by the same process.

(ii) The word 'sin'

But now what about this word 'sin'? We saw in the last chapter (6, A, iii) that it means deliberately missing the mark, which in the last analysis means deliberately turning away from God. And this in turn means that sin as usually defined is a particular act or omission performed (or omitted) by a particular person.

Now in the expression 'original sin' it does *not*, as we have just observed, signify the act of a person, because it is a sin of nature, and so is precisely distinguished from all sins of persons. So it cannot be an actual turning away from God, or a deliberate missing of the mark, because natures as such, being abstractions, neither act nor fail to act in themselves. Nor can acts and omissions be genetic or inherited or originated, not at least properly human acts which are by definition *voluntary*.

The only reason original sin is called 'sin' is because it designates an estrangement from God. But it is a state of estrangement we are born with, a kind of genetic deformity not of the human body but of human nature, inherent in the nature we are all of us, as human beings, born with. And 'sin' does, as we saw in the last chapter, mean alienation or estrangement from God.

Since however 'original sin' does not designate a personal act or omission, perhaps we should rather call it a vice, 'vice' meaning the habit of bad acts. The doctrine states that human nature, as we now know and share it, and receive it or inherit it from our parents, all the way back to the first human beings, is vitiated or flawed. So perhaps instead of the term 'original sin' we should introduce the term 'genetic vice', or 'genetic flaw in human nature'. However, 'original sin' is the term in possession, and no sensible suggestions made in this book are going to dislodge it.

So: what the term 'original sin' refers to is a flaw or distortion in human nature that has marred it from its origins and thus mars all particular human beings from their particular origins, so that infants too are affected or infected by original sin.

B. OLD TESTAMENT SOURCES OF THE DOCTRINE

(i) J's narrative

What makes confusion between original sin and the first sin so difficult to avoid, and difficult to eradicate from people's minds, is not only a natural misunderstanding of the word 'original' but also the fact that there is a close and necessary connection between the two. Original sin, as I have just defined it in line with the tradition, is said to be the effect of the first sin and to derive from it.

This is not explicitly said in Gen 3, or indeed anywhere else in the Old Testament. But it is at least remotely implicit in J's narrative. As we saw in the last chapter, when J makes death and pain and expulsion from paradise the consequences of the sin of the first man and woman, he does not, in spite of the formal structures of his story, envisage these things as purely external and imposed consequences, but much more as the necessary working out of the inner logic of sin, sin as a deliberate turning away from God.

Now it is clear, both from his story and from experience (which his story is partly designed to 'explain'), that these consequences afflict not only the first man and woman but all their descendants too; not only the archetypal man and woman but the whole race also which they represent, including its infant members. Babies suffer and babies die, and babies are not living in paradise. So there is at least a remote implication that the sin of the first man and woman as well as their punishment infects the whole human race; no longer of course as a personal act but as the 'genetic flaw' we have been talking about.

There is just a suggestion of this implication in the two phrases with which J opens and closes his account of the flood, and which we were considering in Chapter 6, C, i, from a slightly different point of view: about the imagination of man's heart being evil from his youth (Gen 6:5, 8:21). It is significant that the author talks about 'man' in the collective singular. There is a universal collective involvement in evil. The word translated 'imagination' by RSV, Hebrew *yetser*, becomes a technical term in rabbinic Hebrew in the phrase *yetser hara'*, 'the evil inclination', which is a very rough Jewish equivalent to the Christian doctrine of original sin.

(ii)   The concept of inherited guilt

There are two concepts which find frequent expression in the Old Testament, and which have a close affinity with the specifically Christian doctrine of original sin, though they must certainly not be simply identified with it. But they do provide it with a wider context or background. The first is the concept of inherited guilt.[3]

This sometimes, perhaps most frequently, takes the form of a hereditary *curse*. Consider the curse of Canaan (Gen 9:25–27), the very ambiguous 'blessing' of Esau (*ibid*. 27:29, 39–40), the hereditary taint incurred by Moabites and Ammonites, which excluded them practically for ever from the fellowship of Israel (Dt 23:2–6; cf. Gen 19:30–38). We find this concept 'moralized' in statements about sins being punished 'to the third and the fourth generation' (Exod 20:5, 34:7), and in the prophet Hosea's suggestion that the nation of Israel is heir to the sins of their representative ancestor Jacob, and liable to the punishment of them (Hos 12:2–4). In Ps 51:5, 'Behold I was brought forth in iniquity, and in sin did my mother conceive me' (see also Job 14:4) the concept is generalized, but generalized, be it noted, by being personalized. The speaker speaks for himself – but anyone could be the speaker.

In none of these texts is the inheritance of guilt traced back to Adam.

(iii)   The concept of collective guilt

This is obviously closely connected with the former concept, but not quite identical with it. It spreads guilt laterally rather than vertically, synchronically rather than diachronically.[4] Thus the tribe of Benjamin shares in the guilt of some of its members (Jgs 20:12–48); all the Amalekites are collectively under the ban of the Lord (1 Sam 15:3); the whole family of Achan (Jos 7:24–25), the whole clan of Dathan and Abiram (Num 16:27–33) are punished for the sins of their principals. The implication, never spelt out because it was so obvious to contemporaries, is that they share in the guilt of their principals.

In one text all Israel is punished for a sin of David, even though their sharing in his guilt is explicitly excluded (2 Sam 24:1–17). But as king he represents the people, and so his kingly sins are also the people's liability and responsibility.

(iv)   Observations on these concepts

The first point to make is that these concepts, though they figure in the Old Testament, are not therefore to be thought of as 'God's truth' or God's revelation, or as thereby for ever receiving the divine sanction. They are concepts that find expression in Israel because they seem to be common, in one form or another, to nearly all comparable societies and cultures, to what we could call pre-scientific or, more precisely perhaps, pre-liberal societies. Nor indeed are they unknown in our contemporary highly developed technological societies, which are becoming more blatantly post-liberal by the day. For with our nationalist/racialist prejudices (and I am not just thinking of South Africa) we very easily attribute a collective or hereditary guilt to whole ethnic and social groups; and the Nazis in the Second World War readily inflicted collective punishments on whole villages and communities – a practice not confined to them in the annals of twentieth-century warfare.

The second point is that these concepts, which in our modern experience or deployment of them usually have such a dubious and negative value, are not simply to be dismissed as irrational, superstitious and wrong-headed. They can indeed be applied irrationally in the service of evil prejudices, and no doubt frequently have been. But they also represent inescapable factors of such positive social values as group loyalty and group pride. These in turn will only be totally rejected by an individualism that is itself an extreme and irrational prejudice. If it is, within limits, natural and laudable for you to feel proud of any group or community you belong to, and to cherish a loyalty to it, then you must be prepared sometimes to feel ashamed of it and acknowledge a group guilt, and be ready to bear a group punishment, and this in a collective or a hereditary, a synchronic or a diachronic sense. If on the other hand you wish to repudiate or disavow some sin of your ancestors or your 'kith and kin', then you must be prepared, perhaps, simply to repudiate your ancestry and your kindred. This the Benjaminites, for example, could have done but chose not to do (Jgs 20:13).

The third point is that these concepts in their more irrational application are in fact also criticized in the Old Testament itself, notably by Ezekiel (18) and with a more commendable brevity by Jeremiah (31:29–30). The prophets reject as a principle of judgement the proverbial saying 'The fathers have eaten sour grapes and the children's teeth are set on edge'. In the New Testament (Jn 9:3) Jesus expressly rejects any simplistic notion of hereditary guilt; but he also there rejects any simplistic connection of suffering with sin, as the author of Job had done before him.

C.   THESE CONCEPTS COMPARED WITH THAT OF ORIGINAL SIN

Given the very considerable moral limitations of these two concepts, it is worth comparing them with the Christian doctrine of original sin. The affinities are undeniable, especially between original sin and hereditary guilt. So too is the fact that these concepts contributed to the development of the doctrine. But there are two crucial differences.

(i) First difference

First, the doctrine of original sin *universalizes* the hereditary and the collective guilt. *All* human beings inherit this genetic flaw of human nature,[5] and therefore no one group may be regarded by the Christian as more guilty than others; and no particular ancestor or founder, like Jacob, or Mohammed, or Luther or Calvin, may be regarded as casting a darker shadow over his group than any others. Concepts of hereditary and collective guilt can be and have been employed to shore up the rickety moral structures of racial and national prejudice; the concept of original sin, if taken seriously, would bring them tumbling to the ground.

(ii) Second difference

Secondly, since the doctrine of original sin makes a very clear distinction between original sin (a sin of nature) and personal sin (a sin of the person), it rules out with complete certainty any notion of the inheritance of personal sins; of holding descendants, therefore, responsible for the sins of their ancestors. Where Christians, including their ecclesiastical authorities, have justified anti-semitism by the text 'His blood be on us and on our children' (Mt 27:25), they have been guilty, to put it at its mildest, of extremely bad doctrine or theology; to put it as strongly as it deserves, they have been guilty of implicitly denying their faith in the redeeming power of Jesus Christ, and of turning a deaf ear to those other, more authoritative, words, 'Father, forgive them; for they know not what they do' (Lk 23:34).

Coming to collective as distinct from inherited guilt, again we must assert that personal active sin can only be shared personally. That is, a group may only be held responsible for the particular sins of its members in so far as its other members enforce or provoke them, consent to them or condone them – which of course they very easily do. But it must be most emphatically stated that mere 'guilt by association', as a notion of Christian moral doctrine, is *out*.

(iii) Sinful structures of society

This brings us to the concept of sinful structures which is frequently employed nowadays and often, if I mistake not, contrasted with the concept of personal sin. This in my opinion is a mistake and a source of confusion. The intention of those Christian moralists who make use of the idea is the very praiseworthy one of prodding the consciences of Christians into an awareness that their Christian moral responsibilities extend far further than their private 'personal' lives; that we must not only examine our consciences about the sins which we personally commit, but also about the sins committed in our name by the society/societies we belong to, sins that are built into the very structures of that or those societies; the structural sins of the 'consumer society' for example, or of the 'apartheid society', or the 'class society', or the 'authoritarian society' which the Catholic Church still is to an excessive degree,

With this I have no quarrel whatever, though of course there will always be room for argument (often, it is true, very specious) about what are and what are not structural sins. But my point is that the *only* way I or anyone else can be involved in structural sins, so as to share moral responsibility for them, is *personally*. Otherwise there would be no point in *me* examining *my* conscience about them. In so far as I am more or less guilty of them and responsible for them, it is because I am more or less personally involved in them – by accepting them, profiting by them, ignoring them, turning a blind eye to them, as well as by actively participating in them. What has to be said is that I cannot and may not be held guilty of them simply by association, simply by being a member of the society in question. If I am a white South African, I cannot simply for that reason be held guilty of the racialist structures of South African society. But if I am a white South African and say, 'Well, how would you like your daughter to marry a black man?', or 'Too bad – but these laws and customs have nothing to do with me, I didn't make them, and anyway you've got to obey the law, and consider what the neighbours might say' – then to be sure I am making myself personally guilty of at least a sin of omission of some sorts; the omission at the very least of formally repudiating the sinful structures in question.

I think the distinction that the proponents of the 'sinful structures' concept are looking for is one between this concept and that of private individual sin; or perhaps between sinful structures, which correspond to the vices or bad habits of a social organism as such, and sinful acts. But the responsibility for both must be personal – or else there is no responsibility or liability at all. This is enough to make it impossible to identify original sin with sinful structures.

NOTES

1 The reader may remember the spectacular feat of some Colombian guerrillas in Bogotá in 1980; and a film starring Robert Morley of 1978, called *Who's Killing off the Great Chefs of Europe?*, but released in Britain as *Too Many Chefs*.

2 See Aquinas, *STh* Ia IIae, 82, i (ET, vol. 26). He quotes the latter expression from Peter Lombard's *Sentences*. He derived it ultimately from St Augustine, who uses the phrase *natura vitiata*, e.g. in *Op. Imperf. contra Julianum*, V, 8 (*PL* 45, 1438).

3 The word 'guilt' can cause vast confusion nowadays, thanks to its use as a technical term in clinical psychology. There is no reason why it should not be so used. But psychology has became such a prestigious profession or science in this century that its technical

language has spilled over into popular use in what one American journalist very aptly termed psychobabble. In psychobabble, then, guilt is a feeling, a bad and neurotic feeling which the sensible person should get rid of, with the help of an analyst if necessary. It appears to have no relation to objective actions of the person concerned.

Let us allow that that is one meaning of the word 'guilt'. But it is a very recent meaning; not the only meaning; and certainly not the meaning of the word as I shall use it from time to time in this book. Long before the psychologists got hold of it, it was a term of *law*, and in law it means responsibility or liability for actions punishable by law. It has nothing to do with the feelings of the person committing those actions, and is objectively related to those actions. Moral theology takes it over from law, from Roman law to be exact, where the term is as closely related to the punishment as to the act to be punished. So in Mt 26:66, when the High Priest asked the Sanhedrin what they thought of Jesus' 'blasphemy', they replied, in the Latin Vulgate, *'Reus est mortis'*, literally, 'He is guilty of death', or as we would say in legal English, 'He is liable to the death penalty'. So in theology 'guilt' means both responsibility for the sin and liability to the corresponding punishment. That is the sense in which it will be used in this book. We will never, if I can help it, be concerned in this book with 'guilt feelings'.

4   'Synchronically' links and compares events happening at the same time; 'diachronically' links and compares events happening successively in time.

5   With the two exceptions of Jesus Christ and his mother the Virgin Mary. These two exceptions cannot be discussed or explained here, but they are exceptions that prove the rule, since they are made with a view to the salvation of the whole human race.

8

Original Sin
II: The New Testament and Tradition

The classic New Testament text for the doctrine of original sin is Rom 5:12–21. The context for St Paul's remarks in these verses is his whole doctrine of justification by grace and faith rather than by the works of the law. In the larger section of the epistle which runs from 5:12 to the end of 7 St Paul is showing us how Christ by his death and resurrection (the universal means or instrument of God's saving grace) has set us free from sin and death – and also from the law.

(i)   The universality of sin

Let us first see what he says about the universal grip of sin in chapter 7. He has already emphasized in several places that all human beings without exception are caught in this grip – 'all have sinned and fall short of the glory of God' (3:23; see also 3:9, 1:18 – 2:24). But in 7:7–25 he describes the grip of sin on 'me' (i.e. on Everyman) as somehow being far more radical than the fact that I am a sinner and liable for the sins which I personally commit. Indeed it is so radical that to some extent I am *excused* from liability for my personal sins! Sin is personified as a kind of living monster and its tentacles are seen as penetrating deep into the constitution of the self, dividing the self: 'For I do not do what I want, but I do the very thing I hate. . . . So then it is no longer I that do it, but sin which dwells within me . . . . I see in my members another law at war with the law of my mind, and making me captive to the law of sin which dwells in my members' (15–23). He is elaborating on that phrase from J, 'the imagination of man's heart is evil from his youth' (Gen 8:21), and showing how law, even the good law of God, is no remedy for this situation, but in some ways even makes matters worse by bringing a knowledge and consciousness of sin. 'I was once alive apart from the law, but when the commandment came, sin revived and I died' (Rom 7:9). Sin was there, in me, from the beginning, but dormant until roused by law.

(ii) The origins of sin

In Rom 5:12–21 St Paul in effect tells us how sin got there, and how it is truly to be got out of there, that is out of 'me'. It is rather a confused and confusing passage, the main purpose of which is to show that in Christ alone is a sufficient remedy for sin to be found. It does this by contrasting Christ with Adam. Although a very great deal of ink has been spilt on v. 12, and especially on the conjunctive phrase at the end, translated in RSV '*because* all men sinned' but in other versions rendered 'in as much as . . . ', or 'in whom [Adam] . . . ', or 'because of which [death] . . . ' or 'because of the one by whom [Adam] . . . ', we can avoid all that tangle here by concentrating on v. 19: 'For as by one man's disobedience many were made sinners, so by one man's obedience many will be made righteous'. I would like to modify this RSV translation slightly by substituting 'the many' for 'many' in each case; it is closer to the Greek, and it helps us to see that by the expression 'the many' Paul in fact means 'all'. He is thinking here in Hebrew or Aramaic, which lack a plural word for 'all', and so use 'the many' in the sense of 'the whole multitude', 'the lot of them'. Paul is thus talking about the whole human race, made sinners by Adam's disobedience, made just (a better word than 'righteous') by Christ's obedience.

That one man's (Adam's) disobedience makes all men sinners is the essence of the doctrine of original sin. The contrast with Christ and his obedience and its effect shows that this doctrine is indeed the necessary negative counterpart to the doctrine of the universal and total efficacy of Christ's saving grace.

This is contrasted precisely with the *inefficacy* of the law. The only thing achieved by the introduction of the law is the crystallization of the generalized and personified Sin, which with its attendant Death entered the world through Adam, into specific transgressions or trespasses. St Paul is not of course making the same distinction as was made in the last chapter between 'sin of nature' and 'personal sin'. But there is a certain analogy between the two distinctions that is interesting. What we do have, very definitely, from him is (a) the all-embracing universality of sin, also attested by other New Testament writers (cf. 'the sin of the world', Jn 1:29; 'if you, who are evil . . . ', Lk 11:13, Mt 7:11); and (b) that its roots go deep beneath visible 'transgressions'; and (c) that it derives somehow from Adam, who is the archetypal man, as well as the first, of the old creation, just as Christ is the archetypal man, the head, the beginning of the new.

B. ORIGINAL SIN IN THE TRADITION

(i) In St Augustine's teaching

Like St Paul, Augustine only raises the doctrine of original sin in the context of *grace*. He was engaged in defending the grace of Christ and its absolute necessity for salvation against the Pelagians,[1] who were the unconscious heirs, I cannot help feeling, of the biblical P tradition.

Augustine develops the doctrine found in embryo in Rom 5 – 7 in two respects. First he makes explicit that it is a matter of human *nature* as such being vitiated in its head and archetype, Adam, as a consequence of his personal sin. Therefore all who share in that nature, viz. the whole human race, through their solidarity with their archetypal head share in his guilt – not personally but by nature. He explicitly excludes the suggestion that sin is derived from Adam to all his descendants 'by imitation', by our all imitating him in our personal sins. No; it is simply not open to us to opt out of human nature as it is. As it is, which is as Adam left it, it is crooked.

The human race is a *massa damnata*. It sounds terrible, and so indeed it is, but not so crudely as it sounds. The expression is a metaphor taken from the bakery, and the batch of dough (*massa*) to be baked into bread. The health inspector finds a batch in which a little dirty water, say, was mixed with the flour and condemns it. It is spoilt, rejected, condemned (*damnata*), and may not be baked into bread. Humanity is a spoilt, condemned batch. Throw the lot away. But in fact God doesn't. He saves some of it through the grace of Christ.

Does he save it all? Augustine, and most of the tradition with him, answers 'No', but that is another question for a later chapter. The point here is twofold: first, God is under no obligation to save any of it, and so if he does save some of it that is pure grace; and secondly, *none* of it is capable of ensuring salvation without his saving grace.

The second development Augustine gave the doctrine was to analyse what this 'sin of nature' actually consists in. Here we may say he is in particular developing Rom 7, and especially 7:7, 'I should not have known what it is to covet if the law had not said "You shall not covet" [Exod 20:17]'. But the law did not put the covetousness there, it only revealed it. Augustine's word for covetousness, from his Latin Bible, was *concupiscentia*, concupiscence. This is much closer in sense and tone to the English 'lust' than to the English 'covetousness', though in fact it covers both, with its centre of gravity nearer to 'lust'. Augustine often substitutes *libido*.

Well, what does it mean? What's wrong with lust or covetousness, or concupiscence or *libido*? Aren't they natural? Yes indeed – *viciously* natural. For in this context they signify disordered or discordant appetites, especially the disordered or discordant sexual appetite, in Augustine's analysis.

There is nothing wrong with appetites as such. They are part of human nature as such, as created, not simply as vitiated. But they are meant to function harmoniously and in an order directed and orchestrated by reason; and this they did in the state of innocence, as we saw in Chapter 5, B, i and ii, but only with the help of the elevating grace of original justice. The *vice* of nature which we inherit from Adam is precisely the disorderliness of our appetites and drives, their rebelliousness against reason – Rom 7 again. This disorderliness, says Augustine, is chiefly manifested in the sexual appetite and the capriciousness of the motions of the sexual organs; hence the appropriateness of original sin being transmitted from one generation to the next through sexual procreation.

(ii)   Certain conclusions from these developments

From each of these developments conclusions were drawn in the course of doctrinal history that are usually felt to be rather disagreeable by people today. From the analysis of original sin consisting essentially in concupiscence or lust, and from the fact (?) of experience that lust is inextricably involved in sexual intercourse, it was concluded by some (though not actually by Augustine) that *all* sexual activity, even the lawful congress of spouses, is at least mildly sinful: and by practically all Christians, including Augustine, that although we cannot actually go that far, and must as Christians say that the intercourse of married couples for the sake of having children is not only not sinful in any way but is actually virtuous, nevertheless even such lawful and virtuous sexual activity is 'using a bad thing [concupiscence, not sex] well', and all other sexual activity, including that of married couples which they indulge in not for the sake of having children but for fun, is in varying degrees sinful; and to abstain from all sexual activity is quite simply better, nobler, more Christian than to get married.

Well, there is no logical necessity in these conclusions, even granted the validity of the premises. You could apply the same principle to eating and drinking, or to doing anything that the average sensual man likes doing. And this, I suppose, is just what the Puritans do. But the more balanced view, which I presume to be the dominant Christian, including Catholic, view today, is that while we can acknowledge the tendency in all of us to go too far, to let one or some or even all of our appetites run away with us, nonetheless this does not *necessarily* happen. *Abusus non tollit usum*; abuse does not rule out proper use. So even sexual activity for fun between married couples can be, and presumably usually is, good and virtuous and not even mildly sinful.

From the universality of original sin, or the human race being a *massa damnata*, Augustine concluded that even innocent infants who die unbaptized are involved in the ruin of the human race, being as Paul puts it 'by nature children of wrath' (Eph 2:3), and thus are not saved. But I shall defer comment on this until the next section.

Here it is only to be noted that it was the practice of baptizing infants (which though not the normal thing was certainly widespread in Augustine's time, and always attempted by Christian parents when the child was in danger of dying) which provided Augustine with one of his main pieces of evidence for the doctrine of original sin. Baptism is the sacrament of the forgiveness of sins, of the justification of the sinner. But babies are of course, in the obvious sense of the words, innocent of all sin. So why the rush to get them baptized if they seem to be dying? It can only be because of their involvement in the collective guilt of the human race, the flaw in the human nature they are heirs to, which cuts them off from fellowship with God unless they receive his grace through baptism.

(iii)   In Thomas Aquinas and the subsequent tradition

The main contribution of St Thomas to the complete formulation of the doctrine lay in his modification of Augustine's view that the vice of nature which original sin actually consists in is concupiscence, or the discordant disorder of the appetites.

This, says Aquinas, is only part of the truth. This is the positive material manifestation of the flaw of nature; but what it arises from, he says following St Anselm of Canterbury, is 'the absence or loss of original justice' (STh Ia IIae, 82, i: ET, vol. 26; Anselm, The Virginal Conception 2 and 3: PL 158, 434–435). This is the true essence of original sin: a lack of something man was graciously endowed with at his creation, over and above his merely natural equipment, an endowment of grace which on a slightly asymmetrical analogy with original sin is called original justice. We discussed it in Chapter 5.

One important consequence of St Thomas defining the essence of original sin as consisting in the lack of original justice is this: it makes possible the continuing dialogue between theology and the natural sciences, in this case the sciences of human psychology. The ideal harmonious state of human nature at the beginning is placed just as firmly in the 'supernatural' sphere as the final glorious state of human nature at the end. So the present condition of man, contradictory and corruptible, is allowed to be natural with reference to the perceptible order of things, and hence to be the proper study of the natural sciences, biological and psychological; while it can still be called a fallen or vitiated nature with reference to God and his grace, about which the natural sciences have nothing to say.

Although Augustine, existentially speaking, was in my opinion a far more brilliant psychologist than Aquinas, yet his approach to things did not really allow for the clear distinction between the fields of theology and the natural sciences and philosophy that we have inherited from Aquinas and the mediaeval Aristotelians.

C. ORIGINAL SIN AND THE FATE OF UNBAPTIZED INFANTS

(i) A common tradition that unbaptized infants are excluded from salvation

We saw above that the traditional Christian practice of baptizing infants led Augustine to the inference that even infants, obviously innocent of any sin in the ordinary sense though they be, are nonetheless involved in the guilt of original sin. I think we may say that this inference has been endorsed by almost the whole Christian tradition. Indeed, if it were not made, there would scarcely be any question of original sin at all. So, in so far as Christians are committed by their faith to accepting the truth of original sin (and Catholics are so committed by the decrees of the Council of Trent: Dz 1510–1516/787–792), they are obliged to accept that it involves infants also in its guilt – unless they wish to deny human nature to infants, or to assert that adults have some other access to human nature than through birth and infancy.

But just as 'sin' does not mean the same here as in its ordinary use, so neither does 'guilt'. It is not a question of personal guilt or responsibility, because it is not a question of personal sin. The guilt is not something therefore for anyone, infants or otherwise, to be personally blamed for, or to have to feel sorry for (except in the sense that one feels sorry at having toothache). It is simply the liability inherent in the genetic flaw in human nature which we have seen original sin to be, the liability of the condemned batch to be thrown away. For since that genetic flaw is lack of God's elevating and sanctifying grace without which there can be no salvation, the inherent liability is to loss of salvation, which means to eternal damnation unless God's grace is restored.

From Augustine's day on it was assumed by practically all Christians in the Western or Latin Church (or at least by all theologians and Church authorities), that the only way through which God's grace can be restored to infants is through baptism, and that therefore all infants who die unbaptized suffer eternal damnation.

This is on the face of it a fairly horrific doctrine, and it is against the evidence and common sense to suppose that either Augustine himself or all theologians and authorities of the Latin Church have been horrifically sadistic characters, or that they have delighted to portray God as a horrific sadist. So from the beginning it was made plain that there is no suggestion of such infants being punished with the pains of hell proper to personal guilt for personal sins. And very soon a kind of 'fringe' place or mode of existence was worked out, on the edge of hell, so to speak, for such 'guilty innocents', in which indeed they do not enjoy the vision of God which constitutes eternal bliss or beatitude, but in which they suffer nothing else. According to one view of human nature, of body and soul, and of death that will be propounded in the next and subsequent chapters, the condition of such infant souls would be most properly assimilated to a deep untroubled sleep. The name that this tradition gives to this fringe place or state of existence is *limbo*, from the Latin *limbus*, a fringe.

(ii) *Assessment and criticism of this tradition*

The first point to be made about this tradition is that in this form it is a purely Western or Latin tradition. About the tradition of the Eastern Churches, whether Greek or Syriac or Coptic or Armenian or Slavonic, on this matter, I confess I am not well informed. That all of them practise infant, or at least child, baptism is certain. But whether they all, or any of them, support the conclusions drawn from this practice by the Western Church about the fate of unbaptized infants – well, that is the question. If they do not, then however widespread or common this tradition may be or have been in the Western Church, it cannot be said to be the universal Christian tradition.[2]

The second thing to note about this tradition is that throughout it is a tradition of *reasoned argument*; it is in fact one long inference argued from premisses of faith. The chief premiss is that Christ is the saviour of *all* mankind (which includes infants), and that *all* human beings (including infants) need his grace in order to be saved, because 'there is no other name under heaven given among men by which we must be saved' (Acts 4:12). This premiss is indeed one that the Christian is bound to hold absolutely and with unshakeable firmness. It is hard to see how you can be a Christian in any full sense if you do not hold it.

The other premiss, which calls for more critical examination, is that the only means of Christ's grace available to infants is the sacrament of baptism. Now the tradition about unbaptized infants which we are assessing argues, in my opinion and that of very many theologians today, on altogether too narrow an interpretation of this premiss. I implied in the preceding paragraph that it is a premiss of faith; but I must here put a big question mark against that implication, and at least state that only on a very wide interpretation can it be treated as a premiss of faith.

For the fact is that the great theologians from Augustine to Aquinas and beyond who established this tradition about unbaptized infants not being saved, did not in general give a narrow interpretation of the principle that baptism is necessary for salvation. They widened it with a number of important qualifications.

First, baptism is said to be normally necessary for salvation because it is the sacrament which signifies and thus effects the grace of regeneration and forgiveness of sins; it signifies and effects the entry of a person into the life of God's grace. But, say all these theologians, it is always possible to receive the grace signified by a sacrament, in this case forgiveness of sins and rebirth in Christ, without actually receiving the sacrament if there are circumstances preventing its reception – such as being taken away to be martyred, like St Alban according to his legend. In this case the tradition talks about 'baptism by blood'. The theologians all enlarge it, to embrace other and less drastic circumstances, where they talk about 'baptism by desire'. And the notion has been enlarged in modern times to include 'implicit desire', a desire the person isn't even aware of, supposing for example that they have never even heard of baptism – or of Christ.

It is true, you may argue (and the particular tradition we are criticizing does argue), that to desire something, even by implication, requires some kind of conscious personal act. It is also true that grace isn't just something given by God like a new coat of paint slapped on a wall, for example. As well as being given, and indeed in order to be given, it has to be humanly and personally received by a personal act. The primary act by which grace is received is the act of *faith*, of trustingly accepting what God offers. That is why baptism is linked especially closely with faith, and often called the sacrament of faith. So, says this tradition, infants being as yet incapable of any personal act, they cannot receive the grace of baptism simply by desiring it.

But now comes the second qualification they make to basic theological principles. For when we ask them how in that case infants can receive the grace of baptism even when they are actually baptized, since not even then can they make the necessary personal act of faith, of personally accepting what God offers, these theologians reply that it is in the faith of the Church that infants being baptized receive what God offers. The Church believes on their behalf, being the believing community.

This principle of vicarious faith, of the personal faith of a believer or the believing community availing another person who is incapable of personal faith, is extended even further by St Thomas to cover the case of those infants who lived and died before the Christian sacrament of baptism existed, in Old Testament times; and some of his successors have extended it also to those who live and die *where* baptism does not yet exist. i.e. where the gospel has not yet been preached nor the Church of Christ yet established. According to this extension of the vicarious faith principle these infants are saved by even the *implicit* faith of their parents or the communities they are born into.[3]

It seems very odd, therefore, to exclude from this capacity to benefit from the personal faith of others the unbaptized infants of Christian parents, or of unbelieving parents in a nominally Christian country. This exclusion, surely, cannot be by a compelling necessity of logical reason. And since, as I have said, this particular tradition about unbaptized infants is a purely reasoned one, it must stand or fall purely by the force of the argument formulating it, and not at all by the number and prestige of its supporters. My first criticism of it, then, is that its basis is so narrow as to make the whole argument extremely wobbly.

My second is that it appears from what has been said to do far less than justice to the grace of Christ, and in particular to what Paul says about the grace of Christ in Rom 5:19. It suggests, first, that the grace of Christ is at least in some particulars more effective where his Church and sacraments are not operative than where they are. Secondly it suggests that the grace of Christ is less effective than the sin of Adam. For the sin of Adam corrupted the entire human nature as well as other human persons. But the grace of Christ, it seems on this hypothesis, is only available to heal and restore persons, and either leaves human nature as such untouched, or at least only reaches it through and in certain persons, but not in its total extensiveness. But what does Paul say in Rom 5:19? 'For as by one man's disobedience many [and he means "all", hence the entire body of mankind, the whole nature] were made sinners, so by one man's obedience many [and he must surely mean "many" in the same sense here] will be made righteous.' It is to be noted that Paul's Greek does not simply say 'many', an indefinite adjective of quantity, but '*the* many' – which is indeed his Semitic way of saying 'all'.

(iii)   An alternative solution

This brings me to the one alternative solution which I shall present. There are a number of others, but this one seems to me by far the best. It is to be found in a little paperback, *From Limbo to Heaven* by Vincent Wilkin, SJ, published posthumously in 1961.

His basic proposition is that Christ, the second Adam, has by his obedience redeemed not only human persons as individuals but the human race as a whole, or to put it in another way, human nature. But during the present period of the grand drama of salvation, the betwixt-and-between period after the first coming of Christ and his saving life, death and resurrection, but before his second coming and the general resurrection of the dead, the effects of his saving work are not fully complete nor fully manifest. The effects of the first Adam's damnatory work are still evident in the régime of sin, sickness and death which we all know by experience. Part of this continued régime is the continued subjection of the whole human race to that genetic flaw of our nature which we call original sin.

In this present dispensation, then, Christ through his saving grace only *actually* saves human beings through their *personal* appropriation of his grace, whether through the visible Church of Christ and the sacraments, which is, so to say, the standard and normal way, or apart from them in extraordinary ways. And therefore his grace does not actually save infants, except through the normal procedure of baptism. Wilkin makes no use of the concept of vicarious faith, let alone implicit vicarious faith, which is perhaps a weakness of his theory when it comes to explaining how actual baptism saves infants.

But infants dying unbaptized, his theory continues, since they bear no personal responsibility for any personal sin, but are only alienated from God through their possession of a flawed and alienated nature, will share in the gracious salvation achieved by Jesus Christ when his redemption of that nature, his restoration of mankind as a whole to grace and glory, takes its full effect. And that will be at the resurrection of the dead. This is the perfect rebirth, the complete re-creation or new creation. It is called the rebirth, *palingenesia*, in Mt 19:28 (RSV translates 'in the new world', an indication perhaps of the transatlantic origins of this version). Then they too will enter into the true glory of the resurrection, which will necessarily include the beatific vision of God face to face.

I have suggested that grace cannot just be given, it also has to be personally received. Who can vicariously receive God's grace on behalf of these infants? The answer would be, I think, that at the resurrection, they will not require vicarious representatives, because they will be delivered by that unimaginable process (the end of the entire human process) from the state of infantile unconsciousness. But in any case they, like the rest of us, will be (and are) perfectly represented by Christ himself, precisely as the second Adam, *the* representative human being, archetype of the whole restored, re-created, re-born human race.

(iv)   Conclusion

This has been a long digression. But I think it has been valuable for several reasons. It has taken us into the final destiny of man which really governs the beginnings that we are at the moment investigating. It has shown how true Christian theological concern goes beyond the merely secular. For secular history and social studies are supremely uninterested in the destiny of those who die in infancy. But Christians cannot be so uninterested because they cannot believe that God is so uninterested. It has also illustrated how Christians must, and have tried to, follow the consequences of their faith to their logical conclusions. At the same time it offers us a warning against making our theological reasoning too rigid and narrow. Lastly, while indeed we have been digressing on a side issue, it has been a side issue that is none the less very firmly and immediately attached to the central point of Christian faith: Christ the saviour of *all* humanity, *all* humanity in need of Christ's saving grace. If one ducks this issue, one is in real danger of tacitly surrendering this central point of faith.

NOTES

1 Pelagius was a British monk (I have been told that his real name, in what we now call Welsh but was then just British, was Morgan) who came to Rome in the first decade of the fifth century, and was much sought after and acclaimed as a spiritual director by the devout ladies of the City. He was indeed by all repute a good and austere Christian, and he and Augustine were prepared mutually to admire each other until he took exception to a prayer in Augustine's *Confessions* (which was also a highly popular and fashionable book of spiritual reading): '*Da quod jubes et jube quod vis*', 'Grant what you command and command what you will' (*Conf*. X, 29 (40), 31 (45), 37 (60): *PL* 32, 796; 798; 804). Augustine makes this prayer during a survey of his present state of soul, after his conversion, and while acknowledging his difficulties with continence in general, and resisting temptations to gluttony and to excessive pleasure in being praised in particular. Augustine recalls Pelagius' objection to this prayer in his work *The Gift of Perseverance*, 20 (53) (*PL* 45, 1026).

Pelagius, the enemy of all determinism and fatalism, stressed not only the importance but also the sufficiency and efficacy of moral effort. To keep you on the right path to salvation God has given you his moral law, and you can keep that law if you want to; you must not go whining to him and asking him to keep it for you. This indeed strikes me as pure P.

2 Since writing this, however, I have received some information on Greek Orthodox teaching and practice from Bishop Kallistos of Diocleia, of the Greek Orthodox community in England. With his kind permission I reproduce his answer to my queries here:

(1) From at least the fourth century onwards, it has been the practice of the Eastern Churches to baptize infants. In the Orthodox Church baptism is normally conferred on the fortieth day after birth – but sometimes it is delayed a good deal later than this.

(2) To the best of my knowledge, no Greek Father draws from this the inference made by Augustine – that unbaptized babies go to hell.

(3) Orthodox theologians do not speak about 'limbo'; they feel this to be a speculation without any clear basis in scripture or tradition. All that we can say about unbaptized infants is that they are in the care of God who is infinitely merciful and loving.

When treating original sin, modern Orthodox writers, in common with the Greek Fathers, lay emphasis chiefly upon the *physical* and *moral* consequences of the Fall: i.e. upon sickness, pain, physical death, weakness of will in resisting temptation, etc. The idea of inherited *guilt* is sometimes present – I have in mind passages from Gregory of Nyssa and Mark the Hermit – but . . . it is not greatly emphasized. Even though there is no fundamental opposition here between East and West, there is certainly an important difference of approach.

Bishop Kallistos refers readers interested in pursuing the subject further to his book: Kallistos Ware, *The Orthodox Way* (Mowbray, Oxford, 1979), chapter 3.

3 Chapter and verse for what I have said about the tradition from Augustine to Aquinas is to be found in the latter's treatise on baptism: *STh* IIIa, 68, ii (ET, vol. 57) for 'baptism by desire', where he quotes Ambrose, *Consolation for the Death of Valentinian* (*PL* 16, 1428); IIIa, 68, ix ad 1 (ET *ibid.*) for the principle of vicarious faith in the baptism of infants, where he quotes Augustine, *On the Deserts and Forgiveness of Sins*, I, 25 (*PL* 44, 131); IIIa, 70, iv, (ET *ibid.*) – note especially the second objection and its answer – for what I call the principle of vicarious implicit faith where the Christian sacrament of baptism does not yet exist, where he quotes Gregory the Great's *Moral Commentary on Job*, IV, 3 (*PL* 75, 635).

QUESTIONS FOR FURTHER DISCUSSION

1   Is a doctrine of original sin necessary for Christian faith?

2   What better expression might be worked out for what is meant by 'original sin'?

3   Does the doctrine necessarily imply the literal truth of Gen 2 and 3?

4   What should be understood by the term 'concupiscence'?

5   What should a contemporary theology of grace contribute to a discussion concerning the salvation of the unbaptized?

RECOMMENDED FURTHER READING

Karl Rahner, *Theological Investigations*, 11, chapter 11: 'The Sin of Adam'.

Selah

Here it is time, I think, to pause and take stock of how far we have come and to see how far we have to go, and to plan how to get there. In many of the psalms there occurs the mysterious rubric or stage direction 'Selah', which some scholars take to indicate a pause in the singing, marked perhaps by some instrumental *obbligato* on the ten-stringed psaltery, the harp or zither, the lute or guitar. I cannot offer any such diversions here. But we can pause, in what is not another chapter but an interlude for revision and reflection.

What we are about, we must never let ourselves forget, is studying the relationships between man (i.e. the whole human race and all human beings of all times and places) and God. These relationships, or the most crucial of them at any rate, are known to us by divine revelation rather than by human experience or discovery. So our study is based on, and must throughout be referred to, the record of that divine revelation which is holy scripture.

But we found at the outset that scripture by and large endorses an insight of a modern school of philosophy, that of A. N. Whitehead (and no doubt others) that being human – being anything, he would say – is more of a process than a state. It is a matter of becoming what you are, both for individuals and for the race as a whole, with the dire possibility attached, realized in the history of sin, of becoming what you are not, or ceasing to be what you are.

It follows then that man's relationships with God are essentially historical or (a preferable word) dramatic; they begin, they develop in one way or another to a climax, they proceed to a term, destiny or goal. And so our method has been historical or, in principle, dramatic. We have examined man's beginning as a creature of God, discussed the topic of evolution and related problems, and seen that from the beginning man's proper and full relationship with God is one of grace, transcending the limits and the possibilities of mere nature. And then we have seen how, practically from the beginning, this relationship of grace has been severed by sin, the counter-process frozen, as it were, in the state of original sin.

That is where we have got so far. Having seen how the relationship with

God has been disrupted, we must go on in our study of the great drama, the 'divine comedy', to see how it has been restored, and how it is to be consummated. But before we carry on in that way, I think we need at this point to step aside from the process of the great human drama, and examine some of its key factors or dimensions, some of the key dimensions of being – and becoming – human. For it is of course within these dimensions that the drama of our human relationships with God is played out.

The first obvious dimension, which we have already encountered several times, is that of life – and death (see above, Chapters 2, A; 3, A, iv; 3, B, i; 6, C, iv). But in order to be able to talk about this pair of contraries in the language which we inherit from the tradition, we must first talk about another pair, and their subsidiary terms, 'body' and 'soul'. On these two we have already stumbled several times, so it is imperative to clear them out of the way (see above, Chapters 4, C, ii; 5, B, i).

Our next step, then, will be to discuss man as 'body and soul'. After that we will proceed to life and death, or to man as 'living and dead'.

But human life, the human process once again, is governed or limited by many other key factors. So after considering life and death we will have to discuss human life as personal and as social: person and community. And because the basic, root community is that of husband and wife, man and woman, we will have to consider human sexuality and at least some of its ramifications; marriage, sexual morality, 'Women's Lib', under the general heading of man as male and female. Lastly, since as we have already noted Christ is the saviour of all men, the whole of mankind, and we are therefore concerned to study the relations of all mankind with God (above, Chapter 8, C, ii), we will have to attend to the unity and the diversity of the human race; our common humanity and the almost infinite variety of our cultures. Into this slot could be fitted a consideration of 'political theology', in particular of 'liberation theology' and 'black theology'.

When we have at least surveyed the scene of these various topics we shall return to the main drama, and the restoration of our proper human relations with God through Jesus Christ. We might have another 'Selah' there.

There are just two further observations to make here, before we end this one. The first is that these topics can be and are studied by the 'human sciences' and by philosophy without any recourse to revelation or reference to theology. We shall therefore in principle (not always in fact, owing to the vast gaps in the writer's knowledge) find ourselves in dialogue with the findings and the hypotheses of these sciences. We will always be interested in the bearing they have on man's relations with God, but at the same time always open to the 'sacred teaching', to what the word of God has to say on these topics, which will always be with reference to man's relations with God.

The second observation is about method. We decided at the beginning that we would make Adam and Christ the two poles of our theology of man (Chapter 1, B), and we are sticking to that decision, putting off a consideration of Christ and his restoration of man's grace-relationship with God until the last part of the book. At the same time I must confess to a considerable sympathy with Karl Barth's view that it is only through Christ that we can come to a real knowledge of what man really is, according to God's intention. So, Barth says, a proper theology of man should begin with Christ, not end with him.[1]

I accept Barth's premiss without reservation, but not his conclusion, which I don't think is really practical – or not practical for this book; it is certainly not logically necessary. Here we are taking the drama as our model; and it is surely true that you don't really know what a play is about (if it is a good play) until you have seen the end of it. The same with novels, especially who-dun-its, which is why I am one of those terrible people who jump ahead to see how it will end before they are half way through. Barth must have been one of them too. I am a natural Barthian. But all the same it isn't practical actually to stage a play by beginning with the last act and ending with the first. It would fairly thoroughly spoil the play. So to begin a theology of man with Christ instead of ending with him, if you are conceiving such a theology in the dramatic mode, will not really work. It is not what the divine dramatist has done. There is quite a big stretch of action between Adam and Christ, in the course of which we learn a great deal about man, though it won't all fall into place until we have seen it 'recapitulated', summed up, fulfilled in Christ (cf. Eph 1:10).[2]

But of course, if readers wish to jump now to the final chapter of this book, I will be the last person to refuse them permission.

NOTES

1 *Church Dogmatics*, III, *The Doctrine of Creation* 2, p. 53: 'In its investigation of man in general, theological anthropology must first look away from man in general and concentrate on the one man Jesus, and only then look back from him to man in general'. This problem of method is the subject Barth discusses in the whole of chapter X, §43.

2 RSV translates the Greek *anakephalaiō*, 'recapitulate', by 'to unite', which seems to me to underplay the historical dimension. But NEB uses the same concept, so it has weighty authority on its side.

9

Body and Soul
I: In the European
Philosophical Tradition

A. INTRODUCTORY REMARKS

In this and the next chapter we shall be discussing body and soul as two words, not as two things. We will indeed have quite a lot to say about whatever realities these two words may signify. But we must carefully avoid begging the question about what those realities might be, and this is what we would inevitably do if we failed to look first at the problems connected with these two words, as words. To be more accurate, the problems really all concern the word 'soul', but 'body' is its natural pair, and so is, as it were, infected by the 'soul' problems.

In very general terms we can all agree that the realities signified by these words amount to the total human reality, to human life, to being human, to human existence. It is true, and worth remembering, that these words can perfectly well be used to talk about living animals, as well as about human beings, but our concern in this book is with human existence. And human life and death will be the subject of subsequent chapters, for which in this and the next we are only clearing the ground by tidying out of the way, we hope, a number of 'soul' problems.

Now 'soul', as we shall see shortly, has become in modern English a predominantly religious word, at least in its normal use. And so people naturally assume that there is a proper Christian doctrine about the soul, which implies that there has been a divine revelation about the soul. This is not however true, in any simple straightforward sense. There is certainly a Christian doctrine, based on divine revelation, about man, about people, about human existence. To anticipate, I will here simply assert that God has revealed two things to us about ourselves that are crucial for our relationship with him. The first is that we have been created in his image and likeness (Gen 1:26f.; 5:1, 3; 9:6). The second is that death has been overcome for us, so that we are in some way or another immortal and have an eternal destiny (e.g. 1 Cor 15).

Both these topics will of course be discussed in detail in later chapters.

But about 'body' and 'soul', we must realize very clearly, God has revealed nothing to us. They are after all two English words, and it would be odd if God had chosen to reveal something to us about English words. It would be equally strange, really, if he had revealed something to us about their Hebrew equivalents – which are by no means exact equivalents anyhow. And here precisely is the point. These are words (there are others also) signifying a certain range of human self-experience; a range which differs, perhaps very considerably, from culture to culture. It therefore produces concepts which differ from culture to culture and are expressed in different languages by words that will overlap in meaning but never coincide exactly. Various philosophies of man, various religions have made use of these and similar terms, modifying and changing their meanings, until it is not altogether easy to be sure what they meant to ancient writers in Hebrew or Greek or Latin. One thing we can be fairly certain of is that they did not mean precisely what we mostly mean by them in twentieth-century English, though we still have to use twentieth-century English terms to analyse the traditions we have inherited, and to trace them back to their roots.

In this chapter we shall be tracing them back to their Greek roots, in the next back to their Hebrew biblical ones. This is simply because these are the main roots of the Christian tradition in Europe, hence of Christian English usage. But of course human beings have experienced themselves as such, and continue to do so in quite other cultures, and their experience and reflection on it, as expressed for example in African or Asiatic languages, will overlap but certainly not coincide with that European tradition. While Christianity, whether European or African or Asian, is obliged to latch on, so to speak, to the Hebrew tradition, since the Bible from that tradition is the record of divine revelation to us, there is no strict obligation on African or Asian or other Christians to take over the whole European, Graeco-Roman tradition too. What God has revealed to us about ourselves as human can be expressed in terms of other traditions, using other philosophies. We really must bring to consciousness, and deliberately reject (I mean, we Europeans), that tacit assumption of so much of our thinking that the only proper way of being human is the European one and in particular the English one.

However, this book is being written in English, mainly for English-speaking readers, and by an Englishman who can only give what he has, and that all comes from the Graeco-Roman European tradition and the Bible. But let us at least realize that in many respects a theology of man cannot be quite universal, but must take as many forms as there are cultures and languages of men.

B. TWO KINDS OF SELF-EXPERIENCE: UNITARY AND DISSOCIATED

I suppose it is true to say that there are as many kinds of self-experience as there are and have been persons; and there is a very important element of the incommunicable about such experience, something that cannot be shared with others, something too that has to be acknowledged and respected by others.

All the same, what *is* communicated or shared has to be so in a language common to some other human beings. So one can also talk about common kinds of self-experience. What I suppose is common to all self-experience, of all human beings, is that it is an experience of living or being alive; although that is not saying very much, since everybody may mean something slightly different from every one else by 'life'.

Still, as I have said, in so far as experience is shared by language it becomes common. And while there have been and are, no doubt, many kinds of common self-experience, most of which you and I, dear reader, are wholly unfamiliar with because we are ignorant of the languages they are expressed in and the cultures they produce and are produced by; still, for our purposes in these chapters I venture to say that two types of self-experience have dominated the European Christian tradition.

(i)   The unitary self-experience

The first one I call the unitary self-experience. We shall see much more of it in the next chapter, because it is the dominant one expressed in the scriptures, which will be our subject there. But it is not absent from the classical Greek and European tradition which is our subject here, and so a few words must be said about it now.

It is, I suppose you could say, the ordinary down-to-earth experience of self, concentrated on the visible self which we call 'the body', 'this somebody' (to use an Afro-English expression) which is *Me, I*. I, the person, am in no sense dissociated from the body which I am. *I* walk, *I* sit, *I* feel hot and cold, just as much as *I* think, or rage, or feel happy or miserable, or make choices and decisions. You beat *me*, kiss *me*, kick *me*, tackle *me*, just as much as you teach me, argue with me, talk to me and so on. I have a unitary experience of myself as living in all these active or passive manifestations of life.

What is totally lacking is any self-experience of death. I am aware of death, of course. Other people die, whom I have known. They quite evidently cease to live. That's what death is. So this unitary self-expression does not take me in any way beyond death, or tempt me to speculate beyond death.

This seems to have been the dominant self-experience of the Homeric Greeks. Life is life in this world, full sensual bodily life. They have a word for 'soul', *psychē*, but it is not a word to distinguish from 'body', or at least from 'living body' (*demas* in Homer), though it will readily be distinguished from 'corpse' (*sōma* in Homer, though in the later language it comes to be used for the living body). *Psychē* means (but this is too precise) 'life principle'. It is, at any rate, a life word. You don't contrast life words with body words but with death words.

There is no *psychē* after death, since death is the end of life, and *psychē* means life. The word is linguistically and imaginatively connected with the word for 'to breathe', *psychō*, and breathing is the most obvious condition and indication of life. At death you breathe your last, you breathe out your soul, *psychē*, breath, and it simply evaporates.

What remains, in the Homeric conception, besides the corpse, is the shade or shadow, a very different symbolic idea from that of *psychē* or soul. The Greek is *skia*, and sometimes the word *eidōlon* is used, meaning 'likeness', when the ghost of a dead person appears to a living person. I have to admit that Homer appears to spoil my theory by sometimes also using *psychē* of the dead, in the sense of 'ghost' or 'departed spirit' (*Odyssey*, XI, 207, for example). But he also uses it in conjunction with *eidōlon* in this sense (e.g. *Iliad*, XXIII, 104), and I suspect that its impact on Greek minds in this context would have been quite different from that of 'soul' on English ones in the same context. It would have struck Greek hearers as an interestingly paradoxical use of words – very much like Virgil's use of the word *vita*, 'life', in the last line of the *Aeneid* to describe the death of Turnus: *vitaque cum gemitu fugit indignata sub umbras*, 'and his life fled with a groan angry beneath the shadows'. 'Shade' is indeed the dominant metaphor for the state of the dead, something unsubstantial and two-dimensional, by no means living, the feeble trace or shadow or impression that a person has made on existence by living.

These shades do have some sort of existence, though, in the 'halls of Hades', the god of the dead in the underworld. They can be consulted by the art of necromancy. Odysseus summons the shades to a consultation (*Odyssey*, XI). But he can only communicate with them after he has filled a trench with the blood of a sacrificial victim for them to drink, and so take on for a few moments a certain three-dimensional substantiality.

In this thought-world, however, there is scarcely any expectation of life after death. Death is to be faced with courage, but hardly with hope. It is the common lot. All a man can hope to do is to leave a *name* behind him, which is perhaps a more positive manifestation of his shade.

(ii)   The dissociated self-experience

There does however seem to have been another, rarer, but sometimes dominant form of self-experience, which I call one of dissociation, or dissociability. It seems to have dominated the culture of the pastoralists of the vast Russian and Asian steppes, whom the Greeks called indiscriminately Scythians; and to have affected Greece through Thrace, the Orphic cult, and Pythagoras and his followers in the sixth and fifth centuries B.C.

A name given by anthropologists to the kind of religion or cult associated with this self-experience is shamanism, which derives from the shamans or medicine men of central Asia. But the phenomenon is not confined to that region. There is a story in Arthur Grimble's delightful *A Pattern of Islands* (Murray, London, 1952), a book of reminiscences from his life as a colonial administrator on the Gilbert Islands in the Pacific in the first half of this century. The story is a striking example of shamanism. Mr Grimble was a thin man, far too thin, his island friends thought, for a man of his rank and authority. 'What you need', said a village chief, 'is a good feast of porpoise meat.' 'But there are no porpoises around here at this time of year', said Grimble. 'As we all know, they are a hundred miles or so out eastward in the Pacific.' 'Never mind', said the chief, 'I will tell my diviner to fetch them.' And he did. A little hut of palm branches was built on the beach for the diviner, into which he retired and went into a trance, during which, in his own words, he sent his soul to summon the porpoises. Some eight hours later he rushed out of his hut shouting 'They're coming, they're coming.' And so they were, a vast school of them swimming quietly in towards the shallows of the lagoon. Well, Mr Grimble is a good storyteller, with all the appropriate arts and licences; but I don't think he was writing fiction.

The body of a man who has sent his soul on such a journey is 'as one dead'. But when the soul returns the body revives. So it is very natural to think of death as no more than the permanent dissociation of soul from body. The soul is therefore easily conceived of as the true self, the true 'I' which continues to live by itself after its permanent separation, or release, from the body. Such a self-experience, whether personally undergone or accepted on faith and admired in others, was probably at the root of Orphic and other mystery cults that came early to Greece. The first incipient philosophical reflection on it was undertaken by the Pythagoreans. It was however given its lasting philosophical form by Socrates/Plato.

C. GREEK PHILOSOPHY

(i) *Platonism*

For Plato then, and the tradition of which he is the prime patron, the true self is the soul; more especially in some refinements of the teaching, the spirit (*pneuma*) or mind (*nous*), over and above the soul (*psychē*). We thus have a tripartite division of man into body, soul and spirit, rather than the simple dualism of body and soul. In such an anthropology the spirit or mind is the true self, while the soul is the subject of that degree of life which human beings have in common with animals – sensation and passion.

But it is not merely a tripartite (or dual) division of man; it is also very definitely a hierarchical division of man, who is given higher and lower, greater and lesser levels of life. The body and its interests and concerns has to be subordinated to the soul, and this in turn to the spirit or mind. Or else body (since we are talking of living bodies) is for practical purposes identified with the soul (*anima* in Latin) which *animates* it; and then the sensuous, 'psychic', *animal* life and its demands, desires and fears have to be subordinated to and disciplined by the intellectual, 'pneumatic', spiritual life, manifested above all in reason.

Death, as Socrates argued in the *Phaedo*, before drinking the lethal hemlock to which his fellow citizens had condemned him, is not a destruction of life to be regarded with dread, but rather the release of the soul, the true self (or of the spirit) into its true and natural habitat or form of existence, an immaterial one, where it is free at last from the 'prison of the body'.

There were a number of subsequent variations on the Platonic theme, notably Stoicism, which became very popular and fashionable in the educated circles of republican and imperial Rome. But we have no time or cause to go into it here.

(ii)   Aristotelianism

But there was one variation, which was really a radical criticism of Platonism in the direction of a more 'unitary' philosophy, and that was the view propounded by Plato's student, Aristotle.

Plato's view of man was part and parcel of his theory of forms and ideas; of the real world being that of these eternal, subsistent, immaterial ideas or forms, the 'universals' of a later terminology; and the soul or mind being by nature and affinity an inhabitant of that real, eternally true world, and a stranger and exile in this less than real world of material things, of which there can be no genuine knowledge because they offer no unchanging reality or truth, but can only be the object of provisional opinion. It is from this no more than semi-real world of opinion that the soul desires to escape into the real world of eternal truth.

Aristotle said, on the contrary, that it is this material world that is really real. Forms and ideas are only abstractions. They are indeed real and the object of genuine knowledge, but only in so far as they are 'realized' in material beings.

Such a form is the soul of a living body. The soul is 'the form of the body' in Aristotle's definition, the principle that makes the living body the kind of living body it is, whether cabbage, pig or king. The soul, *anima*, animates the living body. To live is to be animated (*empsychos* in Greek), to be animated is to live. Therefore 'soul' does not represent a mysterious entity in which some people believe and some people don't. What we mean by the word is 'that which animates', the difference between live bodies and dead ones. We are back again at a formulation of the unitary self-experience.

But Aristotle came to it by way of criticism of the Platonic formulation of the dissociated self-experience. So his terms and to some extent his concerns continue to have a definite Platonic flavour or bias to them. In particular, as regards the human soul (principle of animation, *anima*, *psychē*), he finds that what distinguishes it from the brute souls of *anima*-ls is its capacity for an activity that is completely immaterial, separated or – to use the word we have been adopting – dissociated from bodily matter. He uses the words 'separate' and 'abstract', and the corresponding nouns 'separation', *chōrēsis*, and 'abstraction', *aphairesis*. The activity in question is that of rational abstract thought.

He then argued that if the human *psychē* can in its activity abstract from bodily matter with an act that is separated from bodily matter and therefore immaterial, the *psychē* itself, as subject of this act, must somehow be able to subsist independently or separately from matter. While being indeed the animating form of the human body, and constituting in conjunction with the body, and only in conjunction with it, the complete human being or person, still it can subsist or exist by itself apart from the body – and presumably does so after death, at least for a time. Aristotle himself was not very definite about this conclusion, and remained rather agnostic about the status of the human soul after death; but that was the direction of his argument.

D.   THE BACKGROUND TO MODERN PHILOSOPHY

(i)   *Between Aristotle and Descartes*

Aristotle's philosophy suffered a long eclipse after his death, at least as regards his metaphysics and anthropology. Platonism in one form or another held the field. In particular it enjoyed a remarkable renaissance and development from the third century A.D. in the form usually called Neoplatonic. Its chief exponent was Plotinus, and the Christian thinkers who adopted it were above all Origen (third century) and the Pseudo-Dionysius (fifth). But indeed all the Christian Fathers, Latin and Greek, from the third century onwards were more or less Platonic in their background and thought-world. We shall look at the consequences of this fact in more detail in the next chapter.

In Western Europe there was an Aristotelian revival in the thirteenth century, spearheaded by the two Dominican friars, Albert the Great and Thomas Aquinas. They adopted Aristotle's metaphysics and anthropology, and adapted them to the service of orthodox Catholic theology. Although this work of theirs met with grave suspicion at first, it eventually received the highest official approval in the Catholic Church, an approval that it enjoys to this day. So it might be expected that the Aristotelian formulation of the unitary self-experience would be the dominant anthropology, at least among Catholics.

But this is not the case, and in spite of the enormous prestige of St Thomas Aquinas in the Catholic Church it never has been the case. The long-established Platonic thought forms have been too strong in European culture.

(ii)   From Descartes to the present

So when we come to Descartes, the first great original philosopher after the Renaissance, we find him building with Platonic materials. At that time in any case, in the early seventeenth century, scholastic Aristotelianism was held in very low esteem in leading intellectual circles.

Descartes' prime interests were mathematical, and he had a mathematician's tidy mind, and produced a tidy philosophy of clear and distinct ideas, dominated by the category of quantity because it is the mathematical category, and measurable. His anthropology was a simplified and tidy Platonism, with the soul as the chief and essentially independent constituent entity of the human person, controlling the body it animates from a point at the base of the brain which Descartes called (and no doubt his medical friends did too) the pineal gland (now more often termed the pineal body).

I may have described his anthropology unfairly. But it does seem to be a *reductio ad absurdum* of Platonism, and has in recent years been devastatingly satirized by Professor Gilbert Ryle as the theory of 'the ghost in the machine'.

In reaction to this Cartesianism, in so far as modern English philosophers bother to formulate an anthropology at all, they mostly base it on the unitary self-experience and present it in materialistic language. So they dispense altogether with the word and concept of 'soul' as mere mystification. They are still left, though, with less easily expendable terms like 'life' and 'mind'; thus Ryle's book, *The Concept of Mind*. These will be treated, usually, as functions of the material organism.

Meanwhile the ordinary Christian, with some reason, will think that he cannot do without the concept of 'soul'. But now it has, most unfortunately and inconveniently and to a large extent through the fault of a Platonized Christianity, become a *religious* concept, something you believe in or something you don't, like God. And when it comes to making rational sense of

this concept the Christian remains stymied, transfixed, paralysed, mesmer-
ized, fascinated, dumbfounded and dogged by that magisterial sneer – 'the
ghost in the machine'. We saw something of these difficulties earlier in
Chapter 4, C, ii, where we were discussing the direct creation of every
human soul by God.

Perhaps in the next chapter we may find a way of escape from this situation
– or perhaps not.

10
Body and Soul
II: In Scripture and the
Christian Tradition

I remarked in the last chapter that we have to use the modern English words 'soul' and 'body', and other associated words, in analysing what ancient writers meant by the rough equivalents of these words in their own languages, even though they certainly did not mean precisely what we mean by our words.

We also discovered that we users of modern English no longer really know what we do mean by our words, or at least by the word 'soul', and possibly also by 'spirit', and certainly also by 'spiritual'. The fate that has befallen 'soul' and 'spiritual' in modern English (and corresponding words, I suspect, in other European languages) is that they have become religion words. The soul is something that some people, Christians for example, believe in as part of their religion, like God, and other people don't. But even those who believe in it cannot easily relate it to their experience. They are a little puzzled, or at least inarticulate, about what it is, though they staunchly maintain that it is more important than the body, and they definitely want to save it.

This is a bad fate for the word 'soul'. It lays it open deservedly to Ryle's sneer about 'the ghost in the machine'. It also represents something unfortunate that has happened to modern English (European) religion, and indeed, on this topic, thought. Dissociated from experience (something very different from an experience of dissociation), they have become, the one more and more unreal, the other more and more muddled. So in the following pages it is important for readers to keep on reminding themselves that the same fate had not befallen the Greek and Hebrew words which we shall be trying to understand.

A. HEBREW TERMS AND THEIR GREEK EQUIVALENTS

The dominant self-experience behind the writing of the Hebrew Bible, and the Greek New Testament, was what we have called the unitary one, which was briefly described in the last chapter. Here we shall have to look a little more closely at the Israelite experience, but first we must examine the meanings of the words used to express it.

(i) Nephesh (soul)

Nephesh is the word most universally translated 'soul' in the more traditional English versions. Modern versions will try to avoid it as much as possible, since 'soul' for reasons I have given is so misleading. *Nephesh* then in the Bible is by no means a religion word. It signifies straightforward elements of the ordinary secular unitary experience of self. I shall simply tabulate its range of meaning, and in illustrating with texts I shall invariably put 'soul' for *nephesh*, to show how far it is from designating any 'ghost in the machine'. In the rest of this chapter, then, I shall not be employing the RSV as a rule, because to make my points I will require a very literal translation, which I make myself.

(a) Life, principle of life. Thus the reason given for forbidding the eating of blood runs 'Take care not to eat the blood, for the blood it is the soul, and you shall not eat the soul with the flesh' (Dt 12:23). Again, 'But flesh with its soul, its blood, you shall not eat. And indeed your blood for your souls I shall require; from the hand of every beast I shall require them, and from the hand of man; from the hand of every brother of his I will require the soul of man. Whoever sheds the blood of man, by man his blood shall be shed, for in the image of God he made man' (Gen 9:4–6). When Elijah was so depressed he wanted to die, 'he besought for his soul to die' (1 Kgs 19:4).

In the New Testament the Greek *psychē* has a similar range of meanings, and is the word behind 'soul' in the following illustrations. Thus we have under this heading the truly shocking statement of Jesus (shocking to convinced religious ghost-in-the-machiners), 'He that finds his soul will lose it, and he that loses his soul for my sake will find it' (Mt 10:39). Substitute 'life' for 'soul' as all translations quite correctly do, even the most traditional, and the shock is removed, and the ghost remains undisturbed in the machine, more's the pity.

(b) Self, person. This is a meaning English 'soul' does also have sometimes, as in 'Ole King Cole was a merry old soul'. We never seem to have young souls in English in this sense. Note incidentally, as a sign of hope for the word 'soul', that in this sense it can be synonymous with 'body', especially in Scots: 'Poor wee soul', 'Poor wee body' – you could say either and mean the same thing.

In Hebrew this meaning is more poetic than colloquial. In poetry 'soul' is often used as little more than an emphatic personal pronoun: ' . . . in the hand of those who made you suffer, and said to your soul, Bow down' (Isa 51:23). Elsewhere in biblical language you will afflict your soul with fasting, or bind your soul by an oath (Lev 16:29, Num 30:3 etc.).

In the following text we have senses (a) and (b). 'Each and every one from the house of Israel who eats any blood, I shall set my face against the soul eating blood, and cut it off from the midst of its people; for the soul of the flesh is in the blood, and I have given it [the blood] to you on the altar to expiate for your souls; for the blood, it expiates with the soul' (Lev 17:10–11).

(c) Emotions and appetites or desire. 'Like cold water to a thirsty soul is good news from a distant land' (Prov 25:25). The appetite of the grave is thus described: 'Sheol has enlarged her soul, and opened her mouth without limit' (Isa 5:14). Sheol is the Hebrew equivalent of the Greek Hades, but 'female' instead of 'male'. Incidentally, most modern translators will put 'throat' for *nephesh* in this text (not RSV, which has 'appetite'), as also in Ps 69:1 ('neck' in RSV). It is possible that this is the primary meaning of the word. 'Our soul loathes this very light food' (Num 21:5). In the New Testament we have the telling illustration of the rich fool: 'I shall say to my soul, Soul, you have many goods stored up for many years; rest, eat, drink, be merry. But God said to him, Fool, this night they will demand your soul of you' (Lk 12:19–20). Here we have all three senses, perhaps.

(ii)   Soul, flesh, and other parts of the body

Nephesh is often coupled with other, more concrete words, especially with *basar* (flesh) and *lev*, *levav* (heart). It is worth noting, incidentally, that Hebrew has no distinct word for 'body'. If you come across 'body' in the Old Testament it is probably translating *basar* (flesh), or *beten* (belly). *Nephesh* is often put in parallel with *basar*, almost never in contrast. They are *not* a natural contrast pair like 'body and soul' in English. They are, in fact, often practically synonymous, being two ways of referring to the self, to 'me': 'My soul has thirsted for you, and how much my flesh' (Ps 63:1); 'My soul has pined for the courts of the Lord, my heart and my flesh have exulted in the living God' (Ps 84:2). These are just three poetic, emphatic ways of saying 'I'.

'Heart', by the way, commonly signifies the seat of intelligence or cunning, good or wicked thoughts, pride, humility, joy, never compassion or tenderness. Israelites felt these feelings in their *bowels* or *entrails*. So when Jesus rebukes his disciples for hardness of heart (or the Pharisees), as he frequently does in the gospels, it is their stupidity he is castigating, not their callousness.

(iii)   Ruach (spirit)

This word, unlike *basar* (flesh), is never a practical synonym for *nephesh*, but frequently employed as a contrast term; soul is contrasted with spirit in the Bible, not identified with it. *Ruach* often means much the same as 'spirits' in expressions like 'high spirits'. Thus the queen of Sheba lost her spirit when she saw Solomon in all his glory (1 Kgs 10:5), and Jacob's spirit revived when he heard that Joseph was still alive (Gen 45:27).

Where *nephesh* means 'life', *ruach* means 'vigorous life', transcending the humdrum limitations of the ordinary man's ordinary daily round. God will sometimes take away one spirit from a man and give him another, for better or worse (cf. 1 Sam 10:6; 16:13, 14). In particular, he will give his own spirit to a chosen person, and be asked to bestow it on the petitioner (Ps 51:10–12; here it seems to be parallel, in the first instance, to 'heart').

(iv)   Soul, flesh, spirit in St Paul

St Paul's use of these words (*psychē, sarx, pneuma*) and especially of their adjectives (*psychikos, sarkikos, pneumatikos*) has always been a translator's nightmare. Furthermore, from very early on in the Christian tradition they have been regularly misinterpreted in terms of the Platonic philosophy and the dissociated self-experience.

St Paul's chief contrast is between flesh and spirit, fleshly (carnal) and spiritual. Before seeing what he means by these terms, it is essential to observe that he does *not* mean 'body' and 'soul'. To suppose that he does is precisely the Platonic misinterpretation. Where he introduces *psychē* and *psychikos* ('soul' and ?'soulish'), it is as parallels or synonyms of *sarx* and *sarkikos* ('flesh' and 'fleshly' or 'carnal'), in contrast therefore with *pneuma* and *pneumatikos* ('spirit' and 'spiritual'). In this he simply carries on the Hebrew usage of the Old Testament. Thus fleshly people are also, and by the same token, soulish people, absolutely different from spiritual people. Soul goes with flesh, and together and separately they are contrasted with spirit. The best passage to illustrate this is 1 Cor 2:13 – 3:3: 'We impart this in words not taught by human wisdom but taught by the Spirit, interpreting spiritual things to spiritual people. But a soulish man does not receive the things of the Spirit of God; for they are folly to him, and he is not able to understand them because they are spiritually judged. But the spiritual man judges all things and is himself judged by no one. For who has known the mind of the Lord so as to instruct him? But *we* have the mind of Christ. And I, brothers, could not speak to you as spiritual people but only as fleshly people, as little ones in Christ. I gave you milk to drink, not solid food; for you were not yet capable of it. Indeed you are still not capable, for you are still fleshly.' In 1 Cor 15:44 he contrasts the soulish body with the spiritual body.

For Paul these words do not signify parts of the human make-up or *ensemble*. They signify qualities of life. 'Spirit' and 'spiritual' signify a divine quality of life, received as a gift from God and being a share in his Spirit, which goes with a full active share in the body of Christ, with 'Christ living in me' (Gal 2:20).

'Flesh' and 'carnal', 'soul' and ?'soulish', signify not just a natural or human quality of life, but a corrupt and corruptible, weak and perishable, mortal, self-centred kind of life. That is why it is, in my opinion, totally misleading to translate these words by 'nature' and 'natural'. It is not human nature but the distortion or corruption of human nature that is the enemy of the Spirit. But of course living according to the Spirit does involve a disciplining of nature, of self, particularly since the natural self is in concrete fact corrupted by original sin and personal sin.

B.   ISRAELITE SELF-EXPERIENCE IN THE LIGHT OF ISRAELITE GOD-
EXPERIENCE

(i)   Earliest experience chiefly a group experience

God revealed himself to the Israelites as the God of the ancestors, Abraham, Isaac and Jacob, and then (indeed 'and thus') as the God of Israel the nation (cf. Exod 3:6). Israel, of course, was the new name of the ancestor Jacob (Gen 32:28), in whom one could say the nation had corporate personality.

The point is, he was God of individual Israelites only in so far as they were part of the nation, or of its tribal subsections. They had a group consciousness, a group morality, a group sense of justice. God made a covenant with the nation, the group, which continued through the generations. He dealt with the nation graciously and justly, by delivering them from Egypt, bearing with their infidelities, punishing their transgressions as a group, giving them the promised land, teaching them by the prophets, delivering them once more into captivity and exile for breaking the covenant, bringing a remnant back home again.

It was into this dominating group consciousness, group religion, that what I have called the unitary self-experience fitted. This means that there was even less concern with individual destiny than there was among the Homeric Greeks, and absolutely no thought or concern about life after death. To sleep with one's fathers, to leave one's name behind in children and children's children, that was enough. To be 'cut off from one's people', that was the ultimate and most terrible sanction.

(ii)   Growing interest in personal relations with Yahweh

What has just been said would give quite a false impression if it were taken to mean that there was no room for personal piety in ancient Israel. Quite evidently there was, as can be seen in the psalms and in many of the laws of the covenant. The supreme values of the covenant were *hesed*, *emeth* and *tsedeq*, lovingkindness, faithfulness, justice; and these demand expression in relations between individual persons, as well as between the community and their God. God's concern for these values, expressed in the covenant, shows that he too is concerned for individual persons, e.g. the orphans and the widows and the strangers in your midst, and not just with the group (see e.g. Lev 19:9–14).

Israelite religion, however, right up to the exile and beyond, still remained a completely this-worldly (or rather this-lifely) affair, because it was held in the limits of the unitary self-experience. Now the earliest conclusion from faith in God's *hesed*, *emeth* and *tsedeq* was that he blesses and rewards the just man and punishes the wicked here on earth in this life. This conclusion is stated with the most serene assurance in Ps 37. But sooner or later such a simple view of things breaks down. So very often, especially in unsettled times, it obviously is not true.

Thus an acute crisis arose for the faith of the pious Israelite. What about the justice of God, or his power – or his very existence? It is the problem of evil, of innocent suffering, of the absurdity of existence, presenting itself in the combined context of God's revelation to Israel and the unitary self-experience. The intellectual anguish it caused is expressed in two of the theologically most important books of the Old Testament, Job and Ecclesiastes, both composed a century or two after the exile.

These books are important, not because they solve the problem, which they don't, but because they state it so clearly and honestly, especially Ecclesiastes; clear-sighted honesty is a quality all too often feared and shunned by the genuinely pious, still more by the conventionally religious. The author of Job emphatically states the unaccountability of God (Job 38 – 41). The Preacher even more clearly states his theme of 'Vanity of vanities, all is vanity' (Qo 1:2). So it is – if death is the absolute limit of life. He doesn't see the solution. Nor, for all his scepticism, so shocking sometimes to pious Christian ears, does he choose the false solution of jettisoning God. His is the valuable and difficult scepticism of the *believer* halfway along the process of divine revelation, the scepticism that forces the pace of revelation, so to speak.

(iii) Belief in the resurrection of the dead

The solution offered by the developing divine revelation, finding expression in the faith of believers who refuse to be sceptical for ever, is the strange doctrine of the resurrection of the dead.

We must note: it is *not* a doctrine of the immortality of the soul. There is no such revealed doctrine, or article of either Jewish or Christian faith. God has chosen to make his revelation in the context of a people whose culture was dominated by the unitary self-experience. So when, under the pressure of his self-revelation through their history, they began to penetrate beyond the frontier of death, what they find there in faith is not immortal souls but risen bodies. Living bodies of course, super-living bodies, full selves.

This was the belief inherited by the New Testament, the Pharisee doctrine fully underwritten by Jesus himself (see his reply to the Sadducees who denied the doctrine, Mk 12:18–27); the doctrine amazingly vindicated and illustrated in Christian faith by Jesus' own resurrection from the dead. And so the fullest statement of the doctrine of resurrection, which is expressed in only a few very late passages of the Old Testament (e.g. Dan 12:2), is to be found in 1 Cor 15. The chapter should be read in the light of what we have seen above in A, iv. We shall go through it in some detail in the next chapter.

C. BODY AND SOUL IN CHRISTIAN TRADITION AFTER THE NEW TESTAMENT

(i) *Immortality of the soul an inference from resurrection of the body*

We remarked at the beginning of the previous chapter that God has revealed two things to us about being human: that we are made in his image and that death has been overcome for us. This second revealed truth, we have just been saying, formulated in terms of the unitary self-experience, appears as a doctrine of the resurrection of the body/flesh, not as a doctrine of the immortality of the soul.

I think it is very difficult, if not impossible, to find an unambiguous statement of the immortality of the soul in scripture. Many commentators assume that you have such a statement in the book of Wisdom, a book written in Greek at Alexandria about 100 B.C. or even later, where the influence of Greek thought upon the Jews of the *diaspora* would have been large. Chapters 2 – 5 read rather as if they were composed to be a counterblast to the scepticism of Ecclesiastes. But if you read them in the light of what has been said about *nephesh* and its Greek equivalent *psychē* as employed in both Old and New Testaments; and if then, wherever you find the word 'soul' in Wis 2 – 5 you substitute either 'life' or 'person'; you will I think find the testimony of Wisdom to the immortality of the soul, as distinct from the resurrection of the body, begins to look rather more doubtful.

As for New Testament uses of 'soul' in our modern sense of a religious word, meaning the immortal part of me, I doubt if there are any, though there are instances where the word can be so construed by the unwary, e.g.

Heb 13:17, Jas 1:21, 5:20, 1 Pet 1:9, 2:11, 25. But again, try substituting 'life' or 'person' or 'self' for 'soul' in each case and see what happens.

In Mt 10:28 we do seem to have the 'body and soul' distinction we are used to nowadays: 'Do not fear those who kill the body but cannot kill the soul; rather fear him who can destroy both soul and body in hell'. It is worth noting however that the parallel passage, Lk 12:4, runs: 'Do not fear those who kill the body and after that have no more they can do. But I will warn you whom to fear; fear him who after he has killed has power to cast into hell.' No mention of 'soul'. Again Rev 6:9 and 20:4 mention 'the souls' of those who have been martyred. These texts do affirm the continued existence after death of 'souls'. But Lk's version of Mt (I suspect it is closer to Jesus' own words) shows that the same idea can be conveyed without the concept of soul. It remains that Mt's text does appear to make use of this concept.

What I think we can conclude from these few texts is that the persistence of the life-principle after death is inferred from the doctrine of the resurrection of the body. If I am to rise again, whether to 'life' or to 'judgement' (Jn 5:29), I must continue to exist between my death and the last day; I, my soul. But this concept is the merest appendix, so to speak, to the firmly stated, firmly held doctrine of resurrection.

(ii) Translation of biblical revelation into a culture and language dominated by the dissociated self-experience

However, while the New Testament was being written, the gospel was being preached to Greeks and others whose culture was Hellenistic, whose language was saturated with Platonism and its derivatives, all expressing the dissociated self-experience.

The effects of this translation were most rapidly, and on the whole unfortunately, felt in the realm of Christian ethics. That Platonic sense of hierarchy which first divides body from soul and soul from spirit, and then says spirit is infinitely more valuable than soul, and soul than body – this encouraged Christians simply to take over the Stoic morality with its idea of *apatheia* or passionlessness; to take over and develop a contempt for the body and a fear of it, especially a contempt and fear of sexual activity and feeling.

Christian doctrine, or at least popular belief, was more slowly affected by this transplantation into a Hellenistic, Platonized thought-world. As long as the end of the world was thought to be more or less imminent, and that was for several centuries, the prospect of the resurrection of the body continued to hold the attention of the faithful; and of course it continued to be affirmed in official statements of faith like the Apostles' Creed and the Nicene Creed.

But as serious and general expectation of the last day faded, so did serious belief in the resurrection of the dead. It must be centuries since average pious

Christians ever thought about the resurrection of their bodies except to be puzzled by this odd doctrine. What good Christians have been interested in is the salvation of their souls, and going to heaven (as souls, what else?) when they die. If they belong to the Catholic tradition, they desire to have prayers said for the repose of their souls when they die, but never, so far as I know, for the glorious resurrection of their bodies.

(iii) Some modern incoherences

In the present day things are changing. For some time our culture has been shifting back to a dominance of the 'unitary' self-experience. This shift is catching up with Christians too, at least with the more theologically literate Christians. It is fashionable for theologians and scripture commentators, and even occasionally preachers and teachers and editors of new catechisms, to decry the Hellenistic, Platonic body/soul division and recall us to a more biblical view of man. I think this is a good thing; it is certainly an inevitable thing. We cannot really live for ever with that Rylean sneer, 'the ghost in the machine'.

Should we then scrap the word 'soul'? I myself think it would not be a bad idea; there are plenty of good substitutes, 'self', 'person', even 'personality'. But such a revolution of thought patterns ought, indeed *must* for the Christian be accompanied by a real reassertion of faith and hope in the resurrection. For death has been conquered, and if we play down soul and its immortality, it can only be in favour of the doctrine of the resurrection – if we are Christians.

And yet strangely enough it is just here that we often come across a modern incoherence. The eager abolishers of 'soul' are not too keen on resurrecting the body. The doctrine is as odd, as indigestible as it ever was to St Paul's Hellenistic Corinthians. This is because people are allowing the contemporary culture shift to influence them too much; they are succumbing to the dominant scientific materialism and (in effect) atheism, as well as participating in the dominant unitary self-experience. I am all for abolishing, or rather re-secularizing the word 'soul'; but not for abolishing the central Christian hope, the very sense and meaning of my being embodied in the body of Christ. 'If there is no resurrection of the dead, then Christ has not been raised; if Christ has not been raised, then our preaching is in vain and your faith is in vain' (1 Cor 15:13f.). But more of this in the next chapter.

QUESTIONS FOR FURTHER DISCUSSION

1   In what sense is the human self separable, or even distinguishable, from the human body?

2   Can we dispense altogether with the word 'soul' in our religious and theological vocabulary?

3   How did Israel arrive at a belief in the resurrection of the dead? How does this differ from a doctrine of the immortality of the soul?

RECOMMENDED FURTHER READING

As a background to the whole philosophical issue raised in these two chapters, it would be valuable to read Plato's *Phaedo* and Aristotle's *On the Soul*, both available in English translations (see Bibliography). St Thomas presents a theologized, and perhaps slightly Platonized version of Aristotle's doctrine in *STh* Ia, 75–89 (ET, vols 11, 12).

11
Life and Death
I: Life

A. THE LIVING GOD
(i) Life the primary and ultimate value

From the beginning to the end of the Bible, through all the developments of divine revelation and Israelite and Christian faith, in Old and New Testaments alike, the one constant value shared by both the just and the wicked, by God and man, is *life*. The wise and virtuous know that it is a gift from God, a blessing, and can only be truly enjoyed by keeping his covenant and by sharing life with one's fellows. The wicked and foolish think it can be grabbed and should be exploited ruthlessly at the expense of others, and that human life is no concern of God's: 'The fool says in his heart, There is no God' (Ps 53:1; cf. 10:11). But for all it is the basic and ultimate value.

That is why the God of Israel is the *living* God. He is the author and giver of life. Simply to live is to have a kind of communion with him (cf. Pss 42:2; 84:2). Not to have any communion with him is, for a member of his people, to die or be dead. However, the life of the living God is so much more intense, concentrated, powerful than human life that to come too close to it can be a threat to ordinary human life: 'For who is there of all flesh, that has heard the voice of the living God speaking out of the midst of fire, as we have, and has still lived?' (Dt 5:26).

(ii) God is not the God of the dead, but of the living

This is an axiom of biblical religion as constant as the value of life, and co-ordinated with it. But the consequences drawn from it develop, not to say reverse themselves, as the divine revelation through the people's history unfolds.

(a) The oldest inference drawn was that Israel's and the Israelite's relations with God, and *vice versa*, are confined to this life. The dead do not and cannot worship God, nor has God, the living God, anything to do with the dead. So – 'Please, God, in your own interests as well as mine, keep me alive as long as possible'. This is the tone of Ps 88. Note especially vv. 4–5: 'I am reckoned among those who go down to the Pit . . . like the slain that lie in the grave, like those whom thou dost remember no more, for they are cut off from thy hand'; and vv. 11–12: 'Is thy steadfast love declared in the grave, or thy faithfulness in Abaddon?[1] Are thy wonders known in the darkness, or thy saving help in the land of forgetfulness?' And there is the song of King Hezekiah when he had recovered from an apparently mortal illness and been given fifteen more years of life: 'Thou hast held back my life from the pit of destruction . . . . For Sheol cannot thank thee, death cannot praise thee, those who go down to the Pit cannot hope for thy faithfulness. The living, the living, he thanks thee, as I do this day' (Isa 38:17–19).

(b)   With Ezekiel during the exile we get a certain development. It is in the context of the prophet's doctrine of individual as distinct from collective responsibility, set out at great and repetitious length in chapter 18. The sinner will die for his own sins, the just man on the other hand will live. A man will not live because his father was just while he himself was wicked, nor die for his father's wickedness while he himself is just. And then the prophet proposes to the wicked man the possibility of repentance, an invitation to it indeed from God, who exclaims, 'Have I any pleasure in the death of the wicked, says the Lord God, and not rather that he should turn from his way and live!' (18:23). And later, 'I have no pleasure in the death of anyone, says the Lord God; so turn, and live' (18:32).

The question is, what death and what life does the prophet envisage? The living God does not desire the death of the wicked – and yet as the author of Ecclesiastes was to observe drily one or two centuries later, 'For of the wise man as of the fool there is no enduring remembrance . . . . How the wise man dies just like the fool!' (2:16); ' . . . one fate comes to all, to the righteous and the wicked, to the good and the evil . . . . As is the good man, so is the sinner . . . .This is an evil in all that is done under the sun, that one fate comes to all' (9:2–3).

It would seem that Ezekiel had some glimmerings of a future retribution, 'life' and 'death' in another mode. And yet, though that is the logic of his intuition, it is unlikely that he did have such a glimmering; he gives no further sign of it, at least. Perhaps the prophet is simply thinking of the death penalty, and of the reprieve of the condemned man who repents.

His statement remains, a development of the basic notion that God is the God of the living, not of the dead. God does not desire the death of the wicked, but rather that he should turn from his wickedness and live.

(c)   But when Jesus in the gospel says, 'He is not God of the dead but of the living', the inference he draws from this is absolutely clear, though slightly mysterious; that the dead rise again (Mk 12:26–27). Contrary to the negative inference of the psalmist and Hezekiah, we must conclude that

because he is God of the living and not of the dead, the dead are not dead.
Ezekiel's conviction we must gloss by saying that it is beyond death that God
does not desire the death of the wicked, but rather that he may turn from his
wickedness and live. And so that is why the Son came into the world – that
they may have life and have it more abundantly (Jn 10:10).

B. THE RESURRECTION OF THE DEAD

So now, before considering more closely in the next chapter what death is,
we must go on to understand what life is in its supreme and most abundant
manifestation, life that has triumphed over death, the life of those risen from
the dead. This, presumably, will be the perfection of humanity in itself, the
state of being human in which human beings are intended by God to reach
their final goal of intimate union with him, of seeing him face to face.

The New Testament tells us about the resurrection of Jesus Christ from the
dead on the third day, about the resurrection of the just on the last day in
some detail, and about the resurrection of the wicked on that same occasion
just in passing.

(i)   The resurrection of Jesus Christ

It is, to my mind, curious that not only unbelievers nowadays refuse to accept
the truth of the resurrection of Jesus from the dead in the obvious sense of the
phrase. Many Christians too, in particular many Christian biblical scholars
and theologians, find it extraordinarily difficult to believe it.

At any rate, they devote a vast amount of ingenuity to explaining away the
stories in the gospels about the empty tomb and the appearances of the risen
Christ to his disciples, so that when they have finished with the texts little or
nothing of the traditional doctrine of Christ's resurrection remains. This is
serious, because as we shall hear Paul saying, 'if Christ has not been raised,
then . . . your faith is in vain' (1 Cor 15:14). This is not merely a traditional
Christian doctrine; it is the cardinal, central Christian doctrine and affirmation of faith.

What seems to stick in the intellectual gullet of many such critics is that we
should be expected to believe in the risen Christ as in a 'resuscitated corpse'.
That is indeed a rather horrid expression. But putting a statement in nasty
terms does not make it untrue or irrational, any more than putting it in nice
terms makes it true or rational. One must first observe that a resuscitated
corpse, if it is really resuscitated, i.e. revived, is no longer a corpse but a living
body. The critics are at perfect liberty, as Christians, to reject belief in the
risen Christ as in a zombie. But then no other Christian has ever believed in
such a risen Christ either, nor do the stories even begin to depict him after his
death as a zombie.

A much more important observation is that the stories underline a very definite difference between Christ risen from the dead and other 'resuscitated corpses' (there is no need to be afraid of the expression), like Lazarus, the daughter of Jairus and the son of the widow of Naim, all brought back to life by Jesus. Now these stories of Jesus resuscitating corpses are certainly told in the gospels to demonstrate the power of Jesus Christ over death; they are certainly told as anticipations in a sense of his own resurrection. But it is equally clear that they are told as stories of people being brought *back* to life, to the life they had lost, this life, this time-bound, mortal life. Later on, we must presume, they all died again, definitively.

When we come to the case of Jesus himself we must note: (a) that none of the gospels give us an actual story of his being revived/resuscitated/brought back to life; (b) that when they describe his appearances after the event they have two preoccupations, especially Luke's stories: first to emphasize his *bodily* reality, making it clear that he is not a ghost (not even in its repaired machine – Lk 24:39–43); and secondly to make it clear that he has risen to a new kind of life, life in a new dimension or a new key (Lk 24:15–16, 31–32, 50–51). So it is highly inaccurate to say that the doctrine of Jesus' resurrection from the dead is a doctrine of his being brought *back* to life, or of his corpse being resuscitated. Rather, it is a doctrine of his being carried *onward*, forward through death to a totally new intensity of life. The gospel stories simply bear out, with their simple plain symbolism, culminating in the story of Jesus' being taken up into heaven, Paul's statement that 'Christ being raised from the dead will never die again; death no longer has dominion over him' (Rom 6:9).

The story earlier in the gospels of the transfiguration has something to say about this new mode of life. The transfiguration (Mk 9:2–8 etc.) is a kind of anticipation of the resurrection of Christ. The scene is enacted shortly after Jesus has made his first prediction of his death and resurrection. He is being shown to the chosen three disciples as being already in principle (though not in permanent actuality) endowed with all the fullness of divine and eternal life, which is to transfigure but not to eliminate or destroy his bodily human life.

But the gospels do affirm, what some modern critics find so hard to swallow, but what seems to me a realistic and reasonable thing to affirm, that life in this new mode, risen life, is not compatible with the continued existence in the old dimension of the unresuscitated corpse of the subject of the new risen life. It is not compatible with its subject continuing to be dead. The empty tomb is not only a sign that Jesus has risen from the dead; it is also a *necessary* sign, without which one could not say he has risen from the dead.

Finally it should be remarked that Jesus' resurrection from the dead so understood, though certainly wonderful and a 'mighty work of God' (Acts

2:11), is entirely consistent with the notion of human life we have described as based on the unitary self-experience. It will seem impossible or incredible only to minds still dominated by thought structures derived from the dissociated self-experience, or to a 'scientific' materialism still infected by that kind of idealism.

(ii)   The resurrection of the just

This brings us to what St Paul has to say about the resurrection of the dead in 1 Cor 15. He says it because some of his Corinthian Christians were denying the resurrection of the dead. And they were presumably doing so because of the Platonic presuppositions and assumptions that were in the very air they breathed and the language they spoke. What sense is there, they were no doubt saying to themselves, in this peculiar Jewish idea of the resurrection of the dead, this resuscitation of corpses (which the Athenians had laughed at Paul for mentioning on the Areopagus: Acts 17:32), if our souls are immortal anyway, and we can look forward to a blissful eternity freed from the fetters of the body?

Paul first recites the gospel he had preached, the tradition he had received and handed on, that Christ died for our sins and was raised on the third day (1 Cor 15:1–11). Then he goes on to relate Christ's resurrection to the general resurrection as the first instance, the master instance, the cause of the resurrection of all other people, the first step in the inauguration of the kingdom of God, of which the resurrection of the dead will be the final stage (*ibid*. 20–28, 51–57); 'the last enemy to be destroyed [to be put under Christ's feet; Ps 110:1] is death' (*ibid*. 26).

Thus the Apostle's main concern is to show the theological necessity of the resurrection for the full execution of God's saving plan, that plan which was effectively but still only seminally accomplished in the death and resurrection of Christ. It is a plan for *life*, true to the whole thrust of revelation and Israelite religion, which requires the final destruction of death. No death, no dead bodies; no dead bodies, resurrection of the dead.

Only secondarily is he concerned to deal with the Corinthians' difficulties – they too perhaps were rather put off by the prospect of 'resuscitated corpses'. His answer was more or less what we were saying earlier with regard to Christ's resurrection. They won't be corpses, and they won't be brought *back* to this sort of temporal and thus again *mortal* life. It will be a new kind of life, and thus a new kind of body, but still a real, material body.

He does this in vv. 35–53. The resurrection will be precisely a transfiguration, a *transformation* of which we can perhaps form a dim idea from the remote analogy of a grain dying in the ground to produce a new crop (cf. the use of this image by Jesus in Jn 12:24, to point the necessity of his death). The crucial verses are 42–52, where Paul compares the body as 'sown', i.e. as in our present condition, and as 'raised'. But it is in each case *body*. The fourth contrast is the most significant; that between what the RSV calls 'a physical body' (our present condition) and 'a spiritual body'. This however is an exceedingly regrettable translation which will give the ordinary modern reader a wholly false idea. Of course our bodies are physical, he will assume. 'Physical' and 'bodily' and 'material' are in ordinary modern speech synonymous terms; thus physical violence is the same as bodily violence, physical damage the same as material damage, as distinct from moral or psychological violence or damage. So when a 'spiritual body' is contrasted with a 'physical body' (which is obviously a bodily body') it is readily understood as meaning in fact a non-bodily body, a non-material body, i.e. as spirit pure and simple.

But that is *not* what Paul is saying; he may be obscure, but we should not readily assume that he contradicts himself in two words. His word, translated 'physical' by RSV, is a *psychikon* body, a psychic body, to transliterate. In the last chapter (10 A, iv) we gave 'soulish' as a non-English translation, but here we might with slightly better English talk of an 'ensouled' body. That is what we are now, what Adam was created as, an ensouled body or a 'living soul' (v. 45; RSV: 'a living being'). This ensouled body will be transformed into an enspirited body, a pneumatic body to transliterate Paul's word, a 'life-giving spirit' (*ibid.*). But it will definitely not cease to be *body*, it will not be a *non-body*. The JB translation of the passage is much more satisfactory: 'When it is sown it embodies the soul, when it is raised it embodies the spirit. If the soul has its own embodiment, so does the spirit have its own embodiment. The first man, Adam, as scripture says, became a living soul; but the last Adam has become a life-giving spirit. That is, the first one with the soul not the spirit, and after that the one with the spirit' (vv. 44–46).

When Paul says (v. 50) that flesh and blood cannot inherit the kingdom of God, 'flesh and blood' stand for the untransformed body, the psychic, ensouled body in its mortal weakness. So transformation, transfiguration, is the key to a proper understanding of the resurrection of the body. As he goes on to say, twice (vv. 50, 51), 'we shall all be changed'. The fact that we cannot give a precise description of what it will be like, and can only hint vaguely by fumbling analogies and metaphors at what it will be transformed into, is not an argument against the concept; it is what one would expect. How can our present language describe what is, in the nature of the case, a condition wholly beyond our present experience?

(iii)   *The resurrection of the wicked*

Paul's language in 1 Cor 15 applies only to the resurrection of the just in glory. The resurrection of the wicked or the damned in shame is much more problematic. It is stated very definitely in Jn 5:28–29: 'The hour is coming when all who are in the tombs will hear his voice [the Son of Man's] and come forth, those who have done good to the resurrection of life, those who have done evil to the resurrection of judgement'. See also Acts 24:15, Rev 20:12–13. This was the common Jewish, Pharisee belief, shared by Christ and the Christian apostolic Church: see Dan 12:2.

But the problem remains: what sort of 'transfiguration' can this be? And what kind of conquest of death can a reality or existence be which is precisely called 'the second death' (Rev 20:14)? An interpretation of this, and thus of hell and all its associated imagery, that is popular nowadays is that it means annihilation; the wicked simply cease to exist at all. It is indeed a possible explanation, and it is not beyond the divine power to annihilate a creature, though divine power is what it would call for. But there is no support whatsoever for this explanation in the whole Christian tradition from the New Testament onwards.

The matter will arise again in a later chapter on non-salvation and hell. The suggestion I put forward here is this. The resurrection of the dead will be the chief, but not the only, feature in the final transformation, transfiguration of the whole created universe or cosmos, freeing it from its present temporal condition in which it is 'groaning in travail to be set free from its bondage to decay' (Rom 8:22, 21). Properly speaking, this will mean a full share in the divine glory for every creature, according to the capacity of its nature and the grace it has received (if it is an intelligent creature, human or angelic). It will be transformed into a terminal, achronic, quasi-eternal condition.

But those elements of creation which have definitively turned away from God (wicked spirits and human beings), while involved in the universal or cosmic transposition to an achronic, non-temporal condition, and hence in the resurrection, will be resistant, irremediably so, to that divine glory, at odds with it, burnt up by the fire of a love which they hate.

NOTE

1 The word Abaddon means 'destruction', but comes to be used as a proper noun, the place of destruction, parallel to and synonymous with Sheol. In Rev 9:11 it is personified as 'The destroyer', *Apollyōn* in Greek.

QUESTION FOR FURTHER DISCUSSION

1 In the light of a unitary self-experience, how may we understand the resurrection?

RECOMMENDED FURTHER READING

Gerald O'Collins, *The Easter Jesus*.

Walter Kasper, *Jesus the Christ*, Part II.B: 'Christ, Risen and Transcendent'.

Jon Sobrino, *Christology at the Crossroads*, chapters 7 and 8.

Wolfhart Pannenberg, *Jesus God and Man*, Part One: 'The Knowledge of Jesus' Divinity', chapter 3: 'Jesus' Resurrection as the Ground of his Unity with God'.

12
Life and Death
II: Death

A. THE EVALUATION OF DEATH IN SCRIPTURE

So we come, through the impenetrable murk of the second death to the more familiar obscurity of the first. The Bible, to the best of my recollection, tells us nothing about what death is, but it does attach to death certain tags of *value*; it evaluates death in various ways. So first of all we shall examine these evaluations.

But precisely because we have a doctrine of resurrection, and hence infer a continuation of a person's existence between death and resurrection, a continuation which we also call 'the immortality of the soul', we are also interested, over and above the evaluation of death, in what death is; or rather in what the existence of the human soul or self is after it has ceased to animate the body, which has thereby become a corpse. So we shall go on in the second half of the chapter to consider that question.

(i)   Death as a natural event

We saw reason to believe in an earlier chapter that this was P's view of death (3, B, i; 5, B, ii), implicit in his creation narrative. It is certainly implicit in many other narratives, e.g. of the deaths of the patriarchs (Abraham's, Gen 25:8; Isaac's, 35:29; Jacob's, 49:29–33; Joseph's, 50:24–26). With the dominance of a group consciousness coupled with the unitary self-consciousness, death is no problem – at least not death in a ripe old age. It is as it should be. And this is a perfectly valid and human evaluation of death, one that the Christian should appreciate, and to a large extent share. From the point of view of natural existence in this world, death is indeed a natural event.

(ii)   Death as absurd

But where there comes to the fore a consciousness of a strong personal relationship with God, who is the just God of the covenant, death will soon be perceived as a mark of absurdity (or to use the biblical word, vanity) stamped on God's creation. This is the almost obsessive sentiment of the Preacher, as we have seen (10, B, ii). Life and death, pain and suffering and joy, success and failure, are not conspicuously just in the way that they fall to us. And in any case, however blessed you may be in your life, the fact that sooner or later you will die, simply cease to be (for that is what death looks like), is a kind of cancellation of your worth as a human being made in God's image, personally related through the covenant to the living God. Life is the supreme value; death therefore is sheer anti-value or unvalue. And what is that if not absurd, vanity?

(iii) Death as punishment

The idea of death as punishment is first and foremost a legal one held by human societies, including that of ancient Israel. For certain crimes the death penalty is prescribed. But in Israel, God's own people, whose laws are part of their covenant with their God, it is God who prescribes this penalty, above all for the sin of shedding blood (Gen 9:5–6; above, Chapter 6, B).

But then in J's story of the fall (Gen 3) this notion is generalized. All death is seen as the divinely prescribed penalty for all sin, exemplified in the primal sin of human beings, their disobedience to God's command. If there had been no sin, there would have been no death, says J, as we have also seen in a previous chapter (3, A, iv; 6, C, iv). As we also saw in Chapter 6, this punishment of sin by death is not just the arbitrary sentence of a harsh deity, it is the inner consequence, almost the inner meaning of sin. For sin is essentially the inner turning away, in disobedience and unlove and self-seeking, from the *living* God; and death is nothing but being cut off from the living God, as we saw at the beginning of the last chapter (11, A, i). Death and sin have an intrinsic affinity with each other.

(iv) Death as expiation and atonement

Even acknowledgement that death has the character of punishment for sin (collective punishment on the collectivity of the human race) does not fully relieve it of its quality of absurdity. The writer of Ecclesiastes almost certainly knew J's story of paradise and fall, Gen 2 and 3, and in all probability in the same form and context as we have it now. And he would have accepted it as part of the sacred God-given Torah or Law. But if that is the last word about human destiny – and the author had as yet heard no further word – the situation is still absurd.

So a further word *was* forthcoming; not only the further word of resurrection from the dead, a word *cancelling* death; but also a word *redeeming* death, giving death itself, the final negative, a new and positive meaning.

This word is spoken to us definitively by the death of Christ himself on the

cross, and by the interpretation he gave of his death, which the New
Testament elaborates. Death can be, if its subject so wills, an atonement or
expiation, a making up for sin. And since sin is and produces estrangement or
separation from God, death which as mere punishment is the definitive
establishment of that estrangement, separation, alienation, becomes as atonement or expiation the means of reconciliation and restored unity with God.

Not any death, but only death freely accepted as self-sacrifice, as total self-
dedication to God for man. In Christian faith the only death that qualifies
perfectly in this sense is the death of Jesus Christ. But the possibility of such a
death or of death with such value is envisaged more and more insistently in
the Old Testament. The sacrifices for sin, culminating in that of the Day of
Atonement, suggest the idea. So both Hebrews and the accounts of the institution of the eucharist can interpret the death of Christ in terms of and as the
fulfilment of that sacrifice (Mt 26:28; Heb 9:11–28; cf. Lev 16).

The maturing concept of the 'poor of Yahweh', whose poverty and sufferings and oppressions render them specially dear to him, leads up to the revolutionary statement of the psalmist, 'Precious in the sight of the Lord is the
death of his saints' (Ps 116:15). Above all there is the astonishing insight of
Second Isaiah into the meaning of the sufferings of 'the servant of Yahweh',
supremely in Isa 53. But Jesus Christ, according to our faith, is the only man
capable by his death of perfectly filling this bill.

However, once he has done so, and thereby reconciled mankind to God, it
is then possible, it is normal, it is *de rigueur* for 'his saints', his faithful ones in
another translation, to subsume their deaths under the heading of Christ's
death, and so as members of Christ's body to give their deaths by a voluntary
acceptance the atoning value of a free-will offering, a true self-sacrifice.

B.   THE STATE OF BEING DEAD

Death can only be given this positive value in the light of a hope that goes
beyond death, the hope of the resurrection. In the light of this hope, as we
have seen, we infer some kind of continued existence of the human self even
after death – call it if you like the immortality of the soul (10, C, i). The
question arises, what kind of existence can the human soul or self have after
death, after its separation from the body and before the resurrection of the
body.

(i)   The question of time in such an existence

Before we look at the various answers that may be given to the question what
being dead means, we must dispose of the problem of time in this connection.
I have just used the expression 'the continued existence of the soul or self after

death and before the resurrection'. But we should note that this before-and-after language only really applies within the historical perspective of our present form of existence. Past generations have died at given moments of time; the moment of the resurrection of the dead has not yet put an end to the succession of days, years and ages which constitute human history; so from our point of view in the middle of that history there is 'a time between death and resurrection', and it is quite right to speak in this way. It is the only way in which we can speak in this temporal bodily mode of existence.

But we must realize that by definition this is not the mode of existence of the souls/selves/spirits of the dead. They have been disembodied by death, and if disembodied then 'disentimed', 'distemporalized', since time is a factor or function of bodily existence and movement. So in what sense, from their perspective, can they be said to exist 'between death and resurrection'? It is hard, in fact impossible, to state what sense. The only thing about it that must be said is that one may not ascribe to this 'untimed' or 'detimed' state of being as it is in itself the quality of eternity, as some authors (e.g. Karl Rahner) appear to do – see below, subsection iii. That belongs strictly to God, and by participation to creatures who see him face to face.

(ii) The existence of 'dead souls' as envisaged in terms of the unitary self-experience

What is it like then to be the soul/self/mind/spirit of someone who has died? The answer can only be inferred from what one considers it to be like to be a person who has not died. If you take a view of the person from the vantage point of the unitary self-experience, in which the body, its senses and feelings and emotions are integrally involved in mental self-consciousness, then the state of being dead, disembodied, can only be highly anomalous. Such a disembodied self is cut off from all contact or communication with other created realities, because all our human communication is through the body, through which we receive impressions and give expression to our thoughts and sentiments. So, no receiving impressions, no giving expression, no communications for the 'dead soul'. The dead are held *incommunicado*. As Schillebeeckx puts it, their condition is 'one of spiritual lethargy and isolation', 'the "solitary confinement" of the soul'.[1]

This is indeed death, the logical consequence of sin, which is a kind of deliberate cutting oneself off from others. This is the last word in estrangement or alienation. How very appropriate, when being dragged into this kind of existence, to cry out 'My God, my God, why have you forsaken me'! We are, remember, for the moment considering the state of the disembodied soul/self/mind in itself, abstracting from its relationship to God its creator and redeemer. We will consider that relationship shortly.

(iii)   The existence of 'dead souls' as envisaged in terms of the dissociated self-experience

If one takes a view of the person that opens up from the vantage point of the dissociated self-experience, then one will make rather different inferences. This experience fixes on the unsatisfactory, fragmentary, incoherent quality of our whole psychological experience in this embodied, time-bound mode of life. Wholeness is lacking in our sense-derived knowledge, in the impressions we receive and the expressions we achieve. But wholeness is what we desire.

And wholeness, according to this view, is what is thrust upon us as we die, at the moment of death, and what we are left with in the state of being dead, disembodied, 'disentimed'. Only then, for better or worse, do we possess our life, and what we have made of ourselves in our embodied existence, as a whole.[2]

This view doesn't exactly contradict the one just described above, but it puts a very different complexion on the disembodied state. What the former sees as a state of total isolation from others, this one sees as total self-possession. Does this compensate for that, or does that quite destroy the value of this?

(iv)   The disembodied soul/self/mind in relation to God

However, for the Christian believer that is perhaps an idle question. For while the souls of the dead may be totally isolated from all other creatures, and each other, they are not isolated from God, the ground of their being. And while they may be in total possession of themselves, this is not a self-possession independent of God, who is within even the inmost self (*intimior intimo meo*, in Augustine's phrase, closer to me than I am to myself).

God the creator and redeemer; whichever view you take of the existence of the disembodied soul/self, it is common to the whole Christian tradition that the quality or state of that existence is definitively determined by the quality of the person's relationship with God at death. If you die in God's grace, accepting his redemptive work in Christ on your behalf, sorry for your sins, then for all your disembodied isolation you are not isolated from *him*. So actually or potentially (for those who believe in the doctrine of purgatory) you will enjoy the face-to-face vision of God, and in seeing him will see and communicate with others in him; or in terms of the other view, you will still in such cases possess yourself wholly, but as redeemed and saved and in God.

On the other hand, if you die outside God's grace, alienated from him, definitively turned away from and rejecting him, then precisely because you cannot be cut off from him as creator, your having cut yourself off from him as redeemer and saviour and forgiver will make your isolation all the more terrible (outer darkness), and your self-possession all the more sterile and abhorrent (weeping and gnashing of teeth).

But whatever the state of the disembodied soul/self/mind, it is a state orientated towards resurrection.

NOTES

1   Edward Schillebeeckx, 'The Death of a Christian', *Vatican II, the Struggle of Minds and other essays* (Gill, Dublin, 1963), pp. 64, 73.
2   This is Rahner's 'description' in 'The Life of the Dead', *Theological Investigations* 4 (DLT, London, 1966), pp. 347ff.

QUESTIONS FOR FURTHER DISCUSSION

1   Is the concept of 'abundant life' or 'fullness of life' necessarily religious?

2   Is it possible to make any sense of death in any other way than by abolishing it?

3   What light does the death of Christ throw on our dying?

RECOMMENDED FURTHER READING

There seem to be any number of books about death, but practically none about life – which is perhaps not surprising; life we take for granted, death we never can.

Ladislas Boros, *The Moment of Truth*, has been very popular, to judge from the number of times it was reprinted between 1965 and 1973. It presents a Rahnerian view of death.

Lloyd R. Bailey, *Biblical Perspectives on Death*, gives wide background coverage to what has been said in this chapter.

Marc Oraison, *Death . . . and Then What?* and Ignace Lepp, *Death and its Mysteries*, offer a more meditative approach.

Karl Rahner, 'The Resurrection of the Body', *Theological Investigations*, 2, chapter 6; 'Theological Considerations on the Moment of Death', *ibid.*, 11, chapter 14; and 'Ideas for a Theology of Death', *ibid.*, 13, Part 2, chapter 11.

As I said, nothing on life as such; but F. X. Durrwell, *Resurrection*, is a book that revived the interest of theologians in this hitherto rather neglected doctrine just before Vatican II, and might help to revive the reader's, too.

13

Man as Person and Community
I: The Values of the Person

A. THE HUMAN PERSON IN SCRIPTURE

It is sometimes said that in ancient Israel there was very little sense of individual personal value, since group consciousness was so strong. This is on the whole true; I have more or less assumed it myself in Chapter 10, B, i above, talking about the Israelite unitary self-experience.

But while it is more or less true as a fact, we must resist the temptation to treat it as a *normative* fact, or as a statement having immediate theological value. It is, in itself, a fairly banal fact. The same is true of most if not all comparable societies of relatively simple structure and pre-urban culture. A much more interesting fact is that against the background of such a communal society with a strong group consciousness, some very definite statements on the value of the individual human person should have been made – theological statements which do have a normative value.

(i) Statements of J and P

Let us begin with J. In his account of paradise he has God saying that it is not good for the man to be alone (Gen 2:18). This is clearly a theological, doctrinal statement, a word of the Creator, and its immediate import is to stress the value of the community. But here I just wish to point out an implication of it that is not usually noticed. This is, that though it is not good for the man to be alone, it is still possible for the man to be alone, and that in fact he is at the moment alone, and still a human being, 'a living soul' (2:7; RSV: 'a living being').

In this story, we must remind ourselves, 'the man' is both representative of all mankind and an individual, the first man, Adam. And there he is, a man, a human being – and alone. So at once an extreme form of communalism or collectivism or group totalitarianism is ruled out, according to which

human existence is impossible apart from social existence, and certainly has
no value apart from social existence. This view is sometimes described as the
biblical or Israelite view, which means that the banal fact we have just
referred to is treated as having normative value. And here, in J, that is ruled
out by the Israelite Bible itself. J says that the first man did exist, a man, yet
alone. True, it was not good for him to continue so: but there he is, fully
human, before the complete good is achieved.

Thereby, I suggest, J is implying the absolute and irreducible value of the
individual person. Individual human beings, though needing the company of
others, and finding and fulfilling their humanity in that company or
community, nevertheless exist as individual human beings, logically prior to
community and with a value in God's eyes and a relationship to him that are
not reducible to community values and relationships.

The extreme individualism of much modern society, especially in the
complex urban cultures of Europe and North America, is undoubtedly
mistaken, as the divine utterance of Gen 2:18 indicates. But the element of
truth in it, which must not be lost sight of, and which is implicit in the
context of this statement, is that the individual person as such is precious in
God's sight and in no way expendable for the sake of some community or
collective value.

P reinforces this doctrine with statements that are perhaps rather more
explicit. The crucial one is that man is made in the image and likeness of God
(Gen 1:26–27) – all men, male and female. We shall look much more closely
at this concept in Chapter 19. Here all we need to note is that it implies an
irreducible value, godlikeness, for every single human being as such. A very
practical conclusion, which confirms the seriousness of the principle, is drawn
from this in Gen 9:6: 'Whoever sheds the blood of man, by man shall his
blood be shed; for God made man in his own image'. The *person* then of man,
every human being, is sacred and inviolable, and the supreme sanction is
imposed for violating it, in order to protect it.

(ii)   Statements from the rest of the Old Testament

The laws of the covenant concerning strangers, orphans and widows,
whether from the P or the D tradition, or any other source, indicate that
Israel's strong group consciousness was modified from the beginning in
favour of what is owing to individual persons. For these are precisely the
persons in the community of low social value, the people that 'don't matter',
and if they are to be respected (particularly *strangers* or foreigners), *a fortiori* so
are any other persons as such, including Very Important Persons, not because
they are Very Important, but because they are Persons. Just one example of
such a text, Ex 22:21–23: 'You shall not wrong a stranger [in the contem-

porary English context, read "immigrant"] or oppress him, for you were strangers in the land of Egypt. You shall not afflict any widow or orphan. If you do afflict them and they cry out to me, I will surely hear their cry.'

The psalms which convey God's great and sure concern for the poor and needy and afflicted carry the same lesson. For it is highly unlikely that the poor were conceived of as a *class* community, as the proletariat or the masses of modern jargon. They were poor *persons*, needy and afflicted individuals within the only community the psalmists recognized, namely Israel. For a few random samples see Pss 12:5, 35:10, 86:1, 107:41, 112:9, 113:7, and particularly 109:16, 22, 31. For this is the notorious 'cursing psalm'. Now whoever is being cursed in the middle of this psalm, and the most reasonable view in my opinion is that it is the psalmist himself, telling God what the wicked are doing to him, one of the things he is cursed for in v. 16 is for 'pursuing the poor and needy and the brokenhearted to their death'; then in v. 22 the psalmist claims to be poor and needy himself, and in v. 31 he expresses his confidence that the Lord 'stands at the right hand of the needy'.

Ezekiel, whose outlook has a certain affinity to that of P, launches the most explicit attack on one of the more questionable expressions of group-consciousness morality. He follows Jeremiah in cancelling the proverb 'The fathers have eaten sour grapes and the children's teeth are set on edge' (Jer 31:29). Jeremiah tersely explains this cancellation: 'but each is to die for his own sin'. Ezekiel devotes the whole of his chapter 18 to the laborious spelling out of this principle of individual, personal responsibility, each for his own conduct, in the sight of God. (See above, Chapter 11, A, ii.)

As we saw above in Chapter 10, B, ii, both Job and Ecclesiastes seem to have been written to deal with the thorny problems of God's justice and his wisdom that only really arise when a strong consciousness of individual personal worth begins to break out of and criticize the older and less reflective group consciousness. So both these books may be taken as bearing indirect testimony to the principle of the irreducible value of individual persons.

(iii)   Statements from the New Testament

So prominent, not to say dominant, in the New Testament is the sense of individual personal responsibility, destiny and value that our modern individualists, if they happen to be Christians, take it for granted that their extreme individualism is not merely justified but positively required by the New Testament. They find less disinterested support from our modern totalitarians, or extreme 'communalists' (not quite the same thing as communists since they are also found on the far right of the political spectrum, but including communists), who are only too anxious that 'the Church should keep out of politics' and confine itself entirely to the private sphere of personal concerns. All this is indeed a serious mistake and a very distorted reading of the New Testament, but for all that it is a natural and excusable mistake.

It is a mistake, because at the heart of the New Testament message is the 'kingdom of God', the gospel being precisely the 'good news of the kingdom' (Mt 4:23). And the kingdom of God is certainly a society or community, and one that is proclaimed as being at hand (Mk 1:15), that is to say beginning here and now. But it is a natural and pardonable mistake for honest individualists to make, because the summons to enter the kingdom, which amounts to sharing in the construction of the kingdom, is necessarily addressed to individual persons, to each and every person 'who has ears to hear' (Mk 4:9 etc.). You cannot belong to the kingdom by mere accident of birth or residence, as with other communities; it can only be entered by a personal act of decision, which is the act of faith. The point need not be laboured further.

A good example of the universalization of the value of the individual person achieved in the New Testament is the parable of the good Samaritan. The old law commands the Israelite to love his neighbour as himself (Lev 19:18). But 'who is my neighbour?', asks the lawyer in Lk 10:29. And it is a very important question, although Luke is rather dismissive of the lawyer for asking it. It is, of course, a typical lawyer's question, one designed to establish the precise limits of a legal obligation. In a society dominated by group consciousness, in which community values have pride of place, my neighbour is precisely that – the person living near, a fellow member of my group.

Jesus tells the lawyer in effect that he is neighbour to any and every man, that his group or community is mankind, and even includes his enemy, people of the other group which his own group hates and/or despises. So it is personal, not community or group values that are to have pride of place – taking community and group in their everyday meanings.

B. CONSEQUENCES FOR THE CHRISTIAN VIEW OF MAN

(i) Inviolability of every human being

The Christian conscience has always and consistently taken a very strict view of the sanctity of human life, of *every* human life. When Christianity first broke upon the Graeco-Roman world, the exposure of unwanted infants was a common and legal practice, a crude means of population control. These babies were simply left out to die. The Christians of the first centuries not only did not do this themselves (neither did Jews), but they would also save and rear such abandoned infants as they were able.

It is the same conscience that today makes Christians take up a firm stand against the legalization of abortion – certainly against the practice of abortion. Infants, whether born or unborn, are human beings, human persons, with the same quasi-absolute value, therefore, as any other human persons, and may not be sacrificed either to the interests of other persons, or for the sake of group or community interests and values.

The complaint is sometimes made, and sometimes with a certain justification, that those Christians and Churches (this certainly includes the Catholic Church) that are strongest on the abortion issue, the 'pro-life' groups, are often very weak if not downright reactionary on other human rights issues. If all human life is sacred, then we have as real a responsibility to defend it from abuse, from exploitation and oppression, as from extinction at its beginnings; and from extinction by famine and war and judicial execution as well as by abortion. So why are pro-lifers not infrequently indifferent to these much larger issues?

I suppose the answer is usually to be found in the extreme individualism that underlies so many modern assumptions and attitudes. The issue with abortion (as with the exposure of infants in the ancient world) is simple and clear; the cause of these entirely helpless individuals appeals to the sincere individualist. But with other human rights the issues are by no means clear, on individualist presuppositions. The truth is that such larger human rights as freedom from hunger and exploitation, from oppression and war, cannot be effectively defended or promoted without changes, radical changes in all probability, in all the social and economic structures of the contemporary world. They involve community values as much as personal ones – and to these our modern individualists, including Christians, tend to be impervious if not allergic.

(ii) The equal worth of all human beings

Perhaps this is one reason why the average Christian conscience, and ecclesiastical teaching, is much less sure of itself when it comes to the other main consequence of the biblical revelation of the irreducible value of the individual human person, namely the fundamental *equality* of all human beings.

Of course, given the obvious disparity between people in ability and virtue, intelligence and spirit, not to mention age and sex, and between communities in power and complexity ('civilization'), the assertion of human equality calls for a certain act of faith. The basic act of faith required, and always posited by the official Church teaching, is that all human beings are equal in the sight of God. But Christians, including Church authorities, have more often than not been reluctant to draw the logical conclusion that if people are equal in the sight of God (presumably the 'truest' and most important 'sight' there is) they should *a fortiori* be treated as basically equal in the sight of man. Against this conclusion are cited those disparities we have just spoken of.

Here a distinction can be made that is in fact made by St Paul in 1 Cor 12, where he is talking about differences and varieties of endowment by the Holy Spirit. These differences can and do entail disparities of function within the community, some functions (e.g. prophecy in his view) being more important than others (e.g. speaking with tongues). But there is no reason why these disparities of function should entail disparities of status or dignity, at least of official or legal status and dignity. That people will spontaneously accord special respect to persons of outstanding virtue or wisdom or skill or age and experience is reasonable. That they should accord such extra respect to particular persons merely because of their wealth or rank or noble birth smacks of the vice of 'respect of persons'.

At least it did in the apostolic Christian communities, as you can see at a glance from the epistle of St James (e.g. Jas 2:1–9). In those communities very practical conclusions were drawn from the equality of all in the sight of God. The fundamental conclusion is *brotherhood*. These communities were brotherhoods, as every true Christian community ought to be. The apostles always addressed their audiences and their correspondents as 'Brethren' – except when they addressed them as 'Beloved'. ' . . . They love . . . being called rabbi by men. But you are not to be called rabbi, for you have one teacher and you are all brethren' (Mt 23:6–8). And as St Paul tells us, 'in Christ Jesus you are all sons of God through faith. For as many of you as were baptized into Christ have put on Christ. There is neither Jew nor Greek, there is neither slave nor free, there is neither male nor female; for you are all one in Christ Jesus' (Gal 3:26–28). The differences of function and/or nation of course remain; those of status and dignity disappear. In Christian communities even slaves and free men were first and foremost *brothers*, and one must suppose that they treated each other as such, and that this somehow affected their relationships too when they met about their daily business, outside the confines of the Christian community.

It must be admitted that in the nineteen centuries of the Church's history since then this sense of radically egalitarian brotherhood has rather evaporated, and has certainly had little influence on those societies, mostly European, into which Christianity has most deeply inserted itself. I think three reasons can be given for this, one merely negative, the other two of a theologically interesting ambiguity.

(a) The first, the negative reason, is simple *worldliness*. The Church, embodied in all sorts of different Christian communities and represented by all sorts of prominent ecclesiastics, has succumbed, sometimes more, sometimes less, to the third temptation of Christ by Satan in Matthew's account: 'Again, the devil took him to a very high mountain, and showed him all the kingdoms of the world and the glory of them; and he said to him, All these I will give you, if you will fall down and worship me' (Mt 4:8–9). Satan has been worshipped by the Church in the forms of power, influence and wealth, demonic forces which reck nothing of the basic equality of all in the sight of God. From the beginning the Church has been launched into a world of thoroughly *unequal* societies, a society of vast inequalities of wealth and status in the Roman Empire, the warrior aristocratic societies of barbarian Europe. And chameleon-like it has taken on (in some places more, some less) the colour of these societies, and absorbed their worldly values (of the importance of status and wealth as against the importance of sheer humanity) as much as, if not rather more than it has succeeded in impressing its own proper values of respect for every human person upon them. In a slave-owning society it has become a slave-owning Church; in a feudal society it has become a feudal Church, in a capitalist society a capitalist Church.

(b)   But this worldliness of the Church (its being influenced by the fallen world instead of itself influencing the world) is not the whole story. Another reason, which I call ambiguous, for the Church's not noticeably moving human societies in the direction of Christian brotherhood and egalitarianism, has been the opposite of the first one – precisely the Church's *unworldliness*, combined also with its weakness. The Christian value we are here talking about, namely the equal humanity of all human beings, has been seen and cherished as a value of the kingdom of God, not as a value of this world; hence as an unworldly or otherworldly value.

In the first three centuries of Christianity until the time of Constantine's conversion (*c.* 312), the Church had no power to influence secular society, and in any case did not consider that to be its proper function. Secular society, 'the world' in John's sense of the expression, was doomed; the function of the Church was to proclaim, and in its own confines to embody, the alternative society of the kingdom of God, the society of the future and eternal age to come, and to invite people 'to save themselves from this crooked generation' (Acts 2:40) by believing in Christ and enrolling themselves in this alternative society, whose full perfection would only be realized when Christ came in glory to judge the world.

After the peace of the Church, the Christian community rapidly came to be more or less coterminous with the secular community, so that one could talk of Christendom, and the Christian state and Christian society. This reversal of fortune changed the value and the application of the Church's otherworldliness. It could no longer be the Christian community or the Church as a whole that offered an alternative society, unless it were to undertake a radical transformation of the secular society with which it was more or less coterminous. This it was prevented from doing both by the worldliness we have already remarked on, which was much enhanced by the 'conversion' of so many superficial or merely nominal Christians, and by its continuing to assume, in the light of its traditional 'otherworldliness principle', that this was not its proper function. Instead, the alternative society was now offered by monastic communities. These would henceforth be the concrete expression of the ideal of equal Christian brotherhood, and also of otherworldliness, of the Christian orientation and drive to the kingdom of God, the other world of the future, to be transformed by the power of God.

I call this otherworldliness ambiguous because on the one hand it has the positive value of the authentic Christian gospel of the kingdom, the value of summoning us to go beyond or transcend our present mode of existence and the concerns that arise from it; the value too of reminding us that this 'beyond' is purely in the gift of God and his grace, not something we can grasp and achieve on our own. But on the other hand it has the negative anti-value of often blinding Churchmen, or Christians at large, to their responsibility to do what they can to *transform* secular society, and to criticize its specific values and defects.

Again, we must not exaggerate. Among the Fathers, particularly those of the fourth century, the first century of the Constantinian peace of the Church, there were many severe and trenchant critics of the worldly values of secular society, who asserted in the most thorough-going manner the equal rights of all human beings to justice and to a share in the good things of the earth. Gregory of Nyssa scathingly condemned the institution of slavery as such,[1] while John Chrysostom among the Greek and Ambrose among the Latin Fathers were outstanding in their preaching on behalf of the poor and the oppressed.

(c) The third reason for the Church's not so far having noticeably moved the societies of Europe, America and elsewhere in the direction of universal and equal human brotherhood is what one might call the reason of *incarnational economy*. I use 'economy' in the theological, not the economic sense, to mean the divine plan of salvation as adapted to human needs and accommodated to particular situations. Just as God's plan was to save, and by the same token to judge, mankind, not from the divine vantage point external to mankind, outside the human arena, but from within the human situation, to which end he sent his Son to become man and share the human condition; so too his Church, his new people of God, is to assist in the salvation (and the judgement) of mankind, not from outside concrete human situations but from within. It is the Church's task to incarnate the gospel and itself in any and every type of human society and culture, and then to contribute to the genuine christianization of the values of these societies and cultures from within, rather than merely criticizing them from without. Thus this third reason is in tension, not to say opposition, with the second one of the Church's 'unworldliness'.

The Church's success in thus accommodating itself to different types of human society has of course varied enormously through the ages and in different places. Sometimes it has become too completely naturalized in some type of society or other (e.g. the feudal society of mediaeval Europe), sometimes not enough (e.g. in many mission lands in the last century or so, where it has rather been identified in all sorts of ways with the culture if not the policies of the colonizing power). But accommodate it should. Thus in order to incarnate itself and the gospel in an aristocratic, warrior society, like that of the Vikings, let us say, it would be no use for the Church simply to reject the aristocratic and military values of that society out of hand. It must tolerate and accept them in part at least, and accord a certain special respect in the externals of ecclesiastical deportment and organization to the warrior nobility of that society. But at the same time it has to insist that in the sight of God and the Church all, even the meanest, have equal rights, equal access to the sacraments and Christian instruction; and also gradually to show such a society that there is perhaps a truer aristocracy than that of birth, and a truer manly courage than that of war – the courage of the martyrs, and the aristocracy of sanctity and grace.

Or take the case of nearly all contemporary African societies. They do not traditionally accord equality of status and dignity to women, and they are traditionally polygamous. Should not the Church, at the beginnings of its missions to Africa have at least tolerated polygamy (as it tolerated slavery in the ancient – and modern – world), and allowed criticism of the institution, and of the inferior position of women it entails, to come from within a truly incarnated African Christianity? As it is, insistence by the Churches on marriage laws and customs imported from Europe has been and continues to be treated with that casual insouciance and profound scepticism which is Africa's spontaneous defence against the know-all arrogance of Europe.

To conclude, the Church could never have imposed the Christian ideal of the equality of all human beings on secular societies from without. It could only, at best, foster its acceptance from within. We have seen other reasons why even this has not been done as much as perhaps it ought to have been. But here perhaps we may observe that it has in fact been done, though in rather an odd way. The movement towards political and economic equality has in fact arisen and taken root and proceeded to vigorous, often revolutionary action, above all in European societies – that is to say in thoroughly christianized societies. Such movements occurred sporadically with peasant revolts in the Middle Ages, were more widespread and potent in Reformation times (the Anabaptists of Munster, the Levellers in the England of the Civil War), and finally blossomed in the French and the Russian Revolutions. The roots of the movement are Christian, even though in its modern stages it has in its own terms outgrown Christianity and all religion. The Church has lost what is in fact its own child. In many parts of the Church today, notably in Latin America, there are enthusiastic and powerful moves afoot to reclaim this child, to reclaim it from totalitarian and secularist corruption. Whatever their mistakes, their naiveties and their exaggerations, these moves, I suggest, are inspired by the Holy Spirit, and sanctioned by the teaching of Vatican II.

NOTE

1 *Homily IV on Ecclesiastes* (PG 44, 665). It must be admitted that Gregory of Nyssa was quite exceptional in his criticism of the peculiar institution. A volume of such extracts from the Fathers was published a few years ago in Lima, Peru, by Juan Leuridan, entitled *Justicia y Explotación*; an English translation will, I trust, soon be appearing. But just as Gregory of Nyssa was exceptional in his time, so it is to be remarked that scarcely any of Juan Leuridan's extracts figure among the readings from the Fathers contained in the revised Roman Breviary.

QUESTIONS FOR FURTHER DISCUSSION

1 What is the basis of the dignity of the human person?

2 What problems have arisen from excessive concentration on the value of the individual?

14

Man as Person and Community II: The Values of Community

A. COMMUNITY A FUNCTION OR DIMENSION OF PERSON

We established in the last chapter that human beings as such have a quasi-absolute value, in that they are made in the image of God (and, we could add, redeemed by the precious blood of Christ), and so may not be regarded under any circumstances whatever as expendable; they may not be sacrified to anything, any cause or idea, any community or state thought of as having higher value. Any value such ideas or institutions may have, they derive from tha value of human beings. It is as having such quasi-absolute value that we call all human beings and any human beings 'persons'.[1]

Does the term 'community' represent any value as quasi-absolute as the term 'person'? Well at least it cannot have an independent value of its own, over against and in possible opposition to the value of persons, because a community is made up of persons. If persons, who have their own value as such, are to respect something called community value, it can only be the value of the other persons comprising the community. In other words, just as a community is made up of persons, so the value of community or community value is geared to the value of its member persons. So when persons respect community values, they are in fact respecting (as indeed they should) the value of other persons.

But as well as being seen as an aggregate of persons, community can also be seen as a function or dimension of persons. 'It is not good that the man should be alone' (Gen 2:18). To realize their full value as persons, human beings need the company of others, so that the existence of a community of persons is a function of being a person. This, basically, in two ways.

(i) Community as a complex of relationships

A human being, as such, as a person, is a related being. J, as we observed in the previous chapter, envisaged the abstract possibility of there being just one human being, the first one, all by himself – to make the point, we suggested, of the value of the person as such. But even before he entered upon a relationship with another human being, the woman, he was related, simply in virtue of existing at all, to his creator, to God. In the theological perspective this is the absolutely primary human community: man's community, man's communion with God. *Sancta societate adhaerere Deo* (to adhere to God in a holy association), this is Augustine's surprising and profound definition of true sacrifice (*City of God*, X, 6; *PL* 41, 283). What he means is, that is what religious ritual sacrifices are intended both to signify and effect; and sacrifice being the central act of all religion, this is what all religion is really about. This is what innocent man did at the beginning, without any religious ritual, simply by his grace-endowed creatureliness; this is what fallen man expresses his yearning for in all those thousand and one modes of sacrifice, noble and vile, that he has practised from the beginning, and what they are in themselves ineffectual in achieving (Heb 10:4, 11); this is what redeemed man has been restored to by the perfect self-sacrifice of Christ (*ibid.* 9:12, 28; 10:10), what he shares in and celebrates in the eucharistic sacrifice, and what he will enjoy for ever in glory as the full achievement of this sacrifice.

By 'man' here I mean first and foremost every single human being as a person, and then secondly the community of restored mankind forming a 'holy association', a perfect community with God and hence with each other – with each other in God.

Since we have glanced back again at J's account of the man in paradise, let us notice what God did there, on observing that it was not good for the man to be alone, before he finally established the basic human community of two, the man and the woman. He made the animals 'from the ground' (like the man in the first place), and brought them to the man to see what he would call them, and the man gave them their true names, that is to say he *knew* them (Gen 2:19).

So again, prior to any mutual human relationships, at least materially speaking, there is man's (every human being's) relatedness to other creatures, to nature, to the world we live in. Whatever else we are in addition, we are at bottom, materially speaking, *animals*, along with all the other animals. As such we are 'of dust from the ground' (*ibid.* 7), having gross material bodies, our relatedness to other things being very firmly rooted in *matter*. Indeed our relatedness to other people is likewise very firmly rooted in matter, being at bottom a community, a communion, a contact of bodies. That's the foundation. The true community has no basis in spiritual, heavenly, intellectual pride, but only in material, earthy, bodily humility.

So here already, while the man is still alone, we have some community values, given in the man's relatedness to God and to other creatures: the worship of God, obedience to him, love and desire for him, and the true knowledge of other creatures, and respect and reverence for them. Are they 'quasi-absolute' values? Whether they are or not (and I don't think that in this context that is a real question to be answered), they are in no sense in opposition to the quasi-absolute value of the human person, but factors contributing to it.

So we come now to the community of human beings with each other. Here we say farewell to J for the time being, because he goes on to portray the elemental community of husband and wife, marriage and the family, and that will provide the subject of the next few chapters. Here I do not wish to say anything about the family, except in so far as it is indeed the elemental community, at the centre of the network of relationships in which every human person is involved from the cradle to the grave.

These relationships, marital, parental, filial, fraternal and all the others which we can lump together under the heading of neighbourly, are the essential components of human society or community. They are the supports and buttresses of our personal life, of the human person. They need to be harmonized, and directed. Thus they give rise to the community values, dynamisms, mechanisms of *love* and *justice* (the chief relating virtues) in a regulatory framework of custom or law. The Latin for customs is *mores*. Morals or morality then is the generic term for community values of relationship. Again we observe that they are in no sense in competition with the value of the person, but rather contributory to it.

The individual person should, of course, respect and cherish the community. But this only amounts to saying that individual persons should respect and cherish and love each other. 'Greater love has no man than this, that a man lay down his life for his friends' (Jn 15:13). And there are of course all sorts of lesser loves requiring of us lesser sacrifices – but for our friends, for other people; he did not say 'for the community', 'for his class', 'for his nation or country'. These are in their right place useful concepts – abstractions. To concretize and personify them is to conjure up demons.

(ii) Community as a network of communications

Being *related* to one another in the ways enumerated, we necessarily *communicate* with each other, that is to say we share things with one another. Perhaps you could say that relationships constitute potential or quiescent community, while communication and sharing between those thus related activates community. The basic meaning of the word 'community' indeed appears to be a collection of persons who share or have something 'in common'. We share or communicate, basically, in two ways: by doing things together, and above all (in order to be able to do things together) by talking together, which enables us to think together. So just as community relationships generate, in a word, morality and hence moral values, community sharing and communication generates, in a word, culture: first and foremost language, then all the other forms of cultural expression and communication, art, dance, music, cult, technical skills of all kinds. Just as moral values (the cardinal ones being love and justice) can be summed up under the heading of 'the good', so I suggest cultural values can be summed up under the headings of 'the true and the beautiful'. One of the functions of community is to help us communicate these things, truth and beauty, to each other, to help us to learn, to know, to perceive, to make.

Once more, it is surely absurd to set these values in opposition to the values of the person, or even in tension with them. They are functions, manifestations, extensions of the value of the person. One truth or good or beauty, or at least one perceived good, truth or beauty is often indeed in opposition to another (this is particularly true of beauties). That is what lends a dramatic quality to human life. But such oppositions and tensions cannot really be transposed into an opposition or tension between person and community.

B. VARIOUS GRADES AND TYPES OF COMMUNITY

What has so far been said about community has not been intended, and should not be read, as a *description* of what communities are like, or of how they arise. Rather it has been meant to offer a simple analysis of elements necessarily involved in the association of human persons, and of the values properly embodied in or implied by those elements. Of course, if you proceed to the description of actual societies, you will certainly find some negations of these values, or distortions of them, or anti-values (to your way of thinking) entering into the picture. But that is not our concern here.

However, it will not have escaped the reader that the analysis of relationships and communications which constitute community so far given will only fit, for the most part, the smallest of communities, the family or group of families, the small village, the sub-clan or sept – the community in which all the members know each other.

But in addition to such basic communities (the expression is not here being given any semi-technical meaning such as it may have in some contemporary pastoral theology), there are of course all sorts of wider communities: regions, cities, nations, nation states, confederations and federations (and the United Nations), not to mention inter-community associations such as companies, clubs, schools and so forth. It is the values, and perhaps anti-values, of these that we now have to consider.

Such wider communities have come into existence in all sorts of ways,

from mutual agreement to conquest. And more to our point, they serve all
sorts of purposes, from the preservation of the peace to the furtherance of
trade, the exploitation of resources and the fostering of arts and sciences.
What we are concerned with here is the theological evaluation of such
societies, or rather of the values they may generate, and for this we shall
return to J and P, and to the scriptures in general.

(i)   The different attitudes of J and P

We have already looked in Chapter 3 at the very different attitudes of J and P
to what we loosely call 'civilization'. But whatever that word may mean, it
certainly means something that entails these larger communities we are
talking about. It goes with cities, and urbanization, and the larger organization of human society.

As we saw there, J regards civilization as a consequence of sin. The first to
build a city was Cain the fratricide. The inventors of the basic arts were the
sons of Lamech the multiple murderer and patron of the blood feud or
vendetta in its crudest form (Gen 4:17–24). Even agriculture, the basis of any
advanced culture, is a punishment for sin (3:17–19).

To put the mark of Cain on civilization, however, and to regard it as the
consequence and punishment of sin, is *not* the same as calling it sinful. On the
contrary, it would be sinful not to accept the consequences and punishment
of sin. J may indeed express a certain nostalgia for the wholly simple and non-
civilized life of the garden, but he certainly does not encourage us to try and
recapture it. It is guarded now by the cherubim and the flashing sword
(3:24); the strong equivalent of a notice saying 'Trespassers W'[2] or 'Sinners,
keep out'.

All that J's rather negative attitude to civilization involves in practice is a
refusal to be starry-eyed or complacent about it, and a firm conviction that
the wider communities are there for the sake of the basic communities and of
their members, and not vice versa. So where some wider national or com-
mercial or other interest involves the disintegration of basic communities,
above all of family life, it will be very severely criticized, from the J view-
point; where for example they introduce slavery, or even such a comparatively mild exploitation of human beings as migrant labour, on a massive
scale.

P, on the other hand, the P point of view, will be much more tolerant of
the abuses of civilization, that is to say of these wider forms of community. In
his line of thought it is in working out an ever more perfect form of civilization, or collection of civilizations and cultures, that the human race must
contribute to achieving the destiny which God has laid upon his creation.
And this means precisely evolving these wider forms of community, taking

in our stride the mistakes, the abuses, the sins and cruelties this will inevitably bring with it. Of course we should try to clear up the messes as we go along, but we should not let the fact that there inevitably will be messes deter us from our objective.

The social drives of the two parties, the J-ites and the P-ites, will clearly be very different, one perhaps tending to enthusiasm and optimism, the other to critical protest. Neither need, though either may, deviate, into complacency and ruthlessness for the one or cynical inertia for the other. But even so, they are bound to come into conflict one way or another. We may trace this or similar conflicts of opposing social, cultural and political conceptions in many places in the scriptures. I will take one, which will I hope help us to face the problem squarely of the theological evaluation of wider communities, and the different forms of organization (often conflicting forms) that they involve.

(ii) The issue of monarchy

In 1 Sam 8:5 the people say to Samuel, 'Appoint for us a king to govern us like all the nations'. Samuel warns them of what kings will really be like: oppressive tyrants. But they insist: 'No! but we will have a king over us, that we also may be like all the nations, and that our king may govern us and go out before us and fight our battles' (ibid. 19-20).

This is in a section of the text that is against kings on principle. It is a theme taken up again, in a rather more muted tone, in Dt 17:14-20. It represents what one could call – I was going to say, a conservative republicanism. But it would be better described, perhaps, as a nostalgic anarchism. It had its roots deep in Israel's early history. It was clans set free from the oppression of the monarchy in Egypt, the model and archetype of all monarchies at that time, monarchies with pretensions to divinity, that formed the original nucleus of Israel and then joined forces with other oppressed groups when they began to infiltrate Canaan. There they achieved some sort of further liberation for these other groups by overthrowing a number of petty Canaanite kings. In the light of such a history the ideal Israel was a free brotherhood in which there was no room for the tyranny of kings. The ideal is reflected in a number of the laws of the Pentateuch: e.g. the law of jubilee, Lev 25:8-17; also Lev 19:9-18, 25:35-43, Exod 21:1-2, 22:21-27. The tone of these laws, the ideal of a free and equal brotherhood, reaches its fulfilment in the New Testament with Jesus' remarks to his disciples about their mutual relations, and their ambitions; see Mt 23:8-12, Mk 10:35-45.[3]

The only trouble was, of course, that it didn't work, and couldn't work in any but the simplest and smallest society, barely more highly organized than what we have called the basic community. This was duly noted by a rather more cynical and anyway frankly royalist or monarchist writer in the last chapters of Judges. He tells two or three perfectly horrifying stories of idolatry, rapine, rape, murder and civil war – and observes drily at intervals, 'In those days there was no king in Israel; every man did what was right in his own eyes' (17:6, 18:1, 19:1, 21:25). Might was right, and the devil take the hindermost.

And then to crown it all there were the Philistines . . . . A king was surely essential. So a king they got, and very soon, with David and Solomon and a number of the psalmists, a royal ideology to match, integrating the monarchy which was indeed a pagan institution, borrowed together with the idea of a temple from the other nations, into Israel's covenant with Israel's God. God's old election of Abraham is consummated by his new election of David, and his covenant with David sets the seal on his covenant with Israel made under Moses (see 2 Sam 7:5–16).

The old anarchic ideal, which was also a theocratic one, did not fade away, however. It was kept alive by the prophets, especially in their battles with the kings of the northern kingdom of Israel, people like Ahab and his queen Jezebel, and was inherited from them by the Deuteronomic school.[4]

The issue may be supposed to have been finally settled in a practical way by the destruction of the nation in the exile, and its transformation from Israelite monarchy into Judaic community, never again to be an independent nation except for the brief interlude under the Hasmoneans (c. 140–63 B.C.), when the issue of monarchy versus theocratic 'anarchy' again revived, the Pharisees bitterly opposing the Hasmonean priest-kings.

These two kinds of political establishment, each of which is presented by different biblical authors as divinely ordained, monarchy and theocratic anarchy, are at opposite extremes of the spectrum of possible forms of social organization. Each apparently receives divine sanction; neither is compatible with the other; each receives severe divine criticism; each comes to an end in the course of the sacred history.

The theological inference is obvious, but important. *No* form of society or government or 'wider community' can claim a superiority over others in virtue of divine revelation. The choice is essentially a human one, a secular one, and God is not going to make it for us.

So today we cannot argue politics in terms of religion, on theological premisses. The theory of the divine right of kings was a theological monstrosity, and we should take great care not to replace it with others, such as the divine right of democracy, or capitalism, or socialism. There is no specifically Christian form of political organization.

On the other hand, I think two qualifications must be made to this correct 'secular' view of politics. The first is that according to the scriptural interpretation of Israel's history God did from time to time lend his sanction now to one, now to another form of political or social organization, and all of them provide some analogies for portraying what came to be called, in the final stages of the sacred history, the kingdom of God. About the kingdom of God we shall have to say more in a later chapter.

The second is that whatever kind of political organization a society may have, we must not forget, as Christians, that the basic, quasi-absolute value is that of the human person. The values we have seen attached to or growing out of the elemental or basic communities of family and/or small group are values only in so far as they contribute to the value of human persons. And thus again, any values attached to the larger and wider communities, of nation and so forth, are only genuine values in so far as they contribute to the value of human persons. So all forms of political totalitarianism, which subordinate the value of persons to the value of the social totality, and would control every single aspect of personal life in terms of such 'higher' social values, are theologically taboo – totally so. Christian criticism of the totalitarian aspirations of any parties, any politicians, any political philosophies must be relentless and unsparing.

C. THE SOLITARY LIFE

It may seem strange to have a section on this topic in a chapter about the values of community. But it is a feature of life in general; there are people who lead solitary lives. 'So-and so is something of a recluse', we say. It is a sociological phenomenon which has to be taken account of. And furthermore, it is a specific mode of the Christian life, not very common it is true, but recognized and venerated in the Church ever since the days of St Anthony in the fourth century; indeed a mode of life whose inspiration may well go back to John the Baptist, and before him to prophets like Jeremiah and Elijah. So it has to be accounted for and evaluated.

(i) In the general human perspective

We are not of course here evaluating the solitary life of those unfortunates on whom it is forced, either because they are being held in solitary confinement by the powers that be, or because they have been abandoned or neglected or lost in one way or another by families and friends. These are the victims of socio-political abuse or of social breakdown. Christian communities have a duty, surely, to do what they can either to terminate or to ameliorate such involuntary solitude.

Our concern is with the solitary life voluntarily chosen or at least willingly accepted. And we should begin by recognizing that it is chosen, or accepted, by many besides hermits, anchorites and anchoresses whose choice of it for religious reasons we shall turn to shortly. It is, I rather imagine, sometimes accepted by some of those on whom it is first forced, indirectly, by circumstances; by some migrants from country to big city, for example.

People are always leaving, temporarily or permanently, the basic communities, families, villages, clans, in which they have started life for the vast, anonymous, wider community of the city. Here most of them will slip into other face-to-face relationships or 'basic communities', usually but not necessarily of a more ephemeral and superficial sort. But some won't. Some will continue to be like 'The Cat who Walked by Himself' of Rudyard Kipling's *Just So Stories*. The solitary person is found in an enormous number of guises – the tramp, the pedlar, the eccentric scientist or professor, the wise woman or witch, among sailors and merchant adventurers, geologists, prospectors and 'frontiersmen'.

The question is, given the divine observation that it is not good for the man to be alone, whether this is a permissible or a wise mode of life. Of course it isn't if it is simply motivated by misanthropy or any form of mere selfishness. And of course it isn't for the vast majority of human beings. St Basil the Great, indeed, who was Bishop of Caesarea in Cappadocia in the middle of the fourth century, and wrote a rule for monks that is still observed in churches of the Greek rite, thought it was not a good mode of life for *anybody* (*The Longer Rules*, 7; PG 31, 928–929). It rather looks as if he was very critical of the manner of life of the hermits of the Egyptian and Syrian deserts, who were imitating St Anthony in vast numbers; critical too, perhaps, of St Athanasius of Alexandria, who much admired Anthony and wrote his life in order to popularize this style of life.

But in qualification of Basil's stand we should allow that there can be other motivations besides misanthropy or selfishness or pride, and that while the solitary life does involve cutting oneself off from the 'basic community', it does not necessarily involve rejection of the wider community or humanity at large. If it did, his criticisms of it would stand without qualification. But to separate oneself from the basic community (all basic communities) is often permissible and sometimes necessary. For the basic community, the family and the village, can be very oppressive, can stifle and stunt those personal values and possibilities which are always to be seen as primary. There was a play being performed in the late 1930s, a family comedy called *Dear Octopus*. But the family octopus is not always so dear, and other things being equal it is a good thing to escape from cephalopodic tentacles.

This is particularly necessary for persons who have special talents and vocations. For it is sometimes the case that they can best cultivate these, for the benefit of the wider community, if they are free of any close relationships such as are involved in belonging to a small basic community or family.

(ii) In the specifically religious perspective

The same points can be made with even greater clarity in the case of religious recluses, hermits, anchorites. They cut all their ties with families and friends and neighbours, and by fleeing from the company of others either into a scarcely inhabited wilderness (hermits) or into a cell isolated from the outside world (recluses), they avoid contracting new ones. But they do not leave the wider society of the Church. They provide their fellow Christians with the benefit not only of their prayers but also of their wisdom and illuminations and counsel. How much poorer English Christianity would be, for instance, if Dame Julian of Norwich had not been an anchoress, and in her solitude received those wonderful *Revelations of Divine Love*. And in fact hermits and anchorites have been, and still are, resorted to by great numbers for spiritual counsel.

This is perhaps the answer to Basil's objections to the solitary life; its solitariness is qualified, not absolute. It is put very well by Bede Griffiths in his book *Christian Ashram*. It is true he is writing about monasticism, and the life of the monk, which is a community life. But he is writing about the element of solitude in that life – about which we should remember that the word 'monk' (from the Greek *monachos*) originally meant 'solitary'. He writes:

It is this experience of Christ as the ground of all being which must be the inspiration of a christian monasticism. For this means that in Christ we not only discover the centre or ground of our being, but we also find a meeting point with all other men and with the whole world of nature. There is a necessary separation from the world in a monastic life, a discipline of silence and solitude which is necessary for the discovery of this inner centre of our being. But this separation should not divide a monk from the world but on the contrary enable him to meet the world at the deepest level of its being. 'A monk is one who separates himself from all men in order that he may be united with all men', was one of the sayings of the monastic fathers (p. 25).

But there is another aspect of the religious solitary life that is in tension with this point of Dom Bede's. For it is also part of the vocation of the solitary to be a sign to the Church and the world that 'the form of this world is passing away' (1 Cor 7:31). There is a real sense in which 'the world', as what St Paul means here, and what John usually means by the word (e.g. in Jn 17:9, where Jesus says 'I am not praying for the world'), i.e. human society at large, is beyond redemption. God's plan is not to salvage it or reform it, but simply abolish it and replace it with something better, the kingdom of God, and so he is calling people out of the world, saving them from the world. There is a deep inner corruption in all human society (even in the Church, as a merely human society). The solitary protests against this by his withdrawal from society, and reminds us that there will be no utopias, no perfect, sinless societies in which all corruption and exploitation and injustice is at an end, no perfect Church even, but only a sinful Church, corrupted in its social form by the corrupt world, a Church *semper reformanda*, and never finally *reformata* – until the Day of Judgement. The solitary reminds us, like the patriarchs and prophets of the Old Testament, that 'we are strangers and exiles on the earth', and that we 'look forward to the city which has foundations, whose builder and maker is God' (Heb 11:13, 10).

NOTES

1   At least we do in this book. In some humanist philosophies the concept of person, it would appear, is first defined (in various ways) as a concept of value, and then used as a kind of gauge or yardstick by which to measure human beings, to see how far they actually attain to being persons. If they don't attain very far, if they are mongoloid, for example, or senile, then they don't have much value, and are presumably more expendable.

2   A. A. Milne, *Winnie-the-Pooh*, chapter III.

3   For my brief summary of early Israelite history I am indebted to John L. McKenzie, *The World of the Judges*.

4   I have already referred in passing to this school, or D as it is known to the pundits (see above, Chapter 6, C, ii), but should here give a little more information about it. D really stands for 'Deuteronomist', the school of writers responsible for Deuteronomy and other scattered texts in the Pentateuch. But most modern scholars now credit this school with editing the history of Israel from Joshua to Kings. The school would have come into being about 650 B.C. or earlier, made up of Levites and followers of prophets like Amos and Hosea, who had fled from Samaria when it was destroyed by the Assyrians in 721, and had taken refuge in Judah. The school would have continued in existence for another hundred years at least.

QUESTIONS FOR FURTHER DISCUSSION

1   What are the social and political implications of asserting the absolute worth of the individual human person and the basic equality of all human beings in that worth?

2   Is it true that community values are functions of the value of persons?

3   How can we avoid idolizing cultural values while still respecting and cherishing them?

4   Is there a place for the solitary life? What are the values to which it points?

RECOMMENDED FURTHER READING

For this and the preceding chapter, *Gaudium et Spes*, chapter II, 23–32, 'The Community of Mankind' (in *The Documents of Vatican II*).

15
Man as Male and Female
I: Marriage

A. THE TEACHINGS OF J AND P

(i) J's view of marriage: love and companionship

Let us begin by seeing what J has to tell us about the relationship of man and woman (represented by 'the man' and 'the woman'), and the community they form in marriage – and what he does not tell us.

'Bone of my bones and flesh of my flesh' (Gen 2:23); there is between man and woman, he says, a common nature far surpassing any community between man and the other animals. The creation of the animals has failed to provide the man with 'a helper fit for him' (*ibid.* 20). J wishes to suggest, by his story of Eve being formed from Adam's rib, that there is between them an even closer community of nature than arises from their being members of the same biological species (which is in fact all that P will say about it). To achieve that, God could simply have made a pair of human beings, male and female, from the dust of the ground, as he presumably did in J's view with the other animals. By making Eve from Adam's rib he ensured more than just common humanity; he ensured kinship, a kind of *unity*, unity in diversity, a unity of origin (bone of my bones and flesh of my flesh) that is then realized again in a further mode in the marital union ('they become one flesh'; *ibid.* 24).

So the chief significance for J of the differentiation and union of the sexes seems to be this: the realization of a perfect community of two, the achievement and manifestation of love. The procreation of children he simply ignores at this stage. It is in the companionship of the man and the woman, including their sexual companionship, not in their fertility, that the divine goodness is expressed and experienced, as far as J is concerned. His ideal sinless world (which was not the world, anyway, but the enchanted garden) would not have been heavily populated.

(ii) P's contrasting view of sex: fertility

P shows a very different interest. J's little picture is clearly one of marriage of husband and wife as an institution of creation. P says nothing at all about marriage, simply 'male and female he created them' (Gen 1:27). And he blessed them and said 'Be fruitful and multiply' (*ibid.* 28). No suggestion of just an original couple, let alone of an original individual, simply a statement of the creation of the human species, male and female, and of the blessing of fertility and the command to increase and multiply. A very pragmatic, unromantic view of the distinction of the sexes. As we have observed before, P was a thorough-going rationalist.

Not that P was objecting to J's presentation of marriage as an institution of creation. But he did want to stress the blessing of fertility, a necessary condition for 'subduing' the earth (*ibid.* 28), that is for constructing a civilization. And perhaps, in an altogether more positive vein, he wished to stress against J the essential equality of the sexes. J states much more vividly the unity of human nature in the sexes, but in doing so he undoubtedly subordinates the woman to the man, as St Paul was quite right in remarking (1 Cor 11:8–9). I like to think, and his text permits us to think, that P queried this and offered a correction. And that would be why he did not so much as mention marriage, since in his time marriage as an institution, whether in Israel or among other known peoples, always involved the subordination of women to men.

(iii)   The goodness of sex

Both texts affirm quite unequivocally the goodness of the distinction and therefore of the union of the sexes. For P fertility, the effect of that union, is a divine blessing. For J the union itself is a divine gift for which the man rejoices in his little hymn of Gen 2:23. The unashamed nakedness of the man and the woman tells the same tale.

(iv)   What is not said about marriage

P says nothing about marriage at all, as we have just remarked (which does not of course mean that he disapproved of it as an institution). J combines its institution with the creation of the woman. But in addition to what we have already noticed in his text he says nothing.

He does not, for example, as against the view of many commentators, affirm a preference for monogamy over polygamy. I suspect he was aware that the forms of the institution of marriage varied enormously from culture to culture, and as we have seen (Chapter 3, A, Chapter 14, B, i) all cultures and civilizations were for him the consequence of sin. So he was not going to adjudicate between one culture and another in his picture of the sinless humanity of the original couple.

B. MARRIAGE IN THE SUBSEQUENT TRADITION OF ISRAEL

(i) Sociological specification in Israel

P, then, tells us nothing about marriage and J very little. We have to wait until the New Testament, almost, before we come to any further doctrinal statement about it. And there, very suitably, we find it first in the form of a comment on the texts of J and P.

In between the creation narratives and the gospels we have little more than the particular Israelite cultural expression of the divine, or creational, institution of marriage. In the intention of the creator the union of the sexes is concretized as a *social institution* (marriage). That is a theological statement, a statement of Christian doctrine. But different societies give very different social expression to this universal socialization of sexuality. In Israel, to generalize, we can say that it was given, early in their history, polygamous form, but that through the centuries this polygamous character of marriage seems gradually to have faded. We also observe that the Law made provision for men to divorce their wives, if they wished, with comparative ease, only insisting on the 'bill of divorce' as some guarantee of respectability to the divorced woman (so the suggestion of the New Testament quotation of Dt 24:1 in Mt 5:31 parr.). These are no more than sociological statements.

However, there is one significant theological criticism of divorce in Mal 2:16, put in the mouth of God himself. The practice is simply identified with a man being 'faithless to the wife of his youth' (*ibid.* 14), and equated with violence (which means bloodshed in scripture) in sinfulness (*ibid.* 16).

There are other sociological specifics to Israelite marriage customs, such as the prohibited degrees of consanguinity, and the levirate principle whereby a man is required to take his deceased brother's wife, if his brother dies childless, in order to raise up seed to his brother – and so on (Lev 18:6ff.; Dt 25:5ff.). Such marriage specifications are found in other cultures all over the world, and so are their contraries. I think it is a mistake (Henry VIII's mistake) to suppose that they have revelational, doctrinal authority simply because they occur in scripture, and are there presented as divine legislation. They are really little more than part of the décor for the great drama of salvation, of revelation, like the Hebrew language the Israelites spoke or the clothes they wore, or the food they ate or were forbidden to eat.

In the text of Malachi, and perhaps less forcefully elsewhere (e.g. implicitly in some of the Wisdom literature, like Prov 5:15–23, Prov 31) we do find a divine word criticizing the custom of easy divorce. This itself suggests that Israelite marriage law and custom (which permitted easy divorce) is not to be thought of as necessarily more sacrosanct than the law and custom of other nations.

(ii)   The Song of Songs

There is however one Old Testament text we can scarcely ignore in this context, the Song of Songs. Like P, it says nothing explicitly about marriage,
though a great deal implicitly if it was sung or composed as an epithalamium
at weddings. What it obviously speaks of with voluptuous sensuality is love.
It is surprising, pleasantly so, to find it in the sacred canon. But that we
should be surprised only illustrates, perhaps, how mean and narrow and
culture-bound is our view of what is sacred.

It is probable that the book has only been accepted by both Synagogue and
Church as part of the sacred canon because from the earliest times it has
received a mystical or allegorical interpretation as telling of the loves of the
Lord and his bride: of Yahweh and Israel or of Christ and the Church as the
case may be – or sometimes of Christ and the individual soul.

But this mystical interpretation must not be seen as an exclusive either/or
alternative to the more obvious literal one that the Song of Songs is a collection of love songs in praise of sensual love. If sensual love is a valid analogue
for the love of Christ and the Church, or of Yahweh and Israel, then it is valid
in itself as a human relationship blessed and approved by God.

So much for all the stoics and puritans and the whole dismal strand of
Christian tradition which from Origen (185–253) onwards has tended to
inculcate both fear and contempt of sexual desire and sensual pleasure. The
Song of Songs, elaborating on J's brief paradise scene of Adam rejoicing over
Eve and their innocent lack of shame at their nakedness, tells us unequivocally
– God through these poems tells us unequivocally – that these things are a
vital, essential and excellent part of being human; so excellent that they are
taken up and woven into the very relationship which he himself has forged
with his creation, human kind.

C.   MARRIAGE IN THE NEW TESTAMENT

Coming to the New Testament, we find that what specific teaching there is
about marriage, whether by Christ or Paul or other writers, is purely
accidental and incidental. This is not to say, of course, that it is unimportant;
it is to say that Jesus and Paul took marriage for granted as a human institution, particularized for them mainly by Jewish custom and culture, and made
observations on it or criticisms of current practice as occasion required.

(i)   The gospels: divorce and adultery

As far as the gospels are concerned, everything Jesus had to say on the subject
can be found in two passages of Mark. The parallels in Matthew and Luke
add nothing of significance.

In Mk 10:1–12 Jesus answers the question of the Pharisees about divorce. Here he teaches three things: he confirms the divine hatred of divorce expressed in Mal 2:13–16, and for the same reason – because it is a form of unfaithfulness or adultery; he confirms that marriage is an institution of creation, as it were concreated with man; and he confirms the natural or concreated equality of male and female, and hence of husband and wife within the institution of marriage. It is interesting to see that in referring back to the creation he quotes both from P and J, Gen 1:27 as well as 2:24. It is a most carefully economical quotation.

We have nothing new, then; only a firm criticism and rejection of those corruptions or distortions of the basic community, unity in plurality, unity in equal love and esteem, by sin-ridden human cultures and social systems.

It must be noted that the criticism only bears upon the point of divorce, not on the point of polygamy. It could be argued that the affirmation of equality between husband and wife (in v. 12, where she is put on an exactly equal footing as regards divorcing her husband, something the law of Deuteronomy never envisaged) rules out polygamy as an acceptable, that is divinely acceptable, form of marriage. It is a good argument; but that is what it is, an argument, not a direct expression of the divine will. It is equally arguable that polygamy should sometimes be legally tolerated in the Christian community, as it was in the Old Testament, and as other less than perfect social institutions have frequently been and are still being tolerated – the most obvious example being slavery. To the question of divorce and polygamy in the contemporary Christian scene and the contemporary teaching and practice of the Church we shall return in section D.

(ii)   The gospels: marriage a purely this-worldly institution

In Mk 12:18–25 the Sadducees present Jesus with their conundrum about the resurrection, in terms of the custom of levirate marriage, and he concludes his reply with the statement that 'when they rise from the dead, they neither marry nor are given in marriage, but are like angels in heaven'. Marriage as a social institution (and the sexual relationship which it institutionalizes) does not persist in the kingdom of God as it will be finally established. It belongs only to this order of creation, not to the new creation of the age to come.

Why not? In looking in detail at Jesus' very firm statement we need to be careful. He is *not* arguing, for example, that marriage is a terrestrial but not a celestial, a carnal but not a spiritual institution. He does not say 'they do not marry in heaven', but 'when they rise from the dead they do not marry'. It is not therefore because after death their condition will be spiritual (like the angels in heaven), and no longer material, bodily or carnal. They will be like the angels in heaven (it is the angels who are noted as being in heaven, not those who rise from the dead), not in being disembodied – which they won't be, since they will have risen from the dead – but in enjoying the immediate vision or society of God and of his saints with him, among whom they will be numbered.

In the kingdom, in the resurrection (in heaven, if you like, but it can be a misleading expression) that will be the only and all-sufficient society, and there will be no need or place for lesser social units, hence no need or place for any social institutions. It is not only marriage that will find no place there; neither will government, class, culture, civilization, hierarchy, priesthood, clubs, states, parishes – there will be no institutions at all. It will indeed be anarchy.

(iii)   St Paul: marriage as a sacrament

This firm limitation of marriage and sexual relations to this age and the temporal order, and its exclusion from the age to come has to be balanced against a point we observed when we were considering the Song of Songs. Sexual relations and marriage continue in the New Testament to provide one of the most common and powerful symbols of man's relations with God and of life in the age to come. More than one parable in the gospels features a wedding or wedding feast or bridegroom, and the reference is always eschatological, to the age to come. The same symbolic reference is found in the story of the wedding at Cana (Jn 2:1–11), where Jesus first 'manifested his glory'. And it is of course there in the final vision of the Apocalypse (19:9, 21:2, 9).

This line of thought is taken up briefly in a crucial text, Eph 5:22–33. The passage is for the most part a commonplace exhortation to domestic harmony, to husbands to love and cherish their wives, to wives to love and obey and respect their husbands; and it goes on in chapter 6 with similar exhortations to harmony between parents and children, and to proper relations between masters and slaves. As such it exhibits culture-bound assumptions and sentiments, far more so than any sayings of Jesus about marriage in the gospels; about, for example, the proper subordination of wives to husbands. This is not surprising, nor particulary reprehensible on the Apostle's part. The same is true of 1 Pet 2:18 – 3:7, or of St Paul in the more notorious passage, 1 Cor 11:2–16, which gives a decidedly culture-bound interpretation of Gen 2:24, in marked contrast to the use of that text in Mk 10:1–12.[1]

This merely means, however, that in these moral exhortations we do not automatically have a word of God addressed to Christians in all cultures and all situations. What should be common to all human cultures and situations is the quality of love in marital and family relationships – and justice. But love and justice will find very variable cultural expression.

The theologically important element in Eph 5:22–33 is the quotation of Gen 2:24 with the added comment, 'This is a great mystery, and I take it to mean Christ and the Church' (31–32). The Latin Bible translates the Greek *mystērion* (mystery) by *sacramentum* (in some ways a better translation than 'mystery'), and on this passage is built the Catholic doctrine of marriage as a sacrament.

The doctrine is that the marriage of a Christian man and woman is a sacrament, i.e. a sacred sign, symbol or manifestation of the bridal relation between Christ and his Church. The Greek *mystērion* really means something like 'sacred symbol' rather than something which is beyond comprehension, which is what 'mystery' conveys to most of us.

This then is a Christian value of Christian marriage: that it symbolizes and thus (being an efficacious sign) enhances and participates in the relationship between Christ and his Church; which is in its turn a sacrament (sacred and effective sign) of the potential relationship between Christ and the whole of mankind.

But we have seen that the relationship between Yahweh and Israel was also thought of as a marital one. The great exponent of this theme, with some rather odd twists to it, is Hosea. So one may justly say that Israelite marriage was a kind of sacrament of the old law, symbolizing the covenant between God and his people, and the fidelity of God, which it assured, and of Israel, which it required.

Furthermore, we have seen the love lyrics of the Song of Songs interpreted in this sense. Now while they are indeed Hebrew lyrics, and in the Hebrew Bible, they do not just celebrate Hebrew or Israelite love, but all human sexual love. So we can go further and say that all love of this kind, in so far as it finds expression in a genuine and lasting social relationship, is 'sacramental', a sacred sign or symbol of the ultimate eschatological divine/human relationship as intended by God.

Thus, while marriage and sexual relations are in themselves limited to this temporal age or aeon, and will not persist into the age to come, the kingdom of the *eschaton*, they nonetheless represent sacramentally in this age the perfection of social, community relations in the kingdom of the *eschaton*.

D. DIVORCE AND POLYGAMY IN CURRENT CHRISTIAN TEACHING

The teaching of the Church, of all 'mainline' Churches on polygamy and of the Catholic Church on divorce, is very easy to state. They are not, under any circumstances, permitted. The reasons for this teaching of the Catholic Church on divorce are also very easy to state: the words of Jesus Christ in the text from Mk 10:11–12 which we have already looked at, and which reaffirm Malachi's equation of divorce with marital infidelity. The reasons for the general Christian rejection of polygamy are not so clear-cut, though it is almost universally supposed (wrongly in my opinion) that this too is explicitly forbidden by the New Testament.[2]

However, the simplicity and correctness of the Church's teaching on these points does not prevent it from being both controversial in itself and problematic in its execution. So we must take a closer look at it.

(i) Polygamy

This issue is, clearly, not an important one in Europe or wherever European culture has migrated. This is in itself, I suggest, a significant fact. For polygamy *is* an important issue in other parts of the world, above all in Africa. And from these parts of the world one can very naturally acquire the impression that the insistence of the Christian missionaries on monogamy is more a cultural than a religious 'article of faith'.

This impression is, on the whole, accurate. For Christianity was born into a set of cultures, those of the Graeco-Roman world, that were already monogamous by custom and law. The Jews, perhaps as a result of Hellenistic domination and in spite of their ancient polygamous traditions, had become in fact if not in law monogamous by the time of the New Testament. Monogamy was thus assumed to be the norm.

Then Christianity's first great expansion from the Roman Empire, among the peoples of northern Europe, was again into cultures of monogamous custom. All along then monogamy was taken for granted as the Church rooted itself in European culture.

This is not to deny that monogamy fitted easily into the New Testament moral framework. It did; it harmonized very well with the New Testament teaching on marriage that we have already seen. Where the Church had to challenge these cultures which were the first it penetrated (as the word of God had had to challenge Israelite culture) was in the matter of divorce.

And so when centuries later Christianity came to the polygamous cultures of Africa, its challenge to them was not purely religious, not purely a challenge from the saving and judging word of God, but also a challenge from a rival, stronger, and as it happened more arrogant culture. Perhaps this is one reason why so few African Christians enter into Christian marriage to this very day.[3] In all honesty the Church should at least admit that its marriage laws and policies, those framed by the Council of Trent for Europe in the sixteenth century and adapted, for Europe, in the early twentieth, have been a failure in Africa, because not enough attention has been paid to the cultural factor.

I am not saying there are no good theological or moral grounds for preferring monogamy to polygamy. I am only saying that for historical reasons the

Church does not seem to have thought them out carefully, or distinguished them from cultural grounds. There has, I suspect, simply been an assumption (a European cultural, not a Christian assumption) that polygamy is a licentious, and thus degrading custom, and an almost total unawareness (a European cultural unawareness) of its wide economic and social ramifications – and African cultural justifications.

What then can we say are the theological and moral reasons for preferring monogamy to polygamy? As far as I can see there is really only one, but that is an all-important one: the basic equality, in the divine intention, of the sexes, implicit in P's account of creation, Gen 1:27 (see above, A) and in Jesus' reply to the question about divorce (above, C). The custom of polygamy manifestly assumes the subordination, not to say inferiority, of women and perpetuates it. (It is odd that the much rarer custom of polyandry, whereby one woman has several husbands, does not seem to assume or perpetuate the subordination and inferiority of men.) Only a custom of monogamy can do justice to the proper equality of men and women within the institution of marriage.

And yet the custom of monogamy does not of itself necessarily guarantee the equality of women. And in fact the monogamous Graeco-Roman and European cultures in which Christianity developed from the beginning have been every bit as male-dominated as the polygamous ones into which it has more recently been transplanted. Thus it seems to have happened that the resolute opposition of the missionary Christian Churches to African polygamy has *not* been for the correct theological reason, but for far more questionable cultural reasons wrongly assumed to be genuine Christian and religious reasons.

What should, and still could be the policy of the Churches about polygamy? Not one of sanctioning and blessing it, certainly, in itself. But the Church in its history has tolerated many other much more obviously evil customs and social institutions – male domination of women, for example, or slavery, or imperial conquest; and on the whole rightly so, at least where this has been done with open eyes, and not because of the Church's worldliness (Chapter 13, B, ii). So it is beginning to seem clear to many pastoral theologians in Africa today that the Church should also tolerate polygamy. Many of the new independent African Churches already do. This policy was advocated more than a century ago by the great Anglican missionary among the Zulus in Natal, Bishop Colenso.

But as well as tolerating polygamy, the Church should also have a policy of limiting and discouraging it from within the presuppositions of African cultures. Thus:

(a)   Polygamy should form no bar to conversion and baptism, and a polygamous man should not be required to put away all but one of his wives. This current requirement is of dubious justice to the wives in any case.

(b)   But his wives, perhaps, could be permitted to leave him if they wish, and be regarded as free to marry again.

(c)   A man who is already Christian should be permitted, for a time perhaps, to marry no more than four wives – the Church taking a leaf from the Moslem book; but this could only be with the consent of the wife or wives he already has.

(d)   Men with more than one wife should be disqualified from the Church's ministry and also from any lay position of responsibility in the Church, such as catechist or parish councillor.

Clearly the details of such a policy would have to be worked out by those involved in the actual situation, and would vary from region to region and culture to culture. Here I simply wish to maintain two things: first that such a policy of accommodation or toleration would not be incompatible with true Christian doctrine on marriage; secondly that its discouragement of polygamy should be very explicitly linked with the doctrine of the basic equality of women with men, and therefore coupled with a policy of supporting women's rights in all spheres of social activity – above all in Church activity.

(ii)   Divorce

The matter of divorce is very different. All Christian Churches, I think it is true to say, disapprove of divorce and wish to discourage it. In so doing they set themselves in opposition to the worldly *mores* of practically all cultures, the cultures of the Graeco-Roman and the early Germanic worlds no less than of the modern post-Christian Western world. The Catholic Church is, in this respect, simply more resolutely intransigent in its opposition to these *mores*. The other Churches, in different degrees, have adopted policies of toleration or accommodation with the 'cultural facts', analogous to what we have just been recommending for polygamy.

But the Catholic Church, in adopting its absolute stance on this matter has developed a *doctrine* about marriage, and also what might be called an alternative *practice* or policy (that of annulment), that need closer examination.

The doctrine is that of the indissolubility of marriage; it is seen as indissoluble, not just because Christ said it is, when he said 'What God has joined together, let not man put asunder' (Mk 10:9), but because he made it so in reality. Because the marriage of Christians is a sacrament (above, C, iii), the marriage bond, or the relationship set up between man and wife when they marry, is more than just a legal relationship which is capable of being terminated. It is a kind of sacred, perpetually significant entity which cannot be destroyed; it is something which once done cannot be undone.[4]

The question may be asked whether it is necessary, in order to preserve the sacramental nature of Christian marriage (which is an article of faith, defined by the Council of Trent, Dz 1801/971), that the marriage bond should be seen in this way as something more than a legal relationship. After all, the Church recognizes that not all marriages are sacramental; the marriages of unbaptized persons, namely, which are still for all that lawful and valid. And these marriages it regards as capable of being dissolved, on the strength of what St Paul says in 1 Cor 7:15, although I do not think that the Church wishes to deny that God joins unbaptized persons together as well as Christians. Why then may not the marriages of Christians be regarded as capable of being dissolved by termination of the legal relationship of the marriage bond, once the marriage has in fact broken down and that marriage bond, being no longer a credible sacramental sign of the union of Christ and his Church, has ceased to be anything but a formal legal relationship?

There is a further question to be asked of the Catholic position on divorce. It is based on the supposition that Jesus Christ, in his reply to the Pharisees' question on divorce, made a law about it. Now it was the most natural thing in the world for the mediaeval canonists to cast our Lord in the role of legislator, and in support of this view of him we could cite the evangelists, Matthew in particular, presenting him as a second Moses. This is implicit in the whole structure of Matthew's gospel, and above all in the way in which he stages and arranges the sermon on the mount. And then Jesus is the mediator of a *new covenant*, which betokens a *new law*.

But what the canonists fail to take into account is that legal concepts are here being used *analogically*. When Jesus is seen as a second Moses he is not being seen as a mere successor to Moses, or as doing the same thing as Moses, but as *fulfilling* what Moses did, transposing it into a higher key. And law is fulfilled, not by more law, or by better law (in the univocal sense) but by grace. The new law is not a law of decrees and commandments, written on tablets of stone, but a law written in the heart. St Thomas Aquinas defines it quite simply as the grace of the Holy Spirit (*STh* Ia IIae, 106, i; ET, vol. 30). And that surely cannot be imparted by legislation in any normal sense of the word. It is not theologically tenable or plausible that Jesus Christ came to make laws. So it is theologically eccentric to treat this one saying of his as establishing a law. Can we not then trace this Catholic doctrine about the indissolubility of Christian marriage to the theological eccentricity of canon lawyers, and thus conclude that it is a doctrine which could and should be modified?

As for the Catholic Church's alternative practice of annulment of marriages in place of divorce, it has developed very considerably in recent years as a pastoral response to the actual cultural situation of Catholics in the post-Christian Western world. It is a procedure not for dissolving marriages, but for declaring them, after due investigation, to be null, that is to say never to have been valid marriages from the beginning. The modern development or expansion of this practice since the Second Vatican Council has consisted in the discovery, or elaboration, with the help of theologians, of many more grounds for nullity than used to be admitted by the Church courts.

As a way of helping Catholics to get out of the bind, or dead end, of a broken marriage so that they are free to marry again with the approval of the Church and with access to the sacraments, it is pastorally praiseworthy. It is not as easy as divorce, but it is not meant to be. The only trouble is that it appears in some ways to be just a little less than honest. I remember, after hearing a very distinguished canon lawyer expound the new nullity rules to a gathering of priests in Lesotho, one of his audience observed that if that were so he doubted if one in a thousand of marriages celebrated in the country were valid! In other words, isn't it something of a legal fiction? To which I myself would reply that there is nothing intrinsically dishonest about legal fictions, even though that is how they often strike the non-legal lay mind.

The whole matter is exceedingly intractable. Could one not, in conclusion, say this? Marriage, as the basic social institution intended by the creator (Gen 2:24), forming the basic element of human society, has many dimensions, legal, economic, moral and spiritual. Could the Church not simply leave the legal and economic aspects of marriage to the laws of the secular society (provided they are just), and confine itself to helping its members cultivate the moral and spiritual values of the institution? In other words, could it not accept as legally valid any marriage, including that of divorced persons, which the secular law of a country recognizes as such, and then do what it can to help the partners of the marriage appreciate and consolidate its spiritual and moral values – which means in effect grow in genuine Christian love?

NOTES

1 But see below, Chapter 17, B, ii.
2 The Council of Trent reads this prohibition out of the words of Jesus in Mt 19:6 (= Mk 10:9), and so declares polygamy to be prohibited by divine law (Dz 1798/969; 1802/972) for Christians.
3 See Appendix E of *Christian Marriage in Africa* (SPCK, London, 1973), a report by Adrian Hastings commissioned by the Anglican Archbishops of Eastern, Central and Southern Africa. Hastings there sums up the statistics as follows:

1. In the area as a whole certainly less than half Anglican and Roman Catholic church members now marry in church . . . .
4 . . . The Catholic dioceses of Bukoba, Masasa, Jinja, Tororo, Kisumu and Kisii run round the lake [Victoria] from Tanzania in the west through Uganda to Kenya in the east. They claim between them a Catholic population of 2,317,000 and 4,678 marriages, which gives a marriage rate of precisely 2 [per 1,000; at the beginning of the appendix Hastings establishes 8 as a healthy normal rate]. This means that at least 75% of Catholics, probably more, are never marrying in church.

Hastings' statistics cover the years 1966 to 1970.

4 It would be more accurate to say, perhaps, that it is seen as not just a legal but as an onto-logical relationship, like that of parenthood, for example, which no legal act or judge-ment can abolish. There is an analogy with the sacramental 'character' which the sacra-ments of baptism, confirmation and order are seen as conferring. In the scholastic analysis of the sacraments (which are initially defined as 'sacred signs'), there are observed three levels, so to say, of the symbolic sacramental act. At the superficial, visible level there is the sacramental *sign* itself – the act of baptizing, or here the act of exchanging vows, the public, legal act of getting married. At the deepest, invisible, spiritual level there is the grace of the sacrament, the thing signified by the symbolic sign – the grace of regener-ation in the case of baptism, the grace of being assimilated to Christ and his Church in the case of marriage. But there is also an intermediate level between these two, which the scholastics called 'thing and sign' (*res et sacramentum*); a 'thing', or sacred entity both signified and effected by the visible sacrament, which is also in its turn signifying and effecting the final grace of sacrament. In the case of baptism this is the baptismal *character* of the baptized person; in the case of marriage it is the permanent *marriage bond* between the partners.

QUESTIONS FOR FURTHER DISCUSSION

1 Is it true that the authentic biblical Christian theology of marriage succeeds in maintain-ing the true equality of man and woman, husband and wife, in the teeth of all cultural prejudices, Israelite, Hellenistic, Roman, European, African and Asian, that have favoured male domination?

2 Did Jesus Christ make a definite *law*, in the strict juridical sense, against divorce? Or against polygamy? If not, can Church laws against these options be regarded as irrevocable absolutes?

RECOMMENDED FURTHER READING

James B. Nelson, *Embodiment*, is a valuable and painstaking work, pioneering a rethinking of traditional Christian teaching about sex and marriage. Perhaps inclined to make things a little too easy and plain sailing; and in my view he does not allow at all for the widespread reality of what I have called the dissociated self-experience (what he dismisses as spiritual dualism) until his last chapter, when he suddenly has to admit that it has something to be said for it. But on the whole a sound and sober book.

Walter Kasper, *Theology of Christian Marriage*.

Jack Dominian, *Marriage, Faith and Love* and *Proposals for a New Sexual Ethic*.

Kevin Kelly, *Divorce and Second Marriage*.

16

Man as Male and Female II: Sexual Morality; Religious Celibacy

A. RECAPITULATION

It is with ultimate reference to marriage that sexual morality has to be assessed, marriage being, as J tells us, an institution of creation. So let us begin by recapitulating what we have established about marriage so far.

(i) The distinction of the sexes is essentially relational

This is a point brought out more clearly by J than by P, for whom perhaps the appropriate word would be 'functional'. But the function or purpose of procreation can only be achieved by actualizing the sexual relationship, which is potentially present in the very differentiation of the sexes. So the fundamental relatedness of people to each other is derived from their being male and female – or rather a set of fundamental relationships between them is so derived. For these include the parent/child relationship, and hence sibling relationships, as well as the male/female, husband/wife relationship.

This latter relationship is universally institutionalized in marriage. And this, according to J, in virtue of the design and intention of the creator. But the institution of marriage takes very different forms according to the great variety of human cultures; and divine revelation does not directly or explicitly prescribe any one form in preference to others. It certainly does not, for example, prescribe for universal imitation the Israelite or 'biblical' form of the institution.

(ii) The goodness of the differentiation and union of the sexes

An obvious consequence of this, to be inferred from both P and J, is that the difference between the sexes, and hence the union of the sexes, is good. It is not a point we need linger on, but it is a point we have to stress against a persistent trend in several cultures to depreciate sexuality, to fear and despise its overt expression, and in extreme form to regard it as evil. A combination of ancient cultural developments in Asia and Europe seriously infected the Christian tradition with this virus. It is explicitly excluded by Heb 13:4, 'Let marriage be held in honour among all', and has always been condemned by the Church (at least in its extreme form); but not always with the clarity and consistency that could have been desired.

(iii) The values to be promoted by the institution of marriage

The basic social or community value, both presupposed and promoted by marriage, is mutual love. This in turn presupposes, to be complete and perfect, the equality of husband and wife, man and woman; and it also requires their mutual fidelity. It is in terms of these values, love and equality and fidelity, that the divine revelation and Christian doctrine have to evaluate and criticize the various forms that the institution of marriage takes in different cultures. It was in terms of love and fidelity, for instance, that the divine word in scripture criticized the provision for divorce made in the Israelite form of the institution; and in terms of the basic equality of the sexes that Christian doctrine may rightly criticize the institution of polygamy (and polyandry).

(iv) The symbolic or sacramental meaning of marriage

Because it is an institution of creation in such a fundamental way, marriage has a symbolic meaning which Catholic doctrine expresses by calling it a sacrament. Catholic doctrine explicitly recognizes this value only in the marriage of Christians, whose unions signify and in some way effect and enhance the union between Christ and the Church.

But the concept should certainly not be limited to Christian marriage. Analogous symbolic value (if not sacramental value in the strictest sense of the word 'sacrament') may be discerned in Jewish or Israelite marriages, representing the marital relationship between the Lord, Yahweh, and his people. And furthermore (since marriage is an institution of creation) the analogy may be discerned in all human marriages, representing in their own way that mystery of which the Church itself is 'a kind of sacrament or sign and instrument', namely 'of intimate union with God and of the unity of the whole human race' (*Lumen Gentium* I, 1; Dogmatic Constitution on the Church, Vatican II).

(v) The temporal, this-worldly nature of marriage

But in spite of its sacred character, which it derives from its symbolic or sacramental meaning, marriage is purely a this-worldly, temporal institution. There will be no marriage, no specifically sexual relationship, regular or otherwise, in the kingdom of heaven, in the resurrection of the dead. The pronouncement of Jesus to this effect (Mk 12:25) must in no sense be seen as a devaluation of marriage. The same is true of all social institutions, ecclesiastical as well as secular, of governments, courts, ministries, papacy, episcopacy, priesthood, religious orders; the same is true of all the sacraments. 'When the perfect comes, the imperfect will pass away' (1 Cor 13:10). When what is signified is fully realized, the symbols will fade away.

B.   VARIANT SEXUAL BEHAVIOUR AND RELATIONS[1]

One has to draw the line somewhere between the theology of man, which is our concern in this book, and moral theology, which as such is not. The distinction, to be sure, is highly artificial: 'Manners makyth man', which being translated into modern English is 'Man makes manners', i.e. 'Man makes morals'. So moral theology, properly speaking, is a part of the theology of man. But it is a part that for reasons of convenience has to be separated from the whole. Therefore I do not regard it as my task here to assess the morality of particular kinds of sexual behaviour in detail, of masturbation, fornication, premarital sex, adultery, homosexuality, artificial contraception, artificial insemination, rape, incest, bestiality and public indecency. Rather, we shall try to distinguish and assess the grounds on which moral judgements have been and can be passed on such forms of behaviour.

(i)   Distinction between cultural and theological judgements

We have already touched on this distinction in the previous chapter on marriage (15, B, i; cf. D, i). It is a very simple distinction to make in the abstract, and there is therefore no need to elaborate it any further. But it is a very difficult one to make in practice – and indeed is hardly ever explicitly made in the authorities which control our Christian judgement in these matters, whether in the scriptures themselves or in the later pronouncements of the Church's tradition. There is a good reason for this: that while we can and must make the distinction between cultural norms and theological ones, we can never *separate* the two, because we cannot separate people from their culture (except by transposing them into another one), and should not try.

So in making and applying our distinction we must be clear from the outset that we are not making it in order to eliminate cultural judgements, or to mark them as misguided or as unsuitable for a Christian; but simply in order to prevent ourselves from treating cultural judgements as theological, and so endowing them with a spurious universal and absolute validity. Our principle is that it is proper for a theological standard of judgement to be used to assess the value of all cultural customs, institutions and standards, but not for one cultural standard of judgement (let us say the modern European or ancient Israelite) to be used to judge another culture (let us say modern African or ancient Chinese).

Let us take two cases to show how the two kinds of judgement are sometimes inextricably mixed up together – incest and premarital sex. The first form of variant sexual behaviour is certainly condemned in scripture, though without any reason being given for the condemnation (Lev 18:6–18; cf. 20:11, 12, 14, 17, 19–21). It is also probably true that the condemnation of incest is as universal as the institution of marriage. If I were to hazard a theological reason for the condemnation of incestuous relationships, I would suggest that it is because they cut across, confuse and thus destroy the various basic relationships established by the union of the sexes.

But what precisely does constitute incestuous behaviour? The answer to this question varies from culture to culture. In one (e.g. ancient Egypt) the marriage of brother and sister will not always be regarded as incestuous; in another, rigidly exogamous, that of second cousins will. So what about those tables of prohibited degrees of consanguinity and affinity derived from Lev 18:6–18? Are they universally and absolutely binding on all people, for all time? Not necessarily. They represent the judgement of Israelite culture. Henry VIII was wrong in maintaining the Pope had not had the authority to dispense him from the prohibition of marrying his deceased brother's wife (Lev 18:16); it could be pointed out that he paid insufficient attention to the Israelite cultural law of levirate marriage, Dt 25:5. Clement VII, on the other hand, was right in maintaining that his predecessor had had that authority.

As for premarital sex, the theological censure of it has much the same grounds as that of fornication in general – that it is irresponsible towards offspring, that it offends against the proper permanence of marital love and fidelity. But in this case what is at issue is not casual promiscuity but the more permanent liaisons of couples who are not yet married but may marry in due course. What we have to realize is that such liaisons can only be offences against sexual *mores*, given certain cultural definitions of what is meant by getting married. Thus in some cultures such a regular liaison may simply be identical with marriage. There, 'premarital' sex, as distinct from casual fornication, can have no meaning. In fact it only really has meaning in a culture, such as the contemporary European, in which marriage is conceived as a legal contract entered into at a precise moment by the performance of a precise legal ritual form. Before this takes place the couple are not married, after it they are.

But even in European culture there has been a change in this matter. In earlier times, under the customary law of many European peoples much greater importance was attached to betrothal than is now given to an engagement. A betrothed couple were already half married, and if before the final wedding ceremony they should sleep together, that act, though frowned on at least by the Church, would have the effect of making them fully married – clinching the contract.

Now the modern concept of marriage according to much African custom is not dissimilar to this ancient European one. Marriage is not so much a precise contract entered into at a precise moment as a relationship entered into gradually, step by step. And in this view of it there is no particular reason for regarding the cohabitation of the couple, or their sexual congress, as being properly the final step. Usually it is in fact not so, but comes somewhere in the middle. It is part of the process of getting married which it is faintly ridiculous to censure as premarital sex.

(ii)   Doctrinal judgement distorted by cultural assumptions

There is one matter in which it seems that the common doctrinal judgement of the Church has been distorted by cultural assumptions, and that is the assessment of the gravity of sexual sins. Marriage being, as we have seen, an institution of creation, and thus representing the divine blessing and sanctification of sexuality, it is with reference to marriage as the norm that all non-marital or extra-marital sexual behaviour must be judged. That is the strictly doctrinal, or theological, Christian standard of judgement.

But the judgement can be made in two ways. As I see it, it has commonly been made, up to the present day, in a way that reflects the cultural disparagement, even fear and disapproval of sexuality inherited by the Church from, above all, the Neoplatonic environment of the first Christian centuries. According to this way of seeing things the judgement is that *all* sexual activity is sinful – except within the context of marriage. So it is according to this way of seeing things that we get the maxim of the moral textbooks,'in sexual sins there is no such consideration as smallness of matter'; '*non datur parvitas materiae*'. Generally, in assessing the gravity of a sin one has to take into account whether it is about a trifle, or something serious; for instance, if it is a matter of the sin of theft, if the amount stolen is trifling, a few shillings, then it is not a grave or mortal sin, other things being equal. But in sexual sins, says this maxim, there are no such things as trifles; *all* sexual sins, therefore, are mortal sins, unless there is a lack of full deliberation, unless they are to some extent inadvertent.

Such a maxim of judgement, for which I can think of no justification in scripture, does smack of the neurotic or obsessive. It can certainly promote neurotic attitudes to sex among the faithful. Its *reductio ad absurdum* is given in the story of the military man going to confession, and confessing to having had bad thoughts. 'Did you entertain them?', asked the priest, in order to establish, you see, whether the thoughts had been deliberate; because if they had, the sin would be mortal – no trifles in the matter of sexual sins. But the colonel, being a man of common sense, replied testily, 'Dammit, Padre, they entertained me'.

The other way in which the judgement can be made is this. Sexuality, and its common manifestations, is all good, because it is created by God. But it is properly oriented towards marriage, and it is fully blessed only in marriage. Therefore sexual behaviour that is not oriented to marriage, or is in any way extra-marital or para-marital, is defective, sinful. Thus in this way of making the judgement we do not in any way cut down, so to speak, on the list of sexual sins. But in assessing their gravity we are prepared to make more distinctions, and to jettison that textbook maxim. Our criterion for a mortal sin will be what it is in the rest of classical moral theology, as expounded by St Thomas – a sin that involves a turning away from God by offending against the love of God and neighbour. There are certainly sexual sins that do this, of their nature; they are directly against the good divine institution of marriage: rape and adultery. But other sexual sins? They may, according to circumstances, be against charity, the love of God and neighbour; but then again, it seems to me, they may not. I cannot for example really see how masturbation can be called a mortal sin, of its nature. Clearly it is not oriented to marriage, clearly it is defective sexual behaviour since it has no relational context. But though obviously not in itself an expression of love of another, it is not obviously a sin against love. A bad habit to get into, certainly; a mortal sin – *aikona!* as they say in Southern Africa, meaning 'Get along with you!'

Similar considerations would apply to homosexual behaviour. It is manifestly not oriented to marriage, and thus is of its nature defective sexual behaviour. But it does not seem to be, of its very nature, necessarily against love or charity; it may even be, like heterosexual activity, expressive of genuine love or charity. So on this line of reasoning I would argue that it is not necessarily of its nature a mortal sin. Cultural judgements on homosexuality vary enormously, from the benign, not to say favourable judgement of classical Greece (and of a number of preliterate cultures too), to the severe condemnation of biblical Israel and Christian Europe. It is perhaps worth remarking that the biblical condemnation of it possibly owes something to its connection, in the Israelite experience of it among their neighbours, both with the worship of Canaanite deities and the institution of sacred prostitution, male and female, and also with brutal breaches of the sacred law of hospitality, as in the story of Sodom (Gen 19:4–9) and of the Benjaminites of Gibeah (Judges 19:22–26). Just as the Christian can pass a theological judgement on the deficiencies of the one type of culture, where the acceptance of homosexuality as of positive value seems to contribute to a certain de-

preciation of marriage and also perhaps of the status of women, so he can pass
a theological judgement on the over-severe, oversimplified condemnations of
the other, where official abhorrence of it encourages intolerant prejudice and
perhaps an aggressive type of male chauvinism or *machismo*.

(iii)   Natural law as a standard of assessment for sexual mores

Traditionally these forms of sexual behaviour have been condemned as 'sins
against nature'. But nowadays the natural law gets invoked in Catholic
official teaching mostly in support of this teaching's objection to any artificial
methods of contraception. How cogent this appeal to natural law will be will
depend on many things, but among them will certainly be the validity of the
concept of natural law itself. So this is what we must now examine.

The concept of natural law is one that is widely regarded nowadays as out
of date. In fact, it only appears to hold its own in the official teaching and
among some of the theologians of the Catholic Church. I think it is in
general fair to say that a contributary reason for the scepticism with which
the concept is treated by nearly all moral philosophers and jurists is the fact
that modern Catholic theologians and official documents have employed such
a debased and decadent form of the concept. They have not made it sufficiently clear, indeed they appear themselves not to have sufficiently appreciated, that natural law can be 'law' only in a highly analogous sense. Thus
they seem very often to treat it as a kind of set of legal or moral principles
written into nature, from which it is possibly to deduce a very detailed code
of moral conduct, especially in sexual matters. This is what contemporary
moral philosophers and jurists dismiss, rightly, with a shrug of the shoulders.
And it is certainly a far cry from the much more sober and modest idea of
natural law formulated by St Thomas Aquinas.

The concept can be traced back to the great Roman jurisconsults of the
second century A.D. They first evolved the concept of *jus gentium*, the law of
nations, to account for what they found to be common to all the various
tribal and national customary laws they encountered in the Roman Empire.
Principles of law and institutions that were found in all known bodies of law
were ascribed to this law of nations; for example, the inviolability of ambassadors and the principle that *pacta sunt servanda*, agreements are to be
honoured; and such institutions of diverse moral worth as marriage, slavery
and war. The law of nations was thus a body of universal law, compiled by
empirical observation (and empirical guesswork too, no doubt) and selection.

But under the influence of Stoic philosophy, which was overwhelmingly
influential among the Roman ruling classes in that age of the Antonine
Emperors, one of whom was the 'philosopher king' Marcus Aurelius, the
empirical concept of the law of nations (law in the strict juristic sense) spon-

taneously gave rise to the philosophical concept of natural law. And this, we must emphasize once more, is law only in an analogous sense. Natural law means, not rules, but principles derived from the nature of man and human society which ought to govern and delimit the making of law in the strict sense.

Thus natural law, to use a convenient piece of modern jargon, is 'meta-law'.[2] It pertains to the philosophy of law or of jurisprudence. Now law, whether in the strict or in the analogical sense, is certainly the concern of morals and the moral philosopher and theologian, but all the same it is a much narrower field than morals; and the attempt to reduce morals to law (which seems to be implied by much contemporary Catholic use of the debased concept of natural law) is perverse and back to front. Law has to be reduced and subordinated to morals, not vice versa.

So if natural law is some ultimate principle of human social conduct derived from the nature of man and of society, by which we may judge the validity, the rightness, the morality of law in the strict sense, then your notion of natural law will depend on your notion of human nature and human society. If you take a jaundiced, pessimistic, Hobbesian view of man and society, then you will no doubt reduce natural law to the law of the jungle and the one all-embracing principle 'Might is Right'. I can't help feeling that this, basically, is the deplorable thesis of the voluntarist school of legal philosophy, which defines law, in the strict sense, as the expressed will of the legislator. Here, to be sure, we have a *reductio ad absurdum* of the concept of natural law, which is possibly another reason for the disdain it is regarded with nowadays. Such a view of man and human society, however, is clearly un-Christian, and in the last analysis irrational. So let us now look at Thomas Aquinas' idea of natural law, based on a more positive estimate of human nature.

First of all, his definition of law in the strict sense, what he calls positive law (i.e. law that is posited or made by a legislator of any kind). Law can generally be described (not defined) as a set of enforceable rules, governing men's social relationships. It is also, to carry on describing what we refer to by the word, an essentially *contingent* set of rules, liable to change and repeal as social circumstances change. But to satisfy Aquinas' *definition* of true law, such a body of enforceable rules must be *rational* and *beneficent*. Law, he says, is an ordination of reason, promulgated by the proper authority for the common good (*STh* Ia IIae, 90, i, ii and iv; ET, vol. 28).

Thus all positive law (leaving aside positive laws considered to have been made by God) is subject to criticism, or rather to testing to see if it is true law or not, by the standard of what is reasonable and for the common good. And this standard, in effect, is what is meant by natural law; that our human nature as 'rational social animals' obliges us to be reasonable and to promote the common or social good. How? In *all* our personal conduct? Well, we are indeed obliged morally to be reasonable in all our personal conduct, and at least to ensure that our personal conduct is never detrimental to the common good. But the concept of natural law does not bear generally on all moral conduct, but specifically on positive law; on the laws legislators make to regulate our conduct, not on our personal conduct in itself.

That, at least, is how I would interpret and apply St Thomas. It is a most serious mistake to treat the concept of natural law as though it were a primary source from which to deduce either positive laws or precise rules of moral conduct. For one thing, moral conduct is not mainly a matter of keeping moral rules, but of responding to God's love and grace with love and gratitude in return, and hence of developing by practice those good habits which we call virtues.

For another thing practical rules of conduct, whether moral or legal, cannot be deduced *a priori* from universal principles. It is a logical mistake, a kind of residual Platonism or Cartesianism, an application of the technique of Euclidean geometry to the totally disparate field of concrete human behaviour, to suppose that they can. That is why the attempt, for example, in the encyclical letter of Paul VI, *Humanae Vitae* (1968), to present the teaching of the Catholic Church on the immorality of artificial contraception as *deriving* from the natural law is unconvincing. The teaching may well be in genuine accord with natural law, that is to say reasonable and conducive to the common good, though its opponents argue that it is very definitely not, since the common good, so they aver, calls for strict population control. But it cannot be derived from natural law, as a conclusion necessarily following from its premisses, and thus said to be, as the encyclical would have it, part of the natural law, because natural law properly considered is not that sort of premiss plus conclusion.

So what function does the genuine concept of natural law properly perform? A very similar function, I suggest, to that of the concept still often appealed to by lawyers, 'natural justice'. The two are not perhaps identical, but at least they have this in common that they provide principles (or a principle), not from which positive laws can be deduced, but by which the rightness or wrongness of any positive law and its application can be tested. Perhaps we could say that the difference between them is this: natural law provides us with a standard by which to judge the rightness or wrongness of positive laws as enacted by legislators; natural justice a standard by which to judge the rightness or wrongness of the application of these laws by police and judicial and executive officers.

St Thomas, attempting the logically impossible task (with his tongue somewhat in his cheek, I suspect) of formulating natural law into a rule or rules, said it boils down to saying 'Good is to be done and evil is to be avoided' (*STh* Ia IIae, 94, ii; ET, vol. 28). A fairly useless statement of moral principle, you may feel inclined to remark. And you are right, if what you are expecting is an axiom from which to deduce precise rules of conduct. But as a statement by which to assess the moral, and indeed genuinely legal value of the rules or laws laid down for us by legislators, it is of the greatest use. It establishes that to be binding in conscience these laws must be in accordance with reason and for the common good.

I am writing only a few miles from the Republic of South Africa. By this elementary criterion of natural law (and of natural justice, indeed) volume after volume of that country's laws can be ruled out as not genuine law and therefore not binding in conscience, because they are either designed, with greater or lesser cynicism, to safeguard sectional interests in the teeth of the *common* good (all the separate development legislation, Group Areas Act, influx control laws, pass laws etc.), or because they are based on irrational assumptions about men and society, like the Race Classification Act, for example, or those sections of the Immorality Act which forbid and invalidate marriages between whites and persons of other races. Of course, the defenders of these 'laws' will deny that they are irrational (though not always that they promote sectional interests); but then there are always those who, as the Prophet said, will call evil good and good evil, will put darkness for light and light for darkness (Isa 5:20).

Again, all 'laws' (it is the dominant tendency in most of the contemporary world) that put the government and its agents above any law, beyond any enforceable responsibility, all those security 'laws' that allow for detention without trial, without access, without redress, for any form of administrative punishment before any offence has been committed, like the South African practice of banning certain persons – they are not genuine laws at all and impose no moral obligations whatsoever, because they do not begin to measure up to the most basic standards of natural law or natural justice.

Again, the legalized actions of governments in piling up their armaments and their nuclear weapons are clearly found wanting when tested by the standard of natural law, because they are so manifestly against the common good of mankind, so irrationally out of all proportion even to the apparent good they are supposedly intended to promote ('defence'!!).

So, yes indeed, natural law is an invaluable concept for defending the rights of man and the humanity of humanity; and the Catholic Church can be proud of having clung to this unfashionable idea. But as a concept to enable us to elaborate and justify a complex set of moral rules, nearly all negative, about sexual morality – no, it doesn't work, any more than a motor car will run on skimmed milk, or a horse on a diet of steak and kidney pie.

C. RELIGIOUS CELIBACY

If we take marriage, as we have been doing, as the norm and standard with reference to which all sexual behaviour, or expression of sexuality, should be judged, then we have to state that not all deviations from this norm are regarded by the Christian tradition as reprehensible. The manifest deviation of abstaining from marriage and from sexual relations altogether has been traditionally regarded, if chosen for Christ's sake, as in the highest degree praiseworthy; and even if not chosen as a religious state, as entirely innocent and blameless. Christianity, in other words, insists on a general right to marry and on according great honour to the state of marriage, but knows of no general obligation to marry.

That marriage should not be regarded as obligatory needs little justification, perhaps. But that the choice of a celibate life 'for the sake of the kingdom of heaven' (Mt 19:12) should be regarded as even more honourable than marriage does call for explanation. The New Testament makes it quite clear that it is a genuine Christian option. Besides this passage in Matthew there is what St Paul has to say in 1 Cor 7:25–35. But how can this be if marriage is, as we have seen, an institution of creation established by God, and in addition a sacrament of the Church signifying and in some way even effecting or cementing the union of Christ and his Church?

We have, I think, to concede that the life of religious celibacy would not have been proper to mankind as created, in the state of innocence. Not of course, presumably, that in that state of marriage would have been obligatory – but that abstention from marriage would have had no particular religious significance or merit. But the state of religious celibacy is proper to fallen mankind as in need of redemption and redeemed. In this context much the same may be said about the celibate life as was said about the solitary life above in Chapter 14, C. It may be seen as having two values in the wider society of the Church and of redeemed and redeemable mankind.

In the first place, it is a sign of the kingdom to come, where according to the saying of Christ (Mk 12:25) all will be celibate and virgin (see also, for example, Rev 14:1–5). This is the gist of what St Paul is saying in 1 Cor 7. So celibacy, chosen for the sake of the kingdom of heaven, is an anticipation of the kingdom to come, and a reminder to Christians, both married and celibate, lay and religious, of its total priority over all other values. 'Seek first God's kingdom and his righteousness . . . ' (Mt 6:33).

In the second place the celibate life, whether lived in community or as a form of the solitary life, is or should be a significant protest against the corruption and distortion of human society, and especially of human and sexual relationships and marriage, in this world by sin. It is a kind of response to the prophetic summons to the exiles to 'go out from the midst of her [Babylon]'

(Isa 52:11: cf. 2 Cor 6:14–18). It is a style of life which in itself can state the radical criticism directed by the gospel against merely this-worldly values: wealth, power, prosperity, fame, popularity, pleasure, posterity. It is, as a religious mode of life, a valid way of siding with the humble, the poor, the neglected, the isolated, the outcasts and the scorned, who are the foundation members and the raw material of the kingdom of God.

NOTES

1 The term 'sexual behaviour' can have a wide range of meanings. In this chapter I mean by it genital behaviour, or behaviour likely to lead to genital behaviour.

2 As currently used, the prefix 'meta-' seems mostly to be a shorthand way of saying 'philosophy of . . .'. Thus 'meta-history' means philosophy of history, 'meta-science' means philosophy of science, and so on. But then it can be extended to refer to some concept or principle elaborated by such a 'philosophy of'. It is in this sense that I call the concept of natural law 'meta-law'. It is a concept elaborated by a particular philosophy of law, or philosophical jurisprudence. It is also a concept or principle that lies *behind* (*meta*) law in the strict sense.

But the point I am making with all this is that the word 'law' is not being used univocally but analogically in the expressions 'statute law', 'common law', 'canon law' on the one hand, and 'natural law' on the other. Those other 'laws' designate, or contain, many rules enacted by legislators. Natural law neither designates nor contains any such rules. It lies *behind* the laws enacted by lawmakers.

QUESTION FOR FURTHER DISCUSSION

1 Is it true to say that there are no absolutes in sexual morality?

17

Man as Male and Female III: The Cause of Women's Liberation

A. OLD TESTAMENT DOCTRINE

(i) Recapitulation of J and P positions

We noted above in Chapter 15, A, ii that it rather seems as if P discreetly corrected J on the matter of the equality of the sexes. Gen 1:27–28 says that man, male and female – i.e. the whole human species – was created by God in his own image and likeness, and then blessed and commanded to multiply and rule the earth. The distinction of the sexes is only referred to the utilitarian end of multiplication. By not even mentioning the social institution of marriage, P avoids so much as hinting at any social differentiation of the sexes according to their status and social roles. Each is equally human, equally in the image of God, each equally contributes to the perpetuation of the species and the domination of the earth.

J's earlier story, being more particular and concrete, does appear to have implied the subordination of woman to man, and it is this appearance, so we have suggested, that P deliberately countered with his more 'neutral' and colourless account of the distinction of the sexes. But it is possible that we have been a little unfair to J. Let us then look at his whole account rather more closely.

Let us begin by considering a text we did not notice at all in Chapter 15: Gen 3:16, God's sentence on the woman after the sin in paradise. The obvious, first-level meaning of the whole story of God's sentence on serpent, woman and man is aetiological (see above, Chapter 6, C, iv); why do snakes wriggle instead of walking, why do women suffer the pains of labour; and what particularly concerns us, *why are women subject to men*? That they are so subject is simply a fact of life in J's world (and P's too, for that matter). The answer: it is a punishment for sin; 'your desire shall be for your husband, and he shall rule over you'.

The point I wish to make is that J is not *justifying* the fact of social life which was female subjection; he is explaining it as a consequence of the primordial sin. So it is to be presumed that he did not regard it as a consequence of creation, or as part of the order of nature, whereas we can infer from Gen 2:23–24 that he did so regard the institution of marriage.

We can go on then to make a further inference, that any implication of female inferiority in the story of Gen 2 is not really intended by J. In Chapter 4, D we noted a very profound insight of St Augustine's, which in my view recaptured J's purpose in telling the story as he does, and that was that the woman's being fashioned from the man's rib, and not being jointly and simultaneously created with him, demonstrates the profound unity, and indeed kinship of the human race; the woman was not just the same species as the man, she was bone of his bone and flesh of his flesh.

But does this after all, necessarily imply the woman's subordination to man? So far we have tended to assume that it does. But perhaps all it necessarily implies is that the woman is second to the man. Now wherever you have more than one, one has to be named, or taken, or placed first, before the other or the others. But this does not make the first greater than the others. They can still all be equal. The man may be first, but there is nothing to stop us regarding him as merely *primus inter pares*, first among equals. I suggest that is how J regarded him, and shall return to the point when we come to see how St Paul takes up this passage.

(ii) *Discerning the doctrinal from the cultural content of the Old Testament*

That women on the whole are allotted not only a secondary but an inferior status in the pages of the Old Testament is undeniable. Israel was a patriarchal society. The God of Israel was the God of Abraham, Isaac and Jacob rather than the God (let alone the Goddess) of Sarah, Rebecca, Rachel and Leah. And Israelite society continued to be male-dominated from its beginnings right through to its culmination in the New Testament. We must not exaggerate, of course; women always had their recognized influence not only domestically but also on the larger social and religious stage. Of the matriarchs just mentioned one cannot altogether avoid the impression that at least Sarah and Rebecca would have worn trousers had anyone worn trousers in those days. And they, as much as their husbands, are typical figures as well as being individuals of character. In the time of the monarchy the queen mother was always a person of great importance in the kingdom.[1]

But yes, it was a male-dominated society. This male domination is built into the very structure and bias of all the law codes, which are really laws *for men*, many of which are laws *about women*. However, we are maintaining that the fact of these laws being in the Bible does not mean that it is part of the divine revelation of the divine will that all societies should be patriarchal and male-dominated. We are maintaining that this is a feature of Israelite culture which has to be acknowledged and understood, and even respected, as do all cultures, but which does not necessarily have to be copied, and which is also open, like all cultures, to criticism.

But the reader may legitimately be asking on what principle we decide that some things the Bible says (for example what we have been culling from J and P) are of doctrinal value and to be accepted in faith as conveying God's revelation to us, while other things, such as the acceptance of polygamy and the generally inferior status of women, are of no more than cultural and historical interest, and are certainly not normative.

First of all, in reply to the question, a non-principle. We must at all costs avoid slicing the scriptures up into a series of texts, some of which we label 'revelation', others of which we label 'non-revelation; cultural décor'. If what I have said gives the impression that that is what we are doing, then I have said it very badly. Behind such a misunderstanding lies the assumption that by revelation we mean a whole series of divine utterances, propositions, whether a divine code of laws or divine lectures on the nature of God and man. It is the assumption, which we criticized earlier, that the Bible is some kind of divine textbook on doctrine (Chapter 1, B).

The assumption which I am making here, and inviting readers to make with me, is that the Bible is the script of a tremendous drama, the drama of salvation of which God is the author. Every word of a drama, every stage direction even, is part of the play, and makes some contribution, however minute, to the dramatic whole. But clearly not every word is equally important or central or vital. Much of the text can be cut, and nearly always is, when the drama is staged. The Church invariably cuts most of scripture when it stages the drama – namely in the selection of scripture readings made for the lectionary at mass and in the divine office. The portions cut are not thereby rejected, but they are marked as being judged less important, perhaps even as being ephemeral and out of date.

So our question really is: on what principle is that judgement made? And I answer that it must be on a dramatic principle, culled from the nature of this particular drama. Now it is a drama of universal salvation, of salvation by the self-revelation of the living God to the whole of mankind in Jesus Christ. The basic structure of this particular drama is its division into two parts, the Old Testament and the New. Since we are dealing with a drama of action, there is movement, development, in each testament. The movement in the Old is from the universal mankind to the particular Israel, and by an implicit extension to the most particular and unique, Jesus Christ. The movement in the New is a kind of explosion outwards from the most particular, Jesus Christ, to the universal, all the nations of mankind.

Thus the final and dominant horizon of the drama is the universal, governed by the uniquely most particular, who as the last Adam has universal significance and relevance. In the light of this dominant horizon the particular, Israel, after its role in the drama has been played and its indispensable contribution made, yields to the newly created universal, the Church, the new people of God taken from all nations.

So the particular cultural characteristics of Israel, however much they have had the divine sanction in their own time, cannot be taken as normative for the whole of redeemed and redeemable mankind. After all, this necessarily comprises an enormous diversity of cultures. *But*, where the revelation made to Israel has a universal reference and relevance, as in the book of Genesis and its first eleven chapters in particular, as also in many of the profounder passages of the Old Testament where we find universally valid insights generated from Israel's particular experience (e.g. the ten commandments, the Song of Songs, Job, the Psalms, the heroic story of Saul and Jonathan and David, Amos, Hosea, Jonah, Isaiah); there, we may say, in some sense the Old Testament anticipates the New and provides us with values, doctrines, even norms that persist.

What I am proposing, I trust, is essentially the Pauline solution. The New Testament fulfils the Old, Christ is the end of the law, love is the fulfilment of the law (see Romans and Galatians, *passim*). In its Augustinian form, as stated at the conclusion of the Rule of St Augustine, the principle (which is a principle of Christian living as well as of biblical hermeneutics) runs, 'Let us now live like free people under grace, no longer like slaves set under the law'.

And this brings us at last to St Paul on the equality, or otherwise, of the sexes.

B. THE DOCTRINE OF ST PAUL AND OTHER NEW TESTAMENT WRITERS

(i) *St Paul's central position: Gal 3:26–28*

St Paul is a favourite target for some feminist critics nowadays, but it is possible that they criticize him for positions he did not adopt, and sometimes for statements that are not in fact his.

Let us begin with a statement which is certainly his and for which I am sure feminists do not criticize him but rather applaud him: 'In Christ Jesus you are all sons of God, through faith. For as many of you as were baptized into Christ have put on Christ. There is neither Jew nor Greek, there is neither slave nor free, there is neither male nor female; for you are all one in Christ Jesus' (Gal 3:26–28).

This RSV translation misses two nuances. The last phrase should read 'you are all one man (or person) in Christ Jesus' i.e. you are all simply Christ Jesus.

He is the 'one man' who you are. And in the previous sentence Paul did not preserve exactly the same contrast between the last pair as between the first two pairs. Instead of 'neither male nor female' he actually wrote 'no male and female'. True, it makes no difference to the sense; but it shows that he is directly referring to Gen 1:27, 'male and female he created them'.

Then Paul is in some sense negating Gen 1:27. 'There is *no* male and female', says he; 'male and female he created them', says P. Following my understanding of P, he is stating the *equality* of the sexes in the human species (as against at least the superficial implications of J's narrative). St Paul by negating P does not negate the equality – he negates the very distinction of sex. Things, to be equal, have first to be distinct and different. It is the distinction and difference Paul is negating. So he goes on to say 'You are all one man in Christ Jesus'. In Christ we have totally transcended any talk about equality or inequality, because we have transcended difference and division.

But of course, whatever Paul may say, the distinctions and differences still persist – the national or racial differences, the social and economic differences, and most ineluctably of all the sexual difference. Is St Paul, then, simply being supremely unrealistic, and shutting his eyes to the facts? No; he is only saying that 'in Christ', that is to say in our relations with Christ and in our mutual relations with each other in the context of Christ, these distinctions are of absolutely no significance whatsoever, particularly of no evaluatory significance. Relationships within the kingdom are not based on these distinctions and take absolutely no account of them.

In fact, I think his statement is of the same order as that of our Lord in the gospels that 'when they rise from the dead they neither marry nor are given in marriage, but are like angels in heaven' (Mk 12:25; see above, Chapter 15, C, ii). The distinction of the sexes, and therefore argument about the equality or inequality of the sexes, is a purely this-worldly affair.

So perhaps I was a little hasty in supposing that the supporters of equality of the sexes would applaud St Paul for his statement here in Gal 3:28. He is, in the last analysis, expressing a complete lack of interest in the cause that preoccupies them. You may certainly deduce from his remark that sexism, like racism, is a nonsense theory and an un-Christian prejudice. But you cannot, I fear, deduce any practical consequences about the practical ordering of worldly society. St Paul never deduced the abolition of slavery, for example, from his negating of the distinction between slave and free 'in Christ', and for the same reason he produced no practical conclusions about eliminating the social subordination of women. Whatever the ordering of worldly society – this I think is all that St Paul ever says – don't take it too seriously, don't worry about it too much, either to value or to devalue it, either to venerate it or to cast it down.

(ii) The position of women in the Church: 1 Cor 11:3–16; 14:34–35

Paul, however, did have to deal with the practical ordering of the Christian community in this world, and we are given a glimpse of how he did it in 1 Corinthians. A very good guide here is the commentary on the epistle in the series *New Testament Message* (no. 12), by Jerome Murphy-O'Connor, OP. Paul, he points out, is answering questions submitted by the Corinthians and dealing with problems he sees among them. So we do not rightly understand his answers and solutions unless we know what the questions and problems were – and we can only infer what they were from his answers and solutions! Rather a problem of its own; something of a 'hermeneutic circle'.

However, in 1 Cor 11:3–16 Fr Jerome infers that the problem was not female dress or deportment, as the Jerusalem Bible, for example, supposes with its heading 'Women's behaviour at services', but the deportment of both sexes. In modern terms, there was a tendency to 'unisex' among them – not in clothes, so much, because in those days neither sex wore trousers, just as today both do; but in hair style. St Paul disapproved. We have seen him assert 'unisex' in Gal 3:28 most uncompromisingly – but that is in Christ, in the kingdom, in the resurrection, in the spirit. Here, in the order of time and space, the sexes manifestly *are* distinct and Christians have no business to try and pretend they are not. Murphy-O'Connor guesses that what St Paul is afraid of here, and what embarrasses him so as to make the whole passage messy and unclear, is a tendency to homosexuality. I rather doubt it; if that was what St Paul was afraid of, I cannot imagine him being too embarrassed to say so. I suggest he simply wanted the Corinthian Christians to be respectable and to observe the usual conventions in such matters, in order to avoid the gospel being dismissed as the weird fad of a bunch of Jesus-freaks.

But that is not our concern here. Insisting on men and women doing their hair in conventionally accepted masculine and feminine styles is not in the least damaging to the equality of the sexes. It is Paul's argument in favour of his ruling that appears to be theologically sexist and to give a doctrinal reason for the subordination of women.

The appearance, says Murphy-O'Connor, is deceptive, however. If you read carefully, you will see that Paul is all along *assuming* the equality of the sexes in the Christian community. In v. 5 he assumes that women pray and prophesy (i.e. lead the prayers and do the preaching) in exactly the same way as men. Only he thinks they should do it with their heads covered, and men should do it bare-headed (and with short back and sides). Why? It is to explain why that Paul goes in for his rather involved argument, which depends on a play on the word 'head', and also on an order between man and woman – which is the order, of course, between the first man and the first woman.

Paul is certainly saying 'Man first, woman second'. But he is not saying 'Woman subordinate to man'. Even among equals an order of first and second is unavoidable. Man is only *primus inter pares*, as we inferred above (A, i) was J's view, which Paul here takes up. This essential equality and mutual dependency is made crystal clear in vv. 11 and 12. That the order of man first and woman second is an order among *equals* is proved by the comparison with which Paul starts (v. 3), where he is playing on the word 'head'. How his play on that word should support his practical contention that men should have short hair and not wear hats in church while women should wear their hair long and hats on top of it, I do not understand – nor greatly care. But what *is* clear is that he is saying, following J's creation story, 'Woman comes from man as Christ comes from God', or 'Woman is to man as Christ is to God'. Now, how is Christ to God? For 'Christ' and 'God' we can and should read 'the Son' and 'the Father'. Now on the one hand the Son is *equal* to the Father, equally divine, true God from true God; but on the other hand he is *from* the Father, the second person of the Trinity, never the first. Still, he is equal to the Father. So is woman, then, equal to man, equally human, true human being from true human being in J's account. Thus she is the second of the human pair, and yet equal to the man, to her husband, who is the first.

That putting the woman second and the man first has, however, generally led to the subordination of females to males is certainly true. And that, according to Murphy-O'Connor, is why Paul puts in that strange little passage about angels, in v. 10. This is not yet another reason for insisting on and demonstrating the inferiority of women; on the contrary it is a sign to the angels that women, though second to men as the Son is to the Father, are still their equals in authority. This is how his commentary puts it:

'Therefore a woman ought to have authority on her head, because of the angels' (v. 10). The initial 'therefore' refers to the summary of Gen 2:18–23 in vv. 8–9, which had traditionally been used to prove the subordination of woman to man. For Paul this situation (of subordination) has changed; 'therefore' the woman had to have some symbol on her head to show that she now had the 'authority' to fulfil a role previously denied her. This was 'for the sake of the angels' who were associated with the giving of the Law (Gal 3:19), whose application had been modified.

Readers may feel that this attempt to rescue St Paul is very hard going – whether or not they find it convincing. But surely, they will say, nothing can save the apostle from his feminist critics for what he says later on in the same letter at 14:34–35: 'the women should keep silence in the churches. For they are not permitted to speak, but should be subordinate, as even the law says . . . . For it is shameful for a woman to speak in church.'

Fr Jerome leaps over this hurdle with effortless ease: 'these verses are not written by Paul'. This assertion is supported by the fact that several MSS put these verses at the end of the chapter after v. 40, which does suggest that they began life as a marginal gloss that different copyists inserted into the text at different places. Furthermore, in substance they contradict what Paul had already written in 11:5 and 13, where he took it for granted that women spoke in church just like men. And lastly their appeal to the Law as final authority is entirely at odds with Paul's whole attitude to the Law, which for him had simply ceased to be normative.

Let him then not be taken to task for these sexist verses. If anybody has to be blamed it should be the author of the pastoral epistles to Timothy and Titus – a man who certainly thought of himself as a true disciple of Paul's, but still, according to the almost universal consensus of scholars, was not in fact the apostle.

(iii)   The pastoral epistles: 1 Tim 2:11–15

These letters, most probably a Pauline fiction, fictitiously addressed to Timothy and Titus and composed perhaps some forty years after the apostle's death, were written with Christian communities in mind which were worlds away from the flamboyant Corinthians St Paul had had to deal with. They seem to have been written by a man who indeed thought of himself as a disciple of St Paul, since he would scarcely have written in his name otherwise; but who was again worlds away from the mind of the apostle.

In the matter that we are dealing with, he shared Paul's concern that Christian communities should be 'respectable' in the eyes of the world; but he gives in to the standards of the prevailing culture (or possibly a particular counter-culture) in a way that might, I like to suppose, have rather shocked his master. And so his attitude to women's place in the Church is precisely that of the two verses 1 Cor 14:34–35, which we have just seen were intruded into St Paul's letter. Could those verses perhaps have been this 'pastoralist's' own gloss? They are very much in his style. Or else they had already found their way into the copies of 1 Corinthians circulating among the Churches, and this writer developed them into what he says in 1 Tim 2:11–15: 'Let a woman learn in silence with all submissiveness. I permit no woman to teach or to have authority over men: she is to keep silent. For Adam was formed first, then Eve; and Adam was not deceived, but the woman was deceived and became a transgressor. Yet woman will be saved through bearing children, if she continues in faith and love and holiness, with modesty.'

I have no hesitation in saying this represents a cultural, not a theological, judgement. It is a judgement, to be sure, that is given a little theological dressing, with its reference to J's narrative of Adam and Eve. But if you compare it to Paul's use of this narrative that we have already discussed, which however 'embarrassed' it may have been was certainly profound, you will see how superficial this one is. One suggestion propounded by Ronald Knox (in *New Testament Commentary*, III, London, 1956, p. 7) is that the sentence 'she will be saved through bearing children' should be translated more literally, 'she will be saved through the Child-bearing', i.e. through the bearing of the child Jesus by the second Eve, which is thus presented as the saving of the whole female sex. An interesting, but I fear an unlikely, exegesis.

To call what is said in this passage a cultural judgement is not, let me remind the reader, to call it a bad or wrong judgement; it is merely to assert that it is not doctrinally normative for all Christians at all times. Perhaps it had its validity in the communities for which it was written, round about the end of the first century. I suggested above that rather than being a concession to the values of the prevailing culture (the pagan Hellenistic culture of the eastern provinces of the Roman Empire), it may have represented the stand of a counter-culture. What I mean is that it may represent one element in a process of 're-Judaization' of the *mores* of some Christian communities, in protest and moral self-defence against the general looseness of gentile manners, for which strait-laced Christians may rightly or wrongly have blamed 'emancipated' upper-class women. There were undoubtedly several orgiastic pagan cults in which women took the lead. It is equally certain that the social position of women in Jewish culture was even lower than among the Greeks and Romans.

Whatever the rights and wrongs of it at the time, this purely cultural judgement on the subordinate place of women in the Christian community came to be the general norm in the Church in all the centuries that followed until our own day, so that even those feminine institutions to which the New Testament bears witness, deaconesses (Rom 16:1) and the order of widows (1 Tim 5:3–16), eventually faded out into total obsoleteness. In fact, in this latter passage we can already perhaps observe moves to limit the order of widows and restrict its influence. The author desires younger widows to marry again (v. 14), which will have the effect of preventing them from ever being enrolled in the order if they are widowed a second time (v. 9).

This state of affairs has been unfortunate, to say the least, and has given a cultural judgement the spurious appearance of a doctrinal norm. To be sure, there have been great women saints, women in Church history who have had their influence on affairs. There has been the huge contribution to the life of the Church by the religious orders of women. But the fact is that it is only in the last century or so that women religious in the Catholic Church have out-numbered the men. And I think it is also true to say that women have played an even smaller part in shaping the history of the Christian Church than they have in the secular history of Europe from the beginning of our era until the present day. After all, there have nearly always been women, whether wives or mistresses, in the lives of the men who have made secular history, and many of these women have been able to exercise a strong indirect influence on affairs. But what influence have women ever been able to exercise on papal policy, for example, with the somewhat opposite exceptions of St Catherine of Siena in the fourteenth century, and of Marozia, 'the mother, the mistress and the murderess of popes', in the tenth? John Knox's complaint in the sixteenth about 'the monstrous regiment [i.e. government] of women', aimed at Mary of Guise, Regent of Scotland, and Mary I of England, had no foundation at all where the Catholic Church was concerned.

C. CHRISTIAN DOCTRINE AND WOMEN IN THE CHURCH TODAY

(i) Equality of the sexes, and sex roles

The Church, then, in spite of this long and rather depressing history of a cultural discriminatory judgement on the position of women, is committed to the doctrine of the basic equality of the sexes. What does this mean in practice? I think it means that the Church is committed to sponsoring and promoting the political and economic equality of women with men, equal pay for equal work, equal political rights, equal political and economic opportunities.

In principle this should be so in every society and culture. But in concrete practice and in particular situations a certain reserve, what is traditionally called an 'economy', an accommodation with prevailing cultural patterns, has to be observed. Thus while the Church (in my opinion) can and should support all moves to ensure such equality of women with men in Europe and North America, I would put this cause much lower down on its list of priorities in Asia and Africa. Not that the Church authorities in these parts of the world should care less for women; but that women here, and their menfolk and children, are likely to have more immediate interests to be safeguarded and needs to be met than political and economic emancipation. As it has probably been right sometimes for the Church to tolerate slavery (but never to condone it, though this I fear has at times been done), so it can still be right in some places to tolerate (but not to condone) the social subordination of women.

However, to proclaim the basic equality of women with men is not to be obliged to take up any particular position on the roles of the sexes in society. It is, I grant, to be obliged to say that roles should not be distributed in such a way that all the plums of power and influence go to the men, and all the drudgeries to women, since that would be to negate equality. One cannot in the same breath say that the sexes are equal and that being a member of parliament or a top civil servant are exclusively male roles. But I do not see that the equality of the sexes is necessarily undermined if there is a cultural consensus that being an engine-driver, for example, or a deep-sea diver are exclusively male roles, while being a midwife or a typist are exclusively female ones. Here the decision is purely a cultural one, though it must be judged in the light of Christian doctrine, which at the very least would insist that such distinctions cannot be made absolute.

(ii)   Women in the Church today

We have just observed that one cannot, without contradiction (and indeed without hypocrisy), affirm the equality of the sexes and at the same time earmark all positions of power and influence in society as the exclusive preserve of one of them. But that is what the Catholic Church is, de facto, doing at the moment. The rights, the dignity, the equality of women are being proclaimed and asserted as part of the total Christian view of man with a sureness and clarity never heard in ecclesiastical pronouncements before. And that is excellent, something to rejoice over. But at the same time any suggestions about opening the ranks of the clergy to women meet continually with official disapproval. Now it is true that power in the Catholic Church is not any longer quite the exclusive clerical preserve that it used to be. This is the age of the lay apostolate, of increasingly influential lay movements, in all of which women can and do play as big a role as men. Still, in the last resort authority in the Church continues to reside with the clergy, particularly with the bishops, above all with the Pope and the Roman curia. As long as these bastions of ecclesiastical power are officially closed to women, then so long is the Catholic Church in practice insisting on the subordination of women to men in the Church – whatever it may say to the contrary.

Are there any doctrinal, theological, revealed reasons why women should not, and indeed cannot, be validly ordained? I confess I have never come across any. All the reasons that have been put forward have been based on the premiss of the natural subordination and inferiority of women – which we have been at pains to see is by no means a premiss of revelation. The only reason of any strength that can be put forward is that this has never been done in the Catholic Church or the Orthodox Church or any of the ancient Churches. This argument from custom is a powerful one. But in the light of what may be regarded as the revealed doctrine of the Church on the equality of the sexes, one needs to ask why women have never been ordained. And on examination all the reasons why they have not turn out to be cultural, not doctrinal. As I have suggested above, these reasons boil down to a prolonged and regrettable cultural inheritance from Israel and Judaism, which really has no place in the universal Catholic people of God of the future.

NOTE

1   So she still is in the African kingdom of Swaziland, still a very traditional, male-domin-
    ated society. But there the office of queen mother, or Ndhlovukati, the Great She-
    Elephant, is so important that even when there is no longer an actual queen mother,
    because she is dead, a substitute has to be chosen from among her sisters, or even, as was
    recently the case, from among the king's senior wives.

QUESTION FOR FURTHER DISCUSSION

1   How can we set about promoting women's liberation from male domination in all
    societies, and at the same time respect the great variation in sex roles to be found in
    different cultures?

18
Unity and Pluriformity of Mankind

A. THE PROBLEM SET

(i) Recapitulation

The pluriformity of mankind is a mere fact of experience – the multiplicity of races, nations, cultures and languages is there for all to see. We have already had occasion to make a general and preliminary theological judgement on this fact, a rather negative one; namely that no particular cultural value may, as such, be regarded as absolute, or as normative for the whole human race; nor may any one culture or nation, language or race be properly and fairly judged in terms of the particular values of any other culture, nation, language or race (Chapter 17, A, ii; cf. also 14, B, ii; 15, B, i and C, iii; 16, B, i and ii). When this is done (and I fear it is never not being done), the result is cultural imperialism, and this is a *bad thing*. It amounts to the eye saying to the hand 'I have no need of you' (1 Cor 12:21).

But of course I can only make this judgement about cultural imperialism on the supposition of the unity of mankind. This too, most rational people would agree, is a fact, a biological fact at least. It is not, however, a fact that is so palpably and personally experienced as the fact of human racial and cultural diversity. If it were, we would be spared the wicked nonsense of racism and kindred lunatic social attitudes.

But in any case the unity of mankind has the honour of being what we might call a theological fact, a fact very firmly and theologically attested by both J and P in their stories about origins. Gen 1 – 11 deliberately and explicitly tells the early story not of Israel but of mankind. P gives all men in common the quality of being in the image and likeness of God (Gen 1:26–27; 5:1–3; 9:6), a unifying, specific quality. J gives the whole human race a common ancestor, thus making all men one kin (Gen 2:21–24).

(ii) P and J on human pluriformity

The reader will not be surprised to learn, however, that starting from this common base the two traditions give very different evaluations of the fact of human pluriformity. P does little more than register it, in the genealogy of the descendants of Noah in Gen 10 (there is a fragment of a J genealogy inserted, the piece about Nimrod in vv. 8–12). But this implies P's acceptance of the diversification of humanity into seventy or seventy-two nations[1] as part of the natural course of history, the providential way in which the destiny of mankind was to unfold.

For J, on the other hand, the division of mankind into nations speaking mutually incomprehensible languages is a curse, a consequence of sin, as he makes clear in his story of the tower of Babel, Gen 11:1–9.

P's is the rational, humane, sensible view. J perceives the dramatic, the tragic tension between the created reality of human kinship, universal brotherhood, and the historical reality of human division. Again, we have differences of emphasis rather than stark alternative and mutually exclusive options (see above, Chapter 4, A; also Chapter 3 and Chapter 14, B, i). And though J does perceive that there is a problem, an issue to be resolved, it is still, even for him, only a potential or latent problem, because in his time and in the whole era of the Old Testament there was no actual move or impulse or historical tendency to rediscover the unity that, in his legend, had been shattered on the plain of Shinar.

(iii)   Exclusivism and universalism: Jonah

The issue, or a closely related one, does crop up again however in the Old Testament. After the return from exile the predominant mood of Judaism eventually became one of a severe and narrow exclusivism. The Jews will have nothing to do with the Gentiles; all co-operation and fraternizing with the Samaritans is refused. After the backslidings of their previous history their leaders decided that the only way they could henceforth remain faithful to the Lord their God was by this rejection of all association with Gentiles. They were the chosen nation, and they must keep themselves pure. Their religious and their national identity were entirely fused together; and so of course their religious and their national destiny were entirely fused together, until they came to expect a positive destiny in the age to come, in the *eschaton*, for Israel alone – and for the Gentiles nothing but destruction.

Thus the dominant strand of Judaism came to be tied to a cultural particularism, and indeed to a cultural absolutism, that simply ignored the unity, the common humanity of mankind. This outlook stems mainly from the D theology that took its final form during the exile (see Chapter 14, note 4). Later writings which bear this stamp are Ezra and Nehemiah (Ez 4:1–3, 9 – 10, Neh 2:19–20, 13:23–31), Obadiah, Nahum, parts of Daniel (e.g. Dan 7), and most of the extra-canonical apocalyptic literature. At the time of the

New Testament this point of view is that of the Pharisees, and even more so of the Zealots and the Essenes; less so of the Sadducees.

But there were other voices, other agents of divine revelation in the total Israelite and Judaic tradition; voices trained, one might say, in the J choir. They are heard in the psalms for example (e.g. Ps 87); here and there in the prophets (Isa 19:23–25; 66:18–21; Zech 8:20–23; rather negatively in Amos 9:7). The clearest and the most satirical of these voices, however, proclaiming a doctrine of universalism against the exclusivism we have noted, is that of the author of the book of Jonah. It ought not to need saying, but I fear it does, that this author is *not* writing a piece of history which we moderns cannot swallow quite so easily as the whale swallowed Jonah. He is writing a satirical story; Jonah is his anti-hero, the representative of narrow Israelite exclusivism; and twice over, in the episode of the storm at sea and the whale, and the concluding episode of the castor-oil plant that shrivels up, the laugh is on Jonah for his ridiculous prejudices (as the author considers them). The truth is, in the author's view, that the God of Israel is the God of all men (Rom 3:29, 10:12), and as he sends prophetic warnings, and shows mercy, to Israel, so likewise does he do even to the most hated of the Gentiles, the brutal Assyrians in their great city of Nineveh.

B. THE KINGDOM OF GOD

(i) *The issue between unity and pluriformity resolved in the fullness of the kingdom*

When Jesus Christ came preaching the kingdom of God, the issue between the unity and the variety of mankind that was for the most part only latent and potential in the Old Testament was at once activated and brought to a crisis. For the proclamation of the kingdom initiated a real, active movement for the unification of the human race, for a gathering of the scattered children of God, in John's words, into one (Jn 11:52). And this at once raises the problem of respecting the genuine worth of innumerable varieties of culture, language and nationality that characterize these children of God (potentially the whole of mankind) in their scattered state.

Now in the fullness of the kingdom this problem is transcended. There is fulfilment both of unity and of diversity. We have already seen that in the fullness of the *eschaton*, in the achievement of the destiny for which God's creation was predestined from the beginning, both J's ideal of the garden and P's ideal of the city will be perfectly realized (Chapter 4, A, iii); that both the vision of 'sacred anarchy' and of sacred monarchy will come true in the kingdom of God where everyone shares in the kingship (Chapter 14, B, ii). In the same way all will be one (Jn 17:21), all will be the perfect (and of course symbolic) number of 144,000 from the twelve tribes of Israel (i.e. one nation), and yet they will be a multitude which no man could number from every nation, from all tribes and peoples and tongues (Rev 7:4–9).

Luke has this eschatological fullness of the kingdom, transcending all these tensions, symbolized in his account of its temporal inauguration – I almost wrote 'its *historical* inauguration', but I would not wish Luke to be supposed to be necessarily giving a factual description of the beginnings. Anyway, in the gospel he concentrates Jesus' last appearances to his disciples in *Jerusalem*, the symbolic centre, the city that is 'one united whole' (Ps 122:3, JB translation; 'bound firmly together', RSV); the city that is the mother of men of many nations (Ps 87:5, LXX). And yet from this symbolic centre of unity the apostles are to preach the gospel of the kingdom to all nations (Lk 24:47). This picture of action radiating from a centre provides the whole symbolic structure of the same author's Acts of the Apostles.

But the transcendence of division coupled with the maintenance of diversity in unity is most vividly signified by the actual story of Pentecost. Men from 'every nation under heaven' (Acts 2:5 – a symbolically necessary exaggeration) are gathered in the holy city, the symbol of unity. And when the moment of actualizing or inaugurating the kingdom comes, and the Holy Spirit is poured out 'upon all flesh' (2:17), the disciples are heard to speak the *one* message of salvation, the wonderful works of God (2:11), but in *all* the various languages there represented. The miracle was not that all the nationalities gathered there were suddenly enabled to understand the one sacred language (for there is no such language, not even Hebrew, which was by then a dead language anyway), but that the disciples spoke all the languages, thus lifting the curse of Babel without eliminating the variety of the nations.

(ii)   The issue remains acute in the Church in the New Testament

But if the issue is resolved in the final glory of the kingdom, in a manner which we can state paradoxically but cannot explain or comprehend (for the kingdom of God can only be known as a mystery, Mk 4:11; RSV: 'secret'), it remains acutely unresolved in the life of the Church. The Church is not the kingdom of God in its fullness, but it is committed to the cause of the kingdom, it is the kingdom in the process of coming to be and taking shape. And in its task of inaugurating the kingdom and promoting its values, the Church has throughout its history found itself torn between the claims of *unity* and the claims of *catholicity*, which is another word for pluriformity. Let us first look at the Church struggling with this issue in the New Testament, and then in its subsequent history.

The form it takes in the New Testament is a continuation and a concretization in action of the tension we noted above between exclusivism or particularism and universalism in post-exilic Judaism. But in the New Testament it becomes much more acute, because of the Church's missionary drive to actualize human unity in an *inclusive* universalism. The process inevitably calls forth a reaction from the ingrained particularism of the dominant form of Pharisaic Judaism.

The reaction that we are interested in here is not that of the Jews who rejected Christ and the Christian gospel, who listened to Paul in silence as he described his conversion, until he told them how Christ said to him 'I will send you far away to the Gentiles', and then lifted up their voices and said 'Away with such a fellow from the earth! For he ought not to live' (Acts 22:21–22). It is rather that of the Jewish Christians for whom unity meant in practice uniformity, and hence the conversion of Gentiles not only to Christianity but to Judaism.

They accept (with some surprise) that the gospel of salvation should be preached even to the Gentiles, after Peter has told them all the circumstances of his visit to Cornelius (11:18). But they think all Gentile converts should be circumcised and keep the law of Moses – i.e. adopt Jewish culture lock, stock and barrel (15:1). There had been a kind of presentiment of this clash between Jewish and Gentile culture within the Church in the earlier dissension within the original Jerusalem community itself between 'the Hebrews and the Hellenists' (6:1), i.e. between the native Palestinian Christians and the Greek-speaking 'returned exiles' from the diaspora, both parties being Jews, but with marked cultural differences.

In both crises (Acts 6 and 15) the policy of the apostles was to preserve unity by insisting on a proper tolerance of cultural diversity – which is indeed the only way to preserve any larger unity that is to embrace heterogeneous groups. The most outspoken proponent of diversity in unity among the apostles was St Paul. He was in fact far more vehement in this sense than Luke makes him out to be in Acts. For Luke is inclined to play down (though he certainly does not ignore) internal conflict, and so he has Paul founding Churches on the uniform model of Jewish synagogues with their ordained elders (Acts 14:23, 20:17–28), the model that was to become universally accepted in the post-apostolic Churches, whereas to judge from Paul's letters, especially 1 and 2 Corinthians, several of the Churches he founded did not follow this model, but some like the Philippians (1:1) did. Quite apart, however, from the matter of diversity in ecclesiastical organization, Paul took the line that not only was it wrong to force Gentiles to adopt Jewish customs, it was wrong for them to do so even if they did it willingly. For to do so as a matter of religious obligation was to misunderstand the whole nature of salvation in Christ (Gal 2:11–21, 5:2–6; the whole epistle, indeed).

If St Paul was the champion of pluriformity in the Church and among the

Churches[2] (in the interests of an all-embracing unity), then the 'Paul' who wrote the pastoral epistles, probably several decades after the apostle's death, represents a growing call to more uniformity, in the interests of a more re-assuringly visible unity. This partly consists in the re-imposition to some extent of Judaic customs and attitudes, a re-assertion of the dominance of Jewish culture over Christian communities which was inevitable, given the place of the scriptures in Christian life (see above, Chapter 17, B, iii); and partly in the general insistence on a common form of ministerial organization for the Churches, modelled on that of the synagogue. The ministry as we find it in the pastorals is not yet that which soon became universal in all Churches, a ministry of bishop, presbyters (priests) and deacons; but it is well on the way to it. It is a Church structure which can be held to conflict with the free, charismatic, almost 'anarchic' form of community to be divined from 1 Cor 12:28–31 or Eph 4:7–13.

C.   THE ISSUE OF UNITY AND PLURIFORMITY

(i)   Church history

To appreciate how the issue keeps on recurring throughout Church history, we have to begin by realizing how different in fundamental ways the early Church was from the Catholic Church we know today.[3] There was then no universal organization, with a common centre in Rome, as we now know it. The Church did not begin as an organization but as a movement, which spread rapidly and established itself in local communities of believers. These, to be sure, of necessity developed an internal organization or structure, and by the year 120 or thereabouts all these communities, these Churches, had adopted the same basic organization of one episcopus (bishop) or 'super-intendent' presiding over the community, assisted by presbyters (priests) or 'elders' and by deacons or 'servants'.

These communities were in constant communication with each other, and thought of themselves as forming one world-wide brotherhood, fellowship or communion, which from at least 109 onwards is called the *Catholic* (universal) Church, or simply the *Catholica* for short. The word is first used in a letter of St Ignatius of Antioch, martyred in that year.

But world-wide unity as yet presented few problems, and a superstructure of world-wide organization and relationships, governed by law and custom, only developed slowly. Unity *within* each community or Church was often a pressing concern, as we can already see in the New Testament from Paul's letters to the Corinthians. But on the wider stage, though there was a gradual and quiet move towards a greater cohesion, regional diversity was the general rule – diversity in structure (i.e. in the relationships between the Churches of a region), diversity in liturgy, in language, even in credal formulae. Some Churches were more important than others, and so had great influence and in some cases overriding authority over their smaller neighbours in a region. Such were the Churches of the great cities, of Rome, Alexandria, Antioch, Ephesus, Carthage, Caesarea in Palestine, and from the fourth century onwards, as the supreme centre of Christian pilgrimage, Jerusalem. So while there was great cultural diversity, there was also constant mutual interaction and assimilation of customs going on. But the dominant dynamism of Christianity was expansion accompanied by diversification. Breaches in unity were nearly always of a local or regional character, like the Donatist schism in Africa in the fourth century.

From the fifth century onwards, however, it seems to be the very diversification of Christianity that begins to put a strain upon the unity of the Catholica. It is so *catholic*, so all-embracing, that it finds it increasingly difficult to remain *one*. The tensions are at first greatest in the East between the great sees of Alexandria in Egypt and Antioch in Syria; then more seriously and fatally between Alexandria and Constantinople, newly sprung to prominence and power as the imperial capital.

Christianity provided the people of Egypt and Syria (and other places too, of course) with a means and a context in which to express their own native and ancient cultures in their own languages. But it seems as if, with the official conversion of the Roman Empire to Christianity, the Christian communities in the seats of power, above all the Church of Constantinople, were tempted to launch out on a course of religious cultural imperialism. It was this, and the resentment of it, as much as the power struggles of ecclesiastical patriarchs and genuine doctrinal divisions, that eventually shattered the unity of the Catholica when the large Monophysite Churches broke away after the Council of Chalcedon in 451.

Then in the following centuries a similar cultural rift began between the Christian East centred on Constantinople and the Christian West centred on Rome, until the split became final in 1054. Here the division was almost wholly cultural and political. The doctrinal differences were minimal, and what there were were blown up out of all proportion by the cultural and political animosity with which they were ventilated.

As I see it, it was not in fact the pluriformity of the Catholica that destroyed its unity (so I here qualify what I have just written three paragraphs above), but the growing refusal to accept and welcome that diversity. More and more, this feature of Christendom was barely tolerated, until one was left with two great centres of influence and cultural power, Rome and Constantinople, confronting one another in postures of mutual incomprehension and intolerance, each centre with a vast and enthusiastically loyal, loyally bigoted hinterland behind it. Each in turn was guilty, sometimes more, sometimes less, of cultural imperialism. They were both, perhaps, shown at their worst in the middle of the ninth century during what is called the Photian schism, when they were fighting over who should control the newly converted Bulgars. Photius in Constantinople and Nicholas I in Rome, perhaps miscalled the Great, were two equally forceful and ambitious personalities attempting to extend and consolidate the authority of their sees.

Thus policies of centralization and uniformity, unless pursued within extremely modest limits, are seen to be the real enemies of a truly catholic unity.

From the eleventh century until the present day policies of centralization and uniformity have been consistently pursued by the papacy – and rarely, if one may say so, within modest limits. They have chiefly affected the Western or Latin Church, though they were largely responsible for aborting the two attempts at reunion with the East in the thirteenth and fifteenth centuries. But the diversity of those Eastern Churches that have remained in communion with Rome or been restored to it has often been little more than tolerated in a lordly sort of way, instead of being warmly and fraternally and humbly welcomed. Their missionary expansion, for example, has not been encouraged. When they have spread with immigration to the New World, where their communities are to be found living cheek by jowl with Latin Catholics, they have been forbidden to practise some of their customs, notably that of having a married clergy. One presumes that this prohibition was imposed to prevent them 'scandalizing', or more probably 'tempting', their Latin brethren. This is an instance of cultural imperialism staging a frontal attack on genuine catholicity.

Within the Latin Church the Protestant Reformation, or the Reformatory Protest, was eventually inevitable; and once again it was to a large extent a cultural, frequently a nationalistic, protest against alien cultural domination. The excessive preoccupation with a unity envisaged as uniformity, or at any rate as conformity; the obsession with the unlimited nature and as far as possible the unlimited exercise of papal authority which has been the characteristic Roman, curial neurosis for the last eight centuries; these have not truly served the unity, and have seriously compromised the catholicity, of the one, holy, catholic and apostolic Church. Since the Middle Ages this Church has been increasingly known as the Roman Catholic Church, or the holy Catholic and Roman Church; and I think one has to admit that it has often and in many respects been more Roman than Catholic.

With the ecumenical movement of the present century, finally endorsed by the Catholic Church in the Second Vatican Council, 1962–65, it seems to me that we are seeing one of the truly momentous turning points in the history of the Church, a fitting prelude to the third millennium of that history. For it is not only a movement towards the *unity* of a fragmented Christian people; it is also a movement towards the acceptance and indeed the encouragement of genuine *catholicity*. The realization is being forced on Christians as they seek unity that it will only be possible if they accept in each other an almost unlimited diversity. 'One body, one Spirit, one hope, one Lord, one faith, one baptism, one God and Father of us all' (Eph 4:4–6) – yes indeed. That is what unity is all about. But it cannot be achieved if any of us is going to go on insisting on any kind of *uniformity*. Let us not forget: all those people in Jerusalem at the first Christian Pentecost did *not* suddenly all know Hebrew (let alone Latin); instead they heard the one message of salvation proclaimed in the languages (which means the cultures, the thought forms, the common attitudes and prejudices) of every nation under heaven.

The reader may be wondering what this discussion of unity and diversity in the Church has to do with our topic of the unity and pluriformity of the human race. Well, in the first place it is a kind of paradigm or concrete illustration of the wider issue. But it is also much more than that (for the Christian). It is, at the very least, the master paradigm of the wider issue.

One of the most profound statements of the Second Vatican Council is one that is to be found in the opening paragraph of its Constitution on the Church, *Lumen Gentium*. It says there, 'Since the Church is, in Christ, a kind of sacrament, that is to say a sign and instrument, of intimate union with God and the unity of the whole human race, this sacred synod intends to declare its nature and its universal mission more plainly both to its faithful members and to the whole world' (I, 1). This is as much as to say that one cannot truly think of Christianity and the Church simply as one religion and one religious community among others in human history, simply as one particular feature, one element in the bewildering mosaic pattern of that history.

No, from the point of view of Christian theology the centre of human history is the mystery of the incarnation; and therefore the history of the Church which issues from that centre, and the history of Israel in the Old Testament which leads into it, this total 'sacred history' is as it were the central core or armature of all human history. The Church is a kind of sign and instrument (a sacrament, that is to say) of the unity of the whole human race. It is this because it is also a kind of sacrament of intimate union with God, and the history of the whole human race is directed to the destiny of intimate union with God, and has no meaning without reference to this union.

It follows then that the extent and manner in which the Church succeeds in 'becoming what it is' and in making itself a really visible and effective sign both of an all-embracing unity and a genuine, spontaneously variegated catholicity is of direct relevance to the future geopolitical history of mankind.

(ii)   In the secular world

Though there are not really two kinds of history, secular and sacred, and though the Church's destiny is not really distinct from that of humanity at large, still as a matter of practical convenience one can and does discuss secular and temporal affairs under a heading that is distinct from that of ecclesiastical and spiritual ones. So let us now prescind, to begin with, from the Church and Christianity, and ask ourselves what is the state of the issue between unity and pluriformity in the secular world today.

It is a commonplace that the world today has become a 'global village', with the ease and rapidity of modern world-wide communications. But it is worth observing how this has come about, and what forces are at work in this global village. The 'unification' of world history, so that now there really is such a thing, has taken place under the hegemony of Europe. It began with the discovery and colonization of the Americas in the sixteenth century by the European powers of the Atlantic seaboard. It proceeded at a more hectic pace from the eighteenth to the twentieth centuries with the conquest of India and the other Indies, the discovery of Australia, the humiliation of China, the opening up of Japan, the scramble for Africa, all made possible by the industrialization of Europe and North America and the consequent over-whelming increase in the economic and military and political power of European culture. Echoing, perhaps, the succession of ancient empires which carried Israel's history through its crucial phases, from the Egyptian to the Roman, a modern succession of empires from the Spanish and Portuguese through the French and the British to the present Russian and American 'spheres of influence' has carried the new Israel, the Church, to the four corners of the world and unified world history; constructed, in fact, the 'global village'.

Thus the unity of the human race has at last become as inescapable a fact of experience as its racial and cultural diversity. But it is still, manifestly, a very imperfect and shadowy unity. And more to the point though less commonly remarked upon, it is the result of a stupendously energetic and partly deliberate, partly unconscious, European cultural imperialism.

Now what we are observing at the present moment, since the end of the Second World War in 1945, to be precise, is an increasingly determined reaction all over the world against this cultural imperialism and against Americo-European cultural hegemony. In my opinion the division of the world on the so-called North–South lines, or of Third World against First and Second Worlds, is of far more momentous significance than the division between the Western, free-enterprise capitalist world and the Eastern, Marxist socialist one, that so obsesses Washington and Moscow and their respective satellites. This conflict gets more and more like the rivalry between opposing *magna latrocinia*, great bands of robbers, as St Augustine termed any state or empire which is constituted without justice. Each side represents some aspect of the degradation, the corruption by power of European culture; a degradation that can be summed up in the word 'materialism'; a preoccupation with things, with objects, a valuing of things and above all of the thing of things, money, more than people.

The basic assumptions or philosophies of each side are the product of European culture pure and simple – to be precise of the European Enlightenment and the nineteenth-century variations on its themes. Marxism is really as provincial and as dated to the nineteenth century in Europe as the philosophical formulations of Ricardo and Bentham and Mill and other such political economists who are the fathers of whatever philosophy may be said to support capitalism. The Washington/Moscow confrontation is depressingly out of date – and as fundamentally ridiculous as the quarrel between Tweedledum and Tweedledee,[4] though unfortunately much more deadly.

Each side, admittedly, still partly upholds and represents genuine human values, personal freedom and constitutional government in the one case, human equality and social justice in the other. But in each camp one sees these values, that each claims to be its own proper mark, more and more cynically jettisoned in the name of either security or profit. The most glaring cases in the Western camp are South Africa and the so-called national security states of Latin America, with their atrocious inroads on personal liberty and the rule of law. But what happens in these societies (where precisely the 'West' is confronting the 'Third World' eyeball to eyeball) is symptomatic of a disease of the spirit that is rife also in Europe and North America. Corresponding examples of contempt for genuine equality and social justice can be found where the 'East' (i.e. European Marxism) confronts the 'Third World' eyeball to eyeball, e.g. in Cambodia or Afghanistan.

It is indeed where we have a confrontation between the other cultures of the world and the American-European culture complex, whether of the First or of the Second World brand, that we have more genuine questions of value involved. I am not talking about the confrontation of Third World *governments* and the West, or the East. Many of these are as corrupt and unjust as any in the world – *parva latrocinia*. I am talking rather about what is going on *in* the Third World itself, below government level, and also in the immigrant ghettos of Europe and the United States. It is a shapeless, un-co-ordinated, un-thought-out, but all the same spontaneous and persistent resistance to European *hubris*. For all its limitations and apparent ineffectiveness it is there, and what it is saying is that there are other ways of being human, in many respects better and more humane ways then the materialist ones which are what comes across as the American-European-Russian ways of being human. It is an assertion of the real value of cultural diversity which in no way rejects actual geopolitical unity that is a modern fact of life, but resists the pressure to turn it into a uniformity. Some material uniformity there is bound to be, some world-wide cultural assimilation. There is the uniformity of the jeans-

Coke-football world culture (to which, alas, one can add the uniformity of the arms trade).

But I cannot help feeling that it is only Third World resistance to European cultural imperialism which can save us from the world-wide cultural impoverishment of sheer reduction to the level of these lowest common denominators. It is Third World conceptions of humanity that can, paradoxically, preserve for us the truly humane cultural treasures of the very rich European tradition.

D. THE FUNCTION OF CHRISTIAN POLITICAL THEOLOGY TODAY

Let us now cease prescinding from Christianity and the Church, and consider what the Christian Church can contribute to this modern global village in its ferment of conflicting forces. We have already considered the Church's own proper ecumenical task of working towards its own genuine unity and genuine catholicity. What we must here think about is its more direct involvement in the world's secular affairs, in geopolitics.

Reflection on this involvement and the inspiration and guidance of it is the task of what are being called political theologies. The best known and most dynamic of these is the liberation theology emanating from Latin America. There is a lesser brand one heard more of in the early 1970s, the black theology of the United States, of which I think it is fair to say that it has been both more raucous and less professional (less dull and heavy with jargon, too) than what is coming from Latin America.

The prime concern of these theologies is with racial and economic justice. They thus tend, at least in Latin America and more and more in Africa too, to form links with revolutionary movements of Marxist inspiration, and thus to be drawn into the 'East–West' conflict, as well as the 'North–South' one, the Third World struggle for genuine cultural as well as economic independence. This cannot be helped; it is quite proper that their first concern should be for social and economic justice. But all the same, this is something that has to be watched by Christians, and above all by political theologians, with extreme care.

For the Church, in its encouragement of justice and peace and unity, must on no account let itself again become the unwitting agent of cultural imperialism, of yet another surge of European cultural imperialism in a new, Marxist/socialist guise. So what we need to see emerge on the scene of political theology is a whole range of diverse *cultural* theologies; African of all sorts, Asian of all sorts, Latin American of all sorts. By 'cultural' I do not mean a concern with traditional customs that excludes contemporary politics and economics; I mean a concern for justice, peace, freedom, human rights – the great values – but within the context of local cultures.

Again, it is to the Third World we have to look for these necessary developments. We of the First World can and should strive for a renewal of the genuine human values that are there in our European tradition, try to rediscover 'European man' and reassert him and her in the teeth of our peculiar demon, Mammon, and his agents in high places. Perhaps the best tactical front for European Christians and Christian theologians to concentrate on is that of peace and disarmament rather than on radical structural change.

But the first thing we have to learn, as Europeans, with our four-century-long adventure of demonic cultural pride behind us, is a real cultural humility. And for that reason I think we have to leave it to the Third World to take the theological lead in the quest for human unity in diversity, in the assertion of a true catholic communion of peoples.

NOTES

1   The conventional biblical total of nations; cf. Exod 1:5 with Dt 32:8, following the Hebrew reading, 'he fixed the bounds of the peoples according to the number of the sons of Israel', and count the number of the nations in Gen 10, if you have the time and patience.

2   The word 'church', *ekklēsia*, in the New Testament, and particularly in the epistles of St Paul, far more frequently refers to local communities of believers, the Church in Corinth, in Rome, in Antioch, etc., than to the universal Church. In fact I am not sure that it ever refers to the universal Church in the sense of a world-wide organization. In a text like Mt 16:18, or Eph 1:22, 3:10, Col 1:18, 24, the reference does indeed seem to be to the whole body of believers in Christ, but as a cosmically mysterious totality rather than as a world-wide, empirically observable organization. In Paul's days there was no world-wide organization; all that was empirically observable was a number of local communities sharing in and embodying what would nowadays be called a 'movement'.

3   I am not, of course, denying that it is the same Church as it was in the beginning; I am asserting that it has undergone radical changes in structure and appearance – almost as radical as the change from caterpillar to moth, for instance.

4   Lewis Carroll, *Through the Looking Glass*, chapter 4.

QUESTIONS FOR FURTHER DISCUSSION

1   Is it possible to achieve the Christian unity of the Church or the secular unity of mankind, while maintaining and promoting a genuine pluriformity of cultural, national and linguistic traditions?

2   What is the contribution to be made by the Christian community to the unity of the total human community?

RECOMMENDED FURTHER READING

Yves Congar, OP, *Divided Christendom*, chapters 2 and 3 (on unity and catholicity).

Jürgen Moltmann, *The Church in the Power of the Spirit*, chapter VII.

Walter Buhlmann, *The Coming of the Third Church*.

Edward Schillebeeckx, *World and Church*, chapters 5 and 6.

Selah

It is time for another ghostly interlude on the ten-stringed lyre and the lute, to remind ourselves that we are still engaged in trying to appreciate the drama of man – of each human being and of the whole human race; the drama of man's relationships with God.

For in the last ten chapters we have not been directly considering these relationships, but only some of the key factors or dimensions within which the drama of the human/divine relationship has to be played out. These factors are matters of universal common human experience, and so even though our interest in them has been theological, we have still found that in discussing them we are engaged in judging the merits of non-theological, indeed non-Christian, purely secular cultural assessments of them.

Thus in our examination of the terms 'body' and 'soul' we inevitably got involved in the cases of Ryle and Descartes, of Aristotle and Plato, as we assessed what we call the unitary self-experience and the dissociated one. Going on to investigate the dimensions of life and death, we indeed found that the Christian revelation leads us beyond the limits of common human experience – but not beyond the limits of common human interest or concern, and that our appreciation of what Christian doctrine has to say, for example, about eternal life and the resurrection of the dead is radically conditioned by whatever options we may have taken in those great perennial issues.

Coming to the factors of man as individual and man in community, and of man as male and female, we found that the Christian revelation has only a few, but those crucial, affirmations to make, by which we must judge cultural or secular customs and theories and traditions and practices in these spheres: affirmations about the quasi-absolute value of the human person, about the paramountcy of the imperatives of love and justice in determining human relationships, about marriage as an 'institution of creation', about the fundamental equality of the sexes. And finally, as we turned to observe from a Christian perspective the unity and the pluriformity of the human race, we found ourselves directly involved, as Christians, in the great political and social issues of today, in the so-called 'North–South' confrontation and the so-called 'East–West' confrontation; in the problems of racism, cultural imperialism, nationalism, arms limitation etc.

So even though we have, in the middle section of this book, been considering the permanent, non-dramatic 'given' of human existence, we have nevertheless never got away from the human drama. And more than that, we have constantly found ourselves anticipating the dramatic end of the human story which we are about to investigate in the final section of the book. A consideration of life and death, naturally enough, led us straight to the mystery of our ultimate destiny. Rather more surprisingly, so did our discussion of human sexuality and marriage. And the same was true of the great cosmic issue of human unity and diversity. But these anticipations did not allow us, for the most part, to treat adequately of the great themes of human destiny, and so even at the risk of some repetition we must turn our attention to them now.

At the beginning of the book I said that the two poles of our dramatic presentation of human existence were Adam and Christ (Chapter 1, C). So it must be a study of Jesus Christ as the last Adam, as the last word, so to speak, in human existence, human perfection or completeness, human destiny, that governs this last section of the book. Another book in this series[1] is devoted *ex professo* to the subject of christology, so we will not have to deal with the full mystery of Jesus Christ. But no Christian theology of man can simply leave out Jesus Christ. We shall have to consider him therefore precisely as the last Adam, and as what Edward Schillebeeckx calls 'the sacrament of encounter with God' in a book of that title.[2]

However, reflection on Christ under these headings presupposes reflection on a topic which was introduced at the beginning of the scriptures, and which we have already noted in passing (e.g. Chapter 13, A, i) – man as made in the image and likeness of God. So we shall begin with a chapter on this subject, and then go on to a chapter on Christ, the last Adam.

But the relationship of the rest of mankind to Jesus Christ is perhaps best summed up in Paul's terse expression 'in Christ'. To be in Christ, actually or potentially, means to be, actually or potentially, in the body of Christ, in the Church. The Church too shares in Christ's sacramental quality, being as we have seen a kind of sacrament of the unity of the whole human race and of man's intimate union with God (Chapter 18, B, i).

But as the mode, or ambience, or atmosphere of our being in Christ, and hence our forming the Church, is one of grace, not law, we shall have to lead up to our chapter on the Church with one on law and grace.

Thus our first four chapters of this last section will be: on man in the image and likeness of God; on Christ the last Adam; on law and grace; and on the Church. These must be followed by a few chapters on human eschatology, on our ultimate destiny and that of the cosmos – and on the possibility of our failing to attain that destiny. These subjects have been anticipated fairly thoroughly in the chapters on life and death, and so our final survey of them will be fairly brief.

NOTES

1 Gerald O'Collins, *Interpreting Jesus*.
2 Edward Schillebeeckx, OP, *Christ the Sacrament of Encounter with God*.

19

Man in the Image of God

A. THE DOCTRINE OF P

Then God said, Let us make man in our image, after our likeness; and let them have dominion over the fish of the sea . . . . So God created man in his own image, in the image of God he created him; male and female he created them. And God blessed them, and God said to them, Be fruitful and multiply, and fill the earth and subdue it; and have dominion over the fish of the sea . . . (Gen 1:26–28).

This is really the only text in the Bible which states the doctrine of man being in God's image,[1] so we shall have to suck from it every dram of meaning that we can. But it is also one of the most concentrated theological texts of scripture, and so we may be confident that there is no lack of significance to be extracted from it.

(i)   Context

If it is, in some ways, a very isolated text, it nevertheless has a very broad context; for besides being the climax of P's creation narrative, it may also be said to have as its context the whole of the P corpus. This corpus, we remind ourselves, was in all probability assembled during the Babylonian exile, composed as a kind of defiant statement of Israelite belief and religious practice and above all of the special Israelite covenant relationship with God (see above, Chapter 2, C and D), in the face of an apparently triumphant circumambient paganism.

Thus Gen 1:1 – 2:4a, the P story of creation, is really one of the earliest essays in demythologization, a technique supposedly invented by Rudolf Bultmann for interpreting the New Testament. It is a counterblast, couched in symbolic terms to be sure, to the Babylonian creation myth *Enuma-elish*[2] which glorifies the gods of Babylon, above all Marduk the sun god, for emerging victorious from the great cosmogonic conflict with the monster of chaos Tiamat and then creating men to be the slaves of the gods from the blood of her assistant demon Kingu.

'This is all hogwash', says P in effect – by which he does not mean that it wasn't literally true, since nobody supposed that it was; but that the *Weltan-schauung* it represented was false – a view of a world emerging from the clash of cosmic forces, and of man as the fairly helpless plaything of these forces, with an ineradicably ingrained streak of demonic nastiness in him. 'No', P says to the exiles from Judah in Babylon, 'the world was created, constructed in a perfectly orderly and rational manner by God, the God of Israel of course, our God, the one true God. It was done in much the same way as the Babylonians construct one of their temples for their "non-gods" – or at least we can take that ritual building of theirs as a convenient model.'[3]

And so, just as the Babylonians finish this construction by putting an idol of the non-god in the sanctuary of the temple, God finishes off the work of creating his temple, the world, by putting his idol, man, in it as its crowning achievement or masterpiece. For the word translated 'image' here (quite correctly) is in fact the Hebrew word for 'idol'. And this brings us to the other, wider, context of Gen 1:26–28, the whole P corpus, but in particular P's version of the ten commandments, Exod 20:4: 'You shall not make yourself a graven *image* [i.e. an idol], or any *likeness* of anything that is in heaven above, or that is in the earth beneath, or that is in the water under the earth'. It is the same pair of words as in Gen 1:26.

Thus the prohibition of idolatry is the most significant theological context of the doctrine of man being created in the image of God. You could say that man is forbidden to make images because he does not really need them, being himself the one and only authentic, God-constructed image of God.

(ii) Man as image of God

Here is the place to observe that while our interest in the doctrine of man as God's image, from the point of view of this book, is in what it has to tell us about man, presumably the primary intention of the doctrine is to tell us something about God. After all, the point of images and likenesses is to convey to the beholder a conception of the originals they represent. You look at a picture of the Pope in order, among other things, to see what the Pope is like. You don't look at the Pope to see what his pictures are like.

This is why it is so important to bear Exod 20:4 in mind when interpreting Gen 1:26–28. The prohibition of images (recorded but not of course invented by P) is a much more fundamental feature of Israelite religion than the concept of man as made in God's image. And it tells us something of crucial importance about God: namely that we cannot form any adequate idea or concept of what he is. As Thomas Aquinas puts it, summing up the whole Judaeo-Christian tradition on the matter, 'we cannot know of God what he is, but only what he is not'.[4] Images or idols, then, are forbidden because they are bound to be false.

But (as always in theology) this basic theological principle needs to be balanced, and is, by its opposite. The Bible, to be sure, consistently condemns idolatry. But unlike Islam and extreme puritanical movements in Christendom both before, during and after the Reformation, it never countenances iconoclasm. We need only observe that while forbidding the making of molten and graven images, the Bible itself is a rich source or manufactory of verbal images of God. The Israelite is forbidden to *make* any image of God, but is positively encouraged to *think* or imagine images of God. These are chiefly anthropomorphic: 'the Ancient of days' (Dan 7:9), 'a likeness as it were of a human form' (Ezek 1:26), 'my king and my God' (Ps 5:2), 'he who sits in the heavens' (Ps 2:4), 'The Lord is a man of war' (Exod 15:3) etc., etc.; but occasionally theriomorphic: 'the Lord roars from Zion' (Am 1:2), 'Like an eagle that stirs up its nest' (Dt 32:11), etc.; and yet others apsychomorphic, taken from inanimate objects, rock and fire being the main ones (e.g. Ps 95:1, Heb 12:29).

This verbal idolization of God in the scriptures, chiefly in anthropomorphic terms, is the ground for the common agnostic and atheistic criticism of Judaeo-Christian religion that, like nearly all religion, it is a case of man making God in his own image and likeness. Rupert Brooke voices it wittily enough in his poem about the fish.[5] But this criticism, if intended to destroy the credibility of any religion, is as shallow as the kind of religion it criticizes – which certainly does exist, among Christians no less than among the adherents of other religions. It is an infantile form of religion that is being subjected to adolescent criticism, which usually starts from an *a priori* adolescent assumption that all religious belief and doctrine is infantile.

For these verbal images of God, anthropomorphic and otherwise, in which both scriptures and credal formulations of Christian doctrine abound, must always be interpreted in the context of that prohibition of idolatry, that constant practical assertion that we cannot know about God what he is but only what he is not. They will indeed qualify that assertion, and remove from that prohibition the absolute normative value puritans always ascribe to it – as Aquinas went on to modify his statement by insisting that it is possible to make true affirmative statements about God (e.g. 'God is good') as well as negative ones.[6]

But this context will ensure that the authentic doctrinal tradition never supposes that God can be adequately represented, or in any way whatever be defined or described by these verbal images we apply to him. When we call him a king or a shepherd, a husband or a father, and ascribe to him a footstool or a throne or a chariot, a voice, a countenance or an outstretched arm, we are in no way describing or defining him. We are doing little more than attempting to express our own imaginative and emotional response to the divine mystery as we encounter it.

This, however, is theologically permissible – to attempt to 'know' the unknowable and talk about the ineffable – because, so P assures us, God has made the human in his own image and likeness. It is not an anthropomorphic God we believe in, but a theomorphic man. Of course we must not attempt to make images and likenesses of God – and what is more, we do not need to, because God has made his own images and likenesses of himself – us.

(iii) What we learn about God from his human image

P did not explicitly say in what he considered the divine image in man to consist. It is the question which occupied Christian theologians, and which we shall come to in due course. But it is a question which we cannot put to P. What we can legitimately ask him, I think – that is to say, ask his text – is what in particular he expects us to learn about God from contemplating man, male and female, created in God's image.

It is only of man, after all, that P makes this statement. Of the rest of creation he says repeatedly that God saw that it was good, and the legitimate inference to be drawn is that all creatures genuinely, if at an infinite remove, reflect the goodness of God. But only of man is it said that he is in the image and likeness of God, and so presumably man represents God in a unique way, not shared by other creatures. Man is, in fact, 'God's representative' in the created world, he is 'God' to other creatures.[7] I think that is what P is telling us. And therefore the text goes on to say, 'and let them have dominion' etc. It is not so much that man being in God's image tells us something about God as he is in himself, as that it tells us something about God's relationship to us. God is to man as man is to other creatures. He is the source and the archetype of man's mastery of the world of nature. He cannot therefore (like most pagan gods, for instance) be reduced to a 'force of nature', or regarded as the mythic projection of such a force.

But the text does not leave it at that. It repeats itself with a significant variation: 'So God created man in his own image, in the image of God he created him; male and female he created them' (1:27). What is the author's intention in mentioning the distinction of the sexes in connection with the creation of man in God's image? We have already suggested that one all-important lesson he is teaching is the basic equality of the sexes; women as well as men are in God's image, however reluctant the male chauvinists of any age may be to admit it (Chapters 15, A, ii; 17, A, i). But I do not think that consideration exhausts the exegesis of this statement. Perhaps man being in God's image as male and female also tells us something about God.

But it cannot be just the sexual differentiation of human beings that tells us this, because that is not a characteristic peculiar to the human species – though admittedly P has not mentioned it in connection with other animals.

Also, it is in the highest degree unlikely that he is suggesting a sexual differentiation within the godhead. Such a notion belongs to the Babylonian mythology which he is criticizing.

What he is probably suggesting is that human fertility represents and is derived from divine creativity, just as human dominion represents and is derived from divine lordship. But he may also be hinting at something more, a something more that may throw light on that famous oddity of this text, the divine plural: 'Let *us* make man in *our* image' (1:26).

As we have seen when dealing with J's narrative, man and woman, male and female, constitute the basic human community, a community of equality, reciprocity, complementarity and love (Chapter 15, A, i). Now P does not actually *say* any of this; as we remarked in an earlier chapter, he gives actual expression to an apparently more utilitarian, rationalist view of sexual differentiation (*ibid.*, ii). But all the same, it is possible that such an idea was at the back of his mind as he wrote this passage. And thus he would have been intimating that it is man in his social being, i.e. basically man-and-woman, as well as in his (or her) individual being, who is God's image and representative – representing the God who said 'Let *us* make man'.

The ancient Fathers happily interpreted this turn of phrase as an intimation of the mystery of the Trinity. They were not exactly wrong (in my opinion), but they were a little simplistic. Sticking to our author P (the Fathers stuck to *God* as the author), we cannot suppose he wished to give any intimation of the mystery, since it is a mystery that was only revealed in the New Testament, when in the fullness of time 'God sent forth his Son . . . ' (Gal 4:4–7). Some interpreters have dismissed the expression as simply an oddity of grammar[8] – but that is mere trifling. Others have seen it as a plural of majesty, like the royal 'We'. But that is not a Hebrew mode of speech or etiquette. Still others have taken it as signifying that God was addressing the angels, or indeed other gods. But while in P's source it may well have been El, the father of gods and men, addressing the other gods, P himself cannot have intended this, seeing that he was engaged in a polemic against pagan polytheism. Nor can he even have contemplated angels (as downgraded pagan gods) being addressed and thus again being raised to an equality with God by having man made in their likeness as well as God's.[9]

So what did he intend to suggest? I am inclined to agree with Karl Barth that the author was hinting at some kind of plurality in God; not simply many gods, of course – nothing to compromise the unity and uniqueness of God as stated in Dt 6:4; nor the trinity of persons in God, about which he had not been informed; but still wishing to convey that there must be a richness, an infinite fullness about the divine mystery which could not be adequately expressed by putting God in the grammatical singular, and could not therefore be adequately represented by man as an individual. The Hebrew for God, after all, is a plural form, *Elohim*, and that grammatical oddity must be allowed to have some theological significance.[10] God, P is hinting, also has to be represented by man-in-community, and man-in-community at the most basic is man-male-and-female (cf. above, 14, A, i and 15, A, i). This 'hunch' of P's was verified by the New Testament revelation of the trinitarian mystery. That is why I said that the Fathers were not simply wrong in reading this divine plural as a trinitarian locution – only a trifle simplistic.

To conclude then, it is man in all his dimensions, as individual (whether male or female) and as social (male-and-female) who is in God's image and represents him to the world; and it is only man (in all his dimensions) who is singled out from among all God's creatures for this role.

B.   THE IMAGE IN THE NEW TESTAMENT

The idea of man in God's image is not, to the best of my knowledge, given any further notice in the Old Testament, apart from the two quotations of Gen 1:26 found in Ecclesiasticus and Wisdom which are mentioned below (note 1). It certainly does not seem to have been either anticipated in earlier or developed in later books. This is not surprising. The prophets and the Wisdom writers were not interested in anything as abstract as 'man-as-such'; nor did they have a message for all mankind. Their message was for Israel, even if some of them, like the authors of Jonah and Job, felt it necessary to remind Israelites that they were a part of the human race, and that there were other people around besides themselves.

However, towards the end of the Old Testament period there does seem to have been some theological speculation among the rabbis about Adam, some echoes of which are to be heard in Daniel, in the figure of 'one like a son of man' (7:13). This is a text of crucial importance for the New Testament, to which we shall return in the next chapter. This speculation was carried on in a rather 'mythic' style of thinking, and its effect seems to have been to focus the notion of the image on Adam the first man, with the implication that only he but not his descendants was in God's image. Gen 5:1–3 would have lent support to this view, and perhaps Gen 9:6 (which shows that it certainly was not P's view) was explained away in the light of it. Indeed, according to one school of thought, possibly represented by the Alexandrian Jew, Philo, only a kind of ideal Adam, the archetypal man, the heavenly man (1 Cor 15:48), the 'man' of Gen 1, is this image, not the earthy Adam of Gen 2, who turned away from God and was expelled from paradise and the divine presence.

So it is not surprising that when the New Testament (in fact St Paul) talks about the image of God, it refers the title simply and almost exclusively to Jesus Christ (1 Cor 11:7, 2 Cor 4:4, Col 1:15).[11] Not surprising – but extremely significant. St Paul does not develop the *concept* of the image of God at all, he merely focuses it on Christ, and says *this* man, and this man alone is the image of God. That is to say, as we have worked it out in the previous section, Jesus Christ is God's representative in the cosmos, exercising God's authority and dominion (cf. Mt 28:18). And furthermore, Jesus Christ is God's perfectly representative image, telling us about God and his relationship with us (cf. Jn 14:9, 'He who has seen me has seen the Father'), not only in his unique individuality, but also in his social, corporate and comprehensive being. For it is a property of Christ, made very clear by Paul with his doctrine of the Church as the body of Christ, to include all other human beings, actually or potentially, in himself and his relationship with God.

So while Paul appears to say that Christ alone, properly speaking, is the perfect image of God, he sets before us, all the same, the invitation and task of ourselves being 'conformed to the image of his Son' (Rom 8:29), of 'bearing the image of the man of heaven' (1 Cor 15:49), of 'being changed into his likeness from one degree of glory to another' (2 Cor 3:18), of 'putting on the new nature [he actually says "the new man"] which is being renewed in knowledge after the image of its creator' (Col 3:10).

Thus we are forced to realize that being in God's image is not so much something *given* as something to be realized, to be achieved. It is a dynamic, not a static concept, to use a fashionable jargon. And the word 'image' should not convey to our imaginations the idea of a statue or picture, so much as that of a reflection in a mirror, or the moving image of a film or TV.

C.   THE DOCTRINE OF THE IMAGE IN CHRISTIAN TRADITION

(i)   *Basic development of the doctrine in Hellenistic Christianity*

We saw that the question 'What does the divine image in man consist in?' was not one that P ever asked himself, or one that we could properly put to him. But it was a question inevitably asked by the Gentile Christians of Greek background and culture who by the end of the first century A.D. formed the great majority of believers. And just as inevitably – and rightly – they replied that it consists in, or is located in, the mind, the intelligence, the reason, the rational soul of man. The dominant philosophy of the Graeco-Roman world of the first two centuries A.D. was Stoicism, and after that from the third century onwards it was Neoplatonism. For the Stoics reason was the divine spark in man; for the Neoplatonists, Mind (*Nous*) was the first emanation from the One (God). In both philosophies man was thought of in dualistic terms derived from the dissociated self-experience, as a soul/spirit in a body (Chapter 9 above). So it was inevitable that Christians in that culture should locate the image of God in the mind or reason.

Inevitable – and right; that is to say, it was the correct translation of the biblical, Israelite idea of man in God's image as elaborated above in section A (and the biblical writers, we remind ourselves, thought of man in unitary terms, derived from the unitary self-experience, as a living body, or a living soul) into the language and concepts of Hellenistic culture. For as we have seen, what P seems to have had chiefly in mind was the idea that man is God's representative in the dominion he exercises over the rest of creation. And I imagine we can take it as agreed that it is by his *intelligence* that he is enabled to do this.

However, there are many critics nowadays of this locating of the divine image in the mind or intelligence or rational part of man. It is inferred that doing this detracts from the human significance and worth of the human body; that it is inspired in fact by a contempt for the body and especially by a mistrust or even hatred of human sensual and emotional and affective life; that it is in fact un-Christian because it does not leave any place, let alone the first place, for love in the Christian life.

But these inferences are entirely misguided and stem from a confusion. This sort of criticism may fairly be levelled at much of the content of the Stoic and Neoplatonist philosophies – especially at Stoicism and its influence on Christian moral teaching. But this statement of ours about the location of the divine image does not actually contain the questionable content; it has it read into it by the critics because it is framed in the same dualistic language as was employed by the Stoics and the Neoplatonists. The critics, it seems to me, are here guilty of confusing the language, which was the language of *all* educated Greek-speakers in those centuries, with some of the things said in it. It is not unlike the confusion I have heard attributed to certain zealous French Catholic missionaries in Africa of an earlier era, who are reported to have dismissed English as a 'Protestant language'. It may indeed be the case that there are some good and true things about man's relations with God which cannot be properly expressed in dualist language. But it is certainly not the case that everything expressed in such language implies all the errors that have been characteristically expressed in that language.

What these critics are implicitly doing is refusing to attempt the basic theological task either of translation or of evaluating earlier theological translation. It is universally accepted that this is the task of commentators on scripture, and that contemporary theologians have to translate the teaching of the New Testament into modern, twentieth-century language. But no allowance is made for people having had to do the same sort of thing back in the third century. They are in fact being criticized for not having achieved a good twentieth-century translation, and the critics fail to see that these earlier 'translated' formulations of doctrine also call for understanding in their own terms, their own dualist Hellenistic language, translated into ours of the twentieth century.

So: to locate the divine image in the human mind or reason is not necessarily to undervalue the place of love, or of the affective, sensual, emotional life of man, or of the body, in our relations with God. Human beings, after all, in whatever kind of language you wish to talk about them, are highly complex realities. And whatever language you talk about them in, sooner or later you are going to find yourself saying that one element in the human complex is more important, more essential or significant than others; that hearts, for example, are more essential than toes (anatomical language). Even in our age of predominantly unitary self-experience, and hence of a growing preference for unitary language about man, photographers and portrait painters by and large concentrate on their subjects' *faces*; at least, you would not get very far in your travels if your passport photograph represented your knees or your navel, or even the back of your head. And yet we don't accuse ourselves, our photographers, our portrait painters and our immigration authorities of minimizing the worth and significance of these other portions of the human frame simply because of our unanimous preferential interest in faces.

And why do we concentrate on the face, not only when photographing or painting people, but when describing them, recognizing them, thinking about them, not to the exclusion of the rest of the body but before the rest of the body? It is because the face is the most distinctively human part of us, and our individual characters and personalities, the distinctive styles precisely of our intelligence and hence of our humanity there find the most revealing expression and representation. Well, the same is true of our minds, which are revealed in our faces; they are the most essentially human element in the total human complex.

To say then that it is in the human mind that the image of God is to be found is not to deny that human legs (for example) are in some way godlike. They are, in due measure. But the reason they are more godlike even than the legs of horses or gazelles (which as means of locomotion are much more efficient, and even perhaps more beautiful) is that they are, if we may so put it, rational or intelligent legs, the legs of a type of being that can use them intelligently (to dance with, for instance, or kick footballs with), not just instinctively. And if you go on to remark that the legs of Greta Garbo were almost certainly more godlike or divine than the legs of Bertrand Russell, even though his was in all probability the more brilliant mind,[12] I will not disagree with you, and I am sure Bertrand Russell would not have done so either. But when we all agree on this point we are making a common aesthetic judgement, which is one only intelligent beings can make; and in making that intelligent aesthetic judgement we are showing ourselves to be more godlike in our minds, more representative of God, than are any man's (or woman's) legs (cf. Ps 147:10).

So in locating the image of God in the human mind the Hellenistic tradition of Christian theology was being entirely faithful to the original insight of P. And in this present age of confusion, when rationality and intellect are so often being viciously despised on all sides, on right and on left, by romantic and by cynic, from east and from west, by authoritarian and by anarchist, [13] inside and outside the Church, I for one am determined to go on insisting on at least this element in the Hellenistic tradition: man is a rational animal; being human means being rational, that is to say, it carries a radical obligation to be rational; it is only in the rational activity of intelligence and mind that men and women can properly represent God and realize his image in themselves.

But perhaps I have not yet said enough to allay the genuine fears of the critics I have been counter-criticizing, indeed of the 'anti-intellectuals' in general. They assume, I think, that the nouns 'mind', 'intellect' and 'reason' and their corresponding adjectives and verbs exclude all ideas of love, affection, feeling or will; and then, with that fatal tendency to 'either-or' thinking which is so common a form of defective rationality, they assume that you cannot have both, certainly not both together at the same time. They are suffering, in fact, from the final degeneracy of the dualistic kind of language evolved by the Hellenistic tradition.

But in the most authentic forms of that language, as employed by the great Christian masters of the past (St Augustine and St Thomas Aquinas, for example, to name only the two most influential in the West) these assumptions are simply not valid. They distinguish 'mind' over against 'sense' as representing respectively higher and lower modes of *perception* and *knowledge*; and as being inseparably accompanied in each case by corresponding higher and lower modes of *appetite, affect, feeling*. So each kind of term can be used in a wider sense to include its corresponding affects. Thus 'will' has been defined as 'the intellectual appetite'. Thus Augustine, as we shall see in due course, included the act of willing or loving in the trinity of acts of *mind* which constitute the image of man. Thus Aquinas will associate love or charity, the queen of the Christian virtues, with the gift of wisdom, in such a way that according to him one necessarily requires and engages the other.

Let us illustrate the point again, if his shade and she will excuse the liberty, with Bertrand Russell and Greta Garbo. We assumed earlier on that her legs were more godlike than his, while his *mind*, in all probability, was more brilliant than hers. But now, does this mean, since we are locating the divine image in the human mind, that Bertrand Russell, having the better mind, provided a better image of God than Greta Garbo? That is probably what our critics fear, and on this point we can categorically lay their fears to rest. For

the divine image, though located in the mind, is not to be simply equated
with the mind. It is something, as we have seen, to be realized. And it is only
to be realized by the right use or activation of the mind, of intelligence and
reason. Whatever your degree of intelligence, whether you are a genius or a
bear of very little brain,[14] you can put your intelligence to good or bad use.
And only to the extent that you use it well, that is to say that you use it
lovingly and in the service of charity or true love, do you realize in yourself
the divine image. Now that comparison between Bertrand Russell and Greta
Garbo is one that only God can make. As far as our knowledge is concerned,
it could be made either way.

(ii)   Imitating Christ; the filial image

So whatever human (and hence intelligent) activity you are engaged in,
whether it is acting with Garbo, or philosophizing or mathematicizing or
founding the Committee for Nuclear Disarmament with Russell, or earning
your living by manual labour, or dancing or playing football or making love
or going to school, you are called upon as a human being to represent God in
it, and you do that by the right application of your mind, your whole mind,
to it. To put the matter in specifically Christian terms, you do it by 'being
conformed to the mind of Christ', by imitating Christ. You are called to
model yourself on Christ, to try and think and act as he would have done in
your place, because he is the perfect and complete image of God. It goes
without saying that this presupposes loving Christ, since you may mimic,
but will never set out to imitate a person you do not, in some respect, love.

If then, the image of God is to be realized in us by imitating Christ, the
perfect image, it would seem to be the case that the image we realize or
activate is in particular the image of God *the Son* – what in the sub-heading I
have called the filial image. For Christ is God the Son, the Son who became
man, the Word incarnate. And there is indeed an ancient theological tradition
to this effect. This time, however, it is not exactly a universal tradition, since
it is not the only theological opinion on the subject. There is another, which
we shall see and prefer in the next subsection. Meanwhile, this particular
theology of the image may be set out as follows:

Paul calls Christ the image of God. Since Christ is God the Son, this is
interpreted as saying that the Son is the perfect image of the Father.[15] As God
the Son, the only-begotten, he is the one and only perfect image of the
Father, in all respects equal to that which is represented by the image. Man
(i.e. all human beings, including the man Christ Jesus, or God the Son 'in his
humanity') is therefore not the image of God. For what does Gen 1:26 say
precisely? 'Let us make man in our image, after our likeness', that preposition 'in' being translated in the Greek and Latin, perhaps more accurately,

by one meaning 'according to'. This means that man is modelled on the image of God, which image is God the Son. So man is not the image of God but only approximates, or rather has the potential to approximate, to the image of God. The most perfect approximation is that achieved by, or rather granted to, the man Christ Jesus, through his being assumed into personal union by God the Son, who *is* the image of God. It is this achievement, this grace of Jesus Christ the man that, as it were, provides an opening for his brethren, the rest of mankind, to achieve (i.e. be granted in grace) an ever more perfect approximation to the unique divine image, God the Son, through imitating Jesus Christ.

(iii)   The trinitarian image

An alternative, and more satisfactory, theology of the image was provided by St Augustine, and it has held the field in the Western, or Latin, tradition ever since, though mostly in a somewhat degenerate or dehydrated form.

Augustine, of course, did not ignore or in any way minimize those Pauline texts on which the theology of the 'filial' image was based. He certainly affirmed as strongly as any of the other Fathers that it is by imitating Christ or by being conformed to him that we have to actualize the potential divine image in us. But he considered these texts in a different and wider context, and he refused to make such a hard-and-fast distinction between being the image of God and being in or according to the image of God. And I think we can say that it is implicit in his theory, though I do not think he ever says so explicitly, that Christ is the image of God as man, not as God the Son; that this is a human, not a divine title of Jesus Christ. At any rate, I myself would so interpret St Paul.

The context in which Augustine considers the doctrine of man in God's image is his exploration of the mystery of the Trinity, to which he devoted one of the greatest of his works, the fifteen books of the *De Trinitate*. His main purpose, obviously, is to investigate, to seek to understand, the mystery of the Trinity itself. He spends the first seven books (to over-simplify enormously) discussing the scriptural evidence for Catholic doctrine, the way the mystery was revealed, and the correct use of terms for stating the doctrine. But at the end of all this he still feels (quite rightly) that he does not yet know what it *means* to talk about God as Father, Son and Holy Spirit; he does not yet see why God has to be a trinity of persons, with the Son being eternally begotten of the Father, and the Holy Spirit eternally proceeding from the Father and the Son as Gift. So he decides in book 8 that since he cannot see God directly or look straight into the divine mystery, to examine and understand it in itself (no man can see God and live: no one has ever seen God), he might have some success if he looks at God indirectly as reflected in his image, man. We are assured by scripture that man was made in the image and likeness of God; we are assured by faith based on scripture that God is a trinity of persons; therefore we may infer that man, being in God's image, will somehow reflect or illustrate this uncreated trinitarian mystery on a created scale which our minds should be equal to mastering.

Augustine is therefore bound to criticize the theory of the filial image. He finds it acceptable to regard the Son as the perfect and in all respects equal image of the Father, but not to regard man as created only on the model of the Son. If that were the case, he argues, the text of Gen 1:26 would not have run 'Let us make man in our image, after our likeness', but 'Let us make man in your image, after your likeness'. In any case, since all three divine persons are equal, and equally God, to be like one or in the image of one is to be in the image and likeness of the others, of God in three persons, in fact.

As we saw at the beginning of the chapter, you look at an image to learn what that of which it is the image is like, and not the other way round. So Augustine looks at man to learn what God is like. And since he knows, *a priori*, that God is a Trinity of Father, Son and Holy Spirit (but does not yet know what it really means to say this), he is in a position to assume that there will be a kind of trinitarian structure in man which reflects this divine mystery, and which can be inspected and analysed in order to help us at least to some sort of limited understanding of that mystery.

Let us begin a brief account of Augustine's theology of the trinitarian image, however, with that dehydrated mockery of it that has descended through the centuries to our contemporary Catholic catechisms (or to many of them, anyway), because it is possible that some readers may be familiar with it in this form. And if they are familiar with it, they will almost certainly have been so mystified by it as to shrug it aside as almost meaningless and totally unilluminating. The old so-called Penny Catechism, which is still used in England and Wales in a revised edition (1971) as *A Catechism of Christian Doctrine*, propounds Augustine's doctrine that the image of God in man is the image of the Trinity as follows:

29.   Is there any likeness to the Blessed Trinity in your soul?
      There is this likeness to the Blessed Trinity in my soul: that as in one God there are three persons, so in my one soul there are three powers.
30.   Which are the three powers of your soul?
      The three powers of my soul are my memory, my understanding, and my will.

At the very beginning of the catechism there are the following related statements concerning the image of God:

3.   To whose image and likeness did God make you?
     God made me to his own image and likeness.
4.   Is this likeness to God in your body, or in your soul?
     This likeness to God is chiefly in my soul.

5. How is your soul like to God?
   My soul is like to God because it is a spirit and is immortal.

These answers to qq. 4 and 5 irrevocably commit this English catechism to the view of man satirized by Ryle as the ghost-in-the-machine view (see above, Chapters 9 and 10, especially 9, A and D, ii and 10, C, ii and iii). In virtue of what has happened to the whole language of 'body' and 'soul' in recent centuries, this is unfortunate, if not indeed disastrous. It is very sad to find it still in a catechism revised *after* the Second Vatican Council, when even a sober conservative revision of the old style of catechism could have produced something better and less mystifying. But given this uncritical acceptance of this kind of language, it is not surprising that on the matter of the trinitarian image, the catechism seriously distorts Augustine's doctrine, and empties it of any significant content.

Notice that the catechism language is a distortion even within the old dualistic Hellenistic tradition. For there it was the *mind* that was marked as the locus of the divine image, and in Augustine it is only in the *mind* that we can expect to find the trinitarian image; the word 'soul' is *not* traditional in this context. The fact that the revised catechism fails to use the word 'mind' here suggests to me a deep-seated, if unconscious, anti-intellectualism in the Catholic establishment responsible for it. The mind is something to be distrusted, whereas the soul is something to be saved.

The error perpetuated by this revised catechism goes back to the twelfth-century Master of the Sentences, Peter Lombard. And even though it was expressly corrected by St Thomas Aquinas (*STh* Ia, 93, vi and vii; ET, vol. 13), here it is, still alive and kicking in *A Catechism of Christian Doctrine*, approved by the Archbishops and Bishops of England and Wales, and directed to be used in all their dioceses, in 1971 – and still I presume in 1983.

The doctrine can only be made sense of if we go back to the source of the tradition, St Augustine himself, and discard this dehydrated distortion of his theology, from which the genuine article cannot ever be satisfactorily reconstituted any more than what in the 1940s people seriously called 'shell eggs' can be reconstituted from dehydrated egg powder. Augustine, then, sought the image of God not in the *soul* (far too wide and indefinite a concept here), but in the *mind*, along with the whole early patristic tradition, and he found it, not in 'the three powers of the soul' – as though the soul did not have any number of powers or faculties – but in three particular mental *acts*, the acts of the mind remembering, understanding and willing itself; or in the final perfection of the image, in the acts of the mind remembering, understanding and willing God. The difference between a power and an act is large and crucial. If you just think of the image in the powers of the soul, you think of it as something that is just there; but if you think of it as in the acts of the mind, you perceive it as something that has to be realized and achieved.

Furthermore, the object or objects of these acts (or indeed of the powers, through their acts) is most important. In Augustine's doctrine we see a progress from self-relatedness to God-relatedness in act; in the Catechism doctrine we see mere unrelatedness. It will help us to get things straight if we remind ourselves to think of the 'live images' that we see in mirrors, cinemas and television screens, rather than of the 'dead images' of photographs, statues and pictures.

But why did Augustine pick on these three particular mental acts of remembering, understanding and willing self or God to represent the Father, the Son and the Holy Spirit? The fact is that the first thing Augustine looks for in the human mind is not some mental realities to represent the three persons, but something to throw light, by analogy, on what we call the divine processions, i.e. on the eternal proceeding of the Son, the Word, from the Father, and the eternal proceeding of the Holy Spirit from the Father and the Son together. The eternal procession of the Son is also called a generation or begetting or being born; so we will also look, in our mental analogy, for something to throw light on this reproductive language that theology from the New Testament onwards has applied to the relationship between the Son and the Father.

So Augustine begins by taking what we may agree are the two most basic and general mental acts, those of our perception of things and of our appetite for things. But since the mystery of the Trinity is a mystery of God as he is in himself and not as he is related to things outside himself, we must first look in the mind for a self-contained analogy, not of the mind knowing and loving things outside itself, but of the mind knowing itself and loving itself. In knowing itself it forms an idea of itself; we can and do say it *conceives* an idea of itself. By an association of ideas common to many languages the process of learning, coming to know and expressing what one knows is talked of in reproductive terms of conceiving and bringing to birth. Ideas are also *concepts*, things conceived. So the mind has an idea or concept of itself, and this may also be termed, says Augustine, to drive home the trinitarian analogy, a mental *word*. We must remember that the Greek term *logos,* which Jn 1:1 applies to God the Son, and which is translated by *verbum* in Latin and by *word* in English, also means thought, idea, meaning: the thought word, as yet unspoken, as well as the spoken word. So Augustine is not stretching things when he talks of a mental word.

The mind having thus conceived a mental word of itself, in which it knows itself, spontaneously loves itself as known. The New Testament, as well as talking of the Word, and identifying this with the Son (who is thus conceived as the Father's 'self-thought'), also says God is love (1 Jn 4:8, 16). And without straining the text, this has commonly been applied to the Holy Spirit. So there in the human mind (which we could as well call, in English, the self) in its knowledge of itself and its love of itself as known, we have a kind of image or model, an analogy, of the divine Trinity.

But a moment's reflection will show that it is still a slightly lopsided image or analogy. The trio of mind (self), its self-knowledge and its love of itself corresponds in the divine sphere not to the trio of Father, Son and Holy Spirit, but to the trio of God, Son and Holy Spirit. The point is this: the term 'God', unless particularly qualified, stands indiscriminately and inclusively for any or all of the three persons. As Augustine puts it, it is a term signifying *substance*, whereas the proper names of the persons are terms signifying *mutual relationships*. It is as such mutual relationships that they are really distinguished from each other. Now in the trio of mind, its knowledge of itself and its love of itself, the latter two terms can be seen to connote relationships (indicated by that little preposition 'of'), but the term 'mind' or 'self' signifies substance. The word 'mind' does not, unless qualified, connote relationship.

So to get a more perfect analogy Augustine has to convert the word 'mind' into a relationship word, to make it, if possible into the mind's 'minding itself'. This in fact is what he does; he calls it the mind 'remembering itself'. To see the propriety of this we only need to recollect that 'to mind' does mean 'to remember' in the Scots variety of English. It is indeed likely that there is an etymological connection between the Latin words *mens* (mind) and *memoria* (memory). Thus the complete analogy or image of the Trinity is found by Augustine in the mind's acts of remembering itself, knowing or understanding itself and loving or willing itself. If you wish to turn the verbs into nouns for tidiness' sake, you have memory of self, knowledge or understanding self, and love or will of self. I do not think his change of knowledge and love in the first draft of the mental analogy into understanding and will in the second are particularly significant. It was, if anything, a little unfortunate, as it made it easier for Peter Lombard in the twelfth century to distort Augustine's acts of the mind into the powers of the soul.

What can it mean, though, to remember yourself? After all, memory refers us to things past, and we are always present to ourselves. The idea of remembering oneself was quite as odd in Augustine's Latin as it is in our English. But he met the difficulty by quoting Virgil[16] to show that, just as Ulysses kept his wits about him and did not 'forget himself' in Polyphemus' cave, so we can 'remember ourselves'; by 'memory' of self, he does in fact mean the mind's essential presence to itself: 'presence of mind'. Mind is essentially a kind of luminous or transparent self-awareness, actualized in the primary mental act of simply 'remembering oneself'.

But how does this differ in anything but name from understanding oneself? Are they not just two names for the same act, another one being knowing oneself? To answer this objection Augustine looks at analogous trios of perception and appetite in the lower levels of the soul, in what he calls the outer man: at the levels of sensation (sight), and of memory in the ordinary sense of remembering what you have seen. This is no place to look at his demonstration in detail; but it is worth remarking that although in accordance with the whole tradition he discovers and analyses the divine image in the mind of man, he does not leave the rest of the total human reality out of account.

For Augustine, then, the human mind or self is an image, a model of the divine Trinity of persons in so far as it is in its essence a luminous self-presence or self-memory, which in its act of adverting to itself or remembering itself generates, or begets, an act of self-understanding, an idea or 'word' of itself, just as God the Father, who is indeed the *first* person of the Trinity, begets God the Son, his eternal Word. We can see, when considering the mind or self, how its self-memory and self-understanding must be absolutely equal to each other and coterminous with the mind itself. So by seeing this in the model we can begin to get a glimmering of the corresponding truth in the divine exemplar. Likewise we can see how from the mind's self-memory generating its entirely adequate word or idea of itself there proceeds an act of loving itself, of self-acceptance or self-appreciation which is also entirely equal and coterminous with the self, and yet this final mental act is not thought of in birth language as being conceived, begotten or born. This helps us to a certain hesitant understanding of the mystery of the Holy Spirit.

Augustine's concept of the mind or self as luminous self-presence will not be shared by everyone. It was not accepted in its entirety and without qualification by Aquinas. But if you take it on his own terms for the moment you will find, I suggest, that it does help you to make a little more sense of the mystery of the Trinity. And in any case, it is not Augustine's last word on the image of that divine Trinity in the mind. For, as we have briefly noted, he develops this complete image or analogy of the mind's self-memory, self-understanding and self-willing into what we might call the transcendent image of the mind's remembering, understanding and willing *God*. The mind comes to these transcendent acts through a proper remembering, understanding and willing of itself. God is discovered through the proper discovery or recollection of the self, and the self is discovered through the discovery of God (which is also in a mysterious way a recollection or remembering of one who in Augustine's famous phrase is *intimior intimo meo*, more inward to me than my inmost self). The ultimate perfection of man is to transcend oneself, that is to go beyond oneself, to be taken out of oneself to the deepest ground or cause of one's being, to one's Creator, God. That is why I call this the transcendent image.

To appreciate this, we must always bear in mind what we have stated several times already, that the divine image in man is something to be achieved. But of course it is to be achieved by a creature of God, and therefore as an achievement it is always dependent on God. And therefore it is not what one might call a merely objective likeness to God that we are called to achieve; it is a likeness that, to be true, implies an adherence to God, an adherence of the subject in whom the likeness is to be achieved to the exemplar. 'But for me it is good to cleave to God' (Ps 73:28, after the Vulgate). St Augustine's work on the Trinity was not written without passion – and it is not his fault if my bald account of his theories of the image has failed to convey this to readers. At three crucial places in the work, at the beginning, the middle and the end (I, iii, 5; IX, i, 1; XV, ii, 2), he quotes Ps 105:3–4, 'Let the hearts of those who seek the Lord rejoice . . . seek his presence continually'. He was engaged, and wishing to engage his readers, in a quest for God that demanded of him total concentration. There was nothing 'merely academic' (that tendentious philistine expression!) about this quest. It would have been grotesque if his search had ended in the discovery of himself remembering, understanding and willing – himself!

Again, for Augustine, in contrast with Thomas Aquinas and above all with Aquinas' mentor in philosophy, Aristotle, the proper way to God was through the self and self-awareness, an inner and introspective way rather than an outer, outward-looking way through creatures considered objectively. God is to be discovered within the self. When I do this, and thus remember or recollect him, and understand and will him, he is not in any way an external object of these mental acts of mine, introduced to my apprehension and attention from outside, like the English language, or Pythagoras' theorem, or quantum physics. He is *intimior intimo meo*. 'In him we live and move and have our being' (Acts 17:28). He is the be-all and end-all of existence, always simply waiting to be found, where we really are, that is, where our real selves really are.

Again, none of this would ever need to have been said, because it would all have been 'luminously self-evident'[17] to everyone, had it not been for sin. What may perhaps have been giving a certain air of unreality to what we have been saying so far on Augustine's theology of the image is that nothing has been said about sin. It all seems to be couched in ideal terms, and in a word may seem a little too good to be true. But once more the fault is not Augustine's. *He* doesn't talk about the image in abstract, ideal terms, but sets everything he says in the context of a concrete history of mankind (which is also the personal history of each human individual), a history of sin and redemption, a history according to the basic insight of J (see Chapter 3, A above). We have repeatedly said that the image is not something given, but something to be achieved and realized. This now needs to be qualified and expanded. It *is* something given as a potential, as a capacity which is of the essence of human nature, inherent in the fact of being human. But being

human, as we have also seen, is something we have to become (Chapter 2) –
to become what we are, with the dreadful possibility (in concrete fact the
actuality) of becoming what we are not, or not becoming what we are. That
is what sin is. And it means a thorough shattering or distortion of the image.
The final perfection of the image consists of adhering to God by remembering
him, understanding and willing him. It is the perfection of the cardinal
mental or personal acts of knowing and loving, directed to their one all-satis-
fying object, God, and to everything and everyone else through him and
with reference to him. But sin (as emblematically concretized in the story of
the fall) consists in turning away from God (Chapter 6). In more detail, its
first stage is one of actually forgetting God, and its consequent stages are ones
of misdirecting the cardinal acts of knowing and loving onto knowing and
loving things, above all oneself, without reference to God, or with reference
to any number of misconceptions of God which we can call compendiously
idols or false gods. Thus the sinful self, the darkened and distorted mind,
ceases to be a proper and effective way to the discovery of God.

The situation is irremediable by us, the shattered images, left to ourselves.
But into it, 'when the time had fully come, God sent forth his Son, born of
woman, born under the law, to redeem those who were under the law, so
that we might receive adoption as sons' (Gal 4:4–5). Now we receive
adoption as sons, that is to say, we are converted, or turned round by God's
grace, turned back towards him so that we can once more reflect his image
instead of being turned away from him and just reflecting darkness – this conversion comes to us through *faith* in the man Christ Jesus, born of woman,
faith in the *flesh* of the Word incarnate. Augustine is very insistent on this,
that the object of saving faith is not just God (after all it is only the fool who
says in his heart there is no God, Ps 14:1), but the flesh of the Word
incarnate, that is to say the material humanity of God the Son, Jesus Christ,
as man. It was in the flesh, by his death and resurrection, that he redeemed
us. Believing in the flesh of the Word incarnate is for the spiritual mind of
man a difficult act of *humility*. This at least is how Augustine sees it. The first
and archetypal sin had been one of pride. Spiritual or intellectual pride, manifested in a contempt for the body and material things, was characteristic of
many contemporary intellectuals, Neoplatonist philosophers and Manichees.[18] So it was most fitting that the cure for sin, the restoration of the
shattered image, should be required to begin with an act of humility, an act
of created, sinful but now repentant spirit, acknowledging its creatureliness
and worshipping flesh in the human being of Christ.

The restoration of the image thus begun continues precisely with the
imitation of Christ, that is of the man Christ Jesus, who is the perfect, never
distorted, never shattered image of God, in the cultivation of the virtues.
These, in this context, Augustine regards as instances of 'knowledge'

(*scientia*, a different word from that used earlier for 'knowledge', which was *notitia*); that is, of the mind or self employing itself correctly and with due reference to God, in the use and enjoyment of the external material world. This exercise in the virtues leads the mind to the supreme practice of 'wisdom' (*sapientia*),[19] by which it remembers, understands and loves itself in God and God in itself; by which in fact the perfection of the image is attained. A final note: this perfection is only intermittently and very incompletely attainable in this life. But straining towards it prepares us for its completion in the age to come. 'Now we see in a mirror dimly, but then face to face. Now I know in part, then I shall understand fully, even as I have been fully understood' (1 Cor 13:12).

To conclude: the authentic Christian doctrine of man in the image and likeness of God, whether you prefer to see it as what I called a filial image with many of the early Fathers, or as a trinitarian image with Augustine, is a doctrine that presents us with a programme for Christian living, and challenges us to embark on the search for perfection, which is in essence identical with the search for God. 'You therefore must be perfect, as your heavenly Father is perfect' (Mt 5:48).

NOTES

1   This doctrine is quoted, or referred to, but hardly developed, in the late books Sir 17:3 and Wis 2:23.

2   This is inaccurately called a creation myth, because it in no sense contains any concept of creation. It is a cosmogony, rather, with the world coming to be as it is now out of a vast cosmic conflict between gods and demons. It begins as follows:

When on high the heaven had not been named,
Firm ground below had not been called by name,
Naught but primordial Apsu their begetter,
And Mummu-Tiamat, she who bore them all,
Their waters commingling as a single body;
No reed hut had been matted, no marsh land had appeared,
When no gods whatever had been brought into being,
Uncalled by name, their destinies undetermined –
Then it was that the gods were formed within them
       (*Ancient Near Eastern Texts*, ed. J. B. Pritchard, p. 60).

3   *Ancient Near Eastern Texts* (*ANET* for short) also contains some temple-building rituals, according to which a temple was constructed in a set of stages. This could have provided P with the idea for his six days of creation; that is to say, it could have provided him with the model he used in order to include in his narrative a theological justification of the Jewish practice of keeping the sabbath day holy.

4   *STh* Ia, 3, prol. (ET, vol. 2).

5   Rupert Brooke: 'Heaven':

. . . Fish say, they have their Stream and Pond;
But is there anything Beyond? . . .

But somewhere, beyond Space and Time,
Is wetter water, slimier slime!
And there (they trust) there swimmeth One
Who swam e'er rivers were begun,
Immense, of fishy form and mind,
Squamous, omnipotent and kind;
And under that Almighty Fin
The littlest fish may enter in . . . .

6   *STh* Ia,13, ii and iii (ET, vol. 3).

7   This bold way of talking is employed in Exod 4:16, where God is telling Moses about the function of Aaron: 'He shall speak for you to the people; and he shall be a mouth for you, and you shall be to him as God'. This is not thought to be a P section of the narrative.

8   e.g. E. A. Speiser in his translation of Genesis and commentary for the *Anchor Bible* (Doubleday, Garden City, N.Y., 1964).

9   I have a hunch that P, in fact, did not believe in angels. They are not mentioned at all in his creation narrative, a fact that caused the Christian Fathers a little embarrassment, though not much, since they were ingenious commentators. I see the whole tone of his narrative as essentially rational, even rationalist. I think he would have distrusted the whole idea of angels, or celestial spirits as messengers, because they could so easily become gods once more, and so seduce the Israelite exiles into worshipping them. In this P would have been the forerunner, the intellectual ancestor, of the Sadducees, who were indeed the priestly class in New Testament times (cf. Acts 23:8).

10 My theory is that there were two ways in which Israel came to its monotheistic faith, exclusive and inclusive. The exclusive way is the most obvious in the Old Testament: Yahweh the God of Israel is *not* identical with any other god; Israel must not worship any other gods, the gods of the nations; these are eventually seen to be naught (or demons; Ps 96:5, where RSV translates 'idols'). But the inclusive way is attested by a number of the stories of the patriarchs in Genesis, where the Lord whom Abraham, Isaac and Jacob worship (called Yahweh in the J texts) is happily regarded as identical with the deities worshipped under other names elsewhere; e.g. with El Elyon (God Most High) of whom Melchisedech was the high priest (14:18ff.); with El Shaddai (God Almighty, 17:1); with El Ro'i (God of seeing, 16:13); with El Bethel (God of Bethel, 35:7); with El 'Olam (the Everlasting God, 21:33). So by this way the Israelites arrive at the conclusion that Yahweh, the Lord, is all the gods, all the Els there are; so he is *Elohim*, Gods.

11 The text of 1 Cor 11:7, where Paul calls the man (Adam) the image of God, has already been discussed in Chapter 17, B, ii.

12 The choice of these two distinguished personages rather dates me, it must be admitted. But it is also more prudent to choose figures of the recent past or in honourable retirement instead of any who are in mid-career – about whose legs in any case I am less well informed.

13 I was writing these words just at the end of the Falklands campaign, when a general irrationality seemed to be very strong in the United Kingdom.

14 A. A. Milne, *Winnie-the-Pooh*.

15 See, e.g., *STh* Ia, 35 (ET, vol. 7).

16   nec talia passus Ulixes
oblitusve sui est Ithacus discrimine tanto.

       No such thing did Ulysses endure,
nor did the man of Ithaca forget himself in that momentous hazard
(*Aeneid* III, 628–629; quoted in *De Trinitate* XIV, c.11, 14: *PL* 42, 1047).

17 J. H. Newman, *Apologia pro Vita Sua*. In Chapter 1, entitled 'History of my religious opinions to the year 1833', he mentions the doctrine of 'final perseverance' (which in its Calvinist, or perhaps Methodist, form of an assurance of ultimate salvation he ceased to hold a few years later, at the age of twenty-one) as, among other effects, 'making me rest in the thought of two and two only absolute and luminously self-evident beings, myself and my Creator'. This is sometimes quoted as a position or attitude characteristic of Newman throughout his life. But from the context, which is the account of his juvenile conversion at the age of fifteen, that is doubtful, to say the least.

18 Augustine in his youth had joined the Manichees. When he began to realize that their beliefs were a jumble of irrational nonsense (a mythology that could not be satisfactorily demythologized) he proceeded, via a period of scepticism, to a Neoplatonist position, to which he came on reading the *Enneads* of Plotinus. Some foolish and superficial critics of Augustine, or rather purveyors of a common anti-Augustinian legend, accuse him of unconsciously continuing to be a Manichee after he had become a Catholic Christian. It is simply untrue, a slander first put abroad by his doughty Pelagian antagonist, Julian of Eclanum, in his own lifetime. He did indeed continue, along with most of his Christian contemporaries of any education, to inhabit a Neoplatonist thought-world. But it is my impression from a moderately wide reading in his writings that as he grew older he sat more and more lightly to the assumptions and categories of this philosophy.

19 The pair 'wisdom' and 'knowledge', *sapientia* and *scientia*, are derived from 1 Cor 12:8; 'To one is given through the Spirit the utterance of *wisdom*, and to another the utterance of *knowledge* according to the same Spirit'. Compare also Col 2:3. Searching the scriptures for a definition of this pair, Augustine finds it, in his translation, in Job 28:28: 'Behold, piety is wisdom, while to abstain from evil things is knowledge' (*De Trinitate*, XII, c.14, 22: *PL* 42, 1010).

QUESTIONS FOR FURTHER DISCUSSION

1 What does P's doctrine of man made in God's image and likeness (Gen 1: 26–28) tell us about God?

2 If we regard the human mind rather than the human body as the *locus* of the divine image in man, can we consistently maintain a unitary concept of man, and the validity of the unitary self-experience?

3 Can being in God's image mean both being like Christ the Son, and also being like the divine Trinity – or can it only mean one of these things?

RECOMMENDED FURTHER READING

Edward Schillebeeckx, *God and Man*.

20

Christ, the Last Adam

A. CHRIST, THE PERFECT REPRESENTATIVE OF MANKIND

(i) Comparison with christological approaches

This book is exploring the theology of man, not the theology of Christ, or christology. So while, like the student of christology, we are interested in the humanity of Christ, we look at it, so to say, from the opposite end. Contemporary christology tends to be what they call an ascending christology; that is to say, it starts with the *datum* of the man Jesus of Nazareth and 'ascends' to an awareness of his also being God the Son. The whole drive is to insist on the truth that he was a man, a true, complete human being just like us – a truth of faith which it is widely felt has been underplayed by the more traditional style of christology which is called a descending christology. This starts, like John's gospel, with the person of the Word, God the Son, and 'descends' with the doctrine of the incarnation of the Word to the statement that he is true man as well as true God.

Both approaches, let us say in passing, are not only theologically valid and permissible, but they are also theologically obligatory. It is simply ridiculous to see them as mutually exclusive alternatives, as rivals. But the point I want to make here is that the ascending christology in particular tends to assess the humanity of Christ from what we already know about our own humanity anyhow. What is it to be human? We find out by looking at ourselves, and then say 'Well, that must apply equally fully to Jesus Christ'. This procedure, if followed without careful qualification, can lead (and sometimes does seem to lead some people) to a denial that Jesus Christ can be anything which we obviously are not – sinless, for example, or God, or virginally conceived, or risen from the dead; which is, on the face of it, to clash head on with the authority of the New Testament, not to mention the unbroken tradition of Christian faith.

But in any case, our procedure here is the opposite. Not a descending as opposed to an ascending christology, because we are not engaged in christology at all; but an attempt to learn more about what it is to be human from looking at Jesus Christ. Our starting assumption must indeed be that he is fully and completely human, otherwise we would be unable to proceed with our enterprise. But we do not set *a priori* limits to his humanity – which means that we remain open-minded still about our own. And since we gather from the New Testament, from the consistent tradition of Christian faith and doctrine, that Jesus Christ was indeed sinless, and God (God the Son), and born of a virgin, and risen from the dead, and seated in glory at the right hand of the Father, we are willing and eager to infer that we too, as human beings, may be sinless, and divine, and virgin-born, and risen from the dead, and reigning in glory; that these may be dimensions of our humanity not previously suspected.

To put it briefly, we maintain that as the perfect or final representative of mankind Jesus Christ reveals to us in his person further possibilities of being human, which we would otherwise not have known about, and a programme for achieving those possibilities.

(ii)   Human possibilities revealed in Jesus Christ

Since then Jesus Christ was, or rather is, a human being exactly as we are; and since moreover he is our perfect representative, what Paul means by calling him the last Adam (1 Cor 15:45; cf. Rom 5:14–19); and since, in addition to that, he is also sinless, God, born of a virgin, risen from the dead, and enthroned in glory: he reveals to us new dimensions and possibilities for our humanity. We too can be all these things.

'Now wait a minute', you may say; 'I grant that as Christians we can see how Christ has revealed the possibility of our rising from the dead and sharing in his heavenly glory; that he has opened up the new dimension of eternal life to our humanity, opened to us believers the gates of the kingdom of heaven, as it says in the *Te Deum*. But we are sinners, and we have not been virginally conceived, and we are none of us God (thank heaven). And surely it is logically impossible to make us not to have been what we have been, and to have been what we have not been.'

I concede, of course, that we do not have these possibilities opened up to us in the same way as they were realized in the person of Jesus himself. We do not even have the same possibility of being risen from the dead, namely on the third day and before the end of time. While being fully and completely human, Jesus Christ was and is also human in a unique way, peculiar to himself. But still he enables us to participate in the unique aspects of his humanity, in our own way and measure, without any detriment to his uniqueness.

The key aspect is his risenness, his triumph over death by rising from the dead. It is in the context of the resurrection (our resurrection) that Paul refers to Christ as the *last* Adam in 1 Cor 15:45. The vista is eschatological; Christ is the *eschatos Adam*. The dimensions or possibilities of being human revealed to us by Christ are all eschatological, to be fully realized only at the *eschaton*, the end. It is to the risen Christ, Christ in glory at the Father's right hand, that we have to look in order to discover the full dimensions of our humanity, rather than to the Jesus of Nazareth of the earthly ministry, or Jesus crucified, dead and buried. There, what we will find is the programme Jesus Christ reveals to us, to which we will return shortly in the next sub-section.

To rise from the dead is clearly an eschatological dimension of human existence. But the same is true of those other three dimensions I have mentioned which Christ has opened up for us: being sinless, being virgin-born, and being God. Now in the unique way in which Jesus Christ achieved, or rather was granted the actualization of these possibilities, they were not obviously eschatological. These predicates applied to him throughout his earthly existence, which indeed began by his being virginally conceived as the human being who was one person with the eternal Word of God.

Yet even in Christ these dimensions of his existence were eschatologically oriented. Or rather, they marked him as the eschatological man in whom the fullness of time had come (Gal 4:4), in whom the kingdom of God had finally erupted into the world of time and space. And our participation in them is certainly eschatological. We become sinless in Christ by being newly created in him (that is how we are in him virgin-born). The concept of a new creation (2 Cor 5:17, Gal 6:15) is clearly an eschatological one (Rev 21:5).

So it is the perspective of a new eschatological humanity that is opened up for us in Christ. The key word is 'new', a word of enormous theological weight. We are the new people of the New Testament, who sing a new song and dwell in the new Jerusalem. The point of being new, of course, is that it is contrasted with being old. In ordinary life the new replaces the old. You throw away the old, or pull it down, and start again with the new. Or sometimes you renew what is old and make it 'as good as new' again. Now in the theological sense in which we speak of a new creation and in which we have the real hope of sharing in Christ's prerogatives of sinlessness and divinity, there is a combination of these two modes of newness. There is the radical newness of the first mode, in which something brand new replaces what is old and worn out; and yet there is the continuity of the second mode in which something old is not thrown away and replaced, but renewed. Both kinds of language are used to express the mystery of our eschatological newness in Christ. St Paul in fact mixes them, thus: 'Stripping off the old man with his works, and putting on the new [radical replacement], who is being renewed [continuity] to be recognized in the image of the one who created him [in the Christ image]' (Col 3:9–10); or thus: 'Putting aside the old man who is being corrupted by deceitful desires [radical replacement], be renewed in the spirit of your mind [continuity], and put on the new man created to be like God in the justice and holiness of truth [replacement]' (Eph 4:22-24).[1] The new man is Christ, the last Adam, the old man is the first Adam in his archetypal fallenness.

Another word of Paul's for this new or eschatological dimension of being human is 'spirit' or 'spiritual'. In Christ we see the possibility of an enspirited humanity, a spiritual way of being human. This is not contrasted with a bodily or physical way of being human, but with a fleshly or merely 'ensouled' way (see above, Chapter 10, A, iv). And that it is essentially eschatological is shown by the use of the word in 1 Cor 15:44-49.

But to say that these new or spiritual dimensions to our humanity which we perceive in Christ are eschatological does not mean they are purely and simply in the future. We have already been (or can already be) initiated into them. In us too, as believers, as well as in Christ in whom we believe, the *eschaton* has been anticipated. In baptism we have been born again of our virgin mother, the Church, sinless, risen to newness of life. But it is a hidden form of existence, and it has to co-exist with the old, mortal, sin-ridden mode which is much more evident and palpable.

As for the possibility of our being God, revealed in the person of Jesus Christ, I will just refer the reader to Gal 4:4-7. There Paul talks about our being adopted into the sonship of Jesus Christ. Now his sonship is precisely a *divine* sonship, the relation of God the Son to God the Father. So it is a divine sonship, this particular relationship of God the Son to God the Father into which we are adopted. As the Church Fathers were so fond of saying, especially but by no means only the Greek Fathers, God became man that men might become God. But this, you will object, is only a manner of speaking, a kind of rhetoric. True; but it is good rhetoric and a true and proper manner of speaking. True, adoptive divine sonship is not the same as natural divine sonship, but it is still, in its own degree, real and really divine. If God said 'Let there be light', and there was light, then when God says 'Let these be my Son', and 'I said, You are gods', these are my Son, and you are gods (Jn 10:34; Ps 82:6).

(iii)   The new programme revealed in Christ

What is revealed to us, then, in and through Jesus Christ about our humanity is that it is not locked in the limits of our ordinary experience, limits of sinfulness and mortality and creatureliness. There is the possibility of a full human existence that transcends these limits.

But how is that possibility to be realized? Well, as we have just seen, it has by the gracious activity of God already begun to be realized for Christians initiated through baptism (indeed through the three sacraments of initiation, baptism, confirmation and eucharist) into the mystery of Christ. But, in Paul's striking phrase, 'we have this treasure in earthen vessels' (2 Cor 4:7); or as I have just said, this hidden form of existence (Paul's 'new man'), Christ in us, the life of grace, has here and now to co-exist with the mortal, sinful, obvious form (Paul's 'old man', the old Adam). How are we to cope with such a situation, and nurse our new life, our complete humanity along, until it finally blooms in the glory of the kingdom of God?

Jesus Christ reveals to us the current programme, so to say, of authentic human living by means of his life and death, of which we read in the gospels. It is a paradoxical programme, given the paradoxical situation we find ourselves in. I think it can be summed up in one word – humility. A paradoxical humility, of course, which accepts our present condition of creatureliness, sinfulness and mortality, and so avoids being 'high-minded' (Rom 11:20, 12:16, 1 Tim 6:17),[2] or having big ideas about oneself, but also does not stand in awe in the least at the high-mindedness or high-and-mightiness of others – of anyone, in fact, except God. It is the humility of the *Magnificat* (Lk 1:46–55), in which Mary perfectly represents the response of the Christian to the grace of God in Christ. It is the humility of Ps 8 which we have already commented on in Chapter 1, E, and seen applied by Heb 2:6–9 to Christ himself. So it is the humility of Christ himself, for whom it was necessary to suffer these things and so enter into his glory (Lk 24:26); the humility of Christ the servant of the Lord and of his brethren, who found his own programme prescribed for him in Isa 53.

It might reasonably be objected that love rather than humility is surely what should be the golden thread of the Christian programme of life. I am far from wishing to deny the absolute primacy of love in the Christian life, or, with love, of faith and hope. But the concept of love is in itself too wide to specify this programme. It is, I suggest, humility (not as something separate from love, let alone without it, but as qualifying it) that states the special, peculiar quality of love which was revealed and opened up to us in the life and death of Jesus Christ, oriented to his resurrection.

Other key texts for this programme are, first, the *beatitudes* in all their paradoxicality (not only Mt 5:2–12, but also Lk 6:20–26, where they are four in number, balanced with the counter-paradoxes of four woes); secondly the poignant invitation of Jesus to 'all who labour and are heavy-laden', Mt 11:28–30; and finally the great hymn of Phil 2:5–11, in which Paul sets before us the *curriculum vitae* of Jesus Christ, precisely in an exhortation to 'do nothing from selfishness or conceit, but in *humility* count others better than yourselves . . . . Have this mind among yourselves, which you have in Christ Jesus, who . . . ' (*ibid.* 3–5).

But this is a text of such great importance that we must prepare for a study of it by first trying to see what Jesus meant by calling himself the Son of Man. For this, and related titles, lie behind this hymn, according to Oscar Cullmann in his excellent book *The Christology of the New Testament*.

B. JESUS THE SON OF MAN

(i) Jesus' own use of the title

The title 'Son of man' expresses almost as clearly as 'the last Adam' the representative role of Jesus – that he is 'the Man', from looking at whom we can learn about our own humanity. In fact, it is my guess that 'the last Adam' is simply Paul's equivalent for 'the Son of man' of the gospels. He does not use the expression, but he uses the idea.

Perhaps he did not use the expression because it is in fact an extremely odd expression in Greek (as it is in English if we stop to think about it), and Paul was writing not only in Greek, as were the evangelists also, but for gentile Christians who had no Aramaic or Hebrew background. For in Hebrew and Aramaic 'son of man' is a very common expression, an example of a very common idiom. Yet all the same its use in the gospels, almost exclusively by Jesus and about himself (so it has always been assumed), is also very odd. In itself a commonplace idiom, like the modern American English 'a guy', it is as odd in the gospels as if some famous teacher or guru of today constantly referred to himself as 'the Guy'. It would catch our attention, and set us wondering what he meant by it. So with Jesus' use of 'the Son of man'. People have been wondering what he meant by it ever since.

There are, of course, those who question whether he did use the title about himself, and suggest rather that it was attributed to him by the evangelists or their sources. But this suggestion hardly squares with the evidence, which is that in fact the evangelists, or their sources, never apply the title 'Son of man' to Jesus. They never call him this themselves, nor do they report anyone else doing so. With only one exception (Jn 12:34, of which more in a moment), the phrase is found in the gospels on the lips of Jesus only. So it does not look like a title attributed to him by the first generation of Aramaic-speaking Christians.

A more plausible view (on the evidence) is that Jesus did indeed frequently employ the expression, but applied it to another mysterious eschatological being, not to himself; and that it was his disciples who came to identify him with this coming Son of man of whom he had so often spoken. Thus we do have that text of Jn 12:34 when the crowds say to Jesus, 'We have heard from the law that Christ remains for ever. How can you say that the Son of man must be lifted up? Who is this Son of man?' It is true that Jesus had just said, 'And I, when I am lifted up from the earth, will draw all men to myself' (*ibid.*

32), There is a certain incoherence here, which John does not mind because clearly he identifies the Son of man with Jesus himself. But it is also clear from this passage that the crowd did not make this identification, which means that it was by no means obvious to Jesus' hearers that he himself made it.

But if this view were correct, it would mean that Jesus regarded himself as the forerunner of some greater eschatological figure, rather as John the Baptist was regarded by Christians as the forerunner of Jesus. Historically speaking this is perfectly possible, though historically speaking there is no evidence at all to support it. The first Christians, as represented by the sources behind the gospels, clearly identified Jesus with the Son of man, and clearly assumed that he made the identification himself, i.e. that he talked about himself as the Son of man. That is the evidence. It does not prove that they were right. But historically speaking, since there is no evidence either way that they were wrong, we can prudently give them the benefit of the doubt. Theologically speaking, since the gospels through which their views have come down to us have the authority of inspired scripture, we are obliged to take their view as authoritatively binding. For it is not just their opinion; it is a statement of their faith, which is also our faith.

(ii)   The background to the title and its meaning[3]

Taking the title, then, as applied to Jesus Christ, we shall see that it epitomizes what is revealed to us about our humanity in his person: both its possibilities of eschatological greatness and glory in the future (already anticipated, in a hidden manner, in the present), and its proper programme of modest paradoxical humility in the present. It epitomizes, in fact, Ps 8.

Ps 8:4: 'What is man that thou art mindful of him, and the son of man that thou dost care for him?' This is the idiomatic Hebrew use of the expression. 'Son of man' means 'man', i.e. a member of the species, class or group, a member of the human race, just as 'sons of the prophets' means a group of prophets (1 Kgs 20:35), or 'sons of death' means those who deserve to die (1 Sam 26:16). The only English equivalents I can think of are 'son of a gun' and 'sonofabitch' (I believe it should be thought of as one word in the best American), neither of them, perhaps, very illuminating.

In this usage, and certainly in Ps 8, as we can tell from the context, the expression refers to man in his littleness, modesty, humility. Other instances, where the expression *ben-adam* or *b'ne-haadam* refer to man in his creaturely contrast to God, as weak and little, worthless, sinful, mortal, are Job 25:6 – almost a harsh commentary on Ps 8; Pss 49:2 and 62:9, where *b'ne-adam* is translated in RSV as 'men of low estate' in contrast with *b'ne-ish* (literally 'sons of man/male'), 'men of high estate' – but the psalmist is equally sceptical of either.

So when Jesus calls himself Son of man, one thing he certainly seems to be doing is identifying himself with us in our mortal, feeble, humble, wayward humanity. The method of seeing what Christ was like from the experience of what we are like ourselves, which I remarked on somewhat negatively at the beginning of the chapter, though inadequate as a christological approach, is not without merit after all.

But there is a quite other dimension to the expression 'Son of man'. It is indicated in only one text of the Old Testament, Dan 7:13f.: 'I saw in the night visions, and behold, with the clouds of heaven there came one like a son of man, and he came to the Ancient of Days and was presented before him. And to him was given dominion and glory and kingdom, that all peoples, nations and languages should serve him; his dominion is an everlasting dominion, which shall not pass away, and his kingdom one that shall not be destroyed.' Now it is true that this is only 'one like a son of man', and in Daniel's interpretation of the vision this figure is interpreted as standing for 'the people of the saints of the Most High' (v. 27), i.e. a purified Israel. But Jesus alludes to this text at his trial, in his answer to the High Priest's question whether or not he is the Christ, and he says, 'And you will see the Son of man sitting at the right hand of Power, and coming with the clouds of heaven' (Mk 14:62; cf. Mt 26:64, Lk 22:69). Clearly he, or at least the evangelists, identify this Son of man (no longer one like a son of man) with Jesus as the Christ. Luke in his slightly incoherent text seems also deliberately to identify 'Son of man' with 'Son of God'.

But though Dan 7:13 is the only Old Testament text which employs the phrase 'son of man' in this high sense, this usage was almost commonplace in much of the apocryphal literature that was being produced in late Judaism, from the book of Daniel itself (c. 165 B.C.) onwards. It figures prominently in the book of Enoch, for example. And it seems to represent a line of rabbinic speculation in a somewhat mythical mode about Adam that surfaces in the work of the Alexandrian Jew, Philo, in the early first century A.D.[4]

To put it briefly: the rabbis, the 'scribes' of the New Testament, were as aware as any modern scholar of the discrepancies between the accounts of the creation of man in Gen 1:26–28 and in Gen 2:7. But of course they had no P and J theory to propose as a solution of the problem. For them, Moses wrote the whole thing, under divine inspiration. The solution, then, lay not in two different accounts from two different points of view, but in two distinct acts of creation. Gen 1 describes the creation of the ideal man, the first or heavenly Adam in all his godlike glory; but he is very much a Platonic idea, or a mythical being, laid up in heaven. Gen 2 describes the creation of actual, empirical earth-bound man, the second or earthy Adam, a rather poor concretization of the ideal, who soon fell into even greater trouble by his sin.

Now it is the ideal, heavenly man who is the 'one like a son of man' of

Daniel's vision, and is also the ideal Israel, the people of the saints of the Most High, and who has thus clearly become a figure of eschatological expectation. Laid up in heaven from the beginning of creation, he will be sent at the end of time to bring back the actual material mankind to the perfection of its original idea.[5]

This exegesis may not strike the reader as very coherent. It combines Platonic idealism with frankly myth-making propensities. And while the making of myths is by no means simply an exercise in manufacturing false-hoods, and myths can in their own way be vehicles of truth, still they do not mix easily with other modes of thought. This heavenly man, or Son of man, is clearly not a human being in the obvious empirical sense. As a mythical symbol of what humanity may be or ought to be, he is well enough. But when you start thinking of him as being laid up in heaven until he is sent at the end of time, then you appear to be turning him into a concrete idea – which seems to be a contradiction in terms.

No matter; the myth is there. It is used by the evangelists, by St Paul, by Jesus himself obliquely, to 'put across' the mystery of the person of Jesus, who is identified with the Son of man. Paul seems deliberately to correct the rabbinic scheme of things outlined above by insisting in 1 Cor 15:45–46 that it was the earthy 'psychic' ('ensouled', anima-l) man, Adam of Gen 2:7, who came first, and the heavenly, spiritual man (Christ, and not the man of Gen 1:26ff.) who came second. In other words he puts the myth into a definite framework of salvation history. John gives us the myth, as applied to Christ, in its purest and plainest form, in Jesus' conversation with Nicodemus, for example: 'No one has ascended into heaven but he who descended from heaven, the Son of man' (Jn 3:13). But John also effectively demythologized the notion, and 'entheologized' it by going on immediately in 3:16 to identify this super-human myth figure with God's 'onlybegotten Son'; and he, the only begotten Son, has been identified in the prologue with the eternal Word of God, of which it was said 'and the Word was God' (Jn 1:18, 1).

So, to conclude this subsection: Jesus in calling himself the Son of man applies to himself a title of both unique sublimity and common lowliness or humility.

(iii)   Philippians 2:5–11

This, then, is the network of ideas, concerning the Son of man or the last Adam, in Paul's language, that lies behind this hymn in Philippians, nowadays commonly taken to be an early Christian hymn which Paul quotes, but did not actually compose himself. The patristic tradition, as re-presented particularly by the great post-Nicene Fathers of the fourth and fifth

centuries,[6] interprets the passage in terms of the dialectic between the divine
and the human natures of Christ, just as (see note 3 below) it treated 'Son of
man' as a title designating Christ's human nature, and 'Son of God' as one
designating his divine nature. But this does not fit the text as well as the
interpretation proposed by Oscar Cullmann, which follows, and it has caused
serious theological difficulties over the concept of *kenosis* or emptying himself
(2:7).

2:6 – '. . . Christ Jesus, who though he was in the form of God, did not
count equality with God a thing to be grasped . . .'. 'Form' here should not
be interpreted, as it is in the patristic tradition, as meaning 'nature'. Rather,
says Cullmann, it means 'image'. The composer of this hymn, after all, was
unlikely to be thinking in Aristotelian terms, in which the 'form' of a
substance determines its nature, but in much more material symbolic terms,
in which form means shape, and shape is what makes an image an image. So
the immediate reference is to Gen 1:26–28, man being made in the image and
likeness of God. Throughout the whole passage there is a tacit comparison
and contrast being made between Adam, the first Adam, and Christ, the last
Adam – and we of course are being urged to model ourselves on the latter and
no longer on the former (cf. 1 Cor 15:49). As we saw in the last chapter (19,
B), the notion of 'image of God' had gradually come to be confined to Adam
alone, and then in the New Testament applied, especially by Paul, to Christ
alone. That then is what we have here.

'He did not count equality with God a thing to be grasped.' In this he is
contrasted with the first Adam (and Eve) who precisely did just that (Gen
3:5ff.). The patristic interpretation assumes that equality with God already
belongs to Christ, as the divine Word, and that he did not cling to it. But
that is not what the text actually says. The word translated 'a thing to be
grasped', *harpagmon*, is really a much rougher and ruder word, meaning in
effect 'up for grabs', 'a snatch'. That is what the first Adam did reckon – that
equality with God could be grabbed, seized. Not so the second Adam, even
though he was in the form of God, as his perfect image.

2:7 – 'but emptied himself, taking the form of a servant, being born in the
likeness of men'. This is the heavenly man, in the divine image, putting aside
the glory of that image to become an earthly man, in the form, or image of a
slave; i.e. of Adam after his sin, now the slave of sin. This is a descent in
voluntary humility, contrasted with Adam's fall, after sin, in involuntary
humiliation. Gen 5:3 talks about Adam's son, and hence all his descendants,
including therefore Jesus Christ, being 'in his likeness, after his image'.

2:8 – 'And being found in human form, he humbled himself, and became
obedient unto death, even death on a cross'. The word translated 'form' in
this verse is not the same word in Greek as in the previous two verses, where
we have interpreted it to mean image. Here it is *schēma*, which AV translated

'fashion'. I think it would be best translated 'condition'. So, finding himself in the same human condition as the rest of us, the last Adam became *obedient* unto death, in sharp contrast to the first Adam, who earned death by his *disobedience*. The death Christ obediently accepted was the most shameful, the most grossly punitive death imaginable, death on a cross. So his humility, his self-emptying was perfect and complete. That is the human programme revealed to us in Christ.

2:9 – 'Therefore God has highly exalted him, and bestowed on him the name which is above every name'. Now we are shown the human possibilities revealed to us in Christ. After the humiliation voluntarily accepted out of obedience, out of love, comes the exaltation, the blessing. It is the same pattern as in the *Magnificat*. The name which is above every name that God has bestowed on him is the name 'Lord', *Kyrios* – which in the Greek Old Testament is the substitute for the unnameable name of God himself, YHWH. So the last Adam is graciously *granted*, as a reward for his obedience, that equality with God which he did not count as something to be *grabbed* through disobedience.

2:10, 11 – 'that at the name of Jesus every knee should bow, in heaven and on earth and under the earth, and every tongue confess that Jesus Christ is Lord, to the glory of God the Father'.

Here the name 'Lord' is acknowledged to be that of Jesus by the whole of creation. As he has conquered death by having been obedient unto death, he is acknowledged not only in heaven and on earth, but also under the earth, in the realm of the dead, by death itself.

The theology of this ancient hymn is more primitive, more mythical than the theology of the incarnation of the Word developed by John, and rightly carried on in the Church as its central theology ever since the Council of Nicaea in 325. That is what makes it a little disconcerting. But it also, I am inclined to think, makes it more useful for us in our present concern with a theology of man, since it sets before us with unequalled power both the programme and the ultimate possibilities of redeemed humanity, as enacted by the representative man, Jesus Christ.

NOTES

1   I have not followed RSV here in my quotations, because it is too free for my purpose. It does indeed keep the images of changing clothes, and of renewal. But in both texts it translates Paul's word 'man' (*anthrōpos*) by 'nature'. This misses the allusion to the two Adams, and is in my opinion a mistake. It is true that the expressions 'new man' and 'old man' in such a context are very odd English, and need some explanation; but I am willing to bet that they were also very odd Greek. 'Man' is at least a concrete noun that can conjure up a living, if here rather grotesque image in the imagination. 'Nature' is abstract, and with a very wide variety of meanings and references. JB is better, in talking about the old and the new self.

2 Another case of slightly inadequate RSV translation. Paul is here using a verb, or verbal expression, meaning literally 'to think high things'. RSV translates with the adjectives 'proud' and 'haughty', Now pride and haughtiness are indeed the sins Paul has in mind; but he is actually talking of a particular kind of manifestation of these sins, which is well rendered by the AV term 'high-minded'. It is true that the adjective is nowadays commonly treated as a word of praise, and it is thought virtuous to be high-minded. But perhaps this is a case of a corruption in our contemporary value system, rather than a case of a word changing its meaning.

3 From very early on in the Christian tradition after the New Testament the title was assumed to designate the human nature of Christ, while the parallel 'Son of God' was taken to designate his divine nature. Once the doctrine about Christ, as one person in two natures, had been settled at the Council of Chalcedon, in 451, this was a very convenient pair of phrases for stating the doctrine. But it is not simply what the phrases mean in the New Testament text. The meaning of both is rather more complex, as this subsection explains with regard to 'the Son of man'. About 'the Son of God' I will just say briefly that its basic and primary meaning in the New Testament, when applied to Jesus, is to signify his status as Messiah, or Christ. In this sense it depends on texts like Ps 2:7. The Messiah, a human being like the rest of us, is thought of as having a special relationship with God, which makes him Son of God in a special way. But it must be remembered that the whole people of Israel was called God's son (Exod 4:22, Hos 11:1), and all of us are destined to be so called, and are already so called. However, in later New Testament texts, sometimes in John and Paul, the title 'Son of God' applied to Jesus does come close to signifying his divine sonship. But for this purpose John prefers the plain, unqualified term 'the Son'.

4 I must come clean, and admit that everything that follows is second-hand. I have never read a word of Philo's fairly voluminous writings, and I am far too old to begin now. I owe what follows almost entirely to Oscar Cullmann, in his excellent *Christology of the New Testament*, already mentioned.

5 Something like this curious exegesis, to explain the discrepancies between Gen 1 and Gen 2, was later on to be adopted by Augustine in his *Literal Commentary on Genesis* (*In Genesim ad Litteram*); a work of several volumes which does not in fact get beyond chapter 4 of Genesis. He is there dealing with creation as a whole, not just the creation of man, nor does he envisage a first Adam (Gen 1) and a second (Gen 2), as this rabbinic exegesis seems to. But he does seem to present Gen 1 as an account of the instantaneous (or rather extra-temporal) creation of the cosmos in idea – the idea being unfolded and displayed to the minds of the angels in the device of the six days. The idea, active in what he calls 'seminal meanings/proportions' (*rationes seminales*), begins to be actualized in Gen 2. This is a thoroughly Platonic construction – but it is just possible Augustine may have got the idea for it from some Jewish influence. He does for example make use elsewhere of the typically rabbinic idea of God's having ministered the old law through the mediation of angels, an idea that other Fathers appear to ignore.

6 Notably Augustine, e.g. in *De Trinitate* I, vii, 14 – xiii, 31 (*PL* 42, 828–844); and Leo, *Sermons* 21–30 on Christmas (*PL* 54, 190–234); *Sermons* 52–70 on the Passion (*PL* 54, 313–384), *Letter* 28 to Flavian (the *Tome* of Leo; *PL* 54, 755–781).

QUESTION FOR FURTHER DISCUSSION

1   Is it possible at one and the same time to see Jesus Christ as revealing to us in his own person undreamt-of possibilities of being human (such as being arisen from the dead, being sinless and being born of a virgin), and yet to assess what Jesus Christ must have been like from our own actual experience of being human and its obvious limitations?

RECOMMENDED FURTHER READING

Oscar Cullmann, *The Christology of the New Testament*, is really a first-class book; for our purposes his treatment of the title 'Son of Man' is the most useful part of it.

Edward Schillebeeckx, *Jesus* and *Christ*, though very hard going, could be attempted, and also Aloys Grillmeier, *Christ in Christian Tradition*, which shows us how the Church of the early centuries up till Chalcedon in 451 hammered out its christology, very much in the light of contemporary anthropologies.

And finally, J. Ramsey Michaels, *Servant and Son: Jesus in Parable and Gospel*, published only in 1981, is one of the most pleasurably exciting books on the christology of the gospels I have read for many years. It will certainly rank with Cullmann's work, or ought to. The author is exploring what he calls the personal religion of Jesus himself, and does it by the most lucid, hard-headed, carefully reasoned examination of the texts themselves. Many critical shibboleths are politely but firmly called in question.

21
Law and Grace

A. INTRODUCTION

We have just considered the ultimate possibilities and the immediate programme of being human, which have been revealed to us in the person of Jesus Christ. But we are offered the possibilities and invited to follow the programme not simply as so many individuals. Both possibilities and programme are really social in nature; they both consist in and imply communion, sharing, a community – between man and God and between man and man. This community, established by Christ as he reveals to us the possibilities and the programme of full human existence, is the Church, which we will look at in the next chapter.

But the Church has been adumbrated in advance in Israel, and is indeed reached out to, so to speak, in any and every human society. And a necessary factor in the life of any and every human society is law. It is a given dimension of human existence. But law (like patriotism) is not enough – it can also, indeed (like patriotism), be the last refuge of scoundrels,[1] of the dehumanizers. So the other all-important factor or dimension of human existence is grace. Human social existence cannot be good and lovely and pleasant without this indefinable quality, which finds its expression in simple good manners, in considerateness and courtesy, in freedom and spontaneity, in generosity and love.

We shall be considering both law and grace in a much stricter theological sense. But the theological sense of these terms cannot be justly appreciated unless it is set in this wider context of general human experience. This is particularly true of the term 'grace', because it has become so predominantly a theological word, and is rarely used in a general, secular context.

B. LAW AND GRACE IN THE NEW TESTAMENT

(i) The sermon on the mount

The word 'grace' does not occur in the sermon on the mount, and practically the whole discourse is couched in the language of law – that is of precept and prohibition.[2] And yet the effect of the whole is to dethrone the concept of law from its dominant religious position in the life of God's people and to substitute in its place what we have come to call the principle of grace. The key passage, I suggest, to the whole sermon is Mt 5:17–20, beginning 'Think not that I have come to abolish the law and the prophets; I have come not to abolish them but to fulfil them'; and then after some characteristic hyperbole in elaborating this statement, concluding, 'For I tell you, unless your righteousness exceeds that of the scribes and Pharisees, you will never enter the kingdom of heaven'.[3]

The law is not to be dismantled (Christians may not be antinomians, or even anarchists), it is to be fulfilled. But that fulfilling the law does *not* mean keeping it meticulously is indicated by the final statement. For that is precisely what the scribes and Pharisees did, or set out to do; that at least is what their righteousness consisted in. Theirs, in Paul's phrase, was a justice (righteousness) based on law (Rom 9:31, Phil 3:9). What is needed, as we shall learn in the course of the sermon, is what will there be called the righteousness (justice) of the kingdom (Mt 6:33), which I would interpret as justice based on grace.

Law, properly speaking, is concerned with our external actions, which are the proper objects of commands and prohibitions. But Jesus, still using the language of command and prohibition, directs our attention inwards, to our inner being and dispositions. It is not enough not to kill; you must not even be angry with your brother (5:22). It is not enough not to commit adultery; you must not even lust after a woman (or of course a man; 5:28). Jesus is carrying out the programme foreseen by Jeremiah, and writing the law on our hearts (Jer 31:31–33). But our inner dispositions are precisely the realm where grace operates, not law. The law written on the heart is law that has burst out of its proper category and become law in the most analogical, not to say metaphorical, of senses. It is in fact grace, which is beyond and above the prescriptions of law. 'That which is primary in the law of the New Testament, and in which all its force resides, is the grace of the Holy Spirit, which is given through faith in Christ', says Thomas Aquinas (*STh* Ia IIae, 106, i; ET, vol. 30).

There is a sententious commonplace to the effect that it is not what you do that matters, but what you are. Like most sententious commonplaces it is less than half true. The real point is that what you are governs what you do. So in this case of the sermon on the mount, if we are as Jesus tells us we ought to be, if the law of grace is really written in our hearts, and we really devote ourselves to seeking the kingdom of God and his justice, then our behaviour will be revolutionized. We will find ourselves doing paradoxical things that certainly no law would ever prescribe, and some law would definitely discourage; things like turning the other cheek, not resisting evil, loving one's enemies (Mt 5:39–45). We begin to see that this inner justice or righteousness of the kingdom, this law written in our hearts, must imply that paradoxical humility of which we spoke in the last chapter as being the chief element of the human programme that is revealed to us in Christ.

Then again, this justice of the kingdom, what we are urged to become and to be in our inmost selves and inner dispositions, is shown to involve a very thorough transcendence of, not to say contempt for, the values of common temporal existence which law, any law, naturally upholds; the values of property and wealth in terms of which individuals and communities provide for themselves and make what provision they may for the future. But we, seeking the kingdom of God and his justice, are bidden 'not to be anxious about tomorrow, for tomorrow will be anxious for itself' (6:34); not to worry about what we shall eat or drink or wear, not to lay up for ourselves treasures on earth (not to save or invest money, in other words), because none of it lasts, and anyway God cares for us if only we have the faith to see it, and in any case it is impossible to serve God and mammon (Mt 6:19, 24–32).

But mammon (money), savings, banking, provision for ordinary and extraordinary needs, insurance, development – these are all, very properly, among the chief concerns of law and government in any society – even in the most simple societies in their own measure. People will argue hotly about what are just laws and just systems of government in these respects; but what they are always arguing about, capitalists, socialists, communists, individualists, nationalists and internationalists, anarchists and monarchists and democrats, republicans, aristocrats and oligarchs, traditionalists and radicals, and inevitably and rightly so, is 'the justice which is based on law', not the justice of the kingdom of God; about law, not about grace.

For what else does the 'lawgiver of grace', the Moses of Mount Zion (cf. Heb 12:18–24), who is inscribing the law on our hearts, go on to say about this justice of the kingdom? 'Judge not, that you be not judged' (7:1). But it could well be said that the whole purpose of law is to provide a proper basis for making judgements. And the political arguments we have just alluded to, which are about the justice based on law, involve a whole series of judgements. I think it is true to say that if none of us ever judged any of us, society would collapse.

And yet Jesus has not come to abolish temporal society any more than he has come to abolish the law and the prophets. He has simply come to fulfil them all. Temporal society is to be fulfilled by and in the kingdom. But it is important for us to realize that it is not the kingdom; that its justice is not the kingdom's justice; that therefore in addition to the righteousness based on law and the justice proper to temporal society (in our terms, the virtues of the good citizen, about which we rightly engage in those political and social arguments), we must pursue the justice of the kingdom, or we shall in no wise enter into it. We are, as we have seen before, ineluctably caught in a highly paradoxical situation.

The most 'formal' statement of the paradox is in fact made in the introduction to the sermon on the mount which I have so far not mentioned, the beatitudes (Mt 5:3–12). Here, blessings (not exactly a 'law' concept, but one taken rather from the Wisdom strata of the Old Testament) are pronounced on what for the most part seem to be decidedly unblessed, unfortunate kinds of person and condition. Here is a turning upside down with a vengeance of worldly values. What does it mean? One exploration of its meaning which I strongly recommend to the reader is *Reflections on the Beatitudes* by Simon Tugwell, OP. And I cannot close this subsection more fittingly than by quoting from his introduction:

> God does not come into our world with the toughness of an omnipotent thug, to sort everything and everybody out. He himself has chosen the way of weakness. There is something about God which is better expressed in weakness than in strength, in foolishness than in wisdom, in poverty than in richness. The story of the earthly life of Jesus Christ is a story of human failure, of human poverty, of human foolishness. And yet that is the revelation of God in human terms. And we who are followers of Jesus Christ are called to be imitators of him, and so should not be at all surprised to find that one of the arts we have to learn is the sublime art of weakness.

That's it, that's the justice of the kingdom, that is the grace of the sermon on the mount – the sublime art of weakness.

(ii) St Paul

St Paul deals more explicitly with the issue of law and grace (or law and faith), and so his doctrine on the matter is easier to summarize. What Mt calls the justice of the scribes and Pharisees he calls the justice based on law (Rom 9:31, Phil 3:9), and what Mt calls the justice of the kingdom he calls the justice of God (Rom 10:3) or the justice which is through faith in Christ, the justice from God that depends on faith (Phil 3:9).

I deliberately keep the word 'justice' here rather than RSV's 'righteousness', because it makes clear the connection with *justification*, which is what St Paul is really talking about in these contexts. Justification is a highly legal word, taken from Israelite court procedure. Being justified means being acquitted, or winning your case, judgement being given in your favour. So justification implies something to be justified from, and this, of course, for St Paul is sin.

What he says, then, is that it is impossible to be justified by simply observing the law meticulously, i.e. by the justice which is based on law, which I can claim as my own justice if I succeed in doing that (Rom 10:3).

He quotes Ps 143:2 to the effect that in God's sight can no man living be justified (Rom 3:20). Since we are in fact sinners it is only by God's merciful forgiveness that we can be justified; that is, in Paul's terms, by the justice which is from God, which comes to us through faith in the blood of Christ, which is thus a gift won for us, even in a sense earned for us by Christ, but at all events a gift from God. The justice of the kingdom which we are bidden to seek is only to be found at the hands of God.

Paul could perhaps have been accused with more justice than Jesus of abolishing the law, because he certainly regarded it as abrogated by the saving and grace-giving death and resurrection of Christ. 'For Christ is the end of the law, that everyone who has faith may be justified' (Rom 10:4). He thus related law to grace (or to faith, which in this context means the acceptance of grace) in a historical sequence. The law (meaning always specifically the law of Moses, the Torah) is designed in various ways to prepare for the coming of Christ. It shows up sin in all its evil, and so convinces us of the need for redemption by Christ (Rom 7); it keeps or guards God's people safely till Christ comes, and faith in him; it is a pedagogue (custodian, RSV) leading us to the school of freedom in Christ (Gal 3:19–25). It watched over the 'minority' of God's people, till they should come of age in Christ.

This relating of law to grace in a time sequence fits in very well with the salvation history concept of theology, or the notion of God's revelation as a tremendous drama enacted between God and man, and unfolding towards its climax in Jesus Christ, which has been the central concept of this book. But it does raise certain problems. In the first place, we have to say that on the one hand we Christians, who in the words of St Augustine at the conclusion of his rule are 'established as free men under grace, not as slaves under law' (a contrast borrowed straight from Galatians, *passim*), still for all that find that law is an important and inescapable element in our lives; not indeed the law of Moses, but the law of the land, Church law, moral law. The law of Moses may have been abrogated by the coming of Christ, but surely not law in general. And on the other hand we surely have to say that the grace of Christ was somehow or other available to the people of the old dispensation for their justification, and that they were capable of receiving it inwardly, written on their hearts.

I would answer this pair of problems as follows. As regards the people of the old dispensation before Christ, the law of Moses had a genuine *religious* value as foreshadowing Christ and as representing his grace and providing space, so to speak, for it to be written on the heart. It was possible, it was indeed required, even then to interiorize the law – but only possible, then as now, through the grace of God received through faith in Christ, though this faith was necessarily an implicit 'inarticulate' faith in 'one who was to come' (cf. Mt 11:3).

As regards us now, after Christ has come and redeemed us by his death and resurrection, we can and must believe in him explicitly, and we have his grace represented to us much more effectively by the sacraments of the Church. And so for us absolutely no law has any religious value any more. Law is for us a purely secular, this-worldly matter, even Church law. It is a matter of social order and convenience. It can still impose serious obligations on us, which we are morally bound to observe, but it has nothing whatever to do with our justification.

One may also, perhaps, transpose Paul's temporal sequence of law followed by grace into spatial metaphors signifying order within simultaneity. There is a maxim of Thomas Aquinas that grace perfects nature and does not destroy it. Law is part of man's 'natural' social condition. So we can say that grace perfects law; we can say that grace builds on law; that law regulates the outer shell of human existence, while grace quickens the heart of it. But I think the all-important effect of the New Testament teaching of grace, and of the offer of divine grace in Christ and the invitation to a gracious and graceful form of existence in him, is to *desacralize* law – just as it is to desacralize nature. There is an expression 'the full majesty of the law'. Well, I say that the Christian need no longer be overawed by that majesty, need not take it very seriously any more. Let us think of that other common saying, 'The law is an ass'. Law is a secular convenience, indeed a secular necessity, which has the habit of tying itself into the most inconvenient knots of red tape. It still is this as it always has been. But it has *nothing* to do with the kingdom of God (the only real kingdom there is), and so in fact it does not have any real sacredness or majesty. Just possibly, its majesty is so much flummery.

(iii)   The moral law

Another problem that arises from St Paul's treatment of the law deserves a subsection to itself. That is the problem of the moral law. If the law is abrogated by the saving work of Christ, and outmoded by the grace of the new covenant, does that mean that the ten commandments are no longer binding – or for the matter of that, does it mean that the two great commandments of love are no longer binding, since they occur in the law (Exod 20:2–17; Dt 5:6–21, Lev 19:18, Dt 6:5)? If the question is put like that, it can only be answered that these moral precepts of the law have not been abrogated. In support of this answer, the tradition has analysed the law of Moses into three kinds of law – moral law, ceremonial law, and judicial law – what we might nowadays call constitutional law. Of these kinds of law or precept, it is only the ceremonial and the judicial that have been abrogated by the new covenant and hence are no longer binding on Christians.

I confess that I find this answer profoundly unsatisfactory. Behind it (and the question it answers) lies an assumption that morals are reducible to law. It is an assumption that seems to have governed the teaching of most Catholic moral theology in the last century or so, but that is in fact so deeply un-Christian and uncatholic that it can only be labelled as materially heretical. St Paul in fact makes short work of it. His nameless disciple, the author of the pastoral epistles,[4] makes the point very succinctly: 'understanding this, that the law is not laid down for the just, but for the lawless and disobedient' etc. (1 Tim 1:9). St Paul himself tells the Romans 'You are not under law, but under grace' (6:14). That he included the precepts of the moral law here is plain from how he continues. 'What then? Are we to sin because we are not under law but under grace?' (v. 15). To paraphrase a little: 'Oh good!', say his imaginary opponents, 'that means the ten commandments and all other moral precepts of the law are no longer binding. We can do what we like, sin as much as we want and God won't object.' Now St Paul does *not* answer this objection by saying 'Wait a minute, the moral precepts of the law still bind'. He answers by saying 'You have missed the point. It isn't because there is a law against them that we who are under grace avoid committing the sins that the writer of 1 Timothy is going to list. It is because they are sins, because they are of their nature against justice or righteousness, the justice or righteousness of the kingdom, i.e. the grace which we are now under.'

Elsewhere he says of the ten commandments, 'For the whole law is fulfilled in one word, You shall love your neighbour as yourself' (Gal 5:14; cf. Rom 13:8–10), thus taking up the words of Jesus in the gospel about the great commandments on which depend the whole law and the prophets (Mt 22:37–40). This means, 'If you love, you do all the good things commanded by the law, and avoid all the bad things forbidden by it, not because there is a law about them but because that is what love prompts you to do'. And what about the law of love? you ask. It isn't really a law, I answer, because you cannot legislate love. It is a declaratory teaching of what is so, in the nature of things, in the goodness of God and of his creation.

So, if you are going to ask that question, 'Is even the moral law abrogated by the new covenant?' – which as Paul suggests in Rom 6:15, is a bad question – I will answer boldly, 'Yes, it is'. It is abrogated, because it is not needed for those who are under grace. Grace not law is the all-sufficient principle of right conduct, of justice or righteousness, for Christians, who are led by the Spirit and produce its fruits, against which there is no law (Gal 5:18–23). Moral law is an entirely secondary convenience by which to judge and convict the wickedness of sinners.

C. OLD TESTAMENT BACKGROUND

Both Jesus and Paul were teaching from an exclusively Old Testament background. This background was dominated by the Law, the Torah, and so even
when they are dethroning law and bursting its bounds they still do it in the
language of the law. And conversely, the substance of the concept of grace
which the New Testament disencapsulates from the law is to be found in the
Old Testament, in the Law itself, even though wrapped in the language of
law. It was in fact so found by both Jesus and Paul – the two great commandments of love, for example. So now we will take a closer look at this background by examining, first D's concept of law, and secondly what I call
anachronistically J's conception of grace.

(i)   D's conception of law

We have just observed that Paul was discussing law and grace in a context of
sin. He was in fact saying that law is an ineffective remedy for sin, which only
grace can deal with thoroughly and radically. In this he was going directly
counter to the ideas of P on the subject, as we inferred them back in Chapter
6, B.

D,[5] it is fair to say, had a wider and grander concept of law than as a mere
remedy for sin – too wide and too grand, perhaps Paul would be inclined to
comment. And D is very important to us because he is really the theological
ancestor, first of much of the prophetic teaching of the Old Testament, and
then of the Pharisees in New Testament times.

For D, then, the statutes and commandments and testimonies and customs
that constitute law in the strict sense are all part of the divine *Torah*. This
word, ever since the first translation of the Old Testament into Greek, has
traditionally been translated 'Law', but really means 'Teaching'. Thus in D's
conception, which represents the hard core of Israelite thinking, Law is
essentially didactic or pedagogic in purpose (here Paul is in the D tradition),
meant to teach us what is right and good. We can be taught this also by
stories about God's dealings with our ancestors, and such stories are also part
of the Torah, hence of the Law in the broad sense. The 'statutes and
commandments' of the Law also enforce this divine teaching by sanctions,
punishing us for what is wrong and bad; but that is entirely secondary to the
main instructive function of Law.

More than this: the Torah is the detailed expression of God's *covenant* with
Israel. This is the basic category of D's theology. Yahweh the God of Israel
has entered into a covenant with his people. This is far more than a mere legal
contract, although it has that element about it, or rather it has an essential
element of creating obligations of *justice*. But it is first and foremost a
covenant of *love*; on God's side an expression of his gracious, loving choice or

election of Israel from among all other nations to be his own peculiar people. D is insistent that God did not choose Israel because they were better or nobler than other nations. But because he chose them, he gave them better and wiser laws than any other nations have, and entered into a far closer relationship with them. This was a relationship of *hesed* and *emeth*, lovingkindness and fidelity. Law, the Torah, spells out not only the obligations but also the blessings of the covenant. Israel's sins can, and eventually do, wreck this covenant, according to D, bringing curses (supremely the exile) instead of blessings. But even had there been no sin, there would still have been the covenant and its blessings, God being who he is. And in this context the basic sin is seen not so much as transgression of the law, but rather as *infidelity* or *disloyalty* to the God of the covenant.

Reflection on the essence of the Torah or Law was carried further by the professional sages who produced the Wisdom books of the Bible.[6] They came to think of it as an expression or embodiment of the divine Wisdom. Since this Wisdom is also envisaged in this tradition as the architect of the cosmos, as identical with the 'word' by which God made the world, it is clear that the Law is perceived as echoing the intelligible harmonies that are built into the created universe. Putting it more prosaically, we can say that Law (i.e. in fact the Law of Moses) is seen as being in harmony with either the laws of nature or the natural law, or both, whichever you may prefer. See and compare Prov 8:22–31, Sir 24, especially vv. 23ff., Bar 3:9 – 4:4.

(ii) J's intuition of grace

J gives the impression of having a kind of premonition of the New Testament doctrine of grace, because he has a much more sombre and profound conception of sin than either P or D appear to do. P in particular thinks of God giving man laws as a remedy for sin, which is man, you could say, damaging his lines of communication with God. So God provides laws, with incentives of rewards and punishments, which make it possible for man to repair the damaged lines. D agrees, except that he puts law first very firmly, as part of the creative wisdom of God. So within the framework of God's providence and his external direction and advice, his Torah or teaching, it is up to us human beings to cope with the burden of our sins by repairing the breaches in the lines of communication that our sins have made, both between us and God and between ourselves.

But J, as we saw earlier on in Chapter 6, C, knows that sin is much more than, in effect, blowing up a bridge or severing a telephone wire. It is a turning away from God which damages the inner being of the sinner, indeed of the whole sinful society of mankind. It breaks the relationship between man and man or man and God, not so much as a connecting link, a road or a telephone line, but at the very core of the sinner's capacity to communicate. It causes a decay, a death at the heart of the creature's being. The only remedy, therefore, will be what the New Testament will call 'a new creation' (Gal 6:15, 2 Cor 5:17 – already intimated in the Old Testament by Ezekiel, who looks forward to God substituting a heart of flesh for his people's heart of stone, 36:26; cf. Ps 51:10). God will have to do it all, and keep on doing it, if he wants it done – which of course he is not obliged to want, but our very existence as his people shows that he does want it. It is not enough for him merely to provide the right conditions for us to do all that is necessary, to put us back on the rails, so to say, and then leave the rest to us.

J, needless to say, does not express all this in so many words, but it seems to me to be the implication of his position. He describes what God does by saying that he *calls* certain people that he has *chosen* (divine election), and makes them certain *promises*, and gives them his *blessing*. These are J's key ideas in the texts of Gen 12:1–3 and 15:2–6:

Now the Lord said to Abram, Go from your country and your kindred and your father's house to the land I will show you. And I will make of you a great nation, and I will bless you and make your name great, so that you will be a blessing. I will bless those who bless you, and him who curses you I will curse; and by you all the families of the earth will bless themselves.[7]

And again:

Abram said, O Lord God, what wilt thou give me, for I continue childless, and the heir of my house is Eliezer of Damascus? And Abram said, Behold thou hast given me no offspring; and a slave born in my house will be my heir. And behold, the word of the Lord came to him, This man shall not be your heir; your own son shall be your heir. And he brought him outside and said, Look toward heaven, and number the stars, if you are able to number them. Then he said to him, So shall your descendants be. And he believed the Lord; and he reckoned it to him as righteousness.

All Abraham has to do, then, is to *believe*, or trust God – trust him to keep his promise. The theme is repeated with Jacob, Gen 28:12–15.

The blessing becomes a clearer messianic prophecy in a later J text, Num 24, the oracles of Balaam. The immediate reference of 24:7 and 17, 'A man will arise from his seed' (LXX version), and 'a star shall come forth from Jacob', is almost certainly to David, in whom J considered the promises made to Abraham, Isaac and Jacob to have received their complete fulfilment *so far*. But so far it was. He surely looks beyond David, beyond his own recent past, to some *total* fulfilment which we would now call eschatological. Num 24:5–6 foresees a kind of return to paradise, led and inaugurated by a blessed Israel.

This expectation is taken up in a very much later messianic text, Isa 11:1–9, 'There shall come forth a shoot from the stump of Jesse . . . . The wolf shall dwell with the lamb . . . and a little child shall lead them'; a return to paradise under a divinely appointed messianic or Davidic leader. The foundation text for these further hopes centred on David and his descendants is the prophecy of Nathan in 2 Sam 7. Though most probably later than J, it seems to be in the same kind of tradition: divine promises, made this time to David, in whom earlier promises had been partly fulfilled; but made in such exaggerated terms that their final and complete fulfilment must transcend the ordinary historical limits. But perhaps the clearest Old Testament statement of trust in God's saving grace is to be found in Jer 30 and 31. No one can question the vividness of Jeremiah's awareness of his people's sins and their *irremediable* nature, humanly speaking. But their remedying is not left to man and human speaking. God will intervene, 30:12–24. Why? Because 'I have loved you with an everlasting love' (31:3).That is what grace is, in the last analysis, God's everlasting and *uncovenanted* love. This love is going to issue in, but not be preconditioned by, a new and everlasting covenant, 31:31–34. We noticed this text earlier on in this chapter (B, i). The language is still that of law and covenant, but as we observed there it is law at a new and analogical, or indeed metaphorical level, law transmuted into the grace of the Holy Spirit, which as we also saw is how Thomas Aquinas defines the essence of the new law of the gospel.

It is interesting, incidentally, to see that when St Paul in his protracted arguments with Pharisees and Judaizing Christians about grace and law is looking for Old Testament proof texts to support his case, he chooses for preference texts from J. He did not know about J, of course. But he certainly knew a good text about grace and faith when he read one.

D.   LAW AND GRACE IN THE CHRISTIAN LIFE

The paradoxical, indeed problematical task facing the Christian today is to live the life of grace (a life governed by the radical spontaneity of love) in a wholly secular world of law, a world which the inner drive of the Christian religion has in fact effectively secularized.[8] But before we offer some observations on this task, we must lead up to it by a subsection on how the issue between grace and law has changed since the time of St Paul. Conceptions of law, of course, have also developed during these two millennia, which have seen the elaboration of the important but much misunderstood concept of natural law. But for a brief presentation of this idea I refer the reader back to Chapter 16, B, iii.

(i)   *Grace and free will, grace and morals*

After the New Testament era, in particular after the destruction of Jerusalem by the Romans in 70 A.D., when there ceased to be any significant number of

Jewish Christians, the issue of the binding force of the Law of Moses ceased to be a live one for the Church. It had been settled definitively by Paul. But the basic issue between grace and law remained, as it always will remain, for Christians to wrestle with in different forms. For the excessively legalistic attitude of the Pharisees, or a modification of it into a moralism of law (above, B, iii), remain temptations for any genuinely religious, or even genuinely serious people, agnostics and humanists included. One finds in all Churches what really is a kind of Old Testament Christianity. Certainly an Old Testament Catholicism is deeply entrenched in the Catholic Church. To illustrate how very, very similar early Christians could be in their assumptions to their benighted enemies the Pharisees, we have this charming passage from the *Didache*,[9] probably the earliest Christian text outside the New Testament: 'Your fasts should not coincide with those of the hypocrites. They fast on Mondays and Thursdays; you should fast on Wednesdays and Fridays' (8). The writer is enlarging on Mt 6:16–18 and, one cannot help feeling, rather missing the point.

The issue burst into flame once more in the classic controversy between St Augustine and the Pelagians in the second and third decades of the fifth century. In one way or another it has been smouldering on, at least in the Western Churches, ever since.

Briefly, Pelagius[10] accused Augustine of effectively denying free will with his doctrine of grace. Pelagius and his associates took the straightforward, plain man's view that it is entirely up to you whether you lead a good life or a bad. God has given us every advantage: he has created us with intelligence and free will, he has revealed his truth to us, he has made us wonderful promises, and he has told us, in his moral law, what we have to do in order to receive the promised reward of eternal life and the kingdom of heaven. So it is up to us simply to go ahead with it, thus working our passage to heaven. No doubt it is hard. But if you go into training like a dedicated athlete, leading a life of ascesis or self-denial under a good spiritual director like Pelagius himself (i.e. a good moral director) it is perfectly possible – just a matter of really willing it.

This view of things, Augustine retorted, in denying any need for grace effectively denies any need for us to be saved by God; we simply save ourselves. Therefore it denies any special value to the death of Christ, who of course ceases really to be our saviour.

The radical flaw in the plain, moral man's view of things, I suggest, is that first, it thinks of God as just one more, though the greatest and the top, person over against us, with whom we communicate in exactly the same sort of way as we do with other persons, by means of external signals, symbols, influences and pressures; and secondly, that it thinks of our 'heavenly reward' as again something equally external and extrinsic, really differing very little in anything except quantity and duration from the golden handshake given by benevolent company directors to deserving and respected company servants on their retirement. There is no inkling here either of the transcendence or the immanence of God; nor of the possibility and indeed constant reality of our human transcendence, our capacity to rise to higher levels of existence, our capacity indeed precisely to be divinized; nor of the truth that our 'heavenly reward' consists in our being divinized, in our receiving nothing less than God himself – a gift which by the very nature of things we cannot really earn, and which must therefore in the nature of things be a grace.

Augustine's position, though less simple, is altogether more humane and realistic – and Christian. He does not in fact deny the reality of free will (one of his earliest works after his conversion was *On Free Will*), but says it has been impaired, even enslaved by sin, in particular by original sin, a concept which the Pelagians rejected (Chapters 7 and 8 above). The Latin term, incidentally, *liberum arbitrium*, would be better translated 'freedom of choice', or 'freedom of decision'. This assertion of his does correspond to a widespread, indeed surely universal, experience of psychological compulsion we are all in different ways and measures subject to, an experience the moralistic Pelagians simply ignore. This kind of compulsion, certainly, does not totally destroy our freedom of choice and hence our responsibility for our deliberate acts; but it does seriously diminish it, and so makes it impossible for us to lead morally good lives, to be just in the full biblical sense, entirely on our own psychic and moral resources.

This is where grace comes in. God offers us his liberating love at a level of our being far deeper than these psychological compulsions and hang-ups and our impaired freedom of choice; for God as Augustine knew is deeper within us than our deepest selves, and is not just what Simon Tugwell so happily calls 'the omnipotent thug' out there (above, B, i), whom I suspect all Pelagians and ultra-moralists worship. And to this inner offer of liberating love we respond by faith, explicitly by faith in the saving death of Jesus Christ if we are Christians, implicitly and as it were inarticulately if we are not. And thus we receive God's liberating grace, which becomes precisely an inner principle of *freedom* within us, not a principle of divine compulsion or manipulation.

Just as this liberating or healing grace (which we must remember is a kind of sharing in God's life, an assimilation to his nature) does not abolish free will but sustains it and makes it really free, so neither does it abolish morals or moral obligation. It simply sets us free from them as a network of coercive and irksome 'enslaving' laws imposed from without, and makes us spontaneously free for a kind of inspired moral behaviour which cherishes and practises genuine moral values of goodness and right from within – the 'law' written on the heart. Grace sets us free *from* moral law, free *for* virtue and the virtuous life, free to live it spontaneously, out of love, free spontaneously to struggle against out own continuing propensity to sin, to gracelessness, to slavery.

The study of morals which we call ethics, or at the theological level moral theology, continues of course to be a most necessary and useful guide to right action and good behaviour. We continue, very frequently, to need moral advice. But the advice, or even the commands we receive can never be an effective spring and principle of our behaviour. Nor can 'being moral', 'doing the right thing', ever be a sufficient goal or end of our behaviour. The only vital spring or drive of the truly Christian, which is to say the fully human, life is God's grace issuing in love; and the only sufficient goal or aim of such a life is again love. 'Love – and do what you like'; another very profound, very scandalous and shocking saying of St Augustine's.[11] It will have the respectable, moral Pelagian who lurks somewhere in most of us freeze rigid with horrified disapproval.

(ii) The life of grace in a secular world

We saw earlier on that one important effect of the revelation to us of God's grace in Jesus Christ was to desacralize law. To desacralize is the same as to secularize. So what we mean here by a secular world is a world (i.e. a human society in itself and in its attitude towards the world it occupies) in which practically all aspects of public and social life, political, legal, economic, educational, even moral, have been desacralized; that is to say they are not seen any more as governed by religion, or as enjoying any special religious sanction and support. It is our assumption here that the contemporary European world (and in all probability other worlds too) is for the most part such a secular world. One needs only to compare it, for example, with the contemporary Islamic world (consider in particular the régime of the ayatollahs in Iran) to see the difference between a secular and a sacral world.

A secular world or society is not necessarily a society without God.[12] It is truer to say that it is a society without public religion. Religion is a private affair, purely a matter of free choice for members of such a society. So a secularized society is very often a *plural* society, containing many religions. That is the case with modern Western society, and the fact of its Christian pluralism, the fragmentation of Western Christianity into many different and mutually hostile Churches at the Reformation, has been a potent factor in the secularization of the West. Religious toleration is an important step along the road to secularization, which then makes possible the *comparatively* easy admission to the society of religions and cultures that are quite alien to its Christian origins. Our current troubles with race relations (which means in fact with our European racial prejudices) indicate that there are important areas of our life which remain culturally 'sacral' in a very undesirable way. Another, and more recent, factor in the secularization of our society is of course the abandonment of religious belief altogether by large sections, probably the majority, of the population. Western Europe is a secularized society because it is so very largely a post-Christian society.

So the secularization of society undoubtedly has negative aspects, brought about by what are from the Christian point of view negative causes. The word 'secularism' is often used to signify these negative aspects. But I think it is true to say that the principal architect, so to speak, of the secular world is Christianity itself, indeed the whole biblical revelation. For secularization does not merely mean the transfer of whole sections of life from the sacred to the secular domain, from Church to State, for example. That is merely its superficial aspect, and it is this that so often fills religious people with dismay. What it really means at base is the total abolition of the distinction between the sacred and the secular or profane. The demolition process on this middle wall of partition ('the dividing wall of hostility', Eph 2:14) was begun by Christ himself – indeed by God himself at creation. For what Gen 1 states by implication is that there is no ontological distinction among created beings between the sacred and the profane, the holy and the secular. The only onto-logical distinction that cannot be eradicated is that between Creator and creature. God alone is holy, and eternal; what he creates is by definition 'secular' or temporal and time-bound.

When we get to the New Testament, we not only find Jesus Christ flouting all the cherished 'sacralisms' of the Pharisees about the sabbath and about ritual cleansings, and then talking about the abolition of the temple, and declaring 'all foods clean' (Mk 7:19); we find even the distinction between God and creatures being breached, being plastered over, so to say, by the mystery of the incarnation, God becoming human, and its con-sequence, man being made divine.

What it amounts to is this: if you abolish the distinction between the sacred and the secular, as Christianity in principle does, then you can of course call it secularization if you like; but you can with equal justice call it total sacralization. God is telling us in Christ that we should overcome the distinction between sacred and secular spheres of life because everything and everyone and every aspect of life is in principle holy and sacred. It is up to us to see it so and help to make it so.[13]

So living in a more or less completely secular world, it seems to me, offers the Christian a tremendous opportunity – a field in which the life of grace can have full and spontaneous play. If we see only the negative aspects of secular-ism, see it simply as a threat to our religion and the Church, and to our salva-tion, then we are not going to give the life of grace in us free elbow room; we are going to be far too busy either patching up our 'sacred' defences, or looking for new ones, or we are going to retreat even further into a private kind of religion; to make it a purely personal thing between ourselves and God that has nothing to do with our secular life in the secular world; we are going to 'keep our religion out of politics' and out of our economics and our law and everything else of that kind. In fact we are going to let the world get even more secular in a negative sense as we continue to barricade ourselves into an ever narrower spiritual and mental ghetto. And in such a narrow space (I am talking of spiritual space), the spontaneous, free, generous, graceful life of grace cannot really flourish.

But if we seize the opportunity which the secular world offers us, things will be quite different. Our task is to penetrate this world with God's grace; not to attempt to sacralize it again in the old external way, but to make manifest, to elicit from within, the inner sacred potential of the world that is there, simply because the world has been created, and redeemed by God. To live the life of grace in a secular world is to be free (that's what the life of grace means) and to be free in an infectious way, to elicit spontaneity with spontaneity, to contribute a certain divine elegance, grace, to the life of the secular world.

Very romantic, very high-sounding, very unrealistic, you may be muttering. Come down to earth. What about the evil of the secular world? Well, what about it? The pre-secular world was just as full of evil, or at least the people who lived in it seemed to think so. We must deal with evil as Christ in his grace has always dealt with evil and encouraged his followers to deal with it – by enduring it, by loving both those who also endure it and those who commit it – and by seeing it for what it is and calling it what it is. And I think a sacralized society is often more adept at concealing evil and disguising it as good than a secular society. In both kinds of society the emperor may well have no clothes; but in a secular society it is easier to see so and to say so and therefore to do something about it and get him some. The Christian living the life of grace in a secular society will be making all those airy-fairy contributions I have been talking about to the inner divinization of society by, among other things, facing the social evils he encounters in his secular life, by being committed to the values of justice and truth and liberation, by hardheaded work and study, and conflict, in this sense. He will not be tempted, he will not have the opportunity, to neglect the weightier matters of the law, justice and mercy and faith, by concentrating on tithing mint and dill and cummin (Mt 23:23). He may indeed neglect these weightier matters, because he is a sinner as well as a Christian living the life of grace. But he won't be able to hide it from himself by a 'pious' preoccupation with sacral trivialities.

NOTES

1 With apologies to both Edith Cavell and Samuel Johnson.

2 This is not only because Jesus is teaching within the context of Jewish religion, but also because the Christian community from which and for which the gospel of Matthew came was in all probability a community of mainly Jewish Christians. What was being undertaken was a radical reinterpretation of the whole Judaic tradition, but in its own language. A most useful and interesting book on the Judaic background is *The New Testament and Rabbinic Judaism* by David Daube, himself an orthodox Jew, learned in rabbinic law, who was Regius Professor of Roman Law at Oxford when he wrote the book, in 1956.

3 The word translated 'righteousness' by RSV (following AV) is *dikaiosunē*, for which I prefer the older and more literal translation 'justice' – mainly because 'righteousness' has become, has indeed I suspect always been, a churchy word, not obviously related to ordinary life. I also prefer 'justice' because of its obvious connection with 'justification', which is what many of these texts are in fact concerned with. And in the Bible both are legal as well as moral terms.

4 It is almost universally acknowledged nowadays that Paul himself did not write these. But the suggestion of a Catholic commentator (Robert J. Karris, OFM, *The Pastoral Epistles*) that the writer thought of himself as a disciple of the apostle, and wished to apply Paul's doctrine to changed circumstances in the Church about 100 A.D. is reasonable and a good explanation of why the epistles claim Pauline authorship.

5 D was introduced to the reader in Chapter 14, note 4.

6 The outlook of these sages, who gave us the books referred to here, was not so very different in some ways from that of P.

7 I prefer the translation, given in the RSV footnote, 'in you all the families of the earth will be blessed'.

8 This opinion is elaborated at the end of the chapter. Historically, Christianity was born into a highly sacral world, that of ancient paganism, and of course found itself in bitter conflict with this world, persecuted by it as an 'atheistic madness'. When this world became Christian after Constantine, it continued to be highly sacral, with Christian sacred validation of society and its institutions succeeding to the pagan variety. And this pattern was carried over, with variations, into the new Christian societies of the converted barbarians, from Ireland to Russia and Scandinavia. But this situation, in my view, was never really congenial to the proper nature of the Christian gospel.

9 Its full title is *The Teaching (Didache) of the Twelve Apostles*. Some scholars date it as early as 70 A.D., most at about 90; which means it is earlier than some of the New Testament books, like 2 Peter, or the pastoral epistles.

10 Pelagius (for whom see Chapter 8, note 1) does not seem to have written much himself in the controversy. His most articulate and vehement supporter against Augustine was an Italian, Julian, Bishop of Eclanum, who was the thorn in Augustine's flesh in his old age.

11 In his commentary on 1 John (tract. VIII, 8; *PL* 35, 2033). What Augustine is actually talking about is beating your children. Yes of course, he says, beat them if you think it necessary – provided you do it out of love.

12 A society that is officially atheist, especially if it is intolerant of religious practice, I would hesitate to call secular. It soon produces its own *sacra*, its own absolutes, its own sacred canon, its own hierarchy. At least it seems to have done so in Russia.

13 Why the most diverse human societies have always tended to make the distinction between the sacred and the profane, in an enormous variety of ways, is an interesting question. Is it a necessary accompaniment of the religious sense, of the quest for God? I

would not readily be prepared to concede that it is. I wonder if it is not perhaps rather a kind of defence mechanism, rooted in fear rather than in love of the holy or the divine – a sense that God is dangerous. So to divide life into distinct areas of the sacred and the profane is as much a precaution against God as a precaution against evil. It can indeed sometimes be a means of promoting and sanctioning evil. It is a very great mistake to think of the sacred or the holy as a moral category, as a super good. Holiness has come to be equated with extraordinary goodness in the Christian tradition – but I almost think that is part of the continuing Christian desacralization process! In itself and in its origins the sacred or the holy is morally a completely neutral category. A classic authority on the subject is Rudolf Otto in his book *Das Heilige*, first published in 1917 (ET: *The Idea of the Holy*).

QUESTION FOR FURTHER DISCUSSION

1   Living a life of grace in a world still necessarily and rightly governed by law (including moral law) seems to be a highly paradoxical condition. Is there any possibility of resolving this paradox?

RECOMMENDED FURTHER READING

Simon Tugwell, *Reflections on the Beatitudes*, is a splendid book that brings home to us this Christian paradox.

Roger Haight, *The Experience and Language of Grace*, chapter 2: 'Augustine: Grace and Human Autonomy'.

Charles Davis, *God's Grace in History*.

22

Christ the Last Adam Manifested in his Church

In Chapter 20 we saw how God has revealed to us in Christ the ultimate possibilities of human existence, and the best present programme for realizing those possibilities. This revelation is mediated to us through the Church, not only in the sense that the Church transmits the revelation through its teaching, but also in the sense that the Church manifests or embodies the revelation in its very existence. In the Church we see, and we live, the social dimensions of the programme, and we anticipate the social dimensions of the possibilities of the human existence revealed to us in Christ. For the Church is Christ in his social dimensions.

We have already discussed in Chapter 18 the role of the Church in relation to the whole community of mankind. The Church in its totality forms the subject of another book in this series. Here we are only going to consider the Church insofar as it shows us something about our authentic relations with God; insofar as it is the social dimension of our most authentic human existence. So what we have to do is to explore a little further the statement just made that the Church is Christ in his social dimensions.

A. THE CHURCH AS SACRAMENT OF CHRIST THE SACRAMENT

(i) Christ the sacrament

We shall begin by doing it with the aid of Fr Edward Schillebeeckx, OP. We have already referred to his book *Christ the Sacrament of Encounter with God* (above, Selah 2). This was written as a kind of introduction to sacramental theology, to provide a context for the theology of the sacraments. But as the context provided is christological and ecclesiological, and as in order to relate the sacraments to the Church and to Christ it first has to relate the Church to Christ, it ought to be illuminating for us in our present concern.

Encounter with God, that is man's encounter with God, is basically what the theology of man is about (Chapter 1, A). Schillebeeckx says that like any genuine encounter it means two-way communication; from God to man there is the bestowal of God's grace, the name of God's love of man; and from man to God there is worship, the name for man's love of God. But human encounters are essentially bodily events, since human beings are living bodies. We only encounter each other through our bodies, through bodily signals of one sort or another, and so our encounter with God, in both its directions, also needs somehow to be embodied. Men have always spontaneously embodied their worship in symbolic bodily gestures, i.e. in 'sacramental' acts;[1] and have thought to see the divine communication they desired also embodied in some perceptible symbolic events.

So God, after preparing the ground through the Old Testament revelation in Israel, finally offers man the perfect sacrament of this two-way encounter in Christ, the incarnate Word. It is in the great paschal mystery, in the death, resurrection and ascension of Christ and his pentecostal gift of the Holy Spirit from his throne of glory that the incarnation of the eternal Word is completed and consummated, and thus the Christ sacrament perfectly accomplished. This is both the central, total, visible embodiment of God's gift of grace to man, the grace of forgiveness and reconciliation, and the central, perfect, visible embodiment of man's true worship of God. Christ's death on the cross, as an act of perfect self-giving out of love and obedience to the Father, and love and fellow-feeling for mankind, is the supreme and perfect expression of human worship. And it does not end on the cross; it is accepted by the Father when he raises Jesus from the dead, and Christ now ascended into heaven and seated at God's right hand continues eternally to make intercession for us, to offer the Father our worship (Heb 7:25; 9:24). And all this, from cross to Pentecost, is also his gift to us, first of himself and then of his Spirit, enabling us to be fully identified with him in this two-way encounter with God.

(ii)   Christ invisible and we with him

But with the ascension of the risen Lord into heaven a problem arises. Now that he is no longer visibly present among us, how can he continue to be the *sacrament* of this saving, all-fulfilling encounter of ours with God? For the essence of a sacrament or symbolic sign is that it should be visible, a physically sensible embodiment of what it signifies. Schillebeeckx insists that Christ does continue to be the sacrament of our encounter with God in his heavenly glory – precisely in his glorified bodiliness. And this is partly how he continues to be the sacrament of our saving encounter with God for us; because where he is, we are. We, believing mankind, are already in principle there with him in glory, because we are identified with him, our perfect representative, the last Adam. This truth, that we are already there with

Christ, is treated by Paul as one having practical consequences for our style of life: 'If you have been raised with Christ, seek the things that are above, where Christ is, seated at the right hand of God. Set your minds on things that are above, not on things that are on earth [get your key *values* right]. For you have died, and your life is hid with Christ in God. When Christ who is our life appears, then you also will appear with him in glory' (Col 3:1–4). So Christ in his glory continues to be the model and the final exemplar of our encounter with God. I think the point of doctrine is very neatly stated in a couplet from the hymn for the feast of the Ascension in the last Latin breviary that we Dominicans used before we all went vernacular: *Culpat caro, purgat caro,/Regnat Deus Dei caro*; Flesh has sinned and flesh atoned it;/ Flesh now reigns, God's flesh, as God.[2]

(iii)   Christ visible in the Church

But that is not enough – and is not in fact the way Schillebeeckx sets out his solution to our problem, though nothing he says contradicts it. As well as our already being with the glorious Christ in heaven, it is also necessary to our encounter with God here and now that Christ should continue to be here with us on earth. And the New Testament testifies abundantly that he does so. Note for example the concluding words of Matthew: 'And lo, I am with you always to the close of the age' (28:20), We are with him in heaven, as identified with him; he is with us on earth as identified with us. So he can say 'Where two or three are gathered in my name, there am I in the midst of them' (Mt 18:20); a saying attributed here, to be sure, to Jesus in his earthly ministry, but really heard by the Matthaean Church in which this 'Discourse on the Church' (Jerusalem Bible) was composed as uttered by the risen Christ in his glory. And so this glorious Christ is presented as saying, in the great judgement scene of the parable of the sheep and the goats, 'As you did it (or did it not) to one of the least of these my brethren, you did it (or did it not) to me' (25:40, 45). And finally, when he appears to Saul on the road to Damascus he says, 'Saul, Saul, why do you persecute me?' – not 'my disciples' or 'my brothers', but 'me' (Acts 9:4).

Now in all these cases those with whom Jesus identifies himself are the *community* of his brethren, or of those who believe in him, which we call the *Church*. So, again in virtue of the same principle of perfect representation by Christ, we arrive at Schillebeeckx' further conclusion that Christ, the sacrament of our encounter with God, is still visibly present amongst us in this aeon or age (which is quite distinct from and preparatory to the heavenly or eschatological aeon or age of the glorious Christ seated at God's right hand in the glory of his kingdom) in the visible reality of the Church, the community of believers, of Christ's brothers and sisters. We put this conclusion in the form of the statement that the Church too is sacrament (visible, symbolic embodiment), not this time immediately of our encounter with God, but of Christ (Christ crucified and glorified) who is the immediate sacrament of that encounter. Or perhaps it would be better to say, the Church is the sacrament of our encounter with God inasmuch as Christ identifies himself with the Church. Then the Church (and Christ in and through the Church) lives out its sacramental nature by celebrating for us the seven sacraments of our salvation which, each in its own way, are occasions of our encounter with God, both as God's gift of grace to us and as our offer or worship and prayer to God.

We have already noted the text of Vatican II's Constitution on the Church (*Lumen Gentium*, I, 1) in which the Church is called a kind of sign or sacrament of the unity of mankind and of man's intimate union with God (Chapter 18, C, i), According to Schillebeeckx, and I don't think anyone would disagree with him, it can only be this in and with Christ; it is this because Jesus Christ is this first. It is this kind of sacrament because Jesus Christ, who is this kind of sacrament, identifies himself with the Church. What Schillebeeckx has in fact stressed is Christ, and with and in him the Church, being the sacrament of man's intimate union with God, or as he puts it, of man's encounter with God. Back in Chapter 18, C we were looking at some of the implications of the Church being a sacrament of the unity of mankind. So here let us look at the implications of its representing man's intimate union with God. In particular, what challenge or invitation does this function of the Church present to us its members, precisely as the community of believers in this or that place?

(iv)   The Church, sacrament of Christ's worship of the Father

First then it is our task as the Church, in this or that place, to make visible to the world the authentic worship of God, which can only be the worship which Jesus Christ offered and continues to offer to the Father, the worship of the cross and the resurrection, of the whole paschal mystery. The world should be able to *see*, in our corporate worship (supremely in our celebration of the eucharist), both our generosity of self-sacrifice, of self-giving, and the intensity of our prayer and intercession, and the joyfulness of our praise.

In one very traditional word, the world should be able to see our *devotion*, and through it Christ's perfect devotion. As sacrament to the world of man's intimate union with God we are challenged corporately, not just individually, to *devotion*.[3] It is a challenge which is to a large extent made easier or more difficult to meet by cultural and national factors. For instance, I have experienced Christian Catholic worship mainly in two cultural settings, the English and the Sesotho.[4] And it is undeniable that the Basotho beat the

English hands down in responding to this challenge. They have a strong cultural tradition of popular singing in harmony, and of corporate or collective participation in ceremonies. I fancy the same is true in different ways all over Black Africa. Africa can certainly teach Europe, or at least Anglophone Europe (which includes Ireland) how to worship, which means how in one important respect to be authentically human. Basically, the lesson is, 'Don't presuppose that the worship of God is meant to be stuffy and boring; don't think God requires you to be stiff with inhibitions; let yourself go in generosity and joy'.[5] The impression an outsider ought to get after attending mass in a Catholic Church is, 'See what their religion means to these Catholics; see how wholeheartedly they throw themselves into it, how they enjoy it!' Of course, because we are symbolically demonstrating our intimate union with God.

(v)   The Church, sacrament of Christ's grace

Secondly, it is our corporate task to embody in our community Christian life, in our Church and its sacramental celebrations, the grace of God. And here I doubt if any culture or nation has in its own secular tradition an edge over any other.[6] For the impression the outsider should get from observing our corporate life, not only now in our worship but in our daily living, is, 'See how these Christians love one another!' That is supposed to be what was said about the first Christians by their heathen neighbours.[7] God's grace is unconfined, lavish. We are called on to demonstrate it to the world by perpetually surprising, and no doubt occasionally shocking the world with our corporate openness, generosity, spontaneity, unconventionality, gracefulness – by the *power* with which we witness to the love of Christ that constrains us (2 Cor 5:14; RSV: 'controls us').

But since it is God's grace that we are called upon visibly to body forth, it is not really a question of making an effort, even a corporate effort in this regard. To make an effort to be spontaneous is a contradiction in terms. A certain deliberate recollection is certainly called for, a continuous conversion bringing with it steady growth in self-awareness. But after that by a kind of stillness, of quietening the self, it is simply a matter of letting God's grace shine through – being God's Crystal Palace! This indeed requires a continual cleaning of the glass panes, but not precisely an effort to shine.

B.   THE CHURCH AS THE BODY OF CHRIST

The concept of the Church as sacrament, in and with Christ, of both the unity of mankind and man's intimate union with God presupposes St Paul's doctrine of the Church as the body of Christ. We find this doctrine in Paul's letters in two forms: the first form is that of 1 Cor 12:12–27 (see also Rom 12:4–5); the second that of Eph 1:22–23 and 4:11–16 (see also Col 1:18). Ephesians and Colossians, in the opinion of many, perhaps most, scholars, are not genuine letters of Paul's, but the composition of disciples in the Pauline school. So the second form of the doctrine may be seen as a development from the first.

(i) In 1 Corinthians: our current programme controlled by love

In the first form the community of believers is simply identified as a community with Christ. He is the community, the community is him: 'As the body is one and has many members, and all the members of the body, though many, are one body, so it is with Christ' (12:12). The body of Christ, like any body, is made up of many organs and parts (members) which all differ from each other, each making its own contribution to the life of the whole in harmony with the others, but in its own way. So individual believers are distinct parts, organs or members of the body of Christ, each with their own gifts and graces.

The context, we should not forget, is division and rivalry within the Corinthian Church, jealousies and airs and vanities over the different charismatic gifts of the Spirit. St Paul uses the extended metaphor of the body, with considerable irony, to show the folly of all this. 'If the whole body were an eye, where would be the hearing? If the whole body were an ear, where would be the sense of smell? . . . If all were a single organ, where would the body be? As it is, there are many parts, yet one body. The eye cannot say to the hand, "I have no need of you", nor again the head to the feet, "I have no need of you" ' (12:17–21).

Besides reading these verses in the context of the whole chapter, we should also read 1 Cor 12 as part of the three consecutive chapters 12 – 14. The whole is a doctrine of unity in diversity, of a harmonious toleration, acceptance, indeed admiration of differences – the harmony being provided by *charity* or love. 1 Cor 13 is the key chapter to the section, rightly put in the middle. It is the key to a proper understanding of Paul's doctrine of the body of Christ. We are all different, each with our proper graces and gifts and talents, so that we all need each other but do not need each to possess personally each other's gifts. What we do all need to have personally, however, is *love*, just as all the organs of the body need to have *life*.

In Chapter 20, A, iii we saw that Christ reveals to us what I called our current programme as well as our future possibilities, and that our current programme as individual Christians can be summed up in the one word 'humility'. There I had to put in a little qualification to say that of course this did not exclude love as the all-important Christian virtue. But here, I suggest we now see where love really comes in. It is the one word in which we can sum up the current programme of the Christian *community*, our programme for living the corporate, as distinct from the individual, Christian life. For of course love, unlike humility, is essentially a corporate or a community virtue. Humility means being humble; love means loving *others*. I called Christian humility paradoxical. Christian love is no less so, as we noticed in fact when we were examining the teaching of the sermon on the mount about grace (Chapter 21, B, i). For love or charity is grace made visible in action, and involves loving your enemy, and turning the other cheek, and doing all sorts of impossibly paradoxical things like that. Indeed, is not Paul's hymn to charity in 1 Cor 13 an ode in honour of a supremely paradoxical quality, whose absence renders the grandest moral and religious values worthless, whose unobtrusive presence alone gives wholeness to the fragmentary 'in part'[8] quality of human, temporal existence?

Love does this because it already anticipates the wholeness of the coming perfection, the *eschaton*, the realization of the full possibilities of human existence revealed to us in Christ. But love, as we have just observed, is a social, community, corporate, relating force. It is the life of the corporate body of Christ. As well as reading 1 Cor 12 in the light of 1 Cor 13, we also have to read 13 against the background of 12. So Paul's doctrine of the body of Christ, that is of Jesus Christ corporately embodied in the community of believers, also tells us something of the eschatological possibilities of a perfect community of love, where love no longer has to give wholeness to an otherwise fragmentary 'in part' existence, but ensures perfect communion and communication, total and unreserved and universal sharing in a whole, wholly divinized, eternal mode of existence. Heaven, *pace* Jean-Paul Sartre, will be God and other people.

(ii) In Ephesians: our eschatological possibilities

This brings us to the other form of the doctrine, found in Ephesians. Here the Church (not so concretely the local community of believers as in 1 Corinthians, but 'the Church in general') is still the body of Christ; but not now in the sense of simply being identified with Christ, for Christ in these texts is 'the head of the Church'. The relationship between Christ and the Church is now based on a distinction between them, not on a quasi-identification of them. It is the same relationship that is expressed in the same epistle, perhaps more suitably, in the figure of the Church as the bride of Christ (5:25–32). This figure has earlier been used by Paul (in a genuine letter) in 2 Cor 11:2. The developing Pauline theology of the writer of Ephesians, however, seems to be adjusting the concept of the Church as forming one body with Christ to the concept of the Church as united to Christ (as bride) rather than the other way round.

The background to Ephesians, and even more to Colossians, seems to have been an early form of Gnosticism[9] which threw up rivals to Christ's claim on the total and unconditional allegiance of believers – angels, they are generically called in Colossians. The writer is thus concerned to demonstrate Christ's universal, cosmic supremacy over all such cosmic principalities and powers, and his uniqueness as saviour and mediator. To this end it is necessary clearly to distinguish him from the empirical Church on earth in this age, while keeping the Church most closely united to him. And so God 'has made him head over all things for the Church, which is his body, the fullness of him who fills all in all' (1:22–23).

What does this tell us about the Church, about us in our corporate community existence? Not much, as regards our current programme of being human, except that it does not involve 'self-abasement and worship of angels' (Col 2:18), and does demand that we should remain uncompromisingly faithful to Jesus Christ alone; but much more about our eschatological possibilities and destiny. In the first place, the Church is exalted to share in due measure Christ's superiority over the cosmic thrones and dominations, principalities and powers. For it is 'through the Church' (since it is the fullness of him who fills all in all) that 'the manifold wisdom of God' is now to 'be made known to the principalities and powers in the heavenly places' (Eph 3:10). Our eschatological corporate life takes on cosmic, heavenly proportions. We shall indeed 'judge the cosmos' and 'judge angels' (1 Cor 6:2–3). In this picture Christ is conceived not so much as identified with us in our temporal existence here and now (that is the picture in 1 Corinthians), but rather as the final perfection, the ideal goal to whom as a community we are tending. 'His gifts were that some should be apostles, some prophets . . . for building up the body of Christ, until we all attain to the unity of the faith and of the knowledge of the Son of God, to mature manhood, to the measure of the stature of the fullness of Christ; . . . . Rather, speaking the truth in love, we are to grow up in every way into him who is the head, into Christ, from whom the whole body . . . makes bodily growth and upbuilds itself in love' (4:11–16). Love is again the key concept, but here the stress is even more markedly on its eschatological dynamism that it is in 1 Cor 13.

C. THE CHURCH, LOCAL AND UNIVERSAL

(i) Local Church, or particular community, our primary concern

The Church then, whether envisaged as the sacrament of man's intimate union with God or as the body of Christ, or for that matter as the new people of God,[10] is the privileged 'place' where God's grace is made visible to the secular world, the base from which that grace can most effectively reach out to penetrate the secular world; and also the privileged place where man's worship of God is most authentically accomplished, the centre towards which all the impulses of the secular world to worship are properly drawn. I have just stated in the indicative mood that this is so. Perhaps I should have said in the optative or moral imperative moods that it ought to be so, and if only it were so. But in fact all three moods are called for. Just as being human means becoming (or failing to become) what you are and entails the obligation of becoming what you are, so being Church means the Church ever obliged to become what it is and ever obliged to acknowledge its failure effectively to become what it really is.

But what Church are we really talking about? I don't mean what denomination: that is an issue I leave to the author of another book in this series, though I touched on it above in Chapter 18, C, i. I mean here – Church universal or local? This is an issue I also touched on in the same subsection. But there I was concerned with the problem of unity and pluriformity; here I am concerned with the challenge of being the 'grace base' and the 'worship centre' of mankind, of being effectively Jesus Christ in his social dimensions.

The question for us is whether we should think of this grace base or worship centre as being primarily the Church universal or primarily the Church local. And the answer, I submit, can only be the Church local, the concrete particular community of believers wherever it may be, whatever sort of community it may be, to which each of us belongs. Of course the Church universal, i.e. the Church as a world-wide communion of believers with the Pope at its head, plays a very important part in the consciousness and the lives of Catholics. A very necessary part too, if our Christianity is to be saved from parochialism, or even worse, nationalism, and from degenerating into what the sociologists of religion call 'civic religion'.[11] Members of other Churches (which, let us not forget, also comprise in many cases world-wide communions) also value this 'Catholic' element in their Christianity, and sometimes feel a reasonable envy of Catholics for having in the Pope and the Holy See a very visible focus for this necessary and deeply Christian sentiment.

At the same time a consciousness of belonging to a world-wide communion is not in itself a great help to us in realizing or putting life into the social dimensions of our identity with Christ. The Catholic Church, as a world-wide, highly organized (and centralized) communion, is a social construct, as are nations and/or states, which has a very great effect and influence on the kind of communities its members form and live in, but which is hardly itself such a community. You can, after all, belong to it and be the most lonely, isolated, private, individualistic person in the world, with very few visible social relationships to anyone else. The concrete social dimensions of our lives can only be provided by the particular communities (usually localized) which we live in, with their web of relationships, familial, economic, political, recreational, professional, ecclesial, that involve as a very minimum mutual acquaintance.

(ii) Problems in the concept of local church

But is the local Church such a particular community, and has it ever been? Almost certainly not, after the first few years of the founding of the communities of believers by the apostles. For very soon these communities grew in numbers to such a size as, presumably, to preclude everyone in them knowing everybody else. Already in the first chapters of Acts we find the Jerusalem Church growing from the original, genuinely particular community of disciples, about 120 (1:15), to an extra 3,000 on the day of Pentecost (2:41), and then to 5,000 (4:4 – or does it mean an extra 5,000, bringing the total up to 8,000?), and generally multiplying further (6:1). No doubt these figures are not painstaking historical statistics, but more symbolic than anything else (especially 120 and 5,000). But at least we are given to understand that the number of believers grew beyond the limits of a particular face-to-face community – as it surely was bound to do if the evangelism of the apostles was at all effective. And yet it was in Jerusalem only one local Church, not several.

I would, then, provisionally define a local Church as a 'community of communities' within a fairly restricted area, a social organization articulating itself out of the needs of any number of particular communities, and providing them with the services and structures, the personal and material resources, the means of mutual co-operation, which they require in order to be viable. Very soon such local Churches came to be presided over by one man, called 'bishop' or 'superintendent'; the first such presiding officer, and probably the model for all subsequent ones, being James the brother of the Lord in Jerusalem.

So we can further refine our provisional definition, and say a local Church is a local community of communities of believers, presided over by a bishop, and equipped with a sufficient organization of ministers and personal and material resources to provide for most of the needs of its constituent particular communities. And thus in our modern situation the local Church ought to be the diocese. But is the average diocese in the contemporary Catholic Church such a natural, quasi-spontaneous community of communities? I think the answer must be, hardly ever. One reason for this lies deep in the history of the Catholic Church. For just about the last thousand years the *primary* Church in the Catholic consciousness (which now means the consciousness of Western Latin Christians) has not been the local Church which, being in communion with other local Churches and especially with the local Roman Church, represents the universal Catholic Church in that place,[12] but simply the universal Catholic Church as a world-wide organization, too often simply identified with the Roman Church (which thus loses its proper local identity), which is divided up for administrative purposes into dioceses governed by bishops appointed by the Pope, rather as the old Roman Empire was divided up into dioceses,[13] governed by governors appointed by the Emperor. It is a consciousness of the Church as a world-wide organization (a perfect society[14]), organized and managed from the top down, not as a world-wide 'Church of Churches', built up organically from the bottom. This rather inhibits the modern diocese from being a local Church in any realistic sense; and hence does not make it easy for it to encourage and foster and build up those particular communities of believers, all at least acquainted with one another, which in the concrete must provide Christ with his social dimensions, his 'grace bases' and 'worship centres' in the secular world, and must provide the genuine social dimensions of our Christian life.

If therefore we are fully to learn the lessons Christ has to teach us about our social humanity, at least about its current programme as distinct from its eschatological possibilities, nothing less than a revolution is called for in our Catholic consciousness of the Church. There are indeed signs of such a revolution beginning to occur in various parts of the world. Its slogan seems to be 'Basic communities'. I think one has to say that it is not receiving much encouragement from the Holy See, and is unlikely to do so in the near future, because so much of what the Holy See presently stands for is bound up with the second-millennium consciousness of the Church as a perfect society with the Pope at its head, and in view of Mt 16:18 with the papacy as its foundation. This is a view of the Church sometimes called pyramidal, but with the pyramid balanced on its apex. In more human, but perhaps less reverent, terms, it might be called the Old Father William view of the Church.[15]

(iii)   Problems in the concept of particular community

But the difficulties in realizing the ideal of the body of Christ in particular, vital communities of believers are not peculiar to Catholics and the Catholic Church. It might fairly be asked whether our ideal of a particular community of believers as being 'of one heart and soul' (Acts 4:32) is any more realistic in our actual modern world than the idea of the universal Church as a perfect society. In European culture, at any rate, the sense of community has long been eroded by an ever stronger sense of individualism. It is facile simply to deplore this as a typical example of the corruption of European culture – just as facile as to acclaim it as one of its noble achievements and a liberation of the spirit. Prescinding from all value judgements, we must first see it objectively as a response to changing social conditions, to an increased mobility in human society, both social mobility and territorial. It is a symptom of the shaking apart of tightly-knit communities, of the blurring of the lines dividing communities from each other, of the ever-increasing complexity and in many cases the anonymity of human relationships, of individualization and urbanization and rapid developments in all kinds of communication. It is already spreading to other cultures where ancient patterns of community are being relentlessly, and irreversibly, broken up.

Where are your particular communities in this kind of situation? I don't know. The basic communities movement is, I imagine, aimed at providing some kind of practical answer. But it is important for us to be very clear on one point. There can be no single answer to what is not a single problem. There is a kaleidoscopic range of millions of problems in millions of different situations, calling for millions of different solutions. It is simply up to us, as members of the body of Christ, to join in the search for, or rather in the construction of, solutions for our particular problems.

But then, are our particular problems very easy to define? Is it ever so very clear what particular community we belong to? Let me offer myself to readers as a kind of exercise in deciding what particular community I belong to, what kinds of particular community there are. Here I am, a Dominican of the English province of the Order of Preachers, living in Lesotho with three Dominican colleagues – our numbers, though, fluctuate wildly between one and four. I myself also teach in the national seminary but none of my colleagues do. During term time I spend half the week from Tuesday to Friday at the seminary in a place called Roma, the weekends in our small Dominican house in the capital, Maseru, twenty-five miles away. What is my particular community, or my basic community, if I am to be co-opted into that movement?

There is of course first of all my family, my blood-relations. But are we a community? I do not see any of them very often; I correspond regularly with my mother in England, only very occasionally with my brothers, never with any of my other relations. Yet the relationships are there, and real, as also of course with other friends and acquaintances whom I rarely see and only very occasionally write to. So much, in my case, for the family, the most basic of all basic communities, one might suppose *a priori*.

What about the Order of Preachers, of which I am a member, or more practically the English province of that order? Is that my basic community? There are clearly relationships with my fellow Dominicans in England, but only occasional communication, and I don't even know all of them any more. Then there is the Southern African vicarate of the order to which I am assigned and immediately responsible. This is nearer the mark, no doubt;

there are only about thirty of us, we contrive, more or less, to meet once a year, and all know each other, if in many cases only slightly. But then there is the circumstance that I am prohibited from entry into the Republic of South Africa, where nearly all of these colleagues of mine live and work. So there remains the small group of four of us who live in Lesotho. But we are so few, and our membership so frequently changing, that I wonder if we can really add up to a well-defined particular community.

In any case it would seem that this is not the only local community I belong to. There is the seminary where I teach, and in particular the community of its staff. In addition I teach part time in a high school in Maseru, and three days a week I say mass in another high school in Roma. At weekends my colleagues and I take it in turns to say the two English masses at the Cathedral, and we also say mass in Sesotho at the national teachers' training college – and once a fortnight at the boys' prison, where a friend of mine is temporarily in residence. Our weekday masses in our own house are attended on three days a week by children from the local blind school, who lift the roof off with their cheerful and very varied singing. And the mass, as we all know nowadays, is a community celebration, an assembly of the community, to which the 'president of the liturgical assembly' is surely meant to belong. So that makes about eight possible basic local communities to which I appear to belong in one way or another. At least this little piece of amateur sociological research into me may have shown that the apparently elementary concept of a particular community is not all that elementary after all.

Of course, you will say, my case is not typical. No, but whose case is? But isn't there such a thing, for example, as a typical Sesotho village? Surely that is an obvious candidate for being a basic community. Perhaps; but types are rational constructs, rather than actual realities. Of course there are common features of law and custom, social organization and language and economic circumstances among the thousands of villages in Lesotho. But if you examine the career of a man of my age in any village in the mountains, you will probably find he belongs to quite as many particular communities, in an equally vague way, as I do. His family connections will almost certainly be more extended, more supportive and more demanding than mine. But he will certainly complain that the old family cohesion and discipline and responsibility is breaking down among his sons and daughters, and above all among his grandchildren. And in any case his family relationships will give him community relationships far beyond the confines of his village, extending into the townships of the Rand and the farms of the Free State. He himself will have probably spent most of his working life in the mines in South Africa. One or two of his sons may have settled there. He may be illiterate, but one of his daughters may be working in a bank in Maseru, and one of his grandsons be a student at the university, while others, younger, are still herding sheep and cattle in the mountains and consequently having their schooling delayed. In a word, this apparently simple society is almost as mobile, economically, socially and territorially, as that of the English or Irish.

The last thing I am intending to do is to knock the movement for building up basic Christian communities. All I am wishing to suggest is that communities are not the sort of thing you can pin down, like specimen butterflies, and it would be foolish and wrong to try. And again, in building up a basic or particular community, you will never be starting from scratch. And what you are 'given' to start with will be quite different in one part of the world from what it is in another. A village in the mountains of Lesotho will be rather different from a village in the lowlands, near Roma for example; very different from a suburb or housing estate in Maseru, and totally different from a village in India or Bolivia or Scotland, not to mention a housing estate in Coventry, a shanty town in São Paulo, or a black ghetto in Detroit.

So clearly there can be absolutely no question of a uniform type of Christian community, no question therefore of the imposition of a standard social organization from the top or the centre. Different local Churches, i.e. communities of communities of believers, will certainly be able to learn from each other, as they always have done; but not to provide standard blueprints for each other. *A fortiori* such blueprints cannot be drawn up, for universal application, in Rome. Well, I suppose they can, and perhaps they will – but it will be a complete waste of valuable blue paper. This simply reinforces the conclusion we arrived at a few pages back: that we need a revolution in our Catholic consciousness of the Church, if we as Catholic Christians are more effectively to provide the world with the only benefits that as Catholic Christians we are equipped and intended to provide it with – 'grace bases' and 'worship centres'.

NOTES

1 St Thomas Aquinas, following St Augustine, says that a sacrament is a sacred sign; i.e., that is what we mean by the word in Christian theology. More precisely, it is a sign of the sacred, or a sign of sanctification. This of course is merely a preliminary definition of the term, which can be expanded in all sorts of ways. But it is this notion of sacrament that is presupposed to everything Schillebeeckx says in his book. See *STh* IIIa, 60, especially articles i, ii, iii and iv (ET, vol. 56).

2 *Breviarium juxta ritum Ordinis Praedicatorum* (Rome, 1962), I, p. 496, In ascensione Domini, ad I Vesperas.

3 St Thomas discusses devotion in *STh* IIa IIae, 82 (ET, vol. 39). He defines it (a. i) as 'the will to give oneself wholeheartedly to whatever belongs to the service of God'. And he is led to this definition by the use of the word in ancient Roman religion, illustrated by Livy

in the story he tells of the consul Decius Mus. A battle was going badly for the Romans, so to ensure victory Decius Mus solemnly 'devoted' himself to the *Dii Manes*, the gods of the underworld, or the spirits of the ancestors; which means he devoted himself to death, for having performed the little ceremony he rushed into the thickest of the fray and was promptly slain. The Romans duly won the battle. See Livy's *History*, VIII, 9.

4   Southern African languages modify their words for the most part by prefixes at the beginning, not suffixes at the and. So the country I am living in is called *Le*sotho, its people in the plural are the *Ba*sotho, each individually in the singular being a *Mo*sotho, and the kind of neuter noun to signify anything that pertains to them, above all their language, but also their culture and customs, is *Se*sotho – very roughly equivalent to the adjective 'English'.

5   Sesotho culture is not all positive in this respect. It is very strongly a verbal or rhetorical culture. They will make speeches at the drop of a hat. So as well as enjoying the excellent liturgy of great occasions like ordinations and funerals, with their marvellous congregational singing and participation, one also has to endure the tedium of interminable (and frequently rather bad) speeches. But this is offset by another most amiable and useful feature of local African culture – its casualness or insouciance. So unless you are very important, or billed to make a speech yourself, you can just wander away and chat with your friends on the edge of the crowd, or go and relieve yourself and have a smoke – or just go away. Nobody is offended.

6   Except, in general, poor and simple communities having the advantage over the affluent and sophisticated.

7   Tertullian, *Apologeticus* 39, 7 (PL 1, 471).

8   St Paul's phrase is *ek merous*, used four times in vv. 9, 10 and 12. RSV only translates the last by 'in part' – the previous three being less happily rendered as 'imperfect'.

9   Gnosticism is the name for a vast assortment of mythological, theosophical, quasi-philosophical and religious beliefs that flourished above all in the second century A.D. It was ultra-spiritual, in that at least in some extreme forms it regarded all material being as evil. What was perhaps common to all forms of Gnosticism was a strongly hierarchical conception of the cosmos in which everything emanates from the ultimate source of being in a long ladder or chain of emanations. So by the time the process has got down to us in our visible world, there is a whole line of mediators and saviours between us and the original *One,* or God. Most Gnostic sects were in varying degrees influenced by Christianity, though I think only a few of them can be considered as genuine Christian heresies; and Christ was sometimes allotted a fairly lowly place on this scale of mediation. It is this kind of idea that is being attacked in Colossians and less directly in Ephesians.

10   'People of God' is the way of envisaging the Church which dominates the doctrine of Vatican II's Constitution on the Church, *Lumen Gentium*. Needless to say, it does not exclude these other figures or images, which are indeed all duly discussed in that document.

11   A term devised by the sociologists of religion to designate that kind of religious activity that is undertaken as a civic duty, and seen as a kind of moral buttress or justification of civil society. The ancient pagan cults of the Greek city states and of the Roman Empire were predominantly instances of civic religion. It demands little or no personal commitment of belief. Participation in certain rites and ceremonies are simply a matter of civic loyalty and pride and patriotism. Churches that are part of the established order of society, whether by law established like the Church of England, or simply by popular custom and culture, like the Catholic Church in Spain, or the Dutch Reformed Churches in South Africa, are always in acute danger of degenerating into instruments of merely civic religion. And when they deliberately try to avoid the danger, and refuse to let their

services be merely this or that party at prayer, or even the nation at prayer, they come in for savage criticism. A most illuminating case of this kind was the thanksgiving service for the end of the Falklands campaign held in St Paul's in July 1982. The Anglican Church authorities, in collaboration with their colleagues of other Churches, were at great pains to prevent the service from being a mere show of religious patriotism. And so it is not surprising that they were savagely mauled by a number of Conservative lions who wanted just that. But that is not Christianity. After all, if that was all they wanted, these Conservative patriots, wishing to exult in triumph over the 'Argies' and all such lesser breeds without the law, they could have organized an appropriate service in honour of Thor or Woden.

12   I am suggesting that this is what the Church should primarily signify in our Catholic consciousness, and what it at least implicitly did signify in roughly the first thousand years of Church history. Notice, such a consciousness in no way leaves out either the Catholic or the Roman dimension; it simply puts them in what I suggest is a more realistic, and a theologically more authentic perspective.

13   The word 'diocese' was originally a purely secular word for an administrative area of the Roman Empire, as reorganized by Diocletian at the end of the third century A.D. I do not know when it first came into ecclesiastical use. But that it did come eventually to signify the area over which a bishop rules from his see is evidence of a radical alteration of ideas about the nature of the local Church. Earlier texts would never have talked about the diocese of London, or New York, Westminster or Peking or Maseru, but about the *Church* of this or that place. To call it a diocese is immediately to conceive it as a division of a larger socio-political, or ecclesiastical, entity.

14   The expression, I believe, was first used by Bellarmine at the beginning of the seventeenth century. A perfect society is a social organization that is completely sufficient to itself like, said Bellarmine, the kingdom of France or the Republic of Venice; in other words what we nowadays call a sovereign state. His case was that the Church is such a society – meaning not the local but the universal Church, with the Pope at its head as sovereign, as the king of France was sovereign of the kingdom of France.

15   Lewis Carroll, *Alice's Adventures in Wonderland*, 5:

'Repeat "You are old, Father William" ' said the Caterpillar.
Alice folded her hands, and began:

'You are old, Father William,' the young man said,
    'And your hair has become very white;
And yet you incessantly stand on your head –
    Do you think at your age, it is right?'

'In my youth,' Father William replied to his son,
    'I feared it might injure the brain;
But now that I'm perfectly sure I have none,
    Why, I do it again and again'.

QUESTIONS FOR FURTHER DISCUSSION

1   How is the Church identified with Christ, and how does this offer mankind a true picture, or an effective symbol, of perfect human community?

2   What are the requirements for a local Christian community or Church to exist as such, and to be an effective symbol or sign of perfect human community?

RECOMMENDED FURTHER READING

Edward Schillebeeckx, *Christ the Sacrament of Encounter with God*, is really a most important book for the sacramental, that is to say symbolic and significant, character of the Church. It is written as an introduction to a theology of the sacraments, but is full of valuable insights for our subject here in the way it relates Christ to the Church and its sacraments, and both Christ and the Church to the whole of mankind.

The first two chapters of *Lumen Gentium*, the Constitution on the Church of Vatican II (in *The Documents of Vatican II*) are also well worth reading in this connection.

Karl Rahner, *The Church and the Sacraments*.

Juan Luis Segundo, *The Community Called Church*.

23

Man's Last End
I: The Four Last Things

A. TWO KINDS OF ESCHATOLOGY

We come now almost to the end of our survey of the theology of man. It is time to consider in a little more detail what we have been calling the ultimate possibilities of being human, which have been revealed to us in Christ, and to deal with some of the problems that have always confronted the Christian consciousness in this regard.

The whole subject is usually known as eschatology, the study of the *eschaton* or end. We must begin by noting that there are two fairly distinct kinds of eschatology, both embedded in the Church's traditional teaching, both rooted in the New Testament, and yet neither, to my mind, fitting at all easily into the perspective of the other.

The primary kind I call the horizontal or temporal. It looks *forward* to the *eschaton* as precisely the end of time, the end of the world, the end of salvation history or of the drama of salvation, and thus as the goal and final destiny of the people of God, of the human race in its entirety. It is concerned with the fulfilment of the ultimate possibilities of being human in their social, corporate, community dimensions. We will deal with this theme in the next and last chapter.

The secondary kind of eschatology I call the vertical or spatial, in that it at least uses the metaphors of space.[1] It looks upwards – and downwards – not to the end of time, the world or history, but to the ultimate destination of you and me, of human beings as individual persons. It is the eschatology traditionally codified as 'the four last things: death, judgement, heaven and hell', and it will form the subject of this chapter. I call it vertical and spatial for obvious reasons – so obvious that it is necessary to emphasize that the spatial language of heaven (the sky) up there and of hell (the nether regions) down there is purely and simply metaphorical.

I call this eschatology secondary and the other primary chiefly because the horizontal kind completely dominates the New Testament, not to the total exclusion of the vertical kind, but almost. It continues to dominate the theological tradition for the first thousand years of our era, though less and less thoroughly as the centuries wear on; for as long, that is to say, as the second coming of Christ, the *parousia*, was thought to be fairly imminent. When the year 1000 passed without Christ coming again in glory, this expectation which in various ways had loomed large in the Christian consciousness faded away, and the secondary form of eschatology came to the fore, and has dominated that consciousness ever since.[2] But the other remains primary also in the sense that it is closer to the central revelation of salvation in Christ, which as we have noted so often comes to us in the form of a salvation history, or dramatic story of salvation – which began with creation and will end with the end, the new heavens and the new earth in which righteousness dwells (2 Pet 3:13).

B. THE FOUR LAST THINGS

The traditional list of the four last things makes them death, judgement, heaven and hell. Of these it is only the last two that are purely and simply last things, the ultimate in finality. The first two are, in respect of heaven and hell, the penultimate things, the immediate approaches to those simply final alternative 'destinations'.[3] But in respect of us here and now they are aptly listed among the four last things, because they mark the end of our temporal existence, and our introduction or propulsion into the fully eschatological dimension.

(i)   Death

We have already discussed death at some length above in Chapter 12. But here I think it worth adding a few words precisely about death as seen in the perspective of this vertical eschatology. In the perspective of the horizontal eschatology death is 'the last enemy' (1 Cor 15:26), In Rev 20:14 death and Hades (= death and Death) are the last to be thrown into the lake of fire, even after the devil (20:10) and the beast and the false prophet (19:20).

But in the vertical eschatology, in which we are concerned with our own personal destinies, it is not Death in general that preoccupies us in this rather grand manner, but my particular actual dying and your particular actual dying, as the beginning rather than the end of our personal eschatology, as launching us into a totally new, and final, dimension of existence. St Paul sees the relationship between this life and the next as that between a nomad's tent and a permanent house – one built on rock no doubt (2 Cor 5:1–10; cf. Mt 7:24). This is clearly a variation on the traditional theme of this life as a journey or pilgrimage through the desert to the promised land of the next life. So death, as the point of transition from the provisional to the definitive mode of life, as the crossing of the Jordan, is clearly by far the most important event or moment of our individual lives.

Memento mori is therefore a pretty basic Christian injunction. How am I going to die? That should be my overriding preoccupation. I don't mean that I should worry about whether I shall die in my bed or in a road accident, suddenly or after a 'terminal' illness, in old age or in the prime of my life. That will be as it will be. I mean: how am I going to meet death: ready for it or not, willingly, freely, generously or not, in a state of *metanoia* or not? And, of course, how I die in this sense will be largely (though not totally or absolutely) determined by how I have lived. If I have lived a life of service to others, then I am more likely to be able, with and in Christ, to give my life as a ransom for many (Mk 10:45).

This is called 'dying in the Lord' (Rev 14:13). The author no doubt had dying a martyr's death in mind. But the expression can surely be extended to the death of any Christian who dies, as deliberately as possible, with Christ. And the best way of ensuring, as far as lies in our power, that we will do this is by practising dying every day. This is what is meant by 'mortification' (which is only a long Latin word for 'making dead'). Self-denial – abstaining from the ordinary pleasures of life from time to time, accepting the pains and humiliations and disappointments of life in a good spirit, always putting duty before self-interest – all this should help to put the values of life in this 'tent' in a proper perspective when compared with the values of life in 'a house not made with hands, eternal in the heavens' (2 Cor 5:1). To such a life of self-denial we have really been committed by baptism, which is the cardinal 'practising of dying'. For we were baptized into Christ's death, buried with him so that we too might walk in newness of life (Rom 6:3–4).

(ii) Judgement

Paul concludes his little meditation on death in 2 Cor 5 by remarking that 'we must all appear before the judgement seat of Christ so that each one may receive good or evil, according to what we have done in the body' (*ibid*. 10). There are two points here that should be analysed in some detail: (a) with the whole biblical tradition he is using the language of the law courts, the forensic metaphor, for this ultimate settling of our destiny; and (b) with the whole New Testament tradition he sees Christ, not God, as the final judge and arbiter.

(a) The forensic metaphor of judgement is precisely that, a metaphor (or at most an analogy), and must be interpreted as such, not taken literally. When so taken it too often leads to a picture of God as an arbitrary, capricious, ruthless judge, a kind of divine Judge Jeffreys. I suppose such an idea reflects all too well the all too common human experience of human 'justice' in human courts; also an all too common and distorted view of what justice and law really are. But to appreciate the meaning of the metaphor/analogy when applied to God's definitive assessment of us, we must start with a concept of law and justice that is true to God's revelation and right reason.

As we saw above in Chapter 16, B, iii, law is properly speaking a dictate of reason directed to the common good, and is ultimately derived from, or at least validated by, the divine wisdom. So the law by which God judges is none other than the divine wisdom, none other than God himself as wisdom.

As for justice, whereas we in the tradition of Roman law and ethics tend to contrast justice with mercy (we talk about *strict* justice), the biblical, Israelite tradition sees mercy (*hesed*, lovingkindness) rather as the highest expression of justice, the most notable quality of the just man, *a fortiori* therefore of the just God. God's justice (*tsedeq*, *tsedaqah*) is above all manifested in his two key attributes of 'mercy and truth' (*hesed* and *emeth*, lovingkindness and faithfulness in more modern translations).

Finally, what is the proper purpose of a trial in a court of law, and the proper intention of the judgement that concludes it? Surely, to establish the *truth* of the facts in the verdict, and to decide on them according to the *truth* of the law and justice in the sentence or judgement.

So at the judgement we are talking about (and this seems to me to be the main point of the forensic metaphor) what is going to be established is the real truth about ourselves. At that moment, for the first time without any qualification or ignorance or self-deception we shall see ourselves as we really are, as we have made ourselves in our lives, in the light of God's truth, God's wisdom, God's justice which is the same as God's lovingkindness or mercy and faithfulness. And of course this truth will not have to be laboriously and doubtfully established through the examination of witnesses, and the evidence thus gained to be painstakingly weighed and then pronounced on, without any absolute certainty, by a fallible judge. It will be revealed to us by the infallible and omniscient judge himself; and this not externally but from within, from inside our own consciousness and consciences. We will really judge ourselves, because we will be faced from within ourselves, for the first time in our lives, with 'the truth, the whole truth and nothing but the truth'.

Now here is a very interesting point indeed: Jesus Christ is the truth, and furthermore he 'said to the Jews who had believed in him, If you continue in my word, you are truly my disciples, and you will know the truth, and the truth will make you free' (Jn 8:31f.; cf. 14:6). Knowledge of the truth, then, is essentially a liberating or saving experience. This is emphasized further on in this chapter where Jesus, suddenly changing his tone to these Jews (the style throughout, of course, is entirely Johannine), tells them 'You are of your father, the devil, and your will is to do your father's desires. He was a murderer from the beginning and has nothing to do with the truth, because there is no truth in him. When he lies he speaks according to his own nature,[4] for he is a liar and the father of lies' (8:44).

So falsehood and death (murder – Cain slaying Abel; that was the beginning from which the devil was a murderer, cf. 1 Jn 3:12) go together, just as truth and life are identified with each other in the person of Christ (Jn 14:6). Christ came to save us from the power of the devil, from death, from untruth or lies, which are here, presumably, more or less identified with sin. At the core of every sin, every evil act, is a lie, a heart of darkness and un-truth.

But all this, surely, means that we are forced to the conclusion that judgement and salvation are practically identical, one and the same act or event. The truth by which we are liberated is the same truth as the truth by which we are judged. No judgement, no liberation or salvation. Now part of this saving, judging (or salutary, critical) truth is that we are sinners, i.e. liars. I suppose then that the crucial question for us, as we stand before the judgement seat of Christ, is how we accept this unpalatable truth. To accept it in a spirit of repentance, of *metanoia* or conversion from the heart of darkness to the true light of the heart, is to be saved by it. But this inevitably involves a painful humiliation, a rejection of that part of ourselves which had become wedded to the comfortable lie in our lives, the false image of ourselves to which we are bound to be more or less closely attached.

On the other hand, being unrepentant, unconverted at the moment of judgement means, I suppose, refusing to make this act of self-denial, while being unable to deny (because the whole truth is nakedly revealed to us) the lie in the heart. This is to refuse liberation from the lie, and thus from death, even when it is inescapably perceived for what it is.

Just as we saw that we can practise for death by dying daily, by self-denial; so it is clear we can practise for the judgement by judging ourselves regularly in this life, or rather by letting ourselves be judged. This is the place of the sacrament of penance, which is also significantly known as 'the sacred tribunal of penance', or 'the internal forum'. The sacrament, as a sign of sanctification, enacts the forensic metaphor. It practises us in that humili-ation, that self-denial, of bringing our sins to the light, whereby in being judged and accepting judgement we are set free, released (the meaning of 'absolution') from them.

(b)   The second point to consider is why the New Testament consist-ently, though in various ways, presents Christ, not God, as the judge of the ultimate tribunal. When I say Christ, not God, I am not wishing to deny the divinity of Christ. I mean it is Christ as Man, not the Father, who is presented as the judge. Of course, Christ is also the Son, to whom the Father has given all judgement (Jn 5:22). But he has given it to him 'because he is the Son of man' (*ibid.* 27), because he is the last Adam, the perfect Man, representative of the whole human race, as we explained that title back in Chapter 20, B.

One reason traditionally given for this, valid but in my opinion superficial, and perhaps too enslaved to the forensic metaphor, is that the judge must be seen by those he condemns as well as by those he acquits; justice must not only be done but be seen to be done. This would not be the case if the judge were invisible. But God (Father, Son and Holy Spirit) is invisible, and will never be seen by the wicked but only by the just, whose reward it will precisely be to see him face to face, as we shall discover in the next subsection. The wicked, however, can see the Son of man, for 'they shall look on him whom they have pierced' (Jn 19:37, Rev 1:7 – both quoting Zech 12:10).

But from what we have been seeing about the nature of the final judgement I think we can discover better reasons than this why it should be specifically Christ's tribunal before which we all have to appear. It is because it will be the moment of truth, and he particularly is the truth made manifest to us. He is the wisdom of God (1 Cor 1:24), and the truth will be revealed to us in the light of the divine wisdom. The quotation of Zech 12:10 by John and Revelation is very apposite, but chiefly in the sense that God's truth, by which we are to be judged, was most poignantly and piercingly revealed to us in Christ dying and dead on the cross.

And again, the fact that it will be Christ who judges us supports the point made above that the judgement will not be something imposed on us from outside by a capricious external judge (or even an all-wise, but still external judge), but something we inexorably impose on ourselves in the light of that divine truth. For Christ as man is the perfect and perfectly representative man. He has identified himself with us and us with him; so we will be judged according to 'the measure of the stature of the fullness of Christ' (Eph 4:13); according to how we measure up to the identity with Christ that has been offered us. How we do that will depend to an almost total extent[5] on how far we have observed and respected that identity in others (Mt 25:34–45; see above, Chapter 22, A, iii).

One last observation about the judgement. We have been examining it in the context of the vertical or spatial eschatology, as something that awaits each and every one of us at the moment of death and determines whether we go to heaven (upwards) or go to hell (downwards). But it also figures prominently in the primary, horizontal or temporal eschatology as the event which will wind up the story, put an end to time and history, when Christ comes again in glory – to judge. So the last day is called Doomsday, or the Day of Judgement. The question arises, how are the two judgements connected. The common theological tradition has come to call the first one the particular judgement and the second the general judgement, and to treat

them simply as consecutive moments, so that first we have to face our particular judgement, and then we wait either in heaven or hell till the end of the
world when we all undergo together the general judgement.

This seems to me patently unsatisfactory, and merely illustrates the im-
possibility of fitting one of these eschatologies into the other. I think it better
to treat judgement as a single concept/event/moment which can be viewed
from two different perspectives in the two distinct eschatologies. There is,
after all, a problem about time involved. Time is a coefficient of material or
bodily existence, a 'fourth dimension' of the material world. So while it is
true, from our point of view in this world, that time continues even after
people we know have died, and will doubtless continue after we ourselves
have died, until it is all brought to an end in the unimaginable grand finale;
from the point of view of the dead, disembodied spirits or souls, things must
be rather different. Being disembodied they are outside the sequence of time
as we know it and experience it. The concept of them *waiting*, after one
judgement, to have it all repeated at another is therefore rather bizarre. Now
I concede that this does not mean it is necessarily untrue. The bizarre is something we have to swallow when doing eschatology, because we are simply
venturing beyond the edge of the imaginable. We shall return to the problem
of time for the dead when we consider purgatory and hell. Meanwhile, I
repeat the suggestion that the particular and the general judgement are really
one and the same thing, seen from two different perspectives.

(iii)   Heaven

So the judgement, we hope, will determine definitively that we 'go to
heaven'. Once again we must analyse the metaphor, this time not a forensic
one but a simple spatial one.

The first thing to observe is that the metaphor is scarcely a biblical one –
not at least directly. It is a remote and impoverished and somewhat distorted
derivation from the rich variety of biblical eschatological imagery. If you ask
any average Christian today what they hope for as their ultimate destiny,
they will most likely reply 'to go to heaven'. Had you asked any of our
Lord's disciples this question, or soundly instructed Pharisees of earlier generations and Christians of the first centuries of our era, I don't think any of
them would have given that answer. They would have replied 'to enter into
life, or eternal life', or 'to eat bread in the kingdom of God' (Lk 14:15), or 'to
share in the resurrection of the just' or 'a new heaven and a new earth where
justice dwells' (2 Pet 3:13), or 'life in the heavenly Jerusalem' (Heb 12:22).
But going to heaven would have struck them as a very odd thing to hope for.

So how has it come to dominate the field over all these other images and
metaphors? Heaven, of course, is frequently mentioned in the Bible. It means

the sky. Hebrew hasn't got one secular word, 'sky', and one religious word, 'heaven', just the one word, *hash-shamaim*, meaning 'the skies'. Religiously considered (in a spatial metaphor) it is where God lives. 'The heavens are the Lord's heavens,[6] but the earth he has given to the sons of men' (Ps 115:16) – which is why it would never have occurred to a pious Israelite, or even a pious early Christian, to want to go to heaven. It is what the king of Babylon, modelled on Lucifer, aspired to do, and he had a very nasty and well-deserved fall (Isa 14:12–19).

Being where God lives, heaven comes to be a way, in pious language, of referring to God himself, in order out of respect to avoid naming him as far as possible. We still use this style in such expressions as 'Good heavens!' or 'Heaven preserve us!'. This is the usage in Matthew's recurrent phrase 'the kingdom of heaven'; it simply means the kingdom of God, and in no way designates the locality of the kingdom. It is in this light that we should interpret the expression 'in heaven', which is certainly very common in the New Testament. 'Treasure in heaven' (Mt 6:20); 'your reward is great in heaven' (5:12); 'a house not made with hands, eternal in the heavens' (2 Cor 5:1); 'our commonwealth[7] is in heaven' (Phil 3:20); 'an inheritance kept in heaven for you' (1 Pet 1:4); in all these cases 'in heaven' means 'with God' or 'in God's keeping'. And we should notice it is never *you* or *we* who are talked of as being in heaven, but something of ours, or for us, being kept for us by God.

Christ of course ascended into heaven and is seated there at God's right hand; he has returned to his Father. And as we saw in the last chapter (22, A, ii and iii), our life is invisibly hidden there with him now, and he is visibly with us here (in the sacraments of the Church) on earth. But in the New Testament the expectation is not for the most part that we will go to join him there (though this does seem to be the sense of that passage 2 Cor 5:1–10 which we started with), but that very soon he will return in glory to join us here – on earth.

So how, from all this, do we get the current Christian commonplace 'to go to heaven'? It is all part of the swing of the Christian consciousness from the primary to the secondary eschatology; it is also entirely characteristic of the Platonizing of the Christian consciousness about 'the soul and the body'. The second coming of Christ has receded far into the back of our minds. Meanwhile we believe that the saints are with God, and we pray that the souls of the faithful departed may be with God, and where could that be if not in heaven? We are only concerned with the salvation of our souls now, so we hope our souls will go to heaven while our bodies remain, buried or cremated or otherwise transmuted, among the elements of the earth.

My chief objection, in fact, to the ambition of going to heaven (instead of joining Christ in paradise or entering on our heavenly inheritance or any other of the metaphorical expressions we have noted) is that it leaves the body almost entirely out of account, and is unconcerned to hope for the resurrection of the body. Still, in the context of the vertical eschatology it makes good enough sense, provided we unpack the metaphor and see what it stands for. Actually, we can only express what it stands for by using other metaphors, but this is a very useful exercise. The best of these, the least metaphorical, perhaps quite simply not metaphorical but a proper analogy, is 'eternal life'. And what is eternal life? 'To know thee, the only true God, and Jesus Christ whom thou hast sent' (Jn 17:3). Being in heaven means knowing God and Jesus Christ in a manner in which we do not yet know them. St Paul, with yet another metaphor, tells us what this manner will be: 'Now we see in a mirror dimly, but then face to face. Now I know in part; then I shall understand fully even as I have been fully understood'[8] (1 Cor 13:12). Seeing God face to face is what the bliss of heaven consists in. This is the 'beatific vision' of the technical theological expression. Of course a metaphor, because God hasn't got a face. No, it means knowing God with the mind, but immediately, directly, God so to say occupying or possessing the mind with an immediate presence, so that he is not seen indirectly any more 'in a mirror', dimly reflected through his creatures, which is how we know him now.[9]

This is the last word in 'divinization'. This is our destiny, to be oned with God in this way. But we should not forget that it is always in Christ. Our identification, as human beings, with The Human Being will persist. So we shall see God face to face as Christ does, i.e. within the network of trinitarian relations. Sons and daughters in the Son, we shall see the Father as the Son sees the Father, and be endowed with the Spirit of the Father and the Son, in which we shall cry Abba, Father, no longer in supplication but in perpetual joy and praise.

Having criticized what I regard as the impoverished metaphor of 'going to heaven', I must now defend it against a common form of contemporary attack, which is what I call a pre-emptive sneer. Back in Chapter 9, D, ii we noted what I there called the magisterial sneer of Professor Gilbert Ryle at the Cartesian view of body and soul as 'the theory of the ghost in the machine'. I called it magisterial because it came from a master; but like all sneers it was also pre-emptive (and therefore bad dialectic, though effective rhetoric), because it pre-empted any defence by ridiculing it in advance.

So it is with the common pre-emptive sneer at the Christian hope of heaven: 'Pie in the sky when you die'. Well, all I say to it is, we should not be afraid of such sneers. They parody our metaphorical language, and are only effective on the assumption that we take our metaphors literally. As too many of us do too frequently make that mistake, these sneers can at least remind us of the folly of it. So here: 'pie' parodies the traditional language of the heavenly banquet, of feasting in the kingdom of God. But if we know what this metaphor stands for, namely the ineffable joy of the beatific vision, we will not be worried by the parody of it. Pie in the sky, feasting in heaven? Sure, why not? I hope to enjoy for ever eternal life with God. So now that you have called it 'pie', I can be reminded of it whenever I am enjoying some pie for dinner, or enjoying any good meal – or hungering for a square meal too, for that matter.

'When you die'. There, I think, is the sting of the sneer. It is criticizing what the sneerers see as the offer of joy in the next life *in lieu of* happiness in this, what they see as the religious alibi through which Christians evade their social and political responsibilities to work for the just society and the good life here and now. To this we can only reply that when Christians so evade their earthly responsibilities they are getting their Christianity wrong. Certainly they are not authorized to evade them by their Christian hope, looking forward to eternal life in the kingdom of heaven. But if the pre-emptive sneer of pie in the sky when you die serves to warn us against the temptation to do this, then it is not without value. Only let it not make us falter in our genuine Christian hope.

(iv) Purgatory

Purgatory is not mentioned among the four last things, probably because the list was compiled before a doctrine of purgatory was elaborated, about the twelfth century.

Here again, inevitably, we are knee-deep in figurative language. This time it is the metaphor of the wash-house or the cleaners, with perhaps a sub-sidiary metaphor from the clinic thrown in. But though the metaphor and the elaborated doctrine apparently only date from about the twelfth century, they were developed in order to explain Christian practices that were very old indeed. The evidence for a practical concern for the welfare of the dead, in the form of prayers for them and the celebration of the eucharist and the giving of alms on their behalf, dates back to the earliest Christian centuries, indeed to the New Testament itself. St Paul refers to the practice (whatever it may have been) of 'being baptized on behalf of the dead' (1 Cor 15:29). But whatever it was – it was on behalf of the dead. That prayers and sacrifices on behalf of the dead were accepted practices in late Judaism is clear from 2 Macc 12:38–45. In this text the practice is commended as evidence of a hope in the resurrection of the dead. 'For if he [Judas Maccabaeus] were not expecting that those who had fallen would rise again, it would have been superfluous and foolish to pray for the dead. But if he was looking to the splendid reward that is laid up for those who fall asleep in godliness, it was a holy and pious thought' (*ibid.* 44f.).

This makes it clear that the context at this time for prayers for the dead was entirely the primary, horizontal eschatology. It was to ensure as far as possible that the dead for whom the prayers were offered would rise among the just in glory at the end of the age. Meanwhile, they all simply 'sleep' in the grave, the just and the wicked, and the just who have slipped up like those for whom Judas Maccabaeus offered the sacrifice, all alike. I suspect that the same outlook governed the Christian practice during the first centuries of our era. This is suggested by the traditional prayer, 'May they rest in peace'. The idea of rewards and punishments for the souls of the dead following immediately on death was not, indeed, unknown. It is assumed in the parable of the rich man and Lazarus (Lk 16:19–31). It is there in Christ's words to the good thief (23:43), and in Paul's 'desire to part and be with Christ' (Phil 1:23). But in 2 Tim 4:8 'Paul' (as portrayed by his loyal anonymous disciple) approaches death serenely in expectation of 'the crown of righteousness, which the Lord, the righteous judge, will award me *on that Day*'; that is, on Judgement Day, the day of Christ's *parousia* or second coming. Expectation of this event in the more or less near future inhibited any deep reflection on the status of the dead between now and then.

But by the twelfth century the great change in eschatological consciousness had already occurred. It is the certain conviction now of nearly all Christians that the saints already enjoy the vision of God face to face in heaven; and when Pope John XXII, a somewhat archaic theologian, asserted about 1330 that they do not have this joy until the general resurrection, there was a certain amount of scandal, and his opinion was formally condemned by his successor, Benedict XII (Dz 1000/530).[10] So the question is more urgent: what is the state of the departed souls for whom prayer in the ancient traditional way is offered? They presumably do not yet enjoy the beatific vision, otherwise there would be no need to pray for them; nor yet are they in hell, because then it would be no use praying for them. (They may indeed in fact be either in heaven or hell; we cannot possibly know. But our praying for them is on the basis of a likelihood, or at least a possibility, that they are in neither.) So the traditional practice of praying for the dead implies that they are in a kind of antechamber to heaven, not yet admitted to the divine presence, until they have been purified of all stain of sin.

This is the metaphor of the laundry or the cleaners. Their sins have been forgiven, and they have truly repented of them. But sin has effects that outlive even repentance. It produces, or accentuates, bad habits, defects of character, weaknesses which need to be purged away before a soul is in a fit state to enjoy the beatific vision. Hence the need for some kind of purgation or cleansing. Purifying fires is the usual metaphor adopted, presumably from the processes of refining metals – or from the prominence of fire in the biblical imagery of the final judgement (see 1 Cor 3:13–15). The sufferings of this life are seen in this light by the devout and eager Christian, and are thus accepted not just with resignation but gladly, as purifying the soul or self from these defects. Hence the pious prayer, 'Send me here my purgatory'.

If the metaphor of the refinery or dry-cleaners does not appeal, the matter can be stated in terms of the sanatorium. Sin is a sickness, a mortal malady. It is cured by repentance and forgiveness, but can still leave the patient debilitated and in need of treatment during convalescence of greater or lesser length. So purgatory can be seen as a process or state of convalescence.

The question arises, which we touched on earlier (above, subsection ii) of what we can possibly mean by a 'time' in purgatory, before admittance to the 'eternity' (the total simultaneity) of God's immediate beatifying presence. One suggestion is that it all happens, so to speak, at the moment of death; our language of purgatory has simply transposed into extensive or temporal language what is really an intensive experience. Another is the scholastic idea that in between time, as a dimension of bodily or material being, and eternity, as the equivalent dimension of divine being (a total simultaneity, a comprehensive 'now' in which creatures can participate to the extent of their divinization in the beatific vision of God), there is a kind of dimension proper to created spirits which the scholastics called *aevum*, or *aeon*. But as I don't really understand this, I shall say no more about it.[11]

(v) Hell

Like the other topics we have been discussing in this chapter, hell is presented to us in the Christian tradition in a series of images and metaphors. Given the nature of this topic, they tend inevitably to be gruesome and repellent, not infrequently being expressions of human cruelty projected onto God. That at least is the real danger. If we are in the least little bit literalistic and rigid in our treatment of the doctrine, we can scarcely avoid making God out to be a kind of conscientious ogre. This is particularly true of the forensic metaphor which we have already analysed in our treatment of judgement. This remains the primary metaphor/analogy also for the topic of hell, in so far as hell is conceived of as a punishment, the ultimate punishment, for unrepented mortal sin. Now, as St Thomas remarks in *STh* Ia IIae 72, v (ET, vol. 25), judicial punishment is extrinsic to the sin, just as judgement is in a human court of law (see above, Chapter 6, note 1; also C, iv); something imposed from without, which even though it may be a just judgement and punishment, is not *necessarily* imposed, and is not a *necessary* consequence of the crime. The judge, within the law, usually has a discretion over what punishment to impose; and even if the law obliges him to a particular punishment for a particular crime, that law is not a necessary law, absolutely speaking, but is always capable of being changed.

So then, the forensic metaphor applied to hell, with God as the judge, is too often stated as though this extrinsic relationship of sin (too easily equated with crime) to judgement and punishment were of the essence of the matter. Sin is called 'an offence against God's justice', as crime is an offence against natural justice and the Queen's peace. So God, the argument goes, in his perfect justice, is 'bound to punish it'. Or it may be said, in the same style, that hell is necessary 'to satisfy the demands of God's justice'. At the very best, the picture of God that emerges from such language is of an omnipotent Dr Thomas Arnold, headmaster of Rugby, of whom it was said that he was 'a beast, but a just beast'. To satisfy the inexorable demands of his justice (not biblical justice, this, but the justice of Roman law, which is *contrasted* with mercy) he has at his disposal the very latest thing in dungeons and torture-chambers, to surpass the wildest dreams of the Gestapo, or any of the security forces of our contemporary security states.

It won't do. Something has gone badly wrong with the forensic metaphor. What has gone wrong here, I suggest, is the literal acceptance of the extrinsic relations of punishment to sin. This is true of human punishment of crime defined by human law. It is *not* true of the divine punishment of sin, just as we have seen that it is not true of the divine judgement. As we saw in Chapter 6, C when analysing J's concept of sin, sin is not essentially the breach of externally imposed rules but essentially a turning away from God who is life; essentially an 'offence', not against the justice of a touchy autocrat always standing on his dignity, but against the creator's love for his creature. And so death, the punishment decreed for sin in J's narrative, is also not an extrinsic punishment inflicted by an executioner, but the intrinsic consequence, the necessary manifestation of the true nature of sin. You turn away from life – you die.

That, surely, is how we must also conceive of hell. It is the ultimate inner consequence of turning away from God. Heaven, after all, consists as we have seen in the most intimate and immediate possible union with God. If you turn away from God and spurn his love, and never turn back to him in conversion and repentance, then you necessarily deny yourself the possibility of this union. You lose God. And that is essentially what hell is – the permanent loss of God.

Essentially, I make bold to say, that is *all* hell is. What necessity is there to add further punishments? Loss of God means loss of the good, loss of meaning, loss of value, loss of everything. What *possibility* is there to add further punishments? All suggestions that in addition to this 'pain of loss' we have to maintain the reality of some 'pain of sense', and the almost physical reality of the fires of hell which inflict this pain of sense, seem to me to err by a manifestly neurotic, and I would even say ignoble literal-mindedness, projecting onto God, as I said above, the sadistic cruelty of men. The fires of hell, the apocalyptic lake of fire, are as much figures of speech as the harps of heaven, or the river of life and the heavenly Jerusalem described in the closing chapters of Revelation.

It may be of use to trace this and other images of hell back to their origins. In the earlier writings of the Old Testament there seems to be no clear idea of any life after death, or any future life, and so there is no heaven or hell in our sense.[12] There is only a shadowy 'realm of the dead' called Sheol, an almost exact equivalent of the Greek Hades, which is the word used to translate it in the Greek LXX. The best English equivalent is not 'hell' (as in the older versions), but the 'netherworld' or the 'underworld' (not to be understood, of course, in its sociological sense).

But in the later books of the Old Testament, in order to vindicate the justice of God, a doctrine of future rewards and punishments begins to take shape. It is not a doctrine of heaven and hell in our sense, because it is stated in the framework of a purely horizontal eschatology, of which the climax is the resurrection of the dead. This is because the dominant Israelite self-experience was of the unitary and not the dissociated variety, as we saw above in Chapters 9 and 10. The only conceivable future life was a full bodily life, not a life of the soul apart from the body. And such a life, requiring a resurrection of the dead, has to be put at the end of the age. Of the dead who rise, then, some will rise to eternal life, others to everlasting shame (Dan 12:2). But this will happen, not above in heaven nor below in hell, but here on earth, all in the neighbourhood of Jerusalem, to be precise. The judgement will take place in the Valley of Decision, the Kedron valley to the east of the city, and the everlasting shame will be experienced in the valley of the sons of Hinnom to the south; this becomes in the Greek of the New Testament *gehenna*. In the time of Jeremiah and earlier (especially in the reign of the wicked Manasseh) it had been a grim holy place called Tophet, sacred to the god Moloch, where infants had been sacrificed to him by being 'passed through the fire'. It was thus associated with evil fire. And when this cult was suppressed by Josiah, the pagan sacredness of the place had been deliberately profaned by turning it into the city rubbish dump, where unclean fires continued to burn.[13] There, then, are the literal, physical fires of gehenna, which become the symbol of the fires of hell consuming everything abominable and unclean.

In any case, fire is not the only image of hell nor, I would say, the most telling. The gospels also talk of 'the outer darkness' where 'men will weep and gnash their teeth' (e.g. Mt 8:12). This seems to me a much better image for the loss of the light and the company of God, and for the bitter frustration it necessarily involves – this being lost and cut off in a fearful isolation. Hell is *not* other people, not an imposition from outside; hell is *me* – me saddled with the ruin I have made of myself, for ever and ever. Ugh!

But does it really exist at all? Can we accept it, even when we have cut out the literal torture-chamber stuff, as reconcilable with the goodness of God? Here I propose a double answer, an answer from our point of view and an answer from God's point of view; and it is only the answer from our point of view that I can state with any assurance as the Catholic, Christian answer. From our point of view, then, I maintain that we must accept hell as a *real possibility*. If heaven, i.e. that most intimate possible union with God, is our real destiny, our destiny as free creatures of God in receipt of his elevating and healing grace, then the possibility must be real of our failing to achieve that destiny, of our 'missing the mark'. That the possibility is real, I would argue, is practically demonstrated by the experienced fact of sin or wickedness. Sin is turning away from God, wickedness is being twisted out of true. Hell is sin carried to its logical conclusion, of staying permanently turned away from God, permanently twisted out of true and frozen in the great lie. It is very necessary for our Christian realism that we should understand hell to be a real possibility – *for us*; not so much for other people, though it is salutary for them to realize this too, but for *me*. I am capable of hell, and if I do not face the fact, I fail to face the full, dark truth about myself.

But it is a commonplace of ordinary Catholic instruction that while we have to believe in the reality of hell, we do not have to believe that anybody is actually there (except the demons, I presume, and for a number of reasons, I think we have to accept the existence of demons[14]). And so I propose the second part of the answer, that from God's point of view, I won't say hell is not possible but hell is not actual, not at least for human beings. In other words, God's love and mercy are such that by the power of his grace no human being so persists in evil as to force it to its logical conclusion of hell. God's grace is there to achieve the needed conversion and repentance.

But from our point of view hell remains a real possibility – for *me*!

NOTES

1   It is interesting just to notice that our ordinary language uses metaphors of space in order to talk about *time*. 'Before' and 'after' are really space prepositions meaning 'in front of' and 'behind'. And the fact is, we are not quite certain of which space preposition to use, in order to relate ourselves in time to the past and the future. Is the future behind us, or ahead of us? I am sure you will all answer that it is ahead of us. And yet we talk of the future coming *after* the present, not *before* it. So too the past lies behind us – yet it came *before* us – which means 'in front of us'. Very odd.

2   The expectations of the *parousia* had certainly varied in the first millennium. It is evident that many, perhaps most Christians in the apostolic Churches expected it to happen within their own lifetimes. So Paul, in possibly the earliest of the New Testament writings (*c.* 50 A.D.), has to reassure the Thessalonians on the matter of 'those who are asleep', i.e. have already died (1 Thess 4:13–18). And in 1 Cor 15:51 he declares of the *parousia* 'We shall not all sleep [die], but we shall all be changed', which suggests that he was expecting the event within the lives at least of some of his correspondents.

But then in 2 Pet 3:3 ff., written perhaps fifty or more years after Thessalonians, we find people are becoming rather disillusioned about it, and so the writer has to give some theological explanations of what was thought of as the delay in the *parousia*. God is being very patient with us, giving all a time to repent, and anyway he does not see time as we do; 'with the Lord one day is as a thousand years, and a thousand years as one day' (*ibid.* 8).

In Augustine's time the sack of Rome by the Goths in 410 struck many Christians as a sign of the imminent end of the world. Some years later Augustine was consulted about this by a bishop called Hesychius, and he replied fairly briefly in *Letter* 197 (*PL* 33, 900) that about that day and hour nobody knows (Mt 24:36), and that in any case it would not happen until the gospel of the kingdom had been preached to the whole world and to all nations, which clearly had not yet happened. His correspondent came back with another letter, which drew a very long reply from Augustine (*Letter* 199), in which he repeated these points and had to remind the good bishop that the Lord had promised to include in the seed of Abraham not only the Romans, i.e. inhabitants of the Empire, but all nations (*PL* 33, 922). This indicates that an expectation of an imminent return of Christ often goes with a somewhat narrow outlook which ignores the existence of other peoples and parts of the world besides one's own. But even so, Augustine's thinking was as much controlled by the primary, rather than the secondary, eschatology as anybody else's at that time.

Two hundred years later we find Gregory the Great in his sermons pointing out that the end cannot be far off, seeing all the dreadful things that were happening around them. He was thinking chiefly of the Lombard invasions of Italy.

Throughout these centuries there had been people who were fascinated by the mention in Revelation 20:2, 4 of the reign of the saints with Christ for a thousand years. The text was of course variously interpreted. Augustine among others saw it as a symbol for the time of the Church. If you then add to this exegesis (which he himself did not) a literal mind, it is clear that the year 1000 will have momentous significance for many people. And so it did. But when it passed without Christ coming again the millenniarism associated with that date faded away, and the time was ripe for the swing in consciousness which we have noted.

Not that Christians ceased to think about the second coming, or look forward to it, or predict that it was on the verge of happening. From that day to this, adventist movements have been discernible in Christendom. In the thirteenth century there were the prophecies of Abbot Joachim of Flora who said that an age of the Spirit was about to succeed to the age of the Son (the age of the Church up till that time). That branch of the Franciscans called the Spirituals eagerly followed him in this. At the Reformation there were other adventist movements, notably among the Anabaptists, and again in the nineteenth century we had the Seventh Day Adventists, and after them the Jehovah's Witnesses.

Nearly all these movements and sects suffer from that narrowness of outlook which Augustine gently chided in his correspondent Bishop Hesychius. And they also all seem to have given way to the temptation of calculating when the end was going to be, in spite of Mt 24:36 and similar passages, and in spite of the fact that they are invariably proved wrong. But they should not be simply dismissed from further consideration. They do have a point. They remind us in the mainstream of the Christian tradition that that kind of eschatology is primary, and that we ought to be looking forward to the *eschaton*, to the final and perfect establishment of the kingdom, to the resurrection of the dead, and the coming of Christ in glory.

3   I put this word in inverted commas because it is in fact very mistaken to treat heaven and

hell as alternative destinations. A destination is a place where you are destined, or destine yourself to go. By definition, if you get into the wrong train and go somewhere else by mistake, where you arrive in this way is *not* your destination. You end up at Crewe, or Bletchley or some godforsaken siding in the depths of Galloway; but you certainly don't call it your destination – not unless someone has deliberately and maliciously designed to have you end up there.

Now it is very important to understand (see subsection v of this chapter) that if you have the misfortune to find yourself in hell, it will *not* be because someone has maliciously and deliberately designed to have you end up there; it will be because you have failed to reach your only true destination, which is heaven, through your own fault. This is clearly the place to say a few things about the subject of 'predestination' which is a great worry and anxiety to many people.

Predestination means destining something or someone in advance to reach its allotted destiny. Every time you write a letter you predestine it to reach the person you are writing to. It may go astray, either because you fail to address it properly, in which case you fail to execute your predestining intention, or because of some fault in the Post Office. But in any case it is absurd to talk of its being predestined to go astray. It simply fails to reach its destination, which means your predestining of it to do so proved ineffective.

But if God is the predestiner, intending something, or rather someone, to reach their proper destination, his predestining is bound to prove effective, because he is God. Theologically, predestination means God intending to see to it that someone reaches that proper destiny, i.e. heaven. Then as a result of this divine intention things happen; God gives the person the grace needed to reach that destiny. God's predestining intention in itself makes no difference to the person predestined. The predestined are only personally affected by God's gift of grace which follows upon that intention. The way St Thomas puts it is to say that 'predestination does not put anything in the predestined', i.e. does not in any way diminish or alter their freedom (*STh* Ia 23, ii; ET; vol. 5) – just as your intention to send a letter to So-and-so doesn't actually achieve anything in the matter by itself.

So far, perhaps, no real problems. The problem starts with the supposition that some people do not achieve their proper destiny, heaven, but instead go to hell. This can only be because God did *not* predestine them. It cannot be because he predestined them to hell, because that does not make sense (except on the untenable supposition that God is stupidly malicious), any more than you can be said to predestine your letter not to reach the person you are writing to. Hell, as the inner consequence of sin carried to its logical conclusion (see subsection v), means precisely missing the mark, missing one's proper destiny.

So we are left with God simply having no intention in regard to those who are not predestined. This in itself is a rather staggering idea. But we must remember that just as predestination does not put anything in the predestined, so neither does non-predestination put anything in the non-predestined. Human freedom remains intact. In subsection v I in fact propose the solution that while hell remains a real possibility from our point of view (as the logical inner consequence of human wickedness), from God's point of view it is not an actuality, considering the infiniteness of the divine love. This amounts to saying that all human beings are predestined to salvation. But while I do not think this notion is inconsistent with Christian orthodoxy, or with the doctrine of hell, I certainly cannot say that it is required of Christian belief. However, if you do not agree with me, then you must continue to wrestle with the problem of predestination, or rather of non-predestination, on your own.

4 John's actual expression is *ek tōn idiōn*, 'from what is his own'. The translation 'according to his own nature' could suggest that the devil is evil by nature, naturally evil; and this would be a serious error, implying either that God created an evil nature, or that the devil, as evil by nature, was not created by God. This was certainly not John's intention. In his view the devil is evil by his own malice or ill-will. That is what is 'his own'.

5 I say *'almost* total extent' because I do not wish to appear to rule out the part played by God's grace in the matter. Even if we have gone against the grain of grace for almost all our lives, the possibility of the grace of a final repentance is still here. But then we never can tell how much grace has been operating, and even accepted, in the lives of people who to all appearances are manifestly wicked.

6 A rather odd translation. The more usual and the more correct, in my view, is 'the heavens of heavens are the Lord's'. From this expression the rabbis deduced the existence of three heavens or layers of the heavens, which Paul alludes to in 2 Cor 12:2. He was snatched up to the third heaven (God's very own private apartments, you might say, in his palace), which in v. 3 he equates with paradise – both images suggest the immediate and intimate presence of God, seeing him face to face.

7 Again, I am not too happy with the RSV translation. I prefer 'citizenship' for the Greek *politeuma* here. But it can be argued either way. The Vulgate translates *conversatio*, which means way of life or culture – a rather profound conception.

8 Two points on this translation; the phrase translated 'dimly' is *en ainigmati*, which is in fact changing the metaphor, as Paul so often does. It does not qualify the way we see in the mirror, but is a parallel expression, in apposition to 'in a mirror': 'Now we see in a mirror, which means we see in a riddle'; our present knowledge of God is very enigmatic, not just dim. Secondly, the word translated 'understand fully' and 'fully understood', *epiginōskō*, can also mean 'recognize', and I think there is an overtone of that meaning here.

9 St Thomas discusses the whole question of how we can, and do know God, including the notion of the beatific vision, in *STh* Ia, 12 (ET, vol. 3).

10 This is prevented from being a crux for the doctrine of papal infallibility (a doctrine being elaborated at the time by the Franciscan Spirituals and William of Ockham, to which, and to whom, John XXII was implacably opposed; see Brian Tierney, *Origins of Papal Infallibility 1150–1350;* E. J. Brill, Leiden, 1972), by the assertion that John XXII put forward his views as a private theologian. It is all the same a salutary warning against the modern curial disease of 'creeping infallibility'.

11 It is all explained in *STh* Ia, 10, v and vi (ET, vol. 2).

12 This common view of the scholars is, however, cogently challenged by Mitchell Dahood, SJ, one of the leading Hebraists of our day (he died in the summer of 1982), whose particular speciality has been enriching our knowledge of Hebrew grammar and lexicography by comparison with Ugaritic texts. He maintains that the psalms are full of references to a Ugaritic mythology of an equivalent to the Greek Elysian fields. (See his Introduction to *Psalms I* of the *Anchor Bible*, pp. xxxv ff.). But that there was such a Ugaritic mythology and that it was known to and used by the psalmists, I don't think proves his case. They presumably also knew of Egyptian ideas about life after death. Knowing about is not the same as believing in.

13 When I was in Jerusalem for a few days in 1978 I was shown round the old city by a charming French Dominican from the Ecole Biblique. When we got to the Jaffa gate we looked down over Gehenna, now much prized apparently for artists' studios. My guide said to me, 'Voilà la géhenne! Aujourd'hui la géhenne devient un faubourg très chic' – today gehenna is becoming a very fashionable suburb.

14 I think we have to accept them, not because their existence is 'revealed' to us in scripture

– I don't think it is, any more than the existence of, say, Jerusalem is revealed to us in scripture. Their existence and that of angels is assumed in scripture. But it is not assumed in quite the same way as the existence of Jerusalem, which is a matter of common human sense experience, nor in the same way as most biblical writers assumed, after a fashion, that the earth is flat. This is simply an uncritical inference from ordinary human sense experience. Demons and angels must have been assumed to exist (as they have been and are by the vast majority of the human race) on the basis of a somewhat different kind of experience. We can rule it out as illusory if we wish; but we cannot rule it out as obviously mistaken, or disproved by science, like the assumption that the earth is flat. Though never having shared this kind of experience I think it is something that seems so universal that we have to take it seriously.

But furthermore, there is a theological reason why I think we have to accept the existence of demons – and angels. God's revelation comes to us in scripture, as we have seen frequently in this book, in dramatic form. The chief kind of drama we have in the Bible is *conflict*. For conflict you need opposing forces. Jesus Christ is the hero. Who is the opposing villain? It cannot be another human being, because the task of Jesus is to save all human beings. Who and what from? If you eliminate Satan and i 's fellow demons, then you impossibly emasculate the drama of salvation. So they are necessary. And if you have demons you must have angels too, not for the sake of the drama, in which they play very secondary roles, but in order not to have the demons being evil by nature – to avoid any Manichaean dualism.

QUESTIONS FOR FURTHER DISCUSSION

1 Is there any solution to the problem of applying the concept of time to the dead?

2 If the concept of 'heaven' to signify our ultimate destiny is not altogether satisfactory, what better metaphors or symbols could we use?

3 Is the idea of hell really consistent with the doctrine that God is love?

RECOMMENDED FURTHER READING

I would refer the reader to the books on the subject of death mentioned at the end of Chapter 12.

Also of value for the questions raised in this chapter would be John Hick, *Death and Eternal Life*; Jean Mouroux, *The Mystery of Time*; and G. A. Maloney, *The Everlasting Now*. The first offers a far more radically untraditional eschatology than I can accept. The second deals with time in the context of the whole of salvation history, but includes its eschatological dimensions. The last, in spite of its name, is in fact a useful, up-to-date book on the four last things, and also discusses the point we dealt with in Chapter 8, the fate of infants dying unbaptized.

Karl Rahner, *Theological Investigations*, 4, Part 6: 'Eschatology', chapters 13: 'The Hermeneutics of Eschatological Assertions'; and 14: 'The Life of the Dead'.

24
Man's Last End
II: The Ultimate Destiny of Mankind

A. DIFFERENT KINDS OF HORIZONTAL ESCHATOLOGY

We come now in our last chapter to consider the destiny of the human race as a whole, not just as a vast collection of individuals but as a community, a socially coherent body, the body indeed of Christ the last Adam. The destiny of mankind as a whole is the same as the destiny of the Church as a whole, the universal Church. For the Church is intended at the end to be coterminous and identical with the human race. This identity is not realized yet, of course. But since the Church has been established for the sake of mankind, and has a mission to all mankind, we may conclude that it is intended finally to embrace the whole of mankind in one community of salvation.

The final destiny of the human race is a matter of horizontal eschatology, because it necessarily takes us to the end of history and the end of time. But horizontal eschatology is itself of various sorts, some complementary to each other, others not easily to be reconciled with each other. So we must begin with a brief glance at them.

(i) Realized eschatology

The term 'realized eschatology' was invented by C. H. Dodd as a kind of amendment of the eschatological thesis propounded by Albert Schweitzer at the beginning of this century. The primary kind of eschatology we are dealing with here had, as we noticed in the last chapter, been pushed into the background of the Christian consciousness for many centuries, and never more thoroughly, perhaps, than in the nineteenth century, which tended to see Jesus simply as a sublime moral teacher, or as a kind of utopian prophet who wholeheartedly supported nineteenth-century confidence in the steady progress of mankind – as marvellously represented by European man.

Albert Schweitzer administered a rather rude shock to this somewhat complacent interpretation of the gospel, by pointing out that the heart of the gospel message was Jesus' *eschatological* proclamation of the coming kingdom of God (which had nothing to do with the nineteenth-century concept of progress), and that whatever we moderns may think about such eschatological expectations, they clearly bulked large in the consciousness both of Jesus Christ and of his disciples.

Then, as I say, Dodd offered an amendment to Schweitzer's thesis in the middle of the century with his notion of 'realized eschatology'.[1] He observes that the kingdom is proclaimed in the New Testament not simply as a future event, but as something that is happening here and *now*. The expectations and prophecies of the Old Testament are *now* being fulfilled in the life, death and resurrection of Jesus Christ and in the experience of the Holy Spirit enjoyed by Christian believers. The end has already happened, in Christ, though it also has yet to happen, again in Christ, when he comes again at the *parousia*. So we have in the New Testament a realized eschatology as well as a futurist one. The paradigm text Dodd frequently cites is, 'The hour is coming, *and now is*, when the dead will hear the voice of the Son of God, and those who hear will live' (Jn 5:25; cf. 4:23).

Our concern in this chapter is with the destiny of mankind as fully achieved at the *parousia*, and so with futurist rather than realized eschatology. But in telling us that the ultimate destiny to which we look forward at the second coming of Christ has already been anticipated (in some manner) at his first, realized eschatology tells us some important things about that destiny. First of all, it rules out eschatological speculations of a quasi-historical kind like those of Joachim of Flora (Chapter 23, note 2). There is no room, on the true Christian view of things, for further developments of the divine plan of salvation within history. That plan has been completed, fulfilled in Jesus Christ and by him. So the concept of realized eschatology commits us to transcending history in our expectations, and commits us to appreciating how totally our expectations transcend death. (History, after all, is only the product of death.) Historically speaking, Jesus Christ and the New Testament are two thousand years behind us, like Virgil and Horace and the Emperor Augustus. The world has changed vastly since then – there has been progress, unimaginable either to the apostles or to the Stoic philosophers of that age. But theologically speaking, it is unthinkable to progress beyond the New Testament, to improve on it in any way.[2]

Then again, if the end we are expecting has already been achieved, if the kingdom of God is already ours, it means that in an important sense we already know what that end, that future ultimate destiny, is – because we are already there. It is, to be sure, utterly beyond the capacity of our imaginations, and therefore since we can never express our knowledge without referring to and using symbols provided by our imaginations, it is beyond our capacity to express the knowledge we have of our ultimate destiny. But I think we can put it this way: when that Day comes (2 Tim 4:8) it will not surprise us at all (though it may well catch us by surprise); we shall recognize what we shall then see, we shall realise that we have been there all along, that we have all along possessed what only then shall we see. Isn't this what Paul is saying in Col 3:3–4, 'For you have died and your life is hid with Christ in God. When Christ who is our life appears, then you also will appear with him in glory'; and what John is saying in 1 Jn 3:2, 'Beloved, we are God's children now; it does not yet appear what we shall be, but we know that when he appears we shall be like him, for we shall see him as he is'? Perhaps a better phrase than 'realized eschatology' to express the doctrine of Paul and John on the matter would be 'anticipated eschatology'. All that it lacks, compared with what will be, is the *appearance*, the full manifestation.

So it follows, in a sense, that we can see what the future destiny of mankind is by looking at the Church now, both the Church local and the Church universal. When we look at the Church, it is true, we see much, both good and bad, that belongs to its purely temporal dimension, and that consequently tells us nothing about the atemporal, eternal existence of mankind in the age to come; for example the Church's ownership of property, and its organization and hierarchical structure. But some of its formal temporal activities, like its liturgy and sacraments, though they will clearly not continue as such in the age to come, all the same exemplify and anticipate now in their own mode something that certainly will continue there – the corporate praise of God.

And what the Church for all its shortcomings essentially is now, that is what mankind essentially will be then: a fellowship, a brotherhood, a *koinonia* or communion or sharing of everything with everyone. It will be what the Church essentially is now: the body of Christ which 'God has so adjusted . . . that there may be no discord in the body, but that the members may have the same care for one another' (1 Cor 12:24–25). It will be a perfect community of love. This perfect community of love has already been anticipated in the Church, local and universal, of whose members it is said in an idealized picture that 'they were of one heart and soul, and no one said that any of the things which he possessed was his own, but they had everything in common' (Acts 4:32; cf. 2:44–47). That is an instance of realized eschatology.

(ii)   Utopian and evolutionary eschatology

But the futurist eschatology with which we are concerned in this chapter can be of more than one kind. I will maintain that only one kind (which I shall call 'catastrophic'[3]) is the authentic Christian kind, to which our hopes and expectations as Christians are directed. But first we must look at other kinds which have perhaps a greater appeal to most people nowadays. My criticism of them is not exactly that they are false, but that they are quite insufficient to do justice to the data of the revelation, and furthermore that they are of their nature bound to disappoint.

Utopian eschatology begins, I think we can say, with the fairy tale and ends with Marx. It looks forward to the time when 'they all lived happily ever after'. There can be as many different utopias as there are ideas about what living happily ever after involves. But what they all have in common is that they are projections of ideal happiness to a future *time*. They do not transcend time or history or death.

Nor in fact do they transcend human sin and its more unpleasant consequences. And this means that they invariably end in disappointment because they always contain a substantial element of illusion. There is a danger here, because with the shattering of illusion can come shattering reactions, an irresistible temptation to blame 'the others', to cast them in the role of totally evil enemy, and so to eliminate or liquidate them. Utopian dreams have throughout history tended to lead to 'final solutions', from the *herem*[4] or ban of ancient Israelite holy wars in the books of Joshua and Samuel to the holocaust under Hitler.

Yet utopian thinking is not wholly illusory. To dream about the impossible is a step towards thinking more realistically but with a dash of idealistic motivation about the possible, and so to breaking out of the binding and enslaving spell of the actual. A very stimulating book on some practical utopian thinking in the context of the actual situation in South Africa is *The Eye of the Needle* by Richard Turner (Ravan Press, Johannesburg, 1980).[5]

As I have just intimated, the makings of utopian eschatology are to be found in the Old Testament, which exhibits the dangers of such utopian thinking. But it also has a more positive side to it in illustrating how an inadequate utopian eschatology can lead on to the only genuine, or transcendent, horizontal eschatology, the catastrophic. In the earlier documents of the Old Testament the hopes of Israel were focused on some idyllic, utopian future in which every man would sit under his own vine and his own fig-tree (Mic 4:4) in a land flowing with milk and honey (Exod 3:8). When it did not materialize as dreamt of, besides inevitably blaming the wicked Canaanites, Hivites, Hittites, Perizzites and Jebusites – and Israel for not exterminating these vermin (for failing to apply the final solution) as commanded by Moses (Dt 7:1–2), the Israelite theologians and prophets also blamed their own nation for its unfaithfulness to the covenant (into which it was seduced by these vile indigenes). But they also looked for and promised further salvations from Yahweh if the people repented and returned to him. And after the establishment of the Davidic monarchy these promises and hopes were largely concentrated on that institution, and on an ideal king of the future whose reign would inaugurate utopia (Ps 72). The hopes were expressed in language of such unrestrained hyperbole that of course they were never realized. So then again they were simply extended further into the future, like rescheduled debts – until the breakthrough occurred.

This was when those theologians who produced the apocalyptic writings (and they *were* theologians) realized that utopian eschatology, confined within the limits of time and history, is of its nature illusory. For one thing it does not take account of those who are living now but will be dead then, and who still have a claim on God's saving justice and the fulfilment of his gracious promises. So these theologians made the breakthrough of extending their eschatology beyond death (which means beyond time and history) with their doctrine of the resurrection of the dead.[6]

But of this we shall see rather more in the next subsection. Here I am only pointing out how this radical catastrophic eschatology grew out of an earlier utopian kind.

A modern alternative to utopian eschatology is what may conveniently be called evolutionary eschatology. The most distinguished variety of it is that proposed by Teilhard de Chardin in, for example, *The Phenomenon of Man*. This kind of eschatology is not really utopian at all, at least in intention, because it is not governed by any concept of an ideal society or ideal world which it hopes to see realized in the future. Its tendency is to be deterministic, though I do not think it would be fair to attach this label to Teilhard. But he does commit the mistake, which is characteristic of this kind of eschatology, of regarding human history as simply an extension of the process of biological evolution. If one is thoroughly consistent in this mistake, then I think one is bound to have a deterministic view of the future of humanity. Teilhard is not thoroughly consistent, really because he is Christian.

What it amounts to is that he gives the Darwinian concept of evolution a cosmic extension, and has it controlling the development of the cosmos from creation to what he calls Omega point. This stands for the final infolding of all things, all life, all intelligence (the biosphere and the noösphere, in his terminology) upon Christ. This, one presumes, is Christ at his second coming, when it is translated into the traditional catastrophic eschatology which we will prefer.

One central difficulty with Teilhard's thesis, from a theological point of view, is that it is not easy within its terms to give any very great value to the first coming of Christ. It certainly does not allow for any realized eschatology. By the same token, really, it does not allow for the reality of sin, or moral evil as distinct from physical evil of the lion-eats-lamb variety – certainly not for any concept like that of original sin. All these doctrinal concepts, including the central one of the incarnation, presuppose a dramatic context of a conflict of wills. Teilhard is working within the context of a different kind of drama, that of the interplay of grand cosmic laws, which manifest to be sure the divine wisdom (and which perhaps our old friend P, as well as the Wisdom writers, would have appreciated), but in a fundamentally impersonal, and in the last resort, were he consistent, a deterministic way.

The main defect of evolutionary eschatology is the same as that of utopian eschatology, that it does not go beyond time and history. To put it bluntly: Omega point is all very well, but if it does not occur for another thousand or perhaps million years, it is not of the slightest concern to you or me. It will perhaps have an academic interest for those who are trying to make sense of human history and cosmic development; it will no doubt fire the imagination of some of us in the same sort of way as science or space fiction does. But from a practical, moral, religious point of view it is totally irrelevant (as is the Marxist utopia) because we shall all be dead long before it arrives. Any eschatology, to be relevant to *us* (and to our ancestors from Adam or Neanderthal man onwards) must break the sound barrier of death.

(iii) Catastrophic eschatology[7]

This is only done by traditional catastrophic eschatology. By this term I mean an eschatology that pictures the end of all things as consequential upon a cosmic catastrophe. Such a catastrophe, at any rate, is the dominant biblical symbol of this kind of eschatology. It might also, and perhaps more accurately be called an 'implosive eschatology'. That is to say, it does not anticipate an *eschaton* that is the product of forces within history, whether catastrophically revolutionary or evolutionary, but one that breaks in from outside, from God; it will 'implode' into history, to terminate it. The *eschaton* will, after all, be the end of what is usually called salvation history, in the theological perspective, and which I have preferred to call the great drama of salvation and revelation. Now this *began* with an 'implosion', namely creation of the cosmos by God out of nothing and its launching on its dramatic history; it reached its central climax or fulfilment with another 'implosion' from the divine sphere, the incarnation of the Word of God, a purely divine act which, though it fulfilled the salvation history of Israel that led up to it, can in no way be said to have evolved, or even exploded, out of it. And so it is to be expected that the whole grand drama will be terminated by a similar final divine 'implosion'.

This is not to say that human history (given theological meaning, as we observed in Chapter 18, C, i, by the history of the Church at its heart), as it flows out of that central implosion of the incarnation to the final implosion of the *parousia*, has no meaning or direction or relevance of its own. It is indeed moving towards the *parousia*, just as the history of ancient Israel, theologically central to that of ancient mankind, moved towards the incarnation. So as we take part in this history we can work to prepare for the *eschaton*, to prepare and practise for the kingdom of God by working for justice, unity, truth, peace in human society. But we must not suppose that the *eschaton* will issue from the flow of history, or from our little contributions and efforts of preparation. Our essential preparation, according to the gospels, is to watch and wait for it (Mk 13:32–37); and to wait for it in a human situation that is not simply progressive, but in many ways deteriorating and retrogressive, a situation in which the perennial conflict between good and evil grows ever more intense, and extensive, as the end draws nearer. That is the tenor of Jesus' eschatological discourse (e.g. Mt 24:8–13)[8] and of Paul's otherwise very mysterious 'elucidations' on the whole matter to the Thessalonians (2 Thess 2:1–12).

Since the *eschaton* will break in on the cosmos from outside, from God, there is no possible way of describing it. It can only be talked of in highly coloured symbolic language developed through the course of biblical history; on the analogy of the flood and the destruction of Sodom and Gomorrah, as we have just noted; on the analogy of natural portents like earthquakes and eclipses; with a liberal use of mythical imagery earlier employed to talk about the beginning of things. But we can indicate, still using highly analogical, if not mythical language, some of the things it will necessarily involve.

It will involve an end to history and time as we know them; hence a total transformation of creaturely existence into a new mode of being which we call eternity – a participation by creatures in the divine eternity. Eternity, let us remember, does not mean endless time; it means a timeless 'now' comprehending *all* time. So that new mode of being will not just conclude time and history as we know them; it will comprehend the whole of time and all creatures that have ever existed.

This is an implication of something else which the *eschaton* will necessarily involve:[9] the resurrection of the dead. It is through this event that the catastrophic eschatology meets the theological requirement of Christ being the saviour of all men, the entire human race, which means all generations of the human race. It is this requirement that neither utopian nor evolutionary eschatologies are able to satisfy.

We have already looked at the doctrine of the resurrection and its problems in some detail in Chapter 11, B, and will say no more about it here. What we have to try and reflect on is the nature of this ultimate total universal comprehensive human society of the risen ones, in which we shall, we hope, participate together with *all* our ancestors from the beginning of humanity and *all* our descendants up to its end.[10]

B. UNIVERSAL AND TOTAL MUTUAL SHARING

Of course our reflections on the nature of this ultimate human society can only be couched in symbolic language. There is no question of our trying to describe it, or imagine it, 'literally'. We are not talking here the literal descriptive language we are most familiar with. (Actually, if we have been talking proper theology in this book, we never have been using this kind of language, except incidentally and tangentially.) We are talking the language of 'apocalyptic', the language of the book of Revelation or the Apocalypse. This is a language of elaborate, though often rigorous, symbols and images, with its own special rules of grammar that are of a quite different order from the rules of literal descriptive language. Let us call this language 'apocalyptish' as distinct from the so-called literal language we are more familiar with, which we can call 'literalish', or perhaps 'descriptish', which of course has various subsections or dialects such as 'mathematish', 'scientifish', and 'historish'. The supreme and unsurpassed master of apocalyptish is John the theologian, author of Revelation, and so we will take him for our guide in our reflections.

(i)   Reconciliation and fusion of contrary images

The first thing to note is that in presenting the final state of the risen ones, of a glorified humanity, he employs a number of images or models (all of which he finds prepared for him in the Old Testament) that are in themselves *contrary* to each other. Take the numbers first of all – for of course all his numbers are symbolic, and it is the height of absurdity to try and interpret them, or to criticize them, literally. The first vision of final bliss is to found in Rev 7 – in fact it is two visions. To begin with he hears the number of the servants of God who are sealed on their foreheads to preserve them from the final destruction that is impending;[11] there are 144,000 of them, 12,000 from each of the tribes of Israel. Both numbers and the name Israel are symbolic; it is the new Israel, the new people of God taken from every nation, and the numbers signify perfect completion, totality. Then he proceeds immediately to the vision of the same servants of God *after* they have come out of the great tribulation (v. 14), and they are 'a great multitude which no man could number, from every nation . . . ' (v. 9). Two images for the same reality, but as images they are contrary to each other, as Israel the chosen people had been contrary to the gentiles or nations, as the small remnant (144,000 is not in this context a large number) had been contrary to vast crowds. But both images and what they stand for (you could say 'quality' and 'quantity' respectively, 'selectivity' and 'comprehensiveness') are fulfilled in the *eschaton*. There are no bounds to the saving generosity of God; and yet its beneficiaries are a definitive, perfect, chosen, harmoniously ordered whole.

The author returns more than once to the theme of number, but definitively so in his closing vision of 'the holy city, the new Jerusalem, coming down out of heaven from God' (21:10). It has definite measurements, those of a gigantic box, a cube; its walls being $12,000 \times 12,000 \times 12,000$ stadia in length, breadth – and height (v. 16). It is a cube, incidentally, because it is the ultimate Holy of Holies (see 1 Kgs 6:20). The walls are 144 cubits (thick, presumably) 'by a man's measure, that is an angel's'. What John almost certainly means by this enigmatic phrase is that the walls are built of living stones (cf. 1 Pet 2:5), i.e. of men and of angels. So you have the data provided for you to calculate, if you wish, the number of persons who will constitute the new Jerusalem, each person being presumably a 'cubic cubit' in the walls. (Since the numbers on which the calculation will be based are symbolic, so of course will be the final figure.) All you need to know for your calculations is how many cubits to a stade or furlong. The Jerusalem Bible in its handy table of ancient weights and measures tells us that there are 400. So for a lark I have worked out the number of living stones in the new Jerusalem, the sum being $12,000^2 \times 400^2 \times 144 \times 4$, and it comes to $13,271,040,000,000,000$. But that is counting the corner blocks twice, about which I don't suppose John would have been fussy – to be so, would be to lapse into descriptish. However, if you are fussy and wish to subtract their extra count, they come to $398,131,200,000$ ($144^2 \times 12,000 \times 400 \times 4$). So the final reckoning on this descriptish modification of the apocalyptish number is $13,270,641,868,800,000$. Clearly John's earlier 'great multitude which no man can number', but clearly also an organized, articulated, definite, created number.

This has brought us to the image of the city, which is also that of the temple or holy place. The ancient contrariety or tension between the sacred and the profane has been entirely abolished. The city, as we saw in an earlier chapter (3, B, i; 4, A, ii and iii), represents P's ideal for humanity, the ideal of civilization and the deployment of all the wealth of human talent and resources that it requires, indicated by the wealth and glory of this new Jerusalem. This is the city as the crown[12] and summit of all creation. But as we also saw in those chapters, it is an ideal of which J was highly suspicious (3, A, iii). For him the ideal was paradise, the garden, Arcady, rustic simplicity and innocence. And among the blessed this ideal too is fulfilled; John introduces the paradisal image into his city in 22:1–2. The resurrection of the dead will be paradise regained. And since John takes the details of the image in these verses, not directly from Gen 2, but from Ezekiel's reworking of the paradise image (Ezek 47), his total image is not just paradise but also Canaan, the promised land, turned into paradise. It all represents the ideals of quietness, rest, simplicity, silence, as contrasted with those of activity, creativeness, excitement, bustle, culture. In this life they are not easy to combine; in the resurrection, as modes of social existence and sharing, they will somehow be perfectly combined and equally fulfilled.

The mention of Canaan and the promised land reminds us that it was *conquered*. So we also have the image of victory. The numberless multitude of 7:9 are carrying palms, which shows that they are conquerors in a triumph. But we notice that here there are no conquered enemies, no Canaanites, Hivites, Perizzites, Hittites and Jebusites to be exterminated. For the conflict in which the blessed have conquered has taken place, in the last resort, within them. It is themselves that they have conquered, the 'old man' in them. If it is others in any way, then they have conquered them by forgiveness, conversion and repentance. So perhaps the conquered enemies are there after all – among the conquerors and identical with them.

This reminds us again that in eternity the past is not forgotten, it is comprehended. So our present conflicts with all their sins and defeats are there in the bliss of eternity, as the wounds of Christ are there. But they are there totally shared, which means both totally acknowledged and repented of and totally forgiven. Past enemies are enemies no more, because their past enmity is totally out in the open, with all its causes and tragic misunderstandings and complications and consequences, and so is totally resolved because totally repented of and totally forgiven with a total mutuality.

(ii) God shall be all in all

This total mutuality will not simply obtain between those persons who knew each other, whether as friends or foes, in their lives on earth. It will obtain between all members of the entire human race in all its generations. It will thus offer an unimaginable widening of horizons, an inconceivable liberation of the imagination. Our present horizons are so narrow, our imaginations so limited. But then I shall share my twentieth-century, middle-class, clerical, English experience of life with Neanderthal men and women, who will share their rather different experiences (as persons, not as historical generalizations) with me. I shall receive from and contribute to the riches of all races and cultures that are and ever have been and ever will be. I think this is the significance of the musical image that is so prominent in the biblical presentation of the age to come; all our infinite variety of genuine ways of being human will be orchestrated and harmonized in the massed choirs of human beings and angels into the eternal praise of God. And I (and you) shall know and appreciate and enjoy and share totally with all the other 13,271,039,999,999,999 members of that choir (like John I am not now being descriptishly pedantic about the calculation of that sublime number).

This, however, will only be possible because God will be all in all, or in RSV's not very satisfactory translation, God will be 'everything to everyone'

(1 Cor 15:28). The genuine society of the whole of humanity, its social cohesion and relatedness, will only be possible because it will be 'cleaving to God' (cf. Ps 73:28), and all its members, one body in Christ, will be seeing and knowing each other in God.

God is already all in all, and always has been, as the creator and then the saviour of all things; as their first beginning who keeps them all in the hollow of his hand, maintaining them in being like a dancer keeping a dance in being by dancing it; and as their last end, the goal to which throughout cosmic history all things tend – the magnet drawing them all onwards to their final destiny in him. But when this destiny is achieved, this intimate presence of God to his creatures, this way he fulfils all their desires, will be visible, will be manifestly transparent, will be the principle of cohesion that binds them blissfully together.

I know of few better expressions of this ultimate mystery of our being than Peter Abelard's superb hymn *O quanta qualia*, with which I would like to end. Its splendid, resonant mediaeval latinity defies poetic translation, so I offer as well a prose translation. The Latin text is from *Mediaeval Latin Lyrics*, collected by Helen Waddell (1933; in Penguin Classics, Harmondsworth, Middx, 1952, 1964). I omit two verses.

> O quanta, qualia sunt illa sabbata
> quae semper celebrat superna curia,
> quae fessis requies, quae merces fortibus,
> cum erit omnia Deus in omnibus!
>
> Vera Jerusalem est illa civitas
> cujus pax jugis est summa jucunditas,
> ubi non praevenit rem desiderium,
> nec desiderio minus est praemium.
>
> Nostrum est interim mentem erigere
> et totis patriam votis appetere,
> et ad Jerusalem a Babylonia
> post longa regredi tandem exilia.
>
> Illic ex sabbato succedet sabbatum,
> perpes laetitia sabbatizantium,
> nec ineffabiles cessabunt jubili
> quos decantibimus et nos et angeli.
>
> Perenni Domino perpes sit gloria
> ex quo sunt, per quem sunt, in quo sunt omnia;
> ex quo sunt Pater est, per quem sunt Filius,
> in quo sunt Patris et Filii Spiritus.

O how magnificently marvellous are those sabbaths
which are ever being celebrated by the company above;
rest for the weary, their reward for the strong,
when God will be all in all!

The true Jerusalem is that city
whose continuous peace is supreme felicity,
where desire does not outrun possession,
where reward does not disappoint desire.

Ours, meanwhile, to raise up our minds
and yearn for our native land with all our hearts,
and come back at last from Babylon
after such long exile to Jerusalem.[13]

There holiday follows hard upon holiday,
perpetual rejoicing of holiday-makers;
no end shall there be to the wordless roundelays
which we and the angels will sing through together.

Perpetual glory to the Lord everlasting
from whom, through whom, in whom are all things;
From whom, the Father; through whom, the Son;
In whom, the Spirit of Father and Son.

NOTES

1 C. H. Dodd, *The Apostolic Preaching and its Developments* (1966); *According to the Scriptures* (1952); *Interpretation of the Fourth Gospel* (1958). See also the relevant essay in *The Background of the New Testament and its Eschatology: Studies in Honour of C. H. Dodd*, ed. W. D. Davies and D. Daube (1966).

2 Perhaps not unthinkable, but at any rate heretical. I trust the reader has not understood me, in the previous sentence, to be innocently proclaiming the gospel of progress. Nothing could be further from my intentions.

3 Since writing this, I have come across the perfectly appropriate word *eucatastrophe*, explained as 'the unexpected happy ending', in J. Ramsey Michaels, *Servant and Son* (p. 142), a splendid book. The author gets the word from J. R. R. Tolkien, 'On Fairy Stories', in *The Tolkien Reader* (Ballantine, New York, 1966), pp. 71–73.

   Michaels is not talking about the *eschaton* directly when he uses the word, but about the kingdom of God as proclaimed and inaugurated by Jesus. 'When the cross and resurrection are viewed together', he says, 'we have a perfect example of the eucatastrophe.' *A fortiori* when we consider the *parousia* and the resurrection of the dead.

4 The *herem* was the savage ritual of the holy war by which the enemy was vowed to total destruction, so that all were to be slaughtered without mercy, men, women and children and all cattle and animals. The slaughter was, I suppose, conceived of as a gigantic sacrifice to the God of the victors. It was a custom not confined to the Israelites – and not perhaps as frequently executed as some books of the Bible, notably Joshua, suggest. In the Deuteronomic theology it almost has the status of what I might call a theological fiction

(on analogy with legal fictions). The Fathers very sensibly interpret the command to exterminate the previous inhabitants of the promised land as a figurative way of commanding us to exterminate our vices.

5   Mr Turner was under a banning order when he was murdered in cold blood at the door of his house in Durban. It was undoubtedly a political murder. Mr Turner was a persistent, radical and articulate critic of the South African government's policies, which is why he was banned. There has never been any arrest in connection with the crime – and one cannot seriously believe that there was any genuine investigation. It was committed on 8 January 1978.

But a rather ironic comment needs to be made on his advocacy of utopian thinking; it is precisely the kind of thinking that underlies the whole policy of the National Party in South Africa, of which he was such a staunch critic. From the days of the Voortrekkers in 1836, the Boers had been obsessed by a utopian dream, and still are.

6   See Chapter 23, note 12 for the views of Mitchell Dahood, SJ (who would be critical of this presentation of theological development in the Old Testament in this matter).

7   See note 3 above.

8   See also on the suddenness of the end, Mt 24:37–39, where it is compared to the coming of the flood. Luke in a parallel passage (17:26–30) also introduces the destruction of Sodom and Gomorrah. The point is that both these catastrophes came upon their victims because of their wickedness, because wickedness had increased upon the earth.

9   The necessity is theological, because the doctrine has been revealed by God. St Paul argues the case of this necessity in 1 Cor 15.

10   This is my assumption of the emptiness of hell, for which I argued in the last chapter (23, B, v). But even if that assumption is not made, it can only be saved humanity that will constitute a society, and that will be mankind as a social whole. In hell there can be no society, only a dreadfully atomized number of totally isolated individuals (ibid.).

11   The image is taken from Ezekiel 9:3–6.

12   In his brilliant if baffling commentary on the book, A Rebirth of Images, Austin Farrer observes that there are twelve gates in the city walls, three presumably on each side, and that they consist of pearls; and that the twelve foundations of the city, representing the apostles, are twelve jewels. So you can take each jewel as coinciding with a section of the walls between the gates. The city thus becomes a chaplet or coronet of jewels alternating with pearls – a crown indeed, worn I suppose by God (Rev 21:12–14, 19–21).

13   The notion of return which dominates this stanza is one I have perhaps failed to stress. The return to Jerusalem is also a return to paradise – the only place in the hymn where he implies the paradise image. But when we do return, it will mean that we will be able to say 'We have been here before'. It will be a return to our native land, because it will be a return to God, the source of all our being. Creation will end where it began, in the hand of God, like a wonderful boomerang. The Australian aborigines will clearly have an extremely honoured place there.

QUESTIONS FOR FURTHER DISCUSSION

1   Could the concept of realized eschatology help us to place what is here called the vertical or personal eschatology harmoniously and consistently in the context of futurist horizontal eschatology?

2   If utopian and evolutionary eschatology evaporate in science fiction, does not the catastrophic eschatology here proposed instead so transcend our experience of reality that it vanishes into transcendent mythology?

3   Is there any other way of giving meaning to the lives of *all* human beings who have ever lived or will ever live?

RECOMMENDED FURTHER READING

Besides the books mentioned in the course of this chapter (especially those of C. H. Dodd), Oscar Cullmann, *Christ and Time*, aims at achieving an eschatological perspective, tying in eschatology with salvation history. It is really on the same subject as the book by Jean Mouroux, *The Mystery of Time*, recommended at the end of the previous chapter. Cullmann wrote first, and it would be interesting to compare the conclusions of the two scholars, Cullmann a Protestant, Mouroux a Catholic.

G. B. Caird's commentary on *The Revelation of St John the Divine* cannot really be improved upon for introducing the reader to that extraordinarily difficult, but nonetheless important book of the Bible.

Bibliography

P. Althaus, *The Theology of Martin Luther* (ET; Fortress Press, Philadelphia, 1966).
Ancient Near Eastern Texts (ed. J. B. Pritchard) (Princeton, 1955).
Anselm, *Proslogion* (ed. and ET M. J. Charlesworth, OUP, 1965).
    The Virginal Conception (PL 158).
Thomas Aquinas, *Summa Theologiae* (ET; Blackfriars ed., Eyre and Spottiswoode, London,
    1964–81), vols 1, 2, 3, 5, 7, 9, 11, 12, 13, 14, 15, 25, 26, 28, 30, 39, 41, 56, 57.
Aristotle, *On the Soul* (ET; *Works*, ed. W. D. Ross, III, OUP, 1955).
Augustine, *The City of God*, X, XII *(PL* 41; ET J. Healey, Dent, London, 1945).
    Confessions, X *(PL* 32; ET F. J. Sheed, Sheed & Ward, London, 1944; A. C.
    Outler, SCM, London, 1955; several others).
    The Gift of Perseverance (PL 45).
    Letters, 197, 199 *(PL* 33).
    Literal Commentary on Genesis (PL 34).
    On the Deserts and Forgiveness of Sins (PL 44).
    On Free Will (PL 32).
    On the Trinity (De Trinitate), IX – XIV *(PL* 42).
L. R. Bailey, *Biblical Perspectives on Death* (Fortress Press, Philadelphia, 1979).
K. Barth, *Church Dogmatics*, III, *The Doctrine of Creation* 2 (ET; T. & T. Clark, Edinburgh,
    1960).
Bible: the Revised Standard Version (RSV) is copyright 1946, 1952, 1957 and 1971 by the
    Division of Christian Education of the National Council of the Churches of Christ in the
    United States of America.
L. Boros, *The Moment of Truth* (ET; Search Press, London, 1965; latest reprint 1973).
W. Buhlmann, *The Coming of the Third Church* (ET; St Paul Publications, Slough, 1976).
G. B. Caird, *The Revelation of St John the Divine* (Harper & Row, New York, 1966).
A Catechism of Christian Doctrine (CTS, London, 1971).
R. H. Charles, *Eschatology* (Schocken, New York, 1963).
Y. Congar, *Divided Christendom* (ET; Geoffrey Bles, London, 1939).
O. Cullmann, *Christ and Time* (ET; SCM, London, 1951; reprinted 1971).
    The Christology of the New Testament (ET; SCM, London, 1963).
M. Dahood, *Psalms I (Anchor Bible*; Doubleday, Garden City, N. Y., 1966).
D. Daube, *The New Testament and Rabbinic Judaism* (OUP, 1956).
W. D. Davies and D. Daube (eds), *The Background of the New Testament and its Eschatology:
    Studies in Honour of C. H. Dodd* (CUP, 1954).
C. Davis, *God's Grace in History* (Fontana, Glasgow, 1966).
H. Denzinger, rev. A. Schönmetzer, *Enchiridion Symbolorum*, 33rd ed. (Herder, Freiburg,
    1965) (and 31st ed., 1957).

Dictionnaire de Théologie Catholique, vol. 15, art. 'Traducianisme' (Letouzey et Ané, Paris, 1946).

Didache (ET; *ACW*, 6; Longman, London, 1948).

The Documents of Vatican II (ed. W. M. Abbott) (Chapman, London, 1966; for *Gaudium et Spes* and *Lumen Gentium*).

C. H. Dodd, *According to the Scriptures* (Collins, Glasgow, 1952).
    The Apostolic Preaching and its Developments (Hodder and Stoughton, London, 1966).

J. Dominian, *Marriage, Faith and Love* (DLT, London, 1981).
    Proposals for a New Sexual Ethic (DLT, London, 1977).

F. X. Durrwell, *Resurrection* (ET; Sheed and Ward, London, 1960).

R. B. Edwards, *Reason and Religion* (Harcourt Brace Jovanovich, New York, 1972).

P. F. Ellis, *The Yahwist* (Fides, Notre Dame, Ind., 1968; Chapman, London, 1969).

A. Farrer, *A Rebirth of Images* (Dacre Press/A. & C. Black, London, 1949; Beacon, Boston, 1963).

E. Gilson, *The Spirit of Mediaeval Philosophy* (ET; Sheed and Ward, London, 1936).

R. Gleason, *The World to Come* (Sheed & Ward, London, 1958).

B. Griffiths, *Christian Ashram* (DLT, London, 1966).

A. Grillmeier, *Christ in Christian Tradition* (ET; Mowbray, Oxford, 1965; Sheed & Ward, New York, 1969);

R. Haight, *The Experience and Language of Grace* (Gill & Macmillan, Dublin, 1979).

C. Hartshorne and W. Reese, *Philosophers Speak of God* (University of Chicago Press, 1969).

G. Hibbert, *Man, Culture and Christianity* (Sheed & Ward, London, 1967).

J. Hick, *Death and Eternal Life* (Collins, London, 1976).

A. Hulsbosch, *God's Creation; Creation, Sin and Redemption in an Evolving World* (ET; Sheed and Ward, London, 1965).

Irenaeus, *Against Heresies*, III, IV (*PG* 7).
    Proof of the Apostolic Preaching (ET; *ACW*, 16; Longman, London, 1952).

The Jerome Biblical Commentary (ed. R. E. Brown, J. A. Fitzmyer and R. E. Murphy) (Prentice-Hall, Englewood Cliffs, N.J., 1968; Chapman, London, 1969).

Julian of Norwich, *Revelations of Divine Love* (Penguin, Harmondsworth, Middx, 1966).

R. J. Karris, *The Pastoral Epistles* (*New Testament Message*, 17; Veritas, Dublin/Glazier, Wilmington, 1979).

W. Kasper, *Jesus the Christ* (ET; Burns and Oates, London/Paulist Press, New York, 1976).
    Theology of Christian Marriage (ET; Burns and Oates, London, 1980).

K. Kelly, *Divorce and Second Marriage* (Collins, London, 1982).

I. Lepp, *Death and its Mysteries* (ET; Burns and Oates, London, 1969).

J. Leuridan, *Justicia y Explotación* (CEP, Lima).

B. Lonergan, *Method in Theology* (DLT, London, 1972).

J. L. McKenzie, *The World of the Judges* (Prenctice-Hall, Englewood Cliffs, N.J., 1965; Chapman, London, 1967).

G. A. Maloney, *The Everlasting Now* (Ave Maria, Notre Dame, Ind., 1980).

J. Ramsey Michaels, *Servant and Son: Jesus in Parable and Gospel* (John Knox Press, Atlanta, 1981).

J. Moltmann, *The Church in the Power of the Spirit* (ET; SCM, London, 1977).

J. Mouroux, *The Mystery of Time* (ET; Desclee, New York, 1958).

J. Murphy-O'Connor, *1 Corinthians* (*New Testament Message*, 10; Veritas, Dublin, 1979; Glazier, Wilmington, 1980).

J. B. Nelson, *Embodiment: An Approach to Sexuality and Theology* (SPCK, London, 1979).

G. O'Collins, *The Easter Jesus*, 2nd ed. (DLT, London, 1980).

M. Oraison, *Death . . . and Then What?* (ET; Sheed & Ward, London, 1960).

R. Otto, *The Idea of the Holy* (ET; Pelican, Harmondsworth, Middx, 1959).

W. Pannenberg, *Jesus – God and Man* (ET; SCM, London/Westminster Press, Philadelphia, 1968).

Paul VI, *Humanae Vitae* (CTS, London, 1968).

N. Pittenger, *God in Process* (SCM, London, 1967).

Pius XII, *Humani Generis* (CTS, London, 1950).

Plato, *Phaedo* (ET; *Dialogues*, tr. B. Jowett, I, OUP, 1953).

K. Rahner, *The Church and the Sacraments* (ET; Nelson, Edinburgh and London, 1963).
>   *Theological Investigations* (ET; DLT, London, 1961–   ), 1, 2, 4, 11, 13.

J. A. T. Robinson, *Honest to God* (SCM, London, 1963).

G. Ryle, *The Concept of Mind* (Hutchinson, London, 1949).

Sacramentum Mundi (ed. K. Rahner *et al.*), art. 'Monogenism' (ET; Burns and Oates, London, 1969).

E. Schillebeeckx, *Christ* (ET; Seabury, New York, 1980).
>   *Christ the Sacrament of Encounter with God* (ET; Sheed & Ward, London, 1963/1965).
>   *God and Man* (ET; Sheed & Ward, London, 1969).
>   *Jesus* (ET; Seabury, New York, 1979).
>   *Vatican II, The Struggle of Minds and other essays* (Gill, Dublin, 1963).
>   *World and Church* (ET; Sheed & Ward, London, 1971).

P. Schoonenberg, *Man and Sin: a Theological View* (ET; Sheed & Ward, London, 1965).

J. L. Segundo, *The Community Called Church* (ET; Orbis, Maryknoll, N.Y., 1973).

J. Sobrino, *Christology at the Crossroads* (SCM, London, 1978).

E. A. Speiser, *Genesis (Anchor Bible*; Doubleday, Garden City, N.Y., 1964).

P. Teilhard de Chardin, *The Future of Man* (ET; Collins, London, 1964).
>   *The Phenomenon of Man* (ET; Harper, New York, 1959).
>   *Science and Christ* (ET; Collins, London, 1968).
>   *The Vision of the Past* (ET; Collins, London, 1966).

S. Tugwell, *Reflections on the Beatitudes* (DLT, London, 1980).

G. Vann, *Morals and Man* (Fontana, Glasgow, 1960).

G. von Rad, *Old Testament Theology*, 2 vols (ET; Harper & Row, New York, 1962–65).

J. Wellhausen, *Prolegomena to the History of Ancient Israel* (ET; Meridian, New York, latest reprint 1965).

A. N. Whitehead, *Process and Reality* (CUP, 1929).
>   *Religion in the Making* (CUP, 1926; Meridian, New York, 1960).

V. Wilkin, *From Limbo to Heaven* (Sheed & Ward, London, 1961).

Indexes

INDEX OF BIBLICAL REFERENCES

INDEX OF REFERENCES TO THE *SUMMA THEOLOGIAE* OF THOMAS AQUINAS

General Index